Magnified Capitalism

The new American solution for creating millions of jobs, fixing the economy, and improving government

Peter Naleszkiewicz

Like strapping a rocket engine onto the U.S. economy

www.magnifiedcapitalism.com

First edition

Visit www.magnifiedcapitalism.com for updated information, supporting file downloads, news, contacting the author, volunteering, and ordering additional copies in any format.

Table of Contents

Americans are bold and creative innovators who will not be kept down. Magnified Capitalism represents our next big move toward lasting prosperity and freedom for all. Everything is about to change and it is going to be awesome.

i. Prolog

What you are about to read is a bombshell. It is a big idea that you can participate in. I hope it changes your life.

I have written *Magnified Capitalism* in the form of a narrative presentation to the President of the United States. Given the timing of this publication you might assume that the President in question is Barack Obama. In one sense it is, but my preference is that you, my dear reader, try hard not to look at it this way. Instead, I want you to imagine yourself as our President. *Magnified Capitalism* is written at your request. I wrote this book so you can immerse yourself in this fantasy and become the decision-maker for our nation. If you are uncomfortable with this idea, instead cast yourself in the President's administration as an advisor. After he has read the proposal, imagine he has given you this copy in order to hear your advice on the matter.

At several points in the book I have provided economic data that is current at the time it was written and finalized (end of July 2012). It should be noted that the strategy at the center of this book is relevant outside the current U.S. situation. Magnified Capitalism represents a new higher gear that we can shift into if we choose. It is applicable under many scenarios, even for other democratic countries. The economic data at hand was used in the detailed analysis to reinforce the strategic claims. We should naturally expect other times and situations to require this part of the plan to be reworked. Magnified Capitalism is a powerful option for the United States now and in the foreseeable future. It is a certainty that some countries are not as well prepared for it as we are. As you will see, there are prerequisites. We have all of these prerequisites today in the United States. That is my focus. For other countries to consider a similar move, careful additional analysis is required.

Regardless of who you are and when you pick up this book, I hope you choose to take this ride with me. Put yourself in the seat of power and buckle up. Imagine yourself in a position of authority, able to take action to help yourself, your fellow citizens and your country.

Here is the scenario I'd like you to share with me: You have just been handed a briefing that either you or your boss, the President, commissioned from me a few months ago. This information is a big deal for you because you really want to fix the problems our country faces, but the old ideas are not working any more. You are hoping to see a fresh plan that you can put in place quickly. That is why you cannot wait to read through this report.

i. Prolog

Before I begin the actual presentation, there is something I would like you to keep in mind as you read. Some people think that Americans, as a group, do not care that much about politics, government or the economy. I do not agree at all. On the contrary, most of us closely follow elections, economic news and other reports about how our nation is doing. Unfortunately, much of this information reaches the public in a form that is often unexciting, sometimes even boring. That is understandable. Who, other than Ph.D. economists and their students, wants to read some serious economic thesis? That is why this writing is in the form of an executive briefing. When you are the decision–maker you need to understand the principles and the key points. Lots of jargon or high flown language is for a different audience. The same goes for the details behind details. We do not need that. The information just needs to be clear and logical. Too much more is not helpful to most of us. My goal is to empower you in this very manner. Ultimately, in a democracy each of us is the decision–maker. This writing seeks to give you exactly this level of respect.

It is my deepest wish that reading about Magnified Capitalism in this format will be rewarding and even enjoyable. Perhaps we can even build a consensus that our political leaders should read about it, too. In this way we can once again prove to the world that Americans are shrewder and more thoughtful than our detractors suggest. Let's all gather together around a plan that helps us reinvent ourselves. Let's take on the challenge to re-up our global leadership, but not by the use of military force or political maneuvering. We can lead by showing everyone what it means to be the free-thinking businesspeople, entrepreneurs, inventors, planners, engineers, hard workers, and smart citizens of the finest country in the world.

With that in mind, I now ask you to engage your imagination. Consider yourself transformed and promoted. I have just handed you the report you have been waiting for, Mr. or Madam President. Your country is ready to be transformed if you choose to take the recommended actions. You need only read and decide for yourself.

"It was Americans who retooled democracy when we ratified our Constitution in 1788. Now we finally have a serious proposal for making a profound improvement. Magnified Capitalism will not only pull us quickly out of our economic problems, it will launch us into a new era of global leadership and prosperity."

- a news story excerpt from the near future -

I. Situation

PRESIDENTIAL PRESENTATION

- PRESIDENT'S EYES, OR WITH DIRECT APPROVAL ONLY -

At your request, I have prepared this executive document for you to read and use as an aid in our next discussion. As you had hoped, with my non-political perspective as an experienced business planner and project manager, I have been able to generate a complete, actionable solution to the issues you outlined. The plan in this presentation is politically neutral and based on commercial methods for solving business problems. It features a blueprint for prompt recovery from our economic distress, which was your primary mandate. This specifically means a dramatic reduction in unemployment at the same time as the economy recovers from its current struggles. In addition, this proposal addresses the secondary goals you had requested: lowering the national debt, long-term reduction of income taxes, and a dramatic increase in global competitiveness for the United States.

I call this approach "Magnified Capitalism." For convenience I will frequently refer to our future under Magnified Capitalism as "United States 2.0." The impact of Magnified Capitalism will be profound. It is my sincere hope that reading this strategy gets you excited enough to immediately press for the required legislation.

As a reminder, Mr. President, you had indicated your frustration with the political and economic state of the country. Clearly, this is a feeling most of the American people share. After being discouraged by the failings of supercommittees, secrete negotiations with the opposition party, and the lack of consensus within public dialog, you had what you described as an epiphany. You said you were contemplating the idea that while Americans believe in capitalism, the matter has long since matured beyond theory or philosophy. Our country has prospered to the point of a world leadership role based upon its tenets. Capitalism works. It generates a powerful dynamic for creative business development. Why can't we find a way to apply some of its methods to solve government challenges?

American companies have become world leaders in part due to our ability to master business goals. We are experts at cracking the complex problems raised by economic opportunity. To stay competitive American business processes have evolved into a fine art over the past few decades. Much of this evolution has come about in the ways businesses plan for the future and resolve issues. Yet our government's processes have hardly changed at all in a century or more.

Mr. President, you wondered what would happen if someone trained in modern commercial methods were to tackle our problems. In other words, if the United States were run more like a large corporation, then our economic situation would be addressed in a much different manner. What kind of solution would that produce? The President of a large corporation might assign the matter to an executive business strategist with substantial experience in project management. This manager's task would be to create a strategic plan using established business practices. Your epiphany was to take this idea and make it an actual assignment. You and your team then selected me to execute your mission. Thank you for this honor. It has been a fascinating exercise. Even I am surprised by the outcome. I trust that the results will do justice to your highest hopes.

As you may recall, my background includes formal training in the organization of complex project plans. Therefore, rather than try to guess how it might be done following a government standard, I have provided my presentation to you here in a business-oriented format. This approach lays things out the way most corporate executives would expect, using current standards of project management and business planning.

A Formal Proposal Outline

A professional business proposal follows an outline that includes all the expected elements. Such an outline insures I have addressed the matter thoroughly. In this case we begin with a quick analysis of how we got to this point. It is a picture of our current status as a country, but through the eyes of a commercial analyst. I provide this overview as a continuation of the present discussion. After that I introduce you to Magnified Capitalism itself, laying out the logic that brought about its inception, and then providing an executive summary of the whole strategy. This might seem slightly out of place from a flow perspective, but it is motivated by a basic human need. Most of us want to get to the punch line as quickly as we can. Putting the main point up front in a business proposal allows executives to quickly decide whether or not they think something is a good idea. Only if the big picture sounds promising will most decision-makers then be motivated enough to drill into the particulars. Laying out the basics early also helps set the stage for all the subsequent details. After all, my purpose here is not to wait until the end to reveal the answer, but to propose a strategy and then see how its qualities hold up. So we cover the solution summary early.

Then we walk the path that shows how this plan unfolds. This walk begins with what business managers call a SWOT analysis. SWOT stands for Strengths, Weaknesses, Opportunities, and Threats. It considers both the upsides and downsides of our plan. Much of a SWOT analysis involves trying to shoot the strategy down. We pick on it in every way we can think of. This forces us to improve the plan further. Conducting a SWOT analysis leads us through a plan evolution that can be very interesting. In some business plans, a SWOT kills the whole strategy. This is a good thing, however, because it means we have saved ourselves from a mistake, and the SWOT tells us exactly why. In other words, conducting a SWOT shows us that the idea can withstand everything we can throw at it. I am pleased to advise you that Magnified Capitalism survives the SWOT analysis with interesting improvements.

After the SWOT analysis, we can then describe a solution path that is married with our strategy. This "solution walkthrough" gives us a closer look at the meat of the Magnified Capitalism proposal. I then flesh out the program further by describing an operational plan. That part contains details of how to turn the idea into a something functional and ongoing. Next are the "use cases" which describe examples of how different people and businesses will experience the proposal. Here the projected impact of Magnified Capitalism becomes tangible.

I follow the use cases with a short discussion about finances. I have kept this area high-level, since I expect this part to change once we actually enact the legislation that empowers the program. I do, however, give the summary of a real analysis and offer its details in the appendix for those who are interested. This analysis illustrates the impact of different financial decisions. It will also help you, Mr. President, fight for an aggressive budget that will produce fast, dramatic results. This analysis shows that a serious financial commitment today results in less long-term risk.

No formal plan would be complete without some idea of how to handle the dangers, so this report also provides a discussion of risk management. This differs from the SWOT analysis in an important way. SWOT deals with strategic risks by considering counterpoints and plan improvements before we enact the program. Risk management helps us handle things that might go wrong as we implement the plan. We can have a perfectly good plan but still have trouble turning it into reality. It is helpful to try to predict the critical failure points so I have provided a list of known risks. It is essential that we review methods to handle such potential problem areas in advance. Near the end of this section I include a discussion of risk mitigation as well as plan constraints to conclude the topic.

The last part of this presentation is a discussion of what to do next. This addresses how we get things moving now. From my point of view, this is both the one of the most important parts and the hardest part. The best strategy in the world is of no value if we cannot make it happen. Here I describe the first and most essential steps needed to get the ball rolling.

I. Situation

That is it, the whole proposal outline, formal and business-oriented as requested.

Economic Status of the United States

Mr. President, your request for this proposal implies that you are well aware of our status, as would be expected. However, every examination is an opportunity for new perspective. We are clearly in a difficult economic situation. I promised you details in the spirit of a business analysis, so let's drill down just enough to capture the important issues.

The United States has just experienced an extended economic downturn. Unemployment rates shot up in 2008 from a low of 4.8% in February of that year to 7.3% by that December. By October 2009 unemployment peaked at 10.1% but has still stayed above 8% since then. In historical terms this is terrible. It has not been this bad since the early 1980's. In the 80's we bounced back from those low numbers pretty fast, so most people agree that this time it is far worse. Many have argued that things have not been this bad since the depression era of the 1930's.

Economists tell us that we need to keep unemployment below 5% in order to maintain a healthy economy. We must recognize that some portion of the recent reduction in unemployment is a statistical anomaly caused by people giving up their search for work due to frustration. The reality on the ground is therefore a bit worse than the numbers tell us. Some analysts suggest that effective unemployment is closer to 20% nationally when we consider all these factors.

We also know that with high unemployment come other problems. Fewer people have health insurance. The market for consumer goods suffers due to fewer buyers. Real estate sales drop. Less income means that even if the tax rate remains steady, the government collects fewer taxes. This puts pressure on local, state and federal government budgets. Conversely, if we can dramatically improve the economy, and by this I mean employment in particular, then we will experience improvement in these areas.

I agree with your premise. The culprit of this bad economy is clear. It is the lack of jobs. In a capitalist system the government cannot just hire all those people who are looking for work. To find a solution therefore, we have to examine the source of job creation. Here the high-level answer is easy. About 90% of jobs come from businesses (versus government, which generates about 8% of jobs directly and 13% if we include government contractors and suppliers). Stable jobs tend to come from larger companies but new job growth comes disproportionately from small business. That means if we give a tax break to a big company, we might not create any new jobs because the firm may be careful not to spend cash reserves in a bad economy. But if we provide start-up funds to an entrepreneur, we are virtually assured that all of this money will be spent on hiring or the purchase of products and services. The money here goes either directly to a new job or toward improving the market for a product or service.

Therefore the sweet spot is clearly new business creation. If we can spur that then we should see the best results for our money. But before I go down this road too far we might take notice of a related point. New business creation, a hallmark of start-ups and small businesses, is not found only in these segments. We can also create new business by expanding existing businesses, including mid-sized and large corporations. It is just a question of how to do it, or what motivates such expansions.

In a small start-up, simply having access to investment capital is enough to motivate the task. In an existing business the motivation is more complicated. The larger the company, the more risk-averse they tend to be. That means, the bigger the organization, the more obvious it has to be to the decision-makers that they will make a profit on some new venture under consideration. So the fact is not that larger companies will not generate new jobs, but that they will do it more carefully and at a slower rate than the smallest companies. However, if we can create an environment where the risk of expanding existing business is lowered, than all business expansion should be affected.

There is another important point related to creating new business. Here we might use an economist's terminology. The level of business activity can be measured by how much capital is moved around. This is another way of saying that the more money everyone spends, the more total business is occurring. So if we want to step back even further we can make a broad point like this: Motivate people to spend more and we will motivate an increase in business activity. Capital is the fuel of a capitalist system. If we can burn more fuel our engine will go faster. If we burn less, we will slow down. That is why economists like to measure the state of a country's health with Gross Domestic Product (GDP) and related figures. Essentially, our GDP is just a measure of how much gas our country's economic engine is burning. When GDP growth is high, we are roaring ahead. If GDP growth goes negative, we are stepping backward and in recession if we stay there too long.

According to its numerical definition, the recession of 2009 has ended because the GDP is now showing positive growth. However, that growth is very small, not much above 2% for the past three years, which suggests that we are still trying to climb out of the hole the recession put us in. Though unemployment rates have fallen a bit since 2009, the nationwide unemployment situation hasn't improved enough to make people feel confident about the economy. The recession may be technically over, but most people still feel its pinch, either directly or indirectly.

Regardless, here is the punch line on GDP: It is a real and useful measure of the movement of capital. If we increase it, that means we are increasing the activity of markets (in general). While not directly a measure of generating jobs, increasing GDP will tend to result in business growth. A low or negative GDP[1] tends to scare business planners. It tells them the economy is bad. If someone acquires money in a bad economy, they are likely to stash it in a safe place until things get better. If we give the same person (or business) money in a roaring economy, the odds are much higher that they will do something resembling an investment. Any kind of investment increase pushes GDP up more, which in turn makes the economy better overall. That is because an "investment" typically means this money is going to either buy something or hire someone.

This leaves us with three ways to consider the target of our strategy. First, we can look directly at spurring job growth. The bull's-eye here would be a focus on small business growth. Right next to that sweet spot would be the slightly broader area of business creation and expansion in general. This would mean encouraging growth in businesses of all sizes. And finally we can look at the broadest measure, the amount of capital moving around our country. How are markets for different goods and services doing? Are people spending money or are things tight? We can summarize all of this by seeing if our country's GDP is improving.

Our plan needs to attack all three of these targets aggressively and with maximum efficiency – small business growth, general business growth, and improving capital flow. Efficiency may be the key. We can create a job directly by spending money through a government initiative, like when we build a highway. This is OK but is not a particularly efficient way to generate jobs. In the example of a highway project, a fair portion of every government dollar spent does go directly to creating a term-oriented job. But we can get more jobs per government dollar with other methods. What we must also remember when thinking about job creation is that the highway job goes away as soon as the highway project is finished. We want to create jobs that last in the long term.

A common idea for encouraging job growth is to cut taxes for businesses and the wealthy. While this strategy is popular as political rhetoric, let's first consider whether it actually creates many jobs. Sadly, economists are in wide agreement on this. Even with the most optimistic assumptions, tax cutting is a very inefficient way to create jobs. Most analysts agree that per dollar spent, a tax break in a bad economy produces fewer jobs than even government work projects do. When the government spends money on a tax break, most of the total dollars go to mid-sized and large companies. Especially in a weak economic climate, only a small percentage of a tax break is likely to go into new job

---

[1] "GDP" can be a short for "quarterly GDP rate of change." It is a negative percentage when the economy declines. Actual GDP is a dollar figure representing total U.S. business activity

creation. Rather, these large businesses and wealthy individuals will either save a majority of their tax break money for better times, give it out as pay increases for high-level executives (a sadly growing trend of late), or perhaps use it to buy out other businesses. The buyout of competitors and partners is particularly popular in bad economies because the cost of doing so is relatively cheap. That is, the price of buying other businesses is relatively low in a weak economy because there are fewer takers to compete with. If stock purchases are involved, these prices also trend low. Yet this is a safe way to expand for the companies with enough cash to do it.

These kinds of tax breaks have an unfortunate side effect related to unemployment. When a bigger company buys a smaller one it often results in job reduction. This is because a common post-acquisition (or merger) action is the "down-sizing" phase, which is a euphemism for saying the acquiring company lays off the people they do not need after they buy the other company. Even in the best case where the buyout results in no layoffs there is usually no job creation. Only rarely does a merger or acquisition increase market activity. This means GDP is more likely to reduce than grow with the proliferation of mergers and acquisitions.

The only thing a tax break really does is increase total capital available. Let's specifically consider those companies on the edge of hiring or purchasing something, but falling short before a tax break is enacted. Once we give them the tax break they might then have just enough money to justify the new hire or purchase. This is exactly the logic used by those who push for tax breaks as a means to increase jobs. However, in the real world such a case is nearly unheard of. Business managers almost never say, "If I only had a few dollars from a tax break I could justify hiring that person I need." On the contrary, managers base such decisions on market conditions and business opportunities. If the business move makes sense, they will spend the money. If the environment is too risky, they will not spend the money even if there are plenty of funds available.

The bottom line is difficult for many politicians to accept. In a bad economy tax break dollars go primarily towards activity that has little to no effect on improving jobs and GDP. Tax breaks have somewhat more of a job producing effect when the economy is good, because in a good economy businesses and entrepreneurs are more inclined to make new investments. But even then, history shows us that tax breaks don't have as strong a positive effect on the economy as we might think.

I recognize that there is a political issue involved here. Today, politicians use the issue of tax breaks for businesses as political shorthand for being pro-jobs. But as I noted above, historical analysis shows that the actual effect of taxes on jobs is at best marginal, perhaps even negligible in bad times. This is particularly true as long as the overall tax rate is not historically high, which it currently is not.

We might think with all the noise about cutting taxes to help create jobs that there would be clear data from the past that supports the concept. When I looked at past graphs of tax rates and tax cuts (or increases) and put them next to charts of job growth I was floored. Not only does history fail to support the conclusion, it clearly shows something altogether different. There is essentially no historical relationship between taxes and job growth at all! It does not take a scientist or an economist to see it. Based on the charts, the two issues act as if they have no relationship whatever. Anyone can pull the data off the internet and see that graphs related to taxes move with near complete independence from those related to employment. It looks like the politicians have convinced us of something just by insisting that it's true. But when we look at the data, it is embarrassingly obvious. The emperor has no clothes.

It is vital that we understand this issue; otherwise we will keep making the same detour. So here is another way we can see that taxes have little to do with job growth. Small businesses, especially the startups that generate the most jobs, get no help from a tax break. Many people do not appreciate that startups typically pay no taxes because their costs are generally higher than their income in the first few years. In fact, the act of creating a startup business is itself a popular tax shelter. No matter what the tax rate is, an investor can deduct almost every dollar they invest in an attempt to start a new business.

A similar situation is true for existing businesses. When a company expands and creates new jobs, nearly all of the money they invest in that effort is tax deductible. So a tax break has essentially zero effect on our target sweet spot of new business, as well as our second target of expanding existing businesses. If we want to save money on our taxes, we can start a new company or expand an existing one and deduct all the associated expenses. We don't need a new tax break to improve that. We could even argue that a tax increase might generate more startup businesses because more people would seek this excellent tax shelter.

There is clear historical evidence that small tax increases do not reduce overall job creation even a little. We should not be surprised then that decreasing taxes does not automatically generate new jobs. No amount of huffing and puffing changes the data. This is most obvious over the long term, but it is also the case for mid-term effects. What is most surprising is that in many cases cutting taxes does not even create a short-term improvement in jobs. To be fair, there is no clear consensus on this topic even among economists. There are counterarguments, although they are so technical that they smell wrong. When two graphs act independently, that means they move together as often as they move oppositely. How good is an economic theory that predicts taxes and jobs should move together while history only shows this occurring randomly? Do elaborate excuses really help make such a theory more useful?

Here is the most important point for us to understand on this topic: If we are looking for a job creation strategy, tax rate manipulation is at best terribly inefficient. At worst, it is completely ineffective. If our goal is to grow jobs, we cannot count on tax reduction as a means to get there. As a strategy its efficiency is far lower than a government work program, and government work programs are not efficient enough to solve the problem, either. Everyone should stop talking about taxes as a primary means of controlling job growth, either up or down. Whether we still think there can be some impact with taxes or not, one thing must be true. Taxes are not the problem but they're not the solution, either.

Since there will be some people who just will not concede this point, I will offer what appears to be an exception and explain why it does not undermine my argument. If taxes are *historically* excessive, they can have a repressive effect on economic growth, especially in the long run. This is a macro argument at the same level as GDP, and I agree with it. Similarly, but to a far lesser degree, taxes that are historically ultra-low will likely have some stimulating effect on economic growth, especially in the short run. I say short run because ultra-low taxes are likely starving government budgets, which can come back to bite the economy later on. Regardless, most would agree that these two points are generally true. So the dispute continues even though the actual data shows that at the margins, the real effect of tax manipulation is either zero or something disappointingly close to that. The big point is that if we think our overall rate of taxation is the problem then we need a huge tax change to fix the matter. Small changes may have a big impact on government budgets, yet have little effect on the overall economy. Therefore, we will not waste our time at this waterhole. It is mostly mud.

Let me explain why we can put this question to bed under today's circumstances. We have excellent new data regarding the lower-taxes-for-jobs strategy. Our economy was soaring during much of the 1990's, prior to the Bush tax breaks of the following decade. As a result of Bush's efforts, taxes are lower now than they were then. Strikingly, the economy is far worse now. The first round of tax breaks came after the economy went through a brief recession in 2001. Although things got better for a brief period, we slipped back hard just a few years later even as tax reduction continued. If anyone needs proof of whether tax cutting can fix a problem that wasn't caused by high taxes in the first place, they just have to look at the U.S. economy over the last ten years. Taxes did not cause the 2001 recession and tax breaks were not a good answer. Our debt is now dangerously huge and we are in far worse economic trouble than before.

The dirty problem of tax breaks that their proponents avoid talking about is that they are not free. They require either a cut in government spending or the borrowing of funds to pay for them. Since we are borrowing, we are essentially mortgaging our future on the bet that the tax break will fix everything so we can afford to pay the debt back later. We have tried that over and over. Regardless of how unpopular it might be to point this out, the tax break simply does not fix an economy that was not stifled by high taxes in the first place.

If taxes are not what caused the problem, then the next step is to try to determine what did cause the problem. After all, we did not always have the issues we face today. What happened? What dynamics can we blame?

Let's start by looking at the economic collapse that began in 2008. Officially the recession occurred in 2009, but the tipping point clearly happened the year before. Why did it happen? The answer we get from different experts usually falls into one of three categories. The most common one is to blame Wall Street. This is just a way of saying that investment bankers in particular, and the supporting cast of commercial and real estate bankers (which is ultimately all banks) took advantage of deregulation to ruin everything. It is hard not to empathize with this view.

There is a good argument that those who enjoy government guarantees such as deposit insurance should not use the guaranteed money for any kind of speculation. At the very least it would be reasonable for banks to be required to hold these investments in a completely transparent way. In other words, if a bank is going to do funny things with the money in your savings account, it ought to be easy to look at their books to see exactly what they are doing. This would allow people to change banks if they did not like how their money was being managed. However, we went the other way. The deregulation that came in the Bush era made it easy for the bankers both to do the funny business and to hide it. It is so hard to determine what they are doing with our money that even professional financial analysts cannot tell us. That problem remains today. Deregulation includes the idea that we trust the bankers to tell us what we need to know and what we do not. Apparently we have decided consumers do not need to know anything useful about how the banks manage their deposits.

One conclusion strikes me as obvious. If we believe in loosening the rules of activities a bank is allowed to engage in, then we should add rules to make sure they disclose what they are doing more fully. This way they are less likely to do things approaching unethical or criminal activity. But we did not do that. We essentially created a strategy that said, "We dare you to be under-handed. We will loosen the rules so you can do whatever you want. And on top of that, we will allow you to hide this activity so we cannot tell what you are doing." Really? We did both? It seems to me that those who pushed through deregulation were asking for trouble.

However, this last point leads us to the second most popular target of blame - government. Was it the greedy bankers who did us in or was it the government politicians who set up an environment for greedy bankers to thrive and prosper until their house of cards ultimately collapsed? The capitalist philosopher recognizes that a market will do whatever it can to make money. It is a powerful notion that we should see as inherently neither bad nor good.

Capitalism does what it can to make money legally. If we change the rules to allow behavior we do not like, it will happen as if we had pressed a button. This is a capitalist market dynamic in action. It is actually beautiful in its own way. I, for one, do not excuse unethical behavior simply because we set up a system that does not restrict anyone from it. But I also understand that if we change laws to allow people to profit from behavior we do not really want, people will perform those behaviors.

My opinion therefore is that both arguments have validity: bankers did bad things but government changed laws to invite the bad things. There should be a penalty for working the system in an unintended manner, to the detriment of the masses, especially if the perpetrators hide the facts and lie about it up until the very end. There are many examples of bank CEOs who did this. So we could say, "OK, the mechanics of what they did was not illegal, just marginally ethical. But misleading everyone about what they were doing, that is fraudulent." We should not encourage people of power, very well paid people who are risking more than they ought to, to lie about what they are doing while they are working the system. I therefore believe that prosecuting a few of the worst offenders for fraud might result in a good example for the future.

But such a point is arguably a justice matter and not really within the scope of this project. If I am looking for the actual cause of the problem, I cannot say it was a person or a conspiracy of CEOs. No, here the root cause is obviously the change in banking regulations. We can see an immediate cause and effect in the dynamics of what happened. Once the regulations changed, the undesirable banking behavior quickly became pervasive. This is the hallmark of a root cause. The change in law produced a change in market behavior. Whether we want to prosecute the bastards who did it, or those who lied about doing it, is perhaps secondary. That it happened at all should have been predictable from the change in the rules. So it is really the laws that are bad and should be repaired lest history repeat itself at some point down the road.

I did say there were three arguments regarding whom to blame. I mentioned the two most popular - the bankers and the government (or deregulation). The third argument is that no one is to blame. This argument is most popular among the lawmakers and their advisors who supported the original deregulation. They are essentially saying that the original deregulation was and still is good.

They argue that the abuses were the act of lone individuals and represent aberrant behavior. The implication is that undesired behavior will automatically remedy itself in time. This is similar to the notion that free markets are self-correcting if we just leave them alone long enough.

This is a dangerous argument. Following this logic, we might say that there is no way to determine how many bad-cycles will come before the self-correction sticks. Or we could say that bad cycles are part of the strategy, but they are necessarily temporary. In other words, when the bankers screw up the economy they have to back off for a while before they are likely to do it again (as a group). To say the law should stay as it is without change is to ask for the same thing to happen again and again without any limit. It might take five, ten or twenty years per cycle, or maybe longer. But I do not personally expect so. I think the cycle will exactly match up to an improved economy. As soon as people think things are going well, the banks will try to game the system in yet another way, because it is legal for them to do unethical things, and perhaps more important, it is still legal for them to hide that fact.

There is no real solution to the blame game. I can give my opinion that of the three choices – bankers, government, or no one – I choose deregulation, and the lack of transparency in particular, as the primary root cause. Fixing the deregulation, jailing the bankers who lied, or doing nothing – none of these solve our immediate problem. The first of these does try to prevent the problem from recurring by putting reasonable banking oversight in place. Some might argue that prosecuting people would also be a deterrent against future abuses. Regardless, it strikes me that the argument for deregulation has now proven to be a gross error.

Those who want to keep deregulation say that we shouldn't need laws to keep bankers ethical and transparent. They say that imposing ethics in banking somehow depresses economic activity. Do we need to allow bankers to be shady and risk our future so that they can make a bigger profit? Even aside from the immorality of the matter, this is still a shortsighted strategy. Obviously, allowing bankers to build gains on unethical and hidden behavior is doomed to eventually implode. Whatever short-term economic benefit we achieve will then be erased by a deeper long-term problem.

This is our situation now. Deregulation has almost no long-term benefit. Does anyone really believe that ethical banking cannot prosper without deregulation? Was banking a terribly unprofitable business beforehand? The argument in support of deregulation is nothing less than absurd. It has never benefited most citizens. And although every bank wants it, they are like addicts begging for illicit drugs. Even they have not ultimately benefited because eventually too many of them abused the power. Still, we are only talking about future safeguards in repairing this error. I think there is plenty of room for ethical banking in United States 2.0. So it is part of my recommendation we fully reinstate or even improve banking regulation. We need this to insure the economy does not get ruined again once we do the hard work to fix it. However, this is not at the core of our solution. Magnified Capitalism will thrive in a lawful and ethical environment, but what makes it work is a new dynamic I have not yet explained.

The cause of our overall economic condition is not as simple as the narrow events that triggered our 2008 collapse. That collapse occurred because bankers were doing risky things they thought they could get away with. To be fair though, lots of people became convinced what they were doing was not that risky, at least for a while. Those investments the bankers were making, the ones that turned out to be risky, were largely based on the U.S. real estate market. The real estate market tanked first, which in turn revealed those investments to be risky. Why did that market collapse?

Real estate values had been rising steadily for years, partly due to low interest rates, lower taxes, and increasingly "creative" mortgage broker practices. Home buying continued to increase while prices for those homes rose to levels that could not be sustained. This is the hallmark of a bubble - grow and grow beyond the ability to support the rate of growth. Finally the situation reached a tipping point and the bubble revealed itself. Once people agreed that real estate was way overpriced, the popping began. Real estate prices stopped increasing in 2006. That convinced an ever-growing number of people to stop investing in it. So the pop accelerated. This effect has continued more or less until now.

Today, most investors see real estate as being valued fairly after prices have fallen for six years or so. On the one hand, it might be risky to assume prices will rebound soon. In fact, there is new evidence that they may still decline a bit more. On the other hand, the large decline that comes from a market pop seems to have largely played out. If I need a house or plot of land, I can probably buy it today without unusual risk. However, if I am looking to grow my money in an investment, it is debatable whether the timing is good for real estate. I cannot be sure my investment will increase in value, and it might even decrease a little. So the real estate market is somewhat stable, if a little shaky, after its huge fall, which was one of the biggest real estate corrections in history. From the time prices stopped rising in mid-2006 through the real estate crash in the years 2007 to 2009 to the recent leveling off, the average price of a home in the U.S. fell from its peak value by well over 30%. Some parts of the country were hit harder than others. In Florida, for example, over 40% of all home mortgages have an outstanding debt balance that exceeds today's property value. In other words, all those people are now upside-down in their loans.

Why did this real estate crash happen? We can point to a combination of factors. Investor analysis, an oversupply of mortgages, problems with the stock market, lower taxes and interest rates (increased capital), all of these factors conspired after 2001 to make real estate the most attractive place to put investment dollars. This continued for years because real estate prices just kept going up. Investors have trouble resisting a market that never goes down. After a while people started believing that real estate was incapable of declining. Incidentally, this is an early warning sign for a bubble – when the media provides expert analysis that refutes the warnings of a bubble. This kind of story was becoming popular around 2004. Nay-sayers tend to be too early, but they were correct about their underlying concerns.

Since I was picking on taxes earlier as an ineffective method of improving our economy, I would like to point out an observation related to the real estate bubble. I listed lower taxes as a contributing factor in the real estate collapse. That is right; the lowering of taxes in that time period exaggerated the problem. I want to be clear that lower taxes did not cause the problem. But if a market bubble is generating, and then we add more capital (through lower taxes) to a system that is pumping up the bubble, the bubble inflates faster. Real estate was one of the markets where the extra money from lower taxes was going. Lower taxes contributed to a bigger market and therefore even helped create a few jobs in the short run. But in hindsight we can see that this impact was both artificial and temporary, even as the tax reduction was kept in place.

My point here is not to blame tax cuts for our problems. My point is to warn that even the positive historical examples of tax cutting come with difficult-to-predict negative consequences, in addition to the obvious penalty of pressure on government budgets and increasing debt due to lower tax revenues. The point of the story is to show another aspect of the illusion of tax cuts. It is not that taxes are good. It is just that playing with tax rates, especially when they are already in the fair range, is not a fruitful economic control lever.

Since we are interested in primary causal factors for the troubled economy, we should probably consider why the stock market became less attractive than real estate after 2001. After all, the lack of interest in the stock market was probably the most important contributing factor for why real estate values grew so fast. In 2001 the "dot-com" bubble burst. If we still had money to invest after that, where would we put it? Real estate seemed one of the best choices. The real estate market had been showing steady, unbroken growth for about a decade.

Naturally, when real estate does well, so do real estate related companies, including banks. And when companies do well, so do their stocks. Within a few years whole crowds of investment choices started to improve, all rooted around the idea that real estate is a safe, steady place to invest money. After 2001, the stock market recovered, led by banks, real estate firms, and their related industries. The irony is that much of the economic improvement from 2002 through 2006 was based on blowing up a bubble. There is a lesson here. If we want sustained growth, we need to build it upon real growth of goods and services. If the main pillar of our growth is purely market inflation from short-term stimulants, we should not be surprised if the whole thing falls back when the markets realize there is no new substance.

We could take another step back in time and analyze the "dot-com" bubble that caused the 2001 recession when it burst. If that had not happened perhaps investment in real estate would have stayed more modest. A modest growth in real estate may have been sustainable indefinitely, as with any market. But now we are starting to go back so far that the relevance to today's problems is beginning to appear vaporous.

There is one very important thing I do want to mention about this era. The late 1990's represent our most recent period of widespread prosperity and success. It is useful to point this out because we want to be able to hold up as an example a recent spot in history that represents what it is to be economically successful. It is like saying, "We want a realistic goal. We should define a strong economic status based on what we know can be achieved." In the years 1999 and 2000, the U.S. budget was very nearly balanced for the first time in quite a while, as were most state budgets. Unemployment hovered around a low of 4%. GDP growth was typically over 4% per quarter for years. The lives of U.S. citizens were widely improving. Thus the years 1999 and 2000 can be held up as a peak period for most economic statistics that matter. In fact, if the unemployment rate is our main index, we would have to go back to the late 1960's to find a slightly better period, and then to a few years in the mid 50's before that.

Understanding the history of how we got into this mess is helpful, but the exercise does not automatically produce a solution. It does let us see some facts about what works and what does not. It also lets us see that not very long ago things were going pretty well. Perhaps it means the road to success need not be far away.

That brings us back to today. Other than unemployment and GDP troubles, how is the U.S. doing? What do we have to work with? Is it all bad? What good news do we have?

Here is what I think is the single most impressive economic statistic about our United States. For about the last 100 years the U.S. has been the world's largest economy compared to any other single country. It remains so today, although it appears that China's current growth will put us in the second place spot sometime within the next ten years, give or take five years. That is, unless we do something to dramatically improve our own economic growth. In other words, we are still in the driver's seat, at least for a few years. In my business-oriented view, this is analogous to being the market leader in some business sector, like the company that sells the most cars, or the top provider of internet searches.

I. Situation

Market leadership is the most envious position not just because it represents first place, but also because the market leader has advantages over everyone else. Not all market leaders use their position of power well, but those that do tend to stay in first place.

We have some other strong statistics. Another thing we should be pleased about is a fact that might be news to many. It is about our literacy rate. As you know, Mr. President, we are often bashed for the weakness of our educational system given our economic strength. However, what many do not know is that our illiteracy rate is estimated to be 99.0%. This makes us tied for 23rd place in the world. The interesting part is revealed when we look at the 22 who are slightly better. If we try to find either a major world competitor or close ally on this same list we will discover that only Russia has a higher ranking than we do. The rest are smaller countries, curiously composed largely of former Soviet states and Cuba. Some people are concerned that we are at risk of losing ground on this important statistic, so I do not want to suggest that we should not do better. But still, this is one of the stronger facts about us. It is a solidly justifiable priority to insure that nearly everyone who can read does. That we need more improvement at more advanced educational levels is still true, but it is appropriate to the American sense of equality that we make sure we do not just focus on the more capable students. In this country we work for equality and opportunity even for those young people who have challenges and disadvantages. Our reasonably robust literacy rate suggests our basic education is stronger at being all-encompassing than it is at elevating the majority to a more advanced level. Perhaps there is an interesting angle here to pursue further, but doing so is off my topic.

What other strengths do we have to work with? We are still the number one home of large business. 139 of the top 500 companies in the world are based in the United States. We got this way by being the best country in which to start a business. After all, large companies generally begin as small start-ups. So if a country is the best place to start a business, then it becomes fertile and grows business of all sizes over time.

There is a warning here, however. We are no longer considered the best place to start a business. When economists measure this effect they call it "competitiveness." Recently the World Economic Forum has started formally measuring the competitiveness of the top 30 countries. In 2007, the first year they published this comparison, we were ranked number one in competitiveness. Presumably, we were number one for most of the previous 100 years or so, if they had measured competitiveness during those times.

Regardless, in 2009 we dropped to second place behind Switzerland and have dropped further each year since. In the latest report (2011-2012), we are in 5th place for world competitiveness. Singapore is now second behind Switzerland, with Sweden in 3rd and Finland in 4th! The other big players' positions may be even more important. Germany is 6th and has held pretty steady in that spot. The United Kingdom is 10th due to a modest rise recently. They are just behind Japan which is in 9th place and has been slowly improving. That a communist country like China even made the list (of the top 30) is impressive and illustrates the changes that have occurred there. It should not be a big surprise, then, that they have risen in recent years but are still only in 26th place.

We are no longer in first place for competitiveness, but Switzerland and the others are only beating us by a bit. Who cares about these little guys, right? Wrong. The warning is not that some smaller countries have become more competitive than we are. It is that we are losing our former leadership position and our trend is in the wrong direction. It is not about them. It is about us. The United States is supposed to be the best place to start a business because we believe in the kind of freedom an entrepreneur needs for that. And by freedom I mean not just the laws that allow a person to start a business, but the local infrastructure that makes it easy to do so.

Most countries today allow a person to start a business if they want but there are many more facets involved in setting up a new company. These include obtaining a business loan from a bank, a business license from the government, or a mortgage on the building the startup needs. An entrepreneur might also need to find an investor who is willing to bet on the business plan, or employees who are willing to work for a startup situation. All of these issues, and more, collectively build an environment that defines the ease and attractiveness of starting a business.

Our inherent advantages are slipping in this area of competitiveness. This data regarding our economic competitiveness compared to other nations speaks directly to my proposal's goal. The measure of competitiveness is about small businesses creation above all else. We have already noted that small business is the sweet spot of job creation. In fact, I have said this is the top target of the plan. Now we can come to a new conclusion. If we are focused on new job creation, we must care about improving competitiveness. We will revisit this very important factor as we proceed.

There is another bit of good news that many people do not appreciate, and fewer understand why it matters. 60% of global currency today is in U.S. dollars. Second place goes to the Euro with 24% but this number is declining due to the economic problems the European Union countries are having. Who cares? Nearly every government cares, especially ours, China, Russia and those of the European Union. We care because having such a large proportion of the world's supply of money in the form of dollars gives us a special advantage. In particular, it means we can get away with holding enormous debt with far fewer consequences. That is right. If we were less important economically, the same level of debt we have now would likely be killing our country. We can argue it is killing us anyway, but the effect is less severe because we hold the money standard. This means people all over the world are willing to buy our dollars whenever we need a loan. The government prints more when we increase our debt, and we do not pay as much interest as we would if we were anyone else. Of course, this situation is totally unfair to every other country, especially the other big ones. China wants a different standard world currency, and so do other major players like Russia. But that kind of change would take years, so there is little to worry about in the short term.

What I want to point out, though, is the flip side of this advantage. That is, we know we pay less to borrow money than other nations do. But what if we found a way to stop borrowing and even paid down our national debt? Would holding the world currency have any advantage then? Since the dollar emerged as the global currency around World War II, this has never happened, but we got a taste of what it might look like in the late 1990s. At that time, our government worked hard to try to balance the budget, coming closer and closer as the decade ended. It came so close that by 2000 some news agencies reported that we had in fact balanced the budget, although it turned out we came just slightly short of that goal. Regardless, even though taxes were not reduced, an impressive thing happened to the United States during this period. We experienced the lowest unemployment rate since the 1960's, as I have already mentioned. This time when we nearly stopped borrowing turned out to be our most recent period of widespread prosperity. How are those two issues related? After all, the attempt to lower debt began well before the economy reached its high point. Yet the pinnacle of our economic success occurred in the same years that the national debt just about stopped growing.

We all know we should not increase our personal debt if we can help it. We imagine the same must be true of national debt because we think of the matter in intuitive terms. The problem is that when our country's budget goes negative, it is difficult to see any direct effects from that situation. It has reached the point that some economists say there is nothing really wrong with carrying a large national debt. In other words, what is the penalty? One penalty is obvious: the interest we pay on our debt (which takes the form of treasury bills).

First, let's understand the scale of the problem. Our current (end of 2011) total debt is over $10 trillion (according to the CBO), which equates to 69% of one year's GDP. Other sources who calculate it differently claim our debt to be over $15 trillion at end of July 2012. Ouch. Put another way, we owe roughly about as much as the total value of all the goods and services our nation's businesses generate in one year. Our federal government's income for 2011 was about $2.3 trillion, which is less than one quarter of lower CBO figure for 2011 debt. If we made $100,000 per year and we owed what our government owes, we would have $434,000 of unsecured debt. This is debt that has no collateral, like credit card debt and personal loans – i.e., do not count home mortgages or car loans we might have.

Interestingly, even though our debt has climbed high in recent years, the payment on our debt has not. Why? This is partly because of our leadership in world currency, and partly because other countries have plenty of their own problems. The result is that the interest rate on our debt has fallen to historical lows. In 2008 we paid $253 billion on national debt interest. In 2010, our total debt grew about $2 trillion higher, but our interest payment actually dropped to only $197 billion. This is only a temporary break, though. The CBO estimates that debt payments will climb to $778 billion by 2020. Note that the total federal budget for 2011 was $3.4 trillion. The deficit was a whopping $1.1 trillion (although that is slightly lower than the previous year). To put it simply, we are still borrowing about one third of what our national government spends each year.

To get back to my original point, however, we were trying to project the impact of holding the world currency if we stopped raising our debt levels. One impact would be that we would roughly freeze our interest payments on the national debt we still carry from past years of unbalanced budgets. But we can understand the bigger benefit by looking at what happened in the late 1990's. Recall that this was a period when the economy improved widely and broadly. It is so hard to see the relationship between a balanced budget and low unemployment that not everyone agrees there is one. But nearly the same thing happened in the 1960's, and in the 1950's and just after World War II. It seems that every time we come close to balancing our budget, we find a nearby year where unemployment reached a low point. Numerically, we are talking about an unemployment rate of 4% or less, which is my goal for this plan, too.

The cause and effect relationship is complicated but the correlation on historical charts is readily visible if we just look. It is as if balancing the budget puts in motion a string of positive effects that end up helping our country's economy. We might need a doctorate in economics and the space of an entire book to explain why, but the punch line is right in front of us. Balancing the budget might just turn out to be one of the best things we can do to help our economy. Holding the world's currency may even amplify this positive effect. We could go on by discussing examples of other countries' budgets. Notice that China, Germany and other countries that are prospering have balanced budgets, for instance, but I think I have said enough to make the point for now.

What other aspects of the state of our country today should we examine? There are several other curious tangential points. For example, we have the biggest economy and we spend by far the most per capita on healthcare, yet our country is only in 30th place for life expectancy. That speaks volumes to either the inequality and/or the inefficiency of healthcare in the U.S. Similarly, we are 34th in infant mortality, which strikes me as particularly surprising. However, healthcare is tangential to our plan because we are focusing on the economy. If we greatly improve employment, business growth, and government revenue, we can then expect two healthcare-related factors to improve. First, more people will have employer-provided healthcare. The quality of such plans should also improve in a very competitive job market. Second, the government will have both more resources and (as we will see) more political levers to use in improving healthcare in the U.S. This should be true regardless of which specific strategy we select to improve the economy, as long as the answer is not "do nothing."

Finally, there is an interesting related point that almost no one seems to make. The United States has recently won a major battle for world peace and freedom. Perhaps because it crept upon us, we rarely discuss it. When people do talk about it, the discussion usually centers around the fall of the Soviet Union or the fall of communism in general. But there is a larger picture that may be even more important. Today, capitalism rules. Democracy is the framework in which capitalism thrives best. Most everyone in the world knows that now. Those countries that embrace democracy and capitalism more effectively have become the most prosperous, with minor exception. Those that countries that are exceptions have had their prosperity by making changes that move in a direction of nurturing capitalism.

We can argue that communism still lives (particularly in China), that Russia's democracy is questionable and many other countries' implementation of democratic processes is dubious, and on and on. But we can also argue that these are details and overall, the world continues to gravitate towards the U.S.-led model. China is becoming freer and doing a low-violence slow walk towards democracy as they pursue the fruits of capitalism. The Arab Spring is scaring repressive governments within an internet-connected world. People power can now surpass the will of monarchs and repressive dictators, although the cost is still sadly high. Places like Syria show us the amazing will of people who refuse to be repressed even when their government has no sense of morality. Observe that the wars of today, even those the U.S. wages, are not really about one country taking over another. They are essentially variants of civil wars, wars against repression, or wars against terrorism, as some would put it.

It may not seem obvious, but the world is poised for an unprecedented level of peace. Cooperation and negotiation, even when strained, have largely replaced wars as a method of settling disputes between countries. I suggest that someone should stand up, if meekly, and yell, "Yay, capitalism won!" Maybe we should pick a day and celebrate it. Regardless, this was a battle we led during much of the 20th century, a battle we continue to lead today.

We will go on to have more battles so the fight to spread democracy is not really over. It probably never will be completely so. I can predict that we will always need armies, at least to provide deterrence. And there will still be those rogue leaders who just cannot help themselves by making errant decisions that lead to war. But in general, there has been a major shift in world thinking about what works and what does not. The world has converged on the basic method needed to create economic prosperity: democracy and capitalism. The capitalist approach also elevates the rights of people as individuals. This shift is occurring just as the internet and wireless telecommunications have elevated the individual's ability to speak out. So I will stand up and celebrate this victory, "Yay!"

This brings me to my related point. A part of our victory comes with a penalty. Rather than win by ruling the world directly, we have won a war of competing ideas. The ideas we support now rule much of the world. We achieved this victory by being the example. Even though our example has had, and continues to have flaws, it is a good enough example that most everyone has got the gist of it. The obvious lesson is that the closer we get to implementing a real secular democracy, the less the need for wars and the greater our people's economic fertility.

Democracies with their inherent freedoms are good for people and good for business. The world's nations are starting to focus more on battles of economics rather than those that involve armies and bloodshed, at least between countries (with hopefully minor exceptions). This is good. But we have paid for this achievement directly. One reason we shot to the top economic spot some hundred years ago was that we became the most competitive nation in the world, by far. But now, countries all around the world are duplicating the same types of ideas that made us so successful, with minor modifications. We have stood tall, but in the process we elevated most everyone else to the status of worthy and respected competitor. Therefore, one of the keystones of this proposal is to make a move, a historic move.

In business I can tell you, this kind of move is a constant requirement. When companies update their strategies, their plans often involve the introduction of a newly upgraded product while they phase out the dying old product line. Our product line is old. It works great, but everyone is starting to make and sell the same stuff we have made for years. We do not need to change the kind of product we have, but perhaps it is time to consider an upgrade to our capitalist system. Not a different economic system, but a more powerful version of what we already do so well. If we can make capitalism work better, we may be able to once again become the most competitive country in the world. Such a bold move will produce great economic rewards. We have won the freedom of the world and shown that capitalism rules. Now it is time to show that our innovation can include capitalism itself. We are ready to consider United States 2.0.

"The worst thing that could happen is that we'll spend a lot of money betting on ourselves and then, after we create a zillion jobs, we might have trouble making all the profits that we projected. It's more likely, however, that betting on American ingenuity is as good an investment as it has been for most of the last 200 years. In a few years I expect the argument to change entirely. The issue will become: What do we do with our government profits first – pay down the national debt or cut income taxes?"

- a future U.S. Senator after a briefing on Magnified Capitalism -

II. Magnified Capitalism – Strategy and Executive Summary

Why do jobs exist in a capitalist system? Jobs are performed by employees in order to implement a business plan or a business process. If we want create more jobs, we need to generate and enact more of these plans and processes.

Most active venture capitalists tell us there is an abundance of business opportunities in the United States. These professional investors look for ideas, inventions, business plans, business teams, expansions and extensions to put their money into. But most of the proposals they see are never implemented, and the venture capitalists know they only see a small fraction of the ones out there. Why are so few business plans realized? Because there are far fewer professional venture capital dollars available than all those good ideas call for.

To have any chance of getting funding, an entrepreneur usually needs a very professional team of associates, market studies, and a great business plan. If they vigilantly shop their great plan around they might get hooked up with a special kind of venture capitalist called an "angel investor". These are the people who put up the seed money for a new business. That might be enough for the start-up to build a prototype, launch a pilot program, or prove its business concept in some other way, but nothing more. Only after the viability of their business plan is validated can most start-ups hope to get all the money they need from venture capitalists to launch the full-blown business. Venture capitalists are therefore necessarily cherry pickers.

In these bad times, these same venture capitalists risk even less of their money and therefore fund an even narrower selection of business ventures. Do the venture capitalists make more money this way? No. They choose this safer strategy because they cannot afford to make many bad bets when the economy is slow. The result is that most of the business plans that receive venture capital money today are the high-end, low-risk deals. These are usually situations in which a business has already gotten its feet off the ground. It may just need some money to get through to the next step to the point at which the business starts making a profit on its own. In past good times such businesses would have some chance of borrowing their money from a business banker. The true start-up, the one with a great plan and a skilled management team but no money, can just about forget finding funding in today's climate. It still happens, but the odds of getting the money they need can seem similar to playing the lottery.

Speaking of bankers, are they not still making loans to businesses? It turns out that they are in a situation parallel to that of the venture capitalists, except bankers are an even more conservative group. In these difficult times their loan requirements are so tough that an entrepreneur almost has to show that they do not need the loan in order to qualify for it.

What kind of business loan is a bank likely to provide today? They will consider lending money to an existing business with solid credit and a low-risk reason for needing it. For instance, the company might need some cash to fill a large customer commitment or complete a signed contract. Imagine a plane manufacturer who needs to buy parts to complete a customer order. Or consider a software developer who is a little behind schedule to deliver on a contract that is otherwise going well. Their delay leaves them short on payroll funds. A bank may assist in such a situation and others like it. However, even these examples do not always receive bank support these days, such as a situation in which the company in question has had recent financial troubles.

It was not always this way. In good times banks would take some risks, and in return they would charge a higher interest rate, thus making up for the risk. For example, banks used to be quick to back franchise opportunities, such as the opening of a fast food restaurant, because the franchisee had a proven business plan and established business processes that increased their odds of success. Today, if an entrepreneur wants a loan for a new franchise, they had better qualify for a Small Business Administration guarantee and have enough of their own cash to make up at least 20% of the total working capital they need. That typically translates to the new business owner needing to put up at least $50,000 of their own cash per business location. Often the number is far higher. If they do not qualify for the SBA guarantee for any reason, they can pretty much forget being approved for a franchise loan.

The whole banking industry is affected by this issue; loans for real estate, home improvement, and college expenses have also become much more difficult to obtain. Banks are still making loans, but they have a bit less money to dole out than they used to. This means bank management is being extra careful deciding who qualifies. The net effect is fewer loans for otherwise worthy endeavors. All markets are under downward pressure as a result of this situation. Downward pressure simply means an effect that produces a reduction. In this case, we're talking about a reduction of business in many different parts of the economy. In other words, when businesses or people can't get the loans they need, the people they would have spent that money on also suffer. The result is a reduction in sales. People who can't obtain loans will not buy. Businesses that can't qualify for loans will make less of their own products and services. When banks are making lots of loans, this action can help the economy, which tends to help create jobs. But fewer loans can mean economic growth slows while any related job creation is also stifled.

New startup businesses are the obvious birthplaces of new jobs. However, existing businesses, from small to large, can also be a source of job creation. The problem is that companies need a compelling opportunity to enter a new market, launch a new product line, or make some type of expansion in order to justify hiring more people. The capital for such expansion may already be available to them if they have been successful and managed their finances well. Otherwise they may need to raise funding in any number of ways, from using banks or venture capitalists, to issuing a public stock (or bond) offering in the market. By the way, the latter still generally calls for the participation of a specialized investment banking company. Regardless, in this poor economic climate, all such activity has been greatly reduced. It seems that the business managers who are careful in protecting their bottom line are rewarded more than those who are willing to invest in growth, at least for now.

There is one capital source tied to job creation that is hidden from public view, that is, private funding from non-registered venture capitalists. These are just wealthy people looking to do something fruitful with their money. People with money are everywhere, especially in this country. Here I am talking about people who are rich enough to make direct business investments and still have enough left to live off of. Some of these people sold a business or made great investments that left them very well-off. Others inherited their wealth or made it through fame or good fortune. Regardless, people of means are like "amateur" venture capitalists in that they do not have a formal business for starting or funding new companies, yet they often do so anyway. I will refer to all such people as "private investors." Private investors take some of the highest risks in business. Yet the same negative market pressures in place on professional venture capitalists and bankers also affect these investors. Bad times make everyone more likely to say "no" even when the opportunity in front of them is an otherwise impressive business concept.

I have targeted these four groups on purpose - the venture capitalists, the bankers, existing businesses, and private investors. These are the four sources of funding that create almost all new jobs, in their expected order of impact. When job creation slows down, we can see a comparable slowdown in the activity of these four groups. If we want to create new jobs, these are the four groups that are going to do it. Let us call these four groups the "job financers".

II. Magnified Capitalism – Strategy and Executive Summary

Strategy via Thought Experiment

Being someone who likes to reflect on extreme cases, I could not help but consider this. What if we came up with an idea that lit these job financers on fire? What if we were in a situation in which venture capitalists could not find enough new ideas to fund, bankers wanted to increase their levels of loans, existing businesses were eager to expand, and private investors shared in all these motivations? What would happen to the job market then? We do not need a degree in economics to answer that question. It is obvious. And so we have our strategy for Magnified Capitalism.

Here is the substance of the strategy in just a few words: Magnified Capitalism has a strategic objective to greatly increase the activity of the four groups called the job financers. It seeks to amplify the capability and motivation of the job financers through voluntary programs sponsored by the government. This means government participation in business deals for those job financers who choose to take advantage of a silent partnership. The government will arrange attractive terms for partial funding of various business ventures. The effect is to greatly magnify the capital engine that creates jobs. Our competitiveness will jump to a new level. In return, the government will collect its due portion of the profits under standard terms. Such terms will be highly attractive for most every investor, bank or business. But these terms will still provide a fair return back to the government for its portion of the funding.

It is important to emphasize that any government involvement in business activity will be optional for the job financers, will use standardized terms, and will not allow the government any direct involvement in the selection of deals or decisions about the running of private businesses.

Magnified Capitalism leverages current business activity through the use of government-supplied funds. This money is not provided free and does carry conditions. Importantly, the government expects to make a profit. But the goal is to make the standard terms so compelling that most everyone who qualifies will want to participate.

Magnified Capitalism means the government can be called in to help finance just about any business plan, as long as the government receives an equity share of the deal. But the decision of whether or not the deal qualifies for funding as well as the management of the business afterwards is not part of the government's scope. Rather, the government will rely on existing private-sector sources of business financing – venture capitalists, bankers, businesses, and private investors – to manage the deals themselves. The government will act as a silent non-voting partner that offers excellent terms for its financial contribution. The terms will be so good that people will rush to increase their venture capital activity, their loan activity, their business expansion plans, and their search for the next great idea.

Competitiveness will fly up. Job creation will go on a frenzy.

Our strategy takes our existing capitalist system, and by using government financial muscle, magnifies it. This approach has an amazing side effect. While people rush to take advantage of these programs, the government builds a huge portfolio of business investments that are managed by the private sector. The government becomes a direct benefactor of its own people's business. Why is that so amazing? Because the government will make a fortune, a huge fortune. Those capitalists who help it do so will be thrilled. Let me put a finer point on the matter. If we enact Magnified Capitalism the right way, eventually we will be able to reduce taxes and the national debt. In fact, all our worrisome government funding issues can be made to vaporize over time.

Now we have the core strategy for Magnified Capitalism: The government multiplies the impact of existing capital resources from our four funding sectors - – the venture capitalists, the bankers, existing businesses, and private investors . These job financers can leverage standardized terms to access to extra deal-making federal funds, but otherwise the government keeps out of things.

Hold on, if there are contract terms then there must be some impact on the businesses involved. Those companies that use government capital in their deals will bring upon themselves some new requirements. What are these? In particular, they now have to do some regular reporting to the government. All business activity has to be handled ethically and legally, with full transparency. The biggest impact, however, is this. There is a deadline for paying the government back with interest. All such magnified capital deals must offer a timely, profitable exit to the government in return for its help.

We will drill into the details of of the contract terms and how they are enforced in later chapters. The main thing to know for our summary is this: The government will set up a new agency. I am calling it the Capital Magnification Service or CMS. The CMS will be responsible for allocating funds provided by Congress each year to the four types of existing capital sources we have discussed. Each deal will require that the commercial or private capital source risk a substantial portion of their own money as well as the government's. Funding limits will vary depending on many general factors and deal-specific circumstances. We will discuss these details later.

The result will be dramatic. It will be like the government is strapping rocket engines onto our economy. Job creation will take off, especially if Congress makes enough funds available. All the government-allocated money for the CMS will be amplified by matching private funds. And all the capital will be targeted towards activity that improves competitiveness and creates jobs.

II. Magnified Capitalism – Strategy and Executive Summary

Although job creation is our goal, this program has a bigger impact than just jobs. The jobs this strategy targets are positions in new and expanding businesses. That means this approach magnifies the potential of the whole economy, not just one sector. We will be launching more startup businesses, pursuing more new inventions, and carrying out more good business plans. More people will open new retail shops, go to college, or improve their homes. We hit the target of job creation on the head, but this method of spurring job growth creates new jobs that are not trivial. These are the kinds of jobs that make a better country for all of us. This is the kind of move a market leader makes to keep their leadership. We must do such a thing while we still have the power to do it. Magnified Capitalism might even ensure we remain the top economy in the world even as China continues their improvement.

Questions and Concerns

Of course there are a lot of questions and concerns that pop up when we consider such radical change. The biggest ones are these: Magnified Capitalism sounds expensive, perhaps very expensive. Are we not going to increase our national debt by implementing this plan, perhaps by a huge amount? On a related point, are we not talking about expanding government here? This plan requires a whole new government branch, the Capital Magnification Service (CMS). Do we not want to avoid growing government? What about government involvement in private business? Is it not true that government should stay out of private business and avoid picking winners and losers? I expect the three concerns I just mentioned will be the biggest ones, but I have good news. There are excellent answers to each.

First let us take on what most will consider the single biggest problem, especially at first glance: the cost of Magnified Capitalism. Let me make the matter very clear. We will need to borrow lots of money to set this system up. Just for convenience I will pick a big, round number. Let us say we are talking about one trillion dollars per year for a minimum of four years. On the surface that amount of new debt appears to nearly double our annual budget deficit during this four-year period. However, that analysis is inaccurate. A budget deficit is purely unsecured debt. When we spend more than we take in, that difference is our budget deficit. We have nothing to show for the shortfall.

But the budget for Magnified Capitalism is more analogous to buying a home, or even more closely analogous to borrowing money to buy stocks or mutual funds. Sure there is risk, but the loan is backed by real equity – the value of the business the loan is funding. Furthermore, in the case of Magnified Capitalism, this equity is extremely diversified. That means the borrowed money goes into a multitude of different investments. This spreads the risk out and keeps things safer, as any professional financial advisor can tell us. We will see details later that show how these investments improve in quality over time, as bad partners are weeded out and good ones are given access to more funds. So the system takes advantage of natural capitalist market forces to improve itself.

The bottom line is this: Most accountants would not count the money put into Magnified Capitalism as national debt. Rather, the funding for Magnified Capitalism is an equity-backed investment. It is a collateralized loan with a repayment plan built into it. The loan behind this effort will not only be repaid, it will return a profit. Within about three years the revenue will start coming in, so the amount we need to borrow from the third year onward becomes smaller. If we go beyond four years, by the sixth year, the CMS revenue will exceed its budget, so the program will stop borrowing. Its total debt will be below four trillion dollars at this point. We will recover the first year's trillion dollars by no later than the program's 10th year. The CMS will repay the rest of the $4 trillion loan by the 18th year. From this point forward the CMS will not only be debt free and self-sufficient, but it will pay a portion of its profit into the national budget. That is right. This strategy establishes a new form of income for our government. If we do it right, CMS revenue could eventually become large enough to pay down the national debt, or eliminate the need for most income taxes. Finally, we can see the original suggestion to execute our strategy for at least four years is an unnecessary limitation. As a growing profit center, the far better solution is to run the CMS indefinitely.

The key to making this plan work is two-sided. First, we have to put enough money into the system to produce the huge impact we seek. Second, we need to set up the entire organization in such a way that it makes much more money than it loses. Of course, there will always be losing deals, even if they are set up by well-paid expert capitalists. The key to good investing is to first make sure the losing deals are small in size and few in number. That combination will be the job of the Capital Magnification Service (CMS). They will implement the processes and tweak the rules over time to make sure the government funding activities have a maximum return on investment. The CMS will also enforce the rules, especially to stop the bad eggs as quickly as possible.

This brings us to what I anticipate will be the second-biggest question about this strategy. Do we really want to expand the government by creating a new branch like the CMS? This question is trickier to answer than the first one. Consider that those who believe in smaller government are talking about the kind of government that exists today, without the CMS. For the most part, these are branches of government that do not produce any revenue-generating business. Rather, they are largely enforcers of rules, monitors of various activity, military branches, science and research-related departments, providers of public or infrastructure services, legal branches, the legislature, diplomatic endeavors, the executive branch and so on. The main exceptions are the IRS, which collects money for the government, and some business interfacing departments like the Small Business Administration (SBA).

So when we talk about reducing government, we are really talking about two different goals. The first kind of reduction seeks what a business manager might call the cutting of "obsolete and ineffective projects". Here the focus is to stop offering wasteful services, especially those that do not help commercial businesses. This kind of reduction goal works to identify government programs that have marginal benefits and eliminate them. The result is a cut in the physical size of departments along with their functions. The second kind of reduction goal represents decreasing "overhead expenses". Here the emphasis is on finding inefficient organizations and then streamlining them. This goal is about getting more done with fewer people. Ultimately, both goals seek the same end. Reducing government means cutting the cost of government services, which in turn means saving money and shrinking budgets.

In contrast, the CMS, the organization we will create to implement Magnified Capitalism, is both (eventually) self-funding and will apply business practices for efficiency. That is, within six years the new group will bring in more money than it costs. Some years later it will complete repaying its debt and become a revenue generator. The CMS will increasingly relieve our citizens of their tax burden. We will all be happy that we created this new branch to oversee such business activity.

Since this new organization represents an interface into private business, it is critical that we not set it up like a typical government agency. Rather, we should set it up like an actual business itself. We will reward performance and dismiss those who fail. We will incentivize management just as they are in commercial companies - for effectiveness and efficiency. Since the CMS is new, it represents an opportunity to do things differently than we have before. It should be organized to mirror the best practices of capitalism.

If we set up and run the CMS well it could lead to reform in other agencies. This is not a primary goal of the plan, but there is no reason not to set a good example. After all, we have the self-serving reason. We need the highest possible return on investment. What better way to do that than to run the CMS like any other successful American business? I will expand on what this means in the chapters that follow. The effect will be government efficiency like we have never seen before. Those who seek a new model for government productivity should be delighted.

Here is the answer to our question about whether we really want to build a new branch of government: Yes, we should build or expand agencies of government that can pay their own way. If they go further and produce revenue outside the tax code we should be eager about it. The CMS will be the first government agency that will do that. The larger and more efficient the CMS gets, the fewer taxes we will all need to pay. Those who insist we not grow government cannot apply that requirement here unless they invent a new kind of criticism. No one has ever created a branch that produces money without taxes. I suggest government-growth objectors now modify their rule of thumb. Regardless, I have justified the creation of the CMS based on its contribution to federal income. Remember, however, that the CMS's primary mission is to spur national job growth. That goal is also a strong argument against the no-growth crowd, but the income point is sufficient to make the case here.

Finally, we come to the third big concern we anticipate from early detractors of Magnified Capitalism. This involves the government staying out of private business. It is a vague notion because this worry covers at least two more specific concerns that are largely unrelated. One of these more specific concerns regards the government controlling activities that the private sector should run. The other has to do with government trying to pick market winners.

I will start with the first of these two concerns, the one regarding government control in the private sector. A few people are sure to mistakenly label Magnified Capitalism as a new form of socialism or even communism. Why? Because the result of implementing this plan is that the government will own a substantial portion of new business and private infrastructure. Then how is the comparison to socialism or communism wrong? There are two reasons.

First, the ownership is a technical business mechanism, not a controlling one. That is, the government is holding notes of equity as collateral not unlike a bank would do for a loan. But the only control the bank applies is that the business be honestly, ethically, and legally pursued. In other words, the government will require that the operators overseeing its held collateral not endanger the company with unethical or illegal activity. Anyone who holds collateral for a loan can reasonably expect that the owner will not do anything to risk damaging the value of the collateral. Except for this concern, the government is a silent partner. Essentially, the CMS's purpose is to be a financial backer only. It is counting on commercial partners to set up the deals and risk some of their own money in return for managing the business part of the arrangement. Furthermore, the terms of the government funding, as we will see, reward the private and commercial investors for making sure that these deals succeed. In this system the government does not pick the business deals; the commercial sector does. The government does not control any business decisions. It does not have to. In fact, any attempt to do that will be specifically prohibited.

There is a second reason government ownership of business through this program is not comparable to a communist system. The government's ownership, besides being non-controlling, is only temporary. The terms of every deal the government backs will require a specific timetable (or set of conditions) for the business to repay the government financing with interest. Once the government is repaid, the equity it held in the deal is completely released back into the private sector. Thus the government's ownership is more comparable to that of a bank holding title to an individual's car when they use financing to buy it. The bank is just retaining the equity in the car as collateral. No one from the bank tells the owner how to manage their car, unless they purposefully abuse it or otherwise threaten to damage the value of the collateral. In any case, once the car loan is paid off, the equity is released back to the individual. The car becomes 100% theirs. During the loan period the bank was merely enforcing its financing terms, and nothing more. And so it is with all of the government's equity ownership under Magnified Capitalism.

Now I can address the other kind of concern regarding government involvement in business. In this program the government is not choosing winners and losers because deal selection is conducted by private or commercial capital sources that must also risk their own money. This strategy leverages the existing capitalist system to decide which deals are worthy and which are not. And as I explained above, the government owns equity in these businesses only as a non-voting, non-controlling investor holding collateral, like the bank holding a note. This is not a socialist or communist government trying to directly manage the operations of private businesses.

Therefore, if there is a legitimate accusation along such lines, it would be that the government is starting a business of its own. This business would be a new sort of bank-like service that loans money for a variety of business deals. In other words, the government is modeling itself after the capitalist system that we know works so well. However, in this case, we are not competing with traditional banks at all. On the contrary, the existing banking system will boom under Magnified Capitalism because they will be one of its biggest direct benefactors. So I concede this point. This proposal essentially does call on the government to setup a new business.

People will see the Capital Magnification Service as a sort of bank all right, but it will be of a type that only a government can arrange and that other banks will welcome. To keep things clean, the CMS's rules will be transparent and non-prejudicial. In other words, those who receive money and those who do not will be determined by well-considered processes that everyone can see and anyone can participate in equally. To the degree possible, there will be little human negotiation in handling how capital is assigned to various deals. In fact, most of the actual money management part of the CMS should be implemented by computer. But people will also be needed for running these automated systems, auditing all systems to make sure the system is working correctly, catching rule breakers, and providing legal arbitration to handle unusual cases and complaints.

To be clear, there is a primary question that we must answer. Why does it help us to have the government form a new type of investment bank? The answer is that the CMS will multiply the investment power of the four primary sources of capital in our society, the job financers. This program will profoundly affect each of these four capital sources: the venture capitalists, commercial banks of all types, existing businesses looking to expand, and private investors or entrepreneurs. These four segments will not only explode with activity, but their profits will be amplified. This in turn will attract more competition to these four capital-providing segments.

Not only will existing sources of capital create more business, but expansion will also occur within each of these capital-providing segments. The competition will be on. It will become easier and easier for startup companies to obtain the money they need from venture capitalists. It will become easier to get most any type of loan from banks because banks will become more capable of providing a larger number of loans. Existing businesses will also see an enormous risk reduction when considering whether to expand into new segments or start new product lines. There will even be a menu of deals available to assist individuals directly.

The strategy does not end here. Magnified Capitalism includes an important new kind of control mechanism. All the standard deals the CMS offers will be subject to special incentives. These CMS incentives will be designed to encourage commercial business to make decisions that align with national strategic goals. For example, we will make it more attractive to keep production lines in the U.S., conduct retail expansions in underdeveloped areas, or create solutions that address clean energy. Congress and you, the President, will manage Magnified Capitalism's deal incentives directly. The result will be a new sort of policy steering wheel, except this one is controlled not through direct selection of winners and losers, but by incentives in a market-driven system. If the incentive is misguided, the market will leave it largely unused. If an incentive is well considered, it should nudge business growth into areas that are helpful to our national interests. This is a powerful aspect of capital magnification that I will discuss in more detail later.

Magnified Capitalism is like strapping on rocket engines and adding a new steering wheel to our economic racecar. If we are shrewd enough to embrace this change, our economy will surge forward at an unprecedented pace. Since we are still the world's leading economy, such a step would take unique advantage of our leadership. Suddenly this leadership would become untouchable again and stay that way for some time. We would act as a leader who crafts a bold move to retain their leadership. Our level of world competitiveness would not only return to the number one spot, but it would set the rest of the world on notice.

At first most countries would probably be skeptical, or perhaps stunned and surprised. But as soon as they realized we had out-maneuvered the rest of the world in our ability to generate new business, they would start to try to duplicate our new invention. This is where our other big advantage comes into play.

Since we hold the world currency, our own interest rates are way lower than those of most other countries, certainly less than others who have been as slack as we have in managing their budgets properly. But, because we have this power to access large amounts of money cheaply, the best way to take advantage is not to borrow to increase debt, but to borrow to invest like crazy. We should borrow as much as we can to invest in ourselves. We should put these borrowed funds into revenue-generating secured investments, just as I have described. While we still can, we should grow our investments and ourselves as much as possible. This plan not only creates jobs, grows our businesses, makes us more competitive, and retains our world leadership as the biggest economy, but also produces government riches in fairly short order.

Any good investment advisor would give their client the same advice if they were in such a situation. Our access to money is cheap. We have an opportunity to invest almost as much as we have the courage to. And we can be confident we will receive profits that greatly exceed the cost of the capital we borrow. Our investment advisor would say, "What are you waiting for? Borrow as much as you dare and get this going before someone beats you to it!" That is what I am saying. We can do more than just grow our economy and shrink unemployment. We can turn the United States into a capitalist beast. We will soon start paying off our own debts. We will be able to pay for those Social Security and Medicare programs that might otherwise become insolvent. It will even be possible to support worthy government initiatives that have had to be scaled back.

There is a stunning surprise benefit to this strategy. In our lifetimes we should be able to draw most taxes down to lower rates without any debt increase. We may decide not to go too far, too fast down that road for some good reasons. For example, we might decide to have a new national security policy to keep ourselves financially fat so that we can build a savings fund for bad times, such as unforeseen catastrophes. But regardless of how we manage our newfound riches, this will be a political debate we should all look forward to having.

Before I finish this strategic overview and provide the executive summary for the whole plan, I would like to discuss one more interesting strategic impact that Magnified Capitalism will have. This one is arguably the most surprising of all because it is completely outside the scope of our intentions. It may be unintended but it has an enormously important consequence. I am talking about national security. That is right. Magnified Capitalism coincidentally has a profound impact on international relations, and national security interests in particular.

I could put it this way. If we are sufficiently aggressive and successful with Magnified Capitalism, we will win another world war of sorts. We will do this without killing anyone, without firing any shots or using our military. No other countries should even be particularly offended. What war am I talking about? The war against repressive governments worldwide. This is the war for the individual's right to pursue happiness versus the power of the state to control the masses (i.e., communist systems and governments that are effectively dictatorships). This is perhaps the last war between major countries except for those oddballs that go rogue from time to time, including governments ruled through religious extremists or dictators who become cornered or otherwise behave irrationally. I put these aside.

Why will we win a world war for the freedom of the individual? Because success breeds envy and duplication. Our success over the last hundred years has bred some degree of democratic mimicry throughout the world. What will happen when we show everyone how to do democracy better still? They can either fix up their own governments to be even more like ours or get left behind. No amount of military action could have this degree of impact. We have already proved that our lead-by-example strategy works. Now we just need to do it even better. In an internet-connected wireless world, how long will citizens of other countries allow their governments to stand still while the people of United States take success and happiness to a new level? It will be like pushing a button, although I admit the net effect will take decades.

Incidentally, those who manage commercial businesses realize that with every new product plan, there is an expected problem down the road. If we do something new that works, everyone sees our success and will start to copy us. Eventually, our great idea will be replicated in different flavors all over the place. In a moral sense, this is fantastic. We will infect the world with the peaceful drive towards capitalist success by showing everyone how to do it even better. However, there will come a time when, if we do nothing more about it, we will once again confront the same sort of problem we are facing now. Our world economic leadership may come under threat again, as might our ability to hold the top spot for competitiveness. As I suggested, this would be a wonderful problem to have. It would mean, necessarily, that the other big players are growing and successful, too. That in turn would suggest they found a way to improve both individual rights and business liberties. It would be evidence that we are winning worldwide freedoms, as I just mentioned. So it is a good problem to have.

In the prosperous environment of United States 2.0, we will eventually face a resurgence of international competition, only with fewer difficulties than we have today. We might even be so successful that we do not care that much whether we are number one in these various measures, although I admit that I do not really believe we could ever stop caring. Regardless, we should consider a long-term plan to do more. The commercial business planner would, so I will as well. Part of successful business management today is assuming that even if we initially beat our competitors, eventually they will figure out how to catch up to us. We can do more later to head that off. The earlier we plan for staying in the lead, the more likely we will succeed in that as well. I will discuss my menu of considerations in *Chapter IX, Next Steps and Beyond United States 2.0*.

Magnified Capitalism Executive Summary

The main purpose of Magnified Capitalism is to provide a major economic catalyst for the type of growth that generates jobs nationwide. In order to afford the cost of such activity, this strategy calls for creating a new institution called the Capital Magnification Service (CMS). The CMS is a new kind of organization modeled after commercial businesses - a citizen company. This new structure is a hybrid between a government agency and a commercial company. Its primary goal is to increase the particular kind of business activity that supports job growth. It will achieve this goal by offering a menu of revenue-generating services to four primary types of capital sources: venture capitalists (VCs), bankers, existing businesses, and private individuals. These CMS services will encourage the private sector to increase its support of entrepreneurial activity. The result is an increase in both new business startups and the expansion of existing businesses, because CMS services lower the risk levels and the threshold of resources required to be entrepreneurial. As a citizen company the CMS will necessarily be profitable. However, a difference between it and a regular commercial business is that its senior management will report to the American people through a government-populated Board of Directors. The CMS charter demands that this top management not be incented foremost for profits, but rather for its mission effectiveness based on various real-world measurements. Foremost of these goals is its impact on job growth in the United States.

Through the CMS the U.S. government will offer voluntary commercial services. These services will be so attractive that CMS target customers will be eager to participate. The impact on the economy will be huge because of the level of funding involved and the precise targeting of that money towards commercial job creation activities. Taken together, CMS services could be considered as a new type of investment bank or fund management business, because its services represent investment in a wide range of American businesses. These investments will pay a return with interest over a limited time period. The term will average about 4 years, with a normal range of 3 to 5 years, or up to 6 with a lateness penalty.

We will need a large pool of money in order to offer these investment services. This pool is called the CMS Fund. At first, we will need to borrow money for both the Fund and CMS operating costs. CMS revenues will begin in the 3rd year of operation, since the earliest of its investments from the first year will start to pay off at that time. This incoming revenue will have the effect of reducing borrowing levels needed in that year. By the 6th year, CMS revenues will exceed program costs and the borrowing will completely stop. Such a milestone is called the point of positive cash flow.

This plan estimates that we need a Fund level of one trillion dollars per year to meet the stated goals. The total cost to reach the point of positive cash flow point will be just under $4 trillion. The program will completely repay this debt, with interest, between the 13th and 18th year of CMS operations. That milestone is called the point of net gain. After that, CMS will continue to provide its services debt free and profitably. Since the CMS will no longer need to repay any debt after the point of net gain, most profits will then go towards raising the annual Fund levels above the original one trillion dollar amount. The CMS will return the balance of its profits to the U.S. treasury as new income outside of the tax system. The political leadership at that time will determine the split between reinvestment and income.

Financial analysis shows that in the following decades the CMS will become a major source of government revenue. In the process the CMS Fund will grow to impressive size. This combination will deliver yet another burst in U.S. economic activity beyond that experienced prior to the point of net gain. The level of American prosperity will be so high that it is difficult to predict the upper limit of these positive effects using traditional financial models.

The main challenge to implementing this strategy is that Congress must have a strong political will to pass the needed legislation. The fact that Magnified Capitalism is a politically neutral strategy can be a great advantage towards this end. I suggest that you, Mr. President, claim the position of plan champion before your rival, or some congressional up and comers, do. In addition, this plan seeks to establish both a Magnified Capitalism Political Action Committee (PAC) and a populist grass roots campaign aided by the new website, www.magnifiedcapitalism.com.

The main tenet of Magnified Capitalism is simple: Produce a new pillar of long-term American success. Do this through new financial services that only the government can afford to establish. Steer these services with one eye on economic benefits and the other on profitability. Finally, add a political control through special CMS incentives that encourage business decisions to line up with national policies. We will borrow a lot of money to do this but the program will pay these funds back quickly from service profits. In the meantime we will not only fix the economy but make an impressive surge in world leadership. We will show the world a new capitalist solution towards fixing their problems, too. Repressive governments will fall further behind until they turn themselves around with reforms. Our friends will benefit at first by trading with a resurgent

America, and then later by adopting some version of Magnified Capitalism themselves.

This is the kind of strategy that represents American leadership in a new world. It is at once bold yet carefully considered. Those who support it earliest will be called visionaries. Through their actions, through your actions, Mr. President, we will collectively enter a new era of grandeur I like to call "United States 2.0".

Final thoughts before the details

Magnified Capitalism represents a turning point in the evolution of Americans governing themselves. It is a breakout strategy, a way to pull out of a situation that increasingly frustrates us all. The impact of implementing it is so profound that describing it to the uninitiated is likely to produce initial skepticism. For example, this plan promptly solves our problems of national unemployment. Neither a Republican nor Democratic oriented concept, Magnified Capitalism introduces new methods for running government. It eventually produces windfall national revenues even though its primary purpose is to serve as a business catalyst. It functions within the current framework of our established democracy, although it will have the effect of elevating how our democracy works. If Congress passed the needed bill tomorrow, we would feel direct benefits within little over a year. Indirect benefits would begin immediately. Beyond recovery, we would expect full economic prosperity within a matter of some short years. National debt would begin to draw down not long after that. A menu of other problems would also be addressed very effectively. I hope the details to come will take your breath away.

Magnified Capitalism is remarkable in that it will end up helping all Americans, from rich to poor. Once we implement this plan, our country will become a different place. Welcome to United States 2.0.

People cannot possibly create a perfect plan. There are always downsides, weaknesses and threats to every action we ponder. What we can do is be objective. Consider the competition and those who will be threatened. Identify potential holes and conceivable missteps. Assume there will be those who might respond unethically motivated by their own self-interest. All these issues challenge a plan to either evolve or fail. If the plan survives then our tactics will have improved enough to avoid at least the obvious pitfalls. We may never reach perfection. But for God to recognize our respectable effort, I anticipate She will expect a decent SWOT analysis.

III. SWOT Analysis

I have fashioned myself an "idea person" as far back as I can remember. It can be hard to keep hold of such idealism because eventually we must share our thoughts. Others' opinions and views can tear at the soul of any idealist. One of the most humbling professional experiences I can recall occurred when I was a young product manager at Sprint. It was the first time I was presenting a business plan of my design to a room full of executives. I needed their approval to be able to go forward with my novel business concept. I had no shortage of self-confidence. "Cocky" would be a fair description of my attitude. My new business plan was the awesome creative answer they were looking for, I was sure of it. I was eager to share it with senior management and ready to accept their certain congratulations. Then the presentation began and so did the cold shower.

The head of marketing wanted to understand how we would deal with the customers who would not benefit from my proposed changes. The V.P. of Operations wanted to know where he was supposed to find the resources to implement the technical requirements as quickly as I needed. The finance and pricing director noticed there were some cases in which we would lose money, so how could I prove there would not be too many of those cases? It went on and on like that for hours. It seemed to me that everyone had a problem with my great idea. That meeting ended without approval of either my strategy or the plan behind it. And all those critics were right because the presentation revealed my plan as incomplete.

Ironically, the company eventually approved the same basic business strategy I presented that day, although I had to go through many iterations of adding details to the plan before that happened. Furthermore, that effort became a huge success for both me personally and the company as a whole. But the moral of the story is in that first meeting. It is not enough to have a great strategy. We have to prove to the toughest critics that we thought through how to make it happen, the complexity of how the market will respond, the challenge of keeping within a real budget, the use of available resources, and how exactly we expect to accomplish it all within a believable timeline. We find success in the merger between the idealist and the pragmatist. We only get to be real visionaries if we can make it happen. It turns out that coming up with the idea is the easier part. The inability to implement the concept is what kills most good ideas.

Once we have our great idea laid out, and some notion of a plan to implement it, we need to step outside of ourselves. It is time to take account of both the upside and downside. Shake the idea as if we wanted to tear it down. In this formal plan, critical thinking occurs in two places. The first is the SWOT analysis we are about to discuss, which as a reminder stands for Strengths, Weaknesses, Opportunities, and Threats. The second place is *Chapter VIII: Risk Management*. Risk management tries to prepare for things that might go wrong during the implementation of a plan. In contrast, in the SWOT analysis we consider how the plan will, or might, impact things. This is where we forecast how the plan may fall short or how others might attack it. In this discussion we list the positive effects as well as negative, probable or just potential, intended or not. It is similar to writing down the pros and cons of a decision we are weighing.

Strengths

Unlike a pros and cons list, however, a SWOT analysis encompasses much more than weighing advantages against disadvantages. The exercise involves more than just deciding whether or not the plan holds up, although that is part of its value. The SWOT analysis is useful even if we are so sure of our strategy that we are already committed to following it. By revealing both pluses and minuses, we gain new perspectives that lead us to improve the details of our plan, even while it retains the original strategy. In this subsection I list our plan strengths. Here we can begin to appreciate where we should emphasize the implementation, operational rollout, or core political argument.

The temptation is to focus on the argument alone, especially if we still need to convince any detractors. The real challenge, however, is to consider how each listed strength can impact the plan. For each one we want to ask whether we can adjust the plan so as to take better advantage of the strengths before us. If anyone is still unconvinced about Magnified Capitalism in general, there is something special for them as well. Notice that we adjust this plan, and therefore improve it, throughout the SWOT analysis. The SWOT creates an evolution. Let's follow these strengths first and see how the plan adjusts to each one.

Strength #1: Job Growth We Can Dial Up

There is a direct relationship between the number of jobs we create with Magnified Capitalism and the amount of money we budget towards the effort. Every single dollar the CMS provides to the capital markets will be magnified further by non-government capital, and then applied to the very sort of economic activity that creates jobs. The budget allocation for this magnified capital becomes a job creation dial. We can crank it up as far as we want. The more we do this, the more jobs we generate. It is not possible to turn the system up too far, at least not so far that anything breaks. The reason is that if we run out of opportunities to fund, or if the opportunities dry up because it becomes too hard to find qualified people to fill the jobs, then the CMS will not be able to allocate any more of the money. In other words, if we give the program unlimited funds we will get very close to 100% employment and we will find out exactly how much the CMS needed to achieve that. There will be a natural upper limit. It should be safe to reach that limit no matter what it is.

The main exception to this premise is if the implementation of the program is itself flawed (see the Weakness called *Tuning Problem*). Short of such potential problems, I project that under a well-managed and fully funded capital magnification program, the United States 2.0 should be able to keep its unemployment rate at 5% or less, indefinitely. That is a minimum worst case figure. During a long-term application of this strategy I expect unemployment to hover closer to 4%, perhaps lower. This translates to near full employment, as we can expect roughly 3% of the population to represent those who are "between jobs" at any given time. I might add that my analysis suggests the above figures to be conservative ones. However, there is no need to over-promise on this point. A sustained unemployment rate below 5% is fine and healthy. If the actual number turns out to better that, it is just gravy.

As I mentioned, when we talk about strengths, we do not just want to consider them as reasons to implement our strategy. We want to imagine how each strength can help us improve the plan further. How does knowing we have a job growth dial help us? Because it provides the government, and specifically Congress, with an economic control they have not previously had. In fact, this has been a fundamental problem throughout American history. Congress and the President are always arguing about what they can do to affect the economy, or address the problems of some specific group of people. This problem is pervasive because it is almost always debatable whether a proposed measure will have the intended effect. Should we cut taxes, implement some new industry incentive, or try to enact new laws that regulate or deregulate? Sometimes it seems that our government is a well-intended dart player that cannot aim its darts, let alone agree on where to try to aim.

Magnified Capitalism may forever change this problem, at least regarding unemployment. By allocating more money to the Capital Magnification Service (CMS), and/or by modifying the rules and incentives the CMS offers, the Congress and you, Mr. President, will have new powers. These new governmental powers will typically work swiftly toward the intended target. The United States will be able to direct a near-immediate impact on its own economy, and job growth in particular, whenever Congress decides to do so. This power to dial up job growth will extend to the President as our political leader-in-chief. Hopefully, political arguments will shift away from what to do and instead focus on how much and where special incentives might be placed. It is perhaps naively optimistic of me to say that compromise in such matters is more straightforward than it is with battles that pit one opposing strategy against another. In other words, if we are arguing about how far to turn a dial (i.e., how much money to put into the CMS this year), a compromise of some value in between the extremes seems easier to imagine than in an argument about competing ideologies.

Regardless, the effect of this point on our plan is important. It means that Magnified Capitalism provides a new governmental power, a new way to control the economy. This power is a big deal, perhaps of historic proportions. The plan needs to take advantage by making sure this power is both effectively managed and highlighted as a feature. When we produce our detailed CMS charter it should therefore include standardized control processes. These standards should assume Congress will change CMS funding levels often. Other standard processes should accommodate congressional wishes to pass a variety of incentives and disincentives with great regularity.

In order to keep things working well and effectively, we do not want Congress to be able to accidently mess up CMS processes that have already been debugged. Therefore, the goal is to limit congressional legislation from digging into actual CMS operations. Congressional action should stay at the level of funding and types of incentives, and go no deeper than that. We want to discourage any congressional action that toys with detailed implementation. Imagine changing rules for one kind of incentive so that its process becomes different from another incentive, for example. Eventually we would need experts in CMS rules just to be able to participate in the program. Worse still, the CMS processes would become grossly inefficient due to the nature of congressional micromanagement. That is exactly the sort of problem that adds overhead and inefficiency in government.

As a specific example, just consider the tax code and how that has affected IRS efficiencies. This is why we want to avoid legislative changes that affect most CMS processes. We should keep Congress focused on the issues most appropriate for them to address. They should use the controls provided to set priorities and budget levels. If federal laws change how the CMS executes its duties they could destroy a complex machine by inadvertently throwing a wrench into it. This is an important concern that I am borrowing from the private sector.

Executives and management should not micromanage their projects lest they undermine the well-considered processes established by those under them who really understand the minutiae. In this case, we are not asking Congress to figure out how to run the CMS efficiently, itself a very tricky problem. So they should not be meddling with it once it works. As we will discuss later in some detail, the CMS processes will be largely automated and optimized for high efficiency. This efficiency provides for both CMS internal speed and quality, as well as for the ease-of-use of CMS customers. Those customers will be the venture capitalists, banks, businesses and other private entrepreneurs I mentioned earlier.

If Congress goes about dictating regular changes in CMS rules (versus incentives or funding levels), then there will be ongoing changes in CMS rule books, forms, customer processes, automated systems, and internal processes. We would be forming a new IRS-style nightmare of ever-growing laws, forms, and related problems. Thus we can take a lesson from our strength. Make it easy for Congress to make the kinds of changes they should be making. And, to the degree possible, enact the founding rules of the CMS so that its internal processes and rules remain under its own management outside of congressional reach. Instead, Congress and you, Mr. President, will hold the CMS management responsible for running an efficient and productive agency. For the good of everyone, no one outside the CMS management should dictate how to achieve their goals. The focus should remain firmly fixed only on what those goals are.

Strength #2: Increasing Economic Growth

In order to create jobs, capital magnification helps generate or expand business activity. When we measure such activity by Gross Domestic Product (GDP) we will see a near immediate increase once we implement the program. Given the latest quarterly GDP growth of 2.2% (2nd quarter 2012), I would expect the number to reach 4% within about one year under this Magnified Capitalism plan. However, business activity is not a button that turns on and then stays level. When we start new businesses, the successful ones will grow. Well-managed businesses will continue growing on their own without further intervention. Similarly, when we expand an existing business, the business activity will increase over time if the expansion plan succeeds. So the button we pressed to start an economic activity engine two years ago does not just keep the engine running at the same level as when we started it. Rather, that engine will rev up to some far higher level over time, until it reaches its natural maximum.

For economic activity, this means if we achieve a 4% GDP (quarterly growth rate) within 14 months after starting the program, the rate will rise later on (all other things being equal or stable). GDP will continue to increase on its own from that point forward until it finds a new natural peak. Furthermore, since the plan includes continued funding of capital magnification year after year, we are building new business on top of new business. We should continue to see the GDP growth rate climb to approach levels we have not seen since the mid-1970's, when quarterly GDP growth rates regularly hovered near 10%.

How does the impact of increasing economic growth help us improve our plan further? Consider the analogy of an automobile racecar, which I have used a few times and will return to regularly. If our economy is our car's engine, then capital is the gas, and unemployment is like a health meter. Most cars would turn on warning lights for a health meter function. One such light might blink "Service required" if the unemployment rate goes above 6%. But in our car, we have an actual meter for this. We know the exact unemployment rate all the time. However, in this discussion we are focused on Gross Domestic Product. The GDP growth rate for our car is analogous to our speedometer. Rather than miles per hour, our speedometer is measured as percentage quarterly growth rate. If the GDP growth rate is negative, the economy of the country is going backwards. If it is positive but less than 2%, we are moving slowly forward. If the GDP gauge reads 4% or more, the economy is moving along at a fine, if conservative speed. By the way, historically, we hit our maximum speed briefly in March 1950 when the quarterly GDP growth rate touched 17.2%. We might imagine, therefore, that our speedometer need not go above 20% or so, which is screaming fast.

Knowing Magnified Capitalism has an increasing effect on growth is like saying it presses down on the gas pedal. When the driver holds their foot steadily down on the gas, the car continues to accelerate until it reaches a stable speed sometime later. In other words, we are not just concerned with the short-term effect of speeding up the economy. There is a follow-through effect as well. For our plan this means we want to track not just the result of one year's funding for the next year, but its consequence year after year until we reach a stable speed (GDP growth rate).

The problem is tricky due to the fact that we are stomping on the gas a bit more each year (through continued funding), but that effect peaks after about five years (which is the normal cycle of CMS investments from any given year). Also, we will learn the actual effect of one year's funding after taking an accounting of the results. Then we can subtract a one-year effect from the second year (roughly) to estimate continued acceleration from the previous year. Regardless of the details of how it is done, the point is this: We will learn to control the speed we want to reach (GDP) by how far we press the gas (level of CMS funding), even though it will take about five years to hit that maximum speed.

I mentioned that Magnified Capitalism provides our government with a new kind of economic control. The discussion of this strength underscores the notion that our control's effect is not limited to unemployment, however. Rather, the impact extends throughout the overall economy, as measured by GDP. Although this result is a bit more complicated than the unemployment one, it gives us another reason to focus on improving the plan's ability to act like an effective economic dial. The intricate consequence of an accelerating GDP puts a highlight on making sure we do a good job collecting statistics on CMS deals. We want to become experts at understanding how congressional changes in CMS funding affect the economy.

After considering this strength regarding increasing economic growth, I am left with two conclusions. First, I would reinforce the adjustments motivated by the previous strength, *Job Growth We Can Dial Up*. Those relate to making it easy for Congress to adjust funding levels and incentives, but discouraging congressional rules that change CMS processes. Second, we should create a new plan addition concerning metrics, or the measuring of things. The CMS should value both economic analysis and the compilation of information that improves such analysis.

The complexity of Magnified Capitalism's economic consequences includes how one change made today can having ongoing impacts for several years. The CMS charter needs to support the analysis of economic impacts made by its own services. This analysis should isolate the effect of one year's changes from the next year's. By the way, such economic measurements are far more practical if Congress is largely prohibited from changing process rules. Why? Because measuring the effect of an incentive or funding level is much more straightforward if we keep the rules stable. But if we change the rules and processes, we might face great problems in judging which particular item made the economic impact. Was it the change in funding levels, or was it a change in processes that reduced efficiency or caused heartburn with the customers? This strength reveals another reason for us to allow the CMS to handle its own process optimization. It doubles down on the previously mentioned need to keep optimized processes clean and efficient, only this time we add the notion that stable processes improve our ability to study economic impacts.

Strength #3: U.S. Returns to Number One in Competitiveness

Competitiveness is a notion that encompasses how easy it is to start and conduct business. The whole point of Magnified Capitalism is to make conducting new business easier as long as that business is justified. In our United States 2.0 venture capitalists will help many more businesses expand and start up. Banks will provide more business loans as well as other types of loans. Companies will find it easy to raise funds for their expansion plans. And private citizens will have compelling new motivations to take on new commercial projects. Under the right circumstances these may be gross understatements. The economic situation may even reach a point where there is great demand from capitalists looking for new business plans to fund.

With this plan the United States will quickly return to its number one position in world competitiveness. Furthermore, no one else will even come close until they start trying to copy our strategy, which eventually they will. We should not view this as a deflating point. People will only want to copy us when they see success. The key to being competitive is to do the good stuff first and better. After that, we think of more good stuff and never stop reinventing ourselves. That is how a modern competitive business operates. That is how we should be running our country. Winners, especially in business, are those who learn how to manage change.

Does knowing we will return as the world's most competitive nation itself have an impact on our plan? For one thing, we should be ready for a rush of foreign investors who will try to take advantage. After all, if it were much easier to set up a business in the U.S. than anywhere else, where would we go if we had problems conducting business in some other country? But do we really want to provide capital to foreign-sourced businesses? My answer is a qualified "no". Why? Because the CMS Fund will likely be limited and smaller than it needs to be in order to have maximum impact in the U.S. Therefore, we should use whatever resources we have available for the purpose they were originally intended, spurring U.S. job growth and U.S. economy. Any use that deviates even a little from this aim would represent a misdirection of our goals.

However, down the road, once we have near full U.S. employment and a well-tested CMS machine that has a solid track record of good returns, the answer could change. At some point we might grow to welcome outside investors seeking a friendly new home for their business ventures. We could even decide to loosen rules regarding foreign distribution, production, and support. But I would caution that such loosening be done carefully and slowly lest we subsidize an accidental undoing of many hard-won economic improvements.

Another impact of reestablishing competitive leadership may be that we need to monitor and adjust to the activity of copycats. We should take extra care to watch the results of other Magnified Capitalism implementations as they spread throughout the world. We should assume that each version will have some differences from ours, and therefore should hold both advantages and disadvantages. I expect it a worthy exercise that the CMS conduct a regular annual analysis of each such country. That report should include recommendations for our own consideration based on lessons learned from others. In commercial business, studying rivals and then reproducing some variation of their best new features is a standard practice, more commonly known as competitive analysis.

Strength #4: Economic Leadership Extended

I mentioned that without Magnified Capitalism, China is shortly expected to regain its position as the number one economy in the world. Our hundred-plus year reign as world economic leader will end in roughly ten years. However, implementing this plan in the next year or two will change this projection dramatically. We might argue that China could quickly respond with changes to further their own competitiveness, such as enacting laws to empower the individual more. But it is far more likely that they will take their time before doing anything dramatic in response to our plan. I would not be surprised if we held onto this throne for decades more under our new strategy. The U.S. could even hold it indefinitely if we stay nimble and continue to improve ourselves. Regardless, maintaining our position as the economic leader is more than a symbolic victory. Being number one makes every good move work better, and every mistake gets a bit more tolerance. It is one of those things that are hard to notice unless you lose it.

I can promise you, Mr. President, that China wants this leadership position back, and other contenders would like to have it for a first time. We have held this number one spot for so long, no one is alive who remembers any other way. It would be easy to think it does not matter, but it really does. For example, the effect of introducing Magnified Capitalism here, first, with an aggressively large budget allocation will be tremendous. If we waited to implement this plan until we lost world economic leadership, it would still work, but it will work better if we are still the clear leader. Businesses will be a bit more eager to participate. The money will be a bit cheaper to borrow. Other countries will be a bit more discouraged about whether they can catch up to us so they will be slower to react. It all adds up. Advantage always goes to the current leader, even when it is hard to explain why.

If you, Mr. President, thought being the most competitive nation was important, I suggest remaining the top economy in the world should be a far higher goal in our national interest. This leadership translates directly into fiscal and even geopolitical benefits. We may take it for granted, but China is seeing noticeable benefits as their financial power has recently surged. With the rise of their trade and industry, they have become an international magnet of interest in both obvious and unobvious ways. This growth even spills over into their international clout in matters that seem unrelated to business. Their economic rise has made them more powerful and relevant in ways far more practical than any army could accomplish. Good for them. They earned it with positive changes. Competition is healthy anyway.

For us, however, it is time to be reminded that we are in a battle of global economics and geopolitical power. There is no need to be scared. This is not a military issue. No one should even be mad. This is a battle between respected co-inhabitants, even friends. It is more like a tennis tournament or weekend poker game. If we lose we can always try again next week. But who wants to lose? We are Americans, after all. At the very least it is not our style to go down without a fight. We should consider Magnified Capitalism as a weapon in the battle of global economics.

Why do we care? Because whether we see it as a competition or not, China does. So do India, Russia and a few other long-term contenders. In a world where military wars between countries are distasteful and unpopular for nearly everyone, even with most of the regimes who dislike us, the battle shifts to one based on business and economies. Some may try to use the analogy that this strategy is like an atomic bomb in such a global economic battle. But I think that is a poor comparison. Nukes can be abused. Global security calls for limiting nuclear arsenals once a number of countries have acquired them. No, if we must call upon a military metaphor then I would pick a different comparison. To me, being first with Magnified Capitalism is more like being the first country to have a jet air force, or the first country to have tanks or rockets. Eventually everyone else will have them too, so the advantage will go to those who keep making the better versions.

Now we must consider how extending economic leadership impacts our planning. Our military analogy brings this matter home. Once Magnified Capitalism spurs our economy into taking off, other countries will complain. We can imagine them crying, "Foul! You are unfairly using your economic strength to slingshot your economy into the stratosphere. We are supposed to be working in a global environment of growing free trade and fairness. Now you are implementing economic strategies that use your unmatched borrowing power to subsidize and favor the growth of U.S. companies, U.S. workers, and even U.S.-based production facilities."

Our response should be that there is nothing unfair about it. The strategy is open and public. Anyone in the world can copy it. It is true that we can borrow more money than anyone else can, but that is a nominal advantage. The other countries can quickly overcome their borrowing disadvantage by implementing Magnified Capitalism to whatever degree they can muster.

In the meantime, we can watch our own companies bring more of their products and services back home as the CMS advantages for doing so become increasingly compelling. Those other countries might want to hurry up and copy us better, from the magnification program to improving individual freedoms. However, there is also the possibility that we will become so healthy that other countries may easily become complacent. I would expect our new strength to seep into the global economy and help everyone to some degree. This global trickle-down effect might leave other countries complaining very little. They may even cheer us on for bouncing out of trouble so aggressively. It would certainly be far worse for the other economies in the world if we fell back into recession, or even if we just continued on a pitifully slow rate of improvement.

So what is the impact of global competition on this plan? Think about being the first country with a jet air force. To keep our air superiority we should plan to keep making our jets better, even before other countries copy our initial technology. So it is with Magnified Capitalism. We should see keeping up our renewed world economic leadership as a most important national strategic goal. Perhaps it even qualifies as a national security issue. Regardless, maintaining such leadership means Magnified Capitalism processes and funding need to improve steadily over time, at least until we develop the next major improvement in governing our capitalist system. Our plan needs to include strong consideration for self-improvement or self-optimization. That means the CMS must have a nimble management system and a structure that includes self-analysis and process adjustments. It also means the CMS must report the specifics of its own operations to the public and Congress, transparently and in great detail. This is the best way to insure a minimum of abuse and a maximum feedback loop on continued improvement.

Strength #5: Long Term - Windfall and Strategic Steering
The motivation for creating Magnified Capitalism is rooted in creating jobs and the economic prosperity that comes with them. Assuming we do this soon, I have a prediction that might surprise you. Decades from now we will not characterize this system primarily as a source of job creation. After all, once there are enough jobs for everyone who wants one, markets should pretty much stay that way for as long as we keep such a program going. But there are two effects that we should always associate with Magnified Capitalism. First and perhaps foremost are the eventual riches the government will collect. Yes, I said it. After some decades of operation, the CMS could reach a point where it collects nearly the same amount of revenue from its capital investments as the IRS currently collects in income taxes. CMS revenue could even eventually increase much more than that. *Chapter VII: Financials* will elaborate the details on how that could happen.

The quick reason for our windfall is this. The CMS will offer great terms in return for its participation in deals like funding startups through venture capitalists. Those terms will favor the venture capitalists' controlling partners so much they will take the same terms over and over in their ongoing funding business. However, that does not mean the CMS does not get a fair share. Furthermore, the system will favor the successful venture capitalists who do the greatest volume of CMS business.

Therefore those who continue to have a great track record making the CMS money will gain access to more and more capital. In other words, the system favors the smartest and best capitalist partners. While the CMS's share of profits is notably smaller than that of the commercial partner, it will still receive a strong investment return. Consider this example: If the U.S. co-funds a startup that turns into another Google, then the profits collected will be in proportion to the success. We can expect the best deals to cash out at several hundred percent profit. Of course this will not be the typical case, but if it happens just a bit more often than we need it to, our total profits start to fly way up.

Generally, the longer we run the CMS, the better we will get at tweaking the standard terms, the more successful our capitalist partners will become, and the more funds we will have to reinvest. We will get better at earning the best investment return possible while staying attractive enough that the program remains in use for most new business. In other words, CMS profitability should continue to improve over time. Eventually it will rake in a serious fortune every year. I have not even factored in the benefits of investing in an economy with a healthy GDP. Once the markets start to improve, they build on themselves.

The second effect that will characterize Magnified Capitalism in the long term is its function as a national policy steering wheel. This comes through the powerful CMS incentives and controls designed into the solution. Although we have already touched on this subject, it deserves much further development in our discussion. The ability to adjust CMS incentives and rules amounts to a new shared power between the President and Congress. I will give many more examples of specific kinds of incentives later in the SWOT analysis under *Opportunities*. For now, here is a simple example that I expect we will implement on the first day.

> *CMS for Domestic Use - Rule*
> This is a foundational CMS control that is so strong it is a "hard rule" rather than an incentive, although it has an incentive-like effect.
>
> > Only U.S. companies and citizens qualify for CMS funding and related services.
>
> If a foreign business wants to participate in CMS services, it will need to make sure one or more U.S. citizens own a combined total of at least 51%[2] of the business receiving those services. In other words, foreign investors can participate through a minority holding of a U.S. company that qualifies for CMS services. Otherwise foreign investors are out. There will also be rules to prevent shell games where foreign entities use fake U.S. companies (or even semi-legitimate middlemen) whose purpose is to transfer CMS services to non-U.S. benefactors.

How will this rule impact new business? Foreign companies who want to have a hand in our new economic success will need to invest in real American companies and startups! Furthermore, U.S. investors will have new incentives to keep their money working in domestic growth opportunities. More money will come into our economy from abroad. Less of our money will go overseas.

Now consider what will happen if we make CMS terms slightly less attractive for businesses with production facilities outside the U.S. This could involve a CMS

---

[2] The 51% figure quoted here is adjustable over time to suit political negotiations. It could start out higher, such as 75%. It should probably never be set much higher than 80% unless we want to block the incentive draw of foreign capital into U.S. businesses.

penalty for significant overseas production. Then we might add a positive incentive in the other direction. A basic monetary incentive makes CMS services more profitable if the business receiving the funding has a higher portion of their production in the U.S. than elsewhere. This could include raw materials from U.S. sources, subcontractors, and factory facilities. What impact will this have on new business creation and jobs in the U.S.? Notice that as we turn our steering wheel we are talking about production incentives and disincentives, not requirements. In fact, as we go down the road, our policy controls should increasingly adjust only the incentives part.

I want to urge all future lawmakers to resist creating additional hard rules to implement national policy interests, especially after the CMS is up and running. Whether we wish to favor green energy, or products made in the U.S.A., or any other aspect of business, we should seek to implement this national policy as a positive incentive rather than a hard-and-fast rule. We can optionally consider minor disincentives in some cases, although we should take care to keep these gentle. It will be very easy to create disincentives that are so strong that they take CMS funds out of play. The steering wheel offered here is powerful but dangerously easy to turn too far.

Why so much concern about the government's use of control? It is safer and wiser for the government to nudge the market in a direction of national interest rather than forcing markets in a particular direction. Forcing markets is usually a mistake, as we have learned from the examples of fascism and socialism. Hard rules turn the government into an unwelcome player who is trying to interfere and pick market winners and losers. If we implement a faulty rule, the penalty is the repression of proper business planning and best practices. We are also putting the CMS at higher risk for losing its investments or making itself irrelevant, such as if the market walks away from its services altogether.

The good news is that there is no need to be so heavy-handed. CMS incentives leverage the power of market forces with a gentle touch. If policymakers change an incentive instead of a rule, if they are wrong, then the new incentive just goes unused. We can measure that and learn from it - no harm, no foul. Ultimately, I expect lawmakers will become increasingly skilled at installing new CMS incentives to steer our markets towards useful national goals. Because we will use it continuously, the new policy steering wheel power may turn out to be one of the greatest legacies of long-term importance.

Recall that we are analyzing a forked strength of two prongs. One prong has us generating a new source of revenue; the other one concerns our new policy steering wheel. Now what is the impact of this paired advantage on the plan itself? It is helpful to recognize that we are eventually going to want huge returns from Magnified Capitalism. This pushes us once again to keep our processes both transparent and self-optimizing. It also encourages us further to implement a CMS structure that more closely resembles a commercial company than a government agency. Most of us will trust a commercial fund management company to make successful investments on our behalf. I cannot say the same thing about a government bureaucracy. Having a government agency managing our money should scare anyone. When we combine this with the need for the CMS to become a policy steering wheel the result is even scarier. The total political pressure imposed here would cause most bureaucracies to have a seizure, let alone function well. How do we adjust our plan to protect us and make sure this money is managed professionally?

The answer starts at the top. We should treat the head of the CMS like the president or CEO of any commercial company. Keeping their job should depend solely on their performance. They should pass that disposition on to their staff so that they are in turn incented on performance. This transparency is vital to discourage any kind of funny business, whether it is from within the CMS, from Congress, or even some future President. This will also be the best way to build trust between the public, the legislature, the President and the CMS. Everyone will be better served by highly transparent CMS operations.

This is not enough, however. We must monitor and measure CMS service effectiveness. This means special reporting and analysis of the effects that incentives (and disincentives) have on their targets. I also mentioned this point in the section about the strength of this plan regarding increasing economic growth.

Another previously mentioned adjustment has to do with managing the CMS incentives themselves. This regards the need to implement rules in advance that allow for easy adjustments to incentives in the future. It also reinforces the idea that rules and disincentives should be harder to change than positive incentives.

One new plan modification does result here, since we now have a specific need to manage positive incentives in a more formalized way. This system must manage the modification of incentives, both from the beginning and in on-going ways. Two specific changes accommodate these goals.

First I will speak to the ease of starting up such a system. The CMS will have a package of predefined economic control levers that address a variety of different types of expected strategic goals. In other words, we will give the policy control a menu from which to start. For instance, as I previously suggested, there will be a standard incentive relating to U.S. production that uses locally-sourced supplies. Other standard incentives are also pretty obvious candidates. These include the use of green energy technologies, the production of recyclable goods, and the use of facilities located in economically depressed areas. We will only predefine the definition and existence of the incentive. We will leave open whether or not and to what degree the system triggers such standard incentive types.

On year one, we might leave most of these incentives unused. An unused incentive simply means its incentive level is set to zero. However, you Mr. President, working with Congress, need only pass legislation to turn the economic levers that have already been set up and placed on standby. Rather than get hung up on wording and rules, your work can focus on the simpler issue of how much to turn each available lever. This kind of incentive system ought to reduce gridlock and make compromise a more likely result when dealing with any issues that already have a defined incentive.

The other change that modifies our plan towards improved incentive management is this: We should standardize incentive levels. In other words, when you and Congress decide to trigger an incentive, that means you change its level from zero to some positive value. But what positive value, and how are Congress and the people to know whether a $10,000 incentive per million dollars in a deal is enough, or too much? If it is neither, then we still have a related problem. Was that $10,000 an aggressively high incentive, or is it so weak that it will have little effect? Congress and the President should not have to be experts in CMS financials in order to implement a strategic policy. Rather, the CMS should offer pre-set, standardized levels of incentives that are known to have different degrees of effect. This requirement will come up again soon; I will elaborate more then.

For now we accept the need for the incentive system to have easy-to-understand standard settings, like numbers on a dial. If the incentive is off, then its dial is set to zero. If that incentive's dial is set for "7", this will translate to 70% of full power (maximum incentive). What numerical bonuses are required within each CMS service to translate to 70% effectiveness? Good news! We do not need to figure that out. I make that issue the CMS's problem. Substantially, we can analyze this question in advance with great detail but it is of little immediate concern. For us today, it is sufficient to say that policymakers need their incentives to look like a knob with numbers on it. Furthermore, the CMS is responsible for designing their service incentive system in such a way that it works exactly to the degree Congress has set it for.

Strength #6: Credit is Cheap and Plentiful

Whether it is because we hold the world's currency, or because we are still the number one economy, or just because most of our competition is scarier to work with than we are, we still have a great advantage. We can borrow almost as much money as we want at very low interest rates. As I mentioned, we do not expect this cheap credit situation to last more than another few years, but that is OK. We want to move quickly anyway. We should borrow what we need right now and make our big play under the best credit terms. Later, when money is more expensive, we will be making a profit and will not have the same need to borrow. So our timing for this plan is perfect, at least from a credit perspective. Conversely, if we waste a lot of time arguing about details so that Magnified Capitalism itself is delayed for years, we will be a bit sorry about it. First of all, the problem we have with unemployment is urgent. That is the number one reason to get things going now. But second, the whole plan will be much more expensive if we wait until interest rates climb and the world's willingness to loan us money wanes.

How does the knowledge of a credit advantage impact our plan itself? The primary answer has to do with the timeline. That is, the credit advantage produces an extra sense of urgency, both with starting our plan, and with reaching a stage where the CMS processes are optimized for solid profitability. Therefore we have another political reason to gain quick approval of the program and a strong priority to produce a government agency that is unlike any other: transparent, commercially incented, nimble to process change, self-auditing, quick to assign responsibility for success or failure and take action accordingly. This cannot be an organization of bureaucrats. It should more closely resemble an investment fund management firm, except that its activities are also transparent and self-auditing. We will want to model many aspects of the CMS after a commercial company.

Strength #7: Market Advantage Goes to the First

Magnified Capitalism is an American idea. It is intended to be implemented quickly, before any other country has the chance. Besides the fact that we need this program now to address unemployment and we have a credit advantage today, there is another reason to move fast. As with most good commercial product ideas, the advantage goes to the ones who take it to market first. We will win the biggest rush of business activity by being first. We will be first to learn the detailed lessons of how to improve and optimize this strategy over time. Those great business plans that could not find funding before Magnified Capitalism will be implemented here, instead of in whatever country beats us to it. The benefits go on and on, not unlike the advantage of being a commercial market leader. Sometimes the reason this makes a difference is hard to pinpoint, but it is consistently true in most any competitive situation. Being first has great advantages. Some of these advantages will be easy to spot. Others we may never notice specifically but they nonetheless will be helping in the background. It is about being the powerhouse in capitalism. We should move on this fast and claim our proper pole position.

This strength impacts the actual plan in two areas. First, we gain yet another political reason for prompt approval. As we are deliberating whether to implement Magnified Capitalism in the U.S., we might expect at least a few other countries will be doing so as well. If this is not true now, then it will be very soon. The second impact relates to the importance of setting up the system right the first time. That means the CMS must be set up by professional planners and business people. We must give them the authority they need to run the new agency as if it were a business that just happens to have, you, Mr. President as Chair, and a selection of congressional leaders as the rest of its Board of Directors. If we allow the usual sort of bureaucratic processes to rule the implementation then we should not be surprised to have a disappointing timeline and a disappointing result, at least initially.

Strength #8: Strong Pool of Leverageable Capital

One of the characteristics of a competitive environment is ready access to capital for business growth. Magnified Capitalism increases competitiveness precisely because it increases access to such capital through government-provided magnification services or standard CMS deals. Even though U.S. world ranking in competitiveness has started to fall in recent years, it is still pretty high. One of the reasons it is high is that we have a significant pool of business capital sources. That is, in the U.S. there is a relatively large supply of venture capitalists, banks, businesses with resources, and private investors. As we have noted, these sources are currently underperforming due to the poor economy. Many are strapped for cash. Most are a bit burned from recent events. Nearly all see the current economic climate as a warning to be careful. The result is therefore a collectively more conservative money supply. Our strategy stimulates an improvement in the motivation and the resources of these job-creating sources of capital.

What this strength underscores, however, is that the organizations and people who make capital investments are fairly abundant in the U.S. They could do much more if they had the kind of improved access to attractive funding and other business incentives we will install. This plan will motivate an appetite for these existing sources to take on more risk, and it will multiply the number of deals they can make. This is not equally the case worldwide. Magnified Capitalism works better when more capital infrastructure is in place. Put another way, there must be something there to magnify for the plan to have a big impact. This is the strength I am talking about now. We have plenty of the stuff that needs to be magnified.

As a contrast, consider a country like North Korea, whose world ranking in economic competitiveness is probably last place (only a selection of major countries have been formally ranked and North Korea is not one of them). This communist dictatorship has close to zero business capital sources today. If North Korea were to try to implement Magnified Capitalism they would be very disappointed in the result. With a weak banking system, a tiny pool of successful existing businesses, and virtually no venture capitalists or private investors, they have almost no capitalist system to magnify. They would need to address fundamental capitalist infrastructure before any amount of magnification would help them. This would necessarily include new freedoms and rights for individuals, and laws for the support of business creation and ownership. A nation must set up a decent capitalist system before this strategy can do anything for it. We have already proven to the world that capitalism works best in a free society epitomized by a true democracy. It is too bad for North Korea. They are nowhere near ready for a strategy like this one.

We in the U.S. are on the opposite end of the spectrum. Even in our current weak economy, we still have the fundamental capitalist infrastructure in strong numbers. It might be taking a bit of a nap, but there is the potential to explode our economic activity with a kick from Magnified Capitalism. This is the best situation to motivate a program like this. We have the hot rod. We just have not upgraded it lately. Now we need to strap on our new rocket engines and mount the special steering wheel.

This strength of ours has at least three plan-impacting effects. I will call these three effects scale management, breadth management, and the need for deal efficiency. All of these relate in some way to handling a huge number of capital magnification deals and capital sources.

Scale management refers to the idea that the CMS will need to do two things really well. It will have to be able to manage a large number of participants in Magnified Capitalism programs (a large scale). The CMS will also need to be prepared to grow that large list of participants quickly for an indefinite period of time (scalability, or an inherent ability to grow). The concern is that if the CMS processes are in any way slow, difficult, restrictive, or bottleneck-producing, then the positive impact of our strategy could become threatened.

Breadth management is similar, but it does not refer to the large number of participants per se. Rather, it predicts that such a large number of participants will encompass many variations and special situations. The CMS will be inundated with special requests, special considerations, lots of questions and concerns, ongoing customer support requirements, and even arbitration for parties that have disagreements and grievances. Our plan needs to address such matters head-on for the same reasons we must deal directly with scale management. We must handle complexity and support fairly, transparently, and with great efficiency. Our plan needs to solve this problem well to build confidence and keep government overhead in the CMS to a minimum.

The last impact regards deal efficiency. It means that when a capitalist brings the government in on a deal, that process should be as short and easy as possible, for the benefit of both the private dealmakers and the government. We must create standardized, fair and reasonable terms and conditions. We must insure that automated customer support is helpful. We must strip down commercial requirements, such as for reporting and scoring, to the minimum and provide online tools for customer assistance. We should design rules that make arbitration as unnecessary as possible. We should generate a strong incentive for customers to work out grievances privately. And we should establish significant penalties for the losing party if the government has to step in to settle a matter.

That concludes the list of strengths we should consider. Naturally, more strengths exist but the ones I discussed above provide a good representation of those with a high impact. What I hope you have noticed in the analysis so far, Mr. President, is this. While we could use each strength as a weapon in a political argument, this was only part of the point. The more revealing result is that by considering each strength we could derive some plan-improving impact. This analysis has led to adjustments that help preserve and elevate each strength. This kind of benefit is the nature of a SWOT analysis, a feature that I want to emphasize as we go on.

Weaknesses

As with the information in the previous subsection, the unconvinced might consider a weakness listing as part of their decision-making process regarding the whole of the Magnified Capitalism strategy. Regardless of whether or not you have made a decision on this bigger question, I am more focused on how each weakness will influence change in our plan. Knowing where holes might develop can produce at least two very useful plan-affecting results. First, we can adjust the plan to address these weaknesses as much as possible. We could consider steps to mitigate related risks, answer open issues or concerns, or minimize the impact of the risks. Second, we can prepare pragmatic or political arguments to counter these apparent concerns. In other words, it is possible that something we flag as a weakness is actually addressable with pure reason. Perhaps some apparent flaws will be revealed as mere false impressions once we examine them more closely.

We will consider all of these issues for both kinds of plan response. That is, I will address each weakness with some action-oriented countermeasures. Such measures should work to reduce, fade or even eliminate the weakness. Then I will also offer a counterpoint to each matter with the pure logic of a good argument. Of course, there is always the possibility that a weakness stands up as genuine, even if we can do some things to reduce its impact in our planning. Whatever the case, listing weaknesses includes more than just weighing shortfalls. Knowing where the plan is weak gives us the chance to take appropriate action and otherwise defend the strategy. That is certainly my goal for this plan.

Weakness #1: Borrowing Towards the Untested

I have listed this weakness first on purpose. It is a compound problem with two parts. Specifically, the government must borrow a large sum of money to implement this plan. This is the first part of the weakness, a point that we have already mentioned as one detractors are sure to raise. I have already addressed the borrowing issue directly. Recall that borrowed money goes towards secured diversified investments in U.S. businesses, and these businesses will repay this money in a mid-term schedule of between 3 to 6 years, with interest. Therefore this borrowing falls into a different accounting category than regular unsecured debt. The debt risk is low because the process is designed to keep losses minimal and to take advantage of deals with high returns.

Once we understand the debt issue, where is the real weakness? We must now focus on the second part to see it. Magnified Capitalism is untested. Detractors will likely label it as a theoretical exercise that we must consider a high-risk strategy. After all, it is a totally new idea that has never been implemented before. I recognize well-intended people will insist it is a fair observation, even if that is debatable. Thus, detractors can use the untested aspect of the plan to undermine the argument about the borrowing risk.

In order for the detractor's objections to carry much weight they have to combine the two points into a more powerful complaint: Borrowing money to make investments through an untested plan can produce a loss. This is why the borrowed money could result in new budget debt. I'll walk through this complaint more carefully.

The borrowing required is secured debt, so the detractors must admit this is not the kind debt that makes a budget imbalance. As long as the plan works as claimed, debt is repaid when the CMS cashes the collateral notes a few years down the line. Importantly, we count on Capital Magnification Service (CMS) processes to insure the money lost on bad deals is more than made up by gains on the good deals. But the CMS does not yet exist. We have not fully laid out the processes for the CMS to function. Even considering all the details that come later in this plan I cannot say all CMS processes are documented. Furthermore, I expect that the least efficient return on government investment will occur in the very first years of CMS operation. Why? Because we will learn lessons and improve processes over time. I expect the CMS to get better and better at improving return on investment the longer it exists. This means it will be its least effective on day one.

What is the bottom line? If the CMS does a poor enough job of implementing the strategy, it could lose some portion of the money invested by the government, especially at first. If serious plan problems pop up to undermine investment return, then losses could become substantial. I expect a very pessimistic economic analysis might claim a potential loss as high as 50% of the invested capital. If we were to assume a 50% loss in the first year, even if subsequent years reduced this loss significantly through improvements in rules and processes, our case for this strategy becomes far weaker. It means we would have to write off 50% of the first year's investment as real new debt. Or alternately, we would roll up such loses into the CMS's total debt. Either way, the result would extend by many years our projection of when the plan would start to pay for itself and produce real investment gains.

It is this uncertainty of the program being untested that will cause the heartburn. We are talking about risking a lot of money. The people who should be supporting Magnified Capitalism most include those who want to balance our budget and reduce our borrowing. Yet there is an unavoidable concern that if we have never done this before, anywhere, how can we be certain that there is not some large hole in the investment strategy behind it?

There is a good reason why I listed this weakness first. It really is the biggest drawback. It is big enough to cause pause in the most ardent supporter. This potential defect caused me to question whether or not this was the right strategy to put forward, but not because I agree with the issue itself. Mine is a more pragmatic concern. Consider this: No matter how great an idea could be if it were implemented, there is no point in trying if we are pretty sure it will never be accepted in the political arena. This weakness is potentially powerful enough to block political acceptance. I concluded that it is not enough just to counter this objection. This matter needs a serious hammering.

The punch line is this: For our plan to gain political support, we need to overcome this problem on two fronts. First, we need a solid risk mitigation strategy. That means finding a way to substantially reduce the investment risk of our untested plan. Second, we need a solid, practical counterargument. Preferably, we should have a counterargument that does not refer to our risk mitigation. If we can nail the logic, then adding risk mitigation will make our plan very compelling.

The impact of weaknesses on our plan tends to be more apparent than the impact of most strengths. That is, each weakness calls for strong plan considerations to address the problem. So it is here. This weakness has to do with setting up a complex new function on behalf of our government, the Capital Magnification Service. The CMS will be responsible for implementing and enforcing the Magnified Capitalism strategy. We must accomplish a great deal of work very efficiently to pull this off, both in the setup of the CMS and in its subsequent operations. Those who doubt any government organization could achieve these ends have my sincere empathy. In fact, I believe it very important that we not allow the CMS be set up by government bureaucrats or in the same manner as any other government department. Rather, this proposal specifically calls for the CMS to be set up by professional business leaders with experience in establishing companies that manage investment funds, investment banking divisions, and venture capital firms. We should model the organization itself after proven commercial business establishments and run it almost entirely as if it were a commercial venture.

Here is the biggest single plan modification in this entire proposal: We should set up the CMS as a true commercial business and not a government agency at all. It will not be like any other commercial business, though. It will be a new kind of company. We will grant this business the sole responsibility and license to implement this Magnified Capitalism plan.

By defining itself as a commercial business, the CMS avoids being limited by many kinds of government restrictions. Most specifically, its management will be free to fire people who are under-performing and reward those who contribute to success. But unlike any existing company in the United States, the CMS will be a commercial company with government-managed oversight. More specifically, select members of Congress will fill the company's Board of Directors, with the President as Chair. This was the effect that the plan sought originally. Now I propose to implement it exactly this way. As Chair, you, Mr. President, will have the ultimate power to hire and fire the CMS Chief Executive Officer (CEO). Unlike a regular commercial company though, you and the rest of the CMS Board will set the goals that the CMS is expected to achieve. I will more fully explain why later, but I call this new kind of organization a "citizen company".

This approach should greatly reduce the risks inherent in setting up a brand new government department. Although government representatives have oversight, the CMS CEO and the rest of that organization will be composed of the same kind of people who already run successful investment firms. Not only that, but they will be expected to implement the same sorts of commercial processes and practices already proven to work. Our odds for the CMS working efficiently and successfully have just gone way up.

Never heard of the government setting up a private company to do its work? There is some precedent. The United States government set up a company called COMSAT Corporation in the 1960's. COMSAT was established to seed the start of the commercial satellite industry by being the first company with the bankroll to afford to do it. Our government set them up and provided their initial funding. COMSAT had the mandate to build and launch satellites. The government expected the company to figure out how to make money doing that, back when no one else was. They did. COMSAT had no permanent tie to the government, though. This is the main reason why it is not an example of a citizen company. By the way, decades later another company bought out COMSAT. The new owner, Lockheed Martin, now continues this business with fair success. Most consider that the COMSAT effort worked well, even in its first years. Regardless, turning the CMS into a new, special kind of commercial company is an aggressive step, but this is not enough for me.

Therefore I will add another major plan addition that should also greatly improve the odds of success. This idea comes from the world of commercial software development. Let me explain. Whenever a company develops software, especially if it is mission critical or if lives depend on it, they experience a problem similar to the one our plan faces. The software is brand new, never before used. So how do they make sure it works well enough to put it into the marketplace? The answer is to test it. If the software were just a computer game, or some kind of tool like a calculator, the testing process would be relatively simple. The company would start by having a pool of their own people test it. These testers would try to make the software fail in different ways and under different circumstances. At a later stage, many software developers also conduct a beta test, which is a limited trial using friendly customers.

But beta tests are not a great way to debug software that runs a heart-lung machine or the software running an aircraft controller's console. If the software must work right the first time, the company instead does something a bit trickier. How do they pretest their software against every possible real life situation? These developers create special testing software which is essentially a simulator that replicates some part of the real world. By the time the doctors plug the heart-lung machine into a real person, it has been tested against millions of simulated patients with every combination of symptoms imaginable. If the heart-patient simulator software was well designed, the beta test is no longer required. In the real world, this method of testing works well.

Let us now come back to our problem. First we recognize that most of the CMS will be computerized, although people following written processes will certainly be integral to CMS services. While we are setting up the CMS, we will establish a major software development effort to design and build the automated systems that provide much of CMS's function. The plan change I am putting forward is this: During this same period, a software developer separate from those working on the main systems should launch a parallel development effort. This second developer will be responsible for creating a U.S. market simulator and testing system.

To simulate the CMS customers, the software will generate deal requests in the way we expect all four capitalist segments to do. It will then simulate deal results in a wide variety of economic scenarios. This testing system will even simulate customer service problems, arbitration issues, and illegal activities. Its goal will be to try to break the CMS. The main difference will be that the testing will occur on accelerated time scales. That is, this testing software will be able to simulate years of CMS requests in a matter of hours. The emphasis will be on testing the automated portion of the real CMS software once that is ready. However, the testing system will also exercise the real people in CMS operations using their draft processes. The goal will be to flush out both the automated and the human procedures against a large pool of possible simulated situations. This kind of testing should expose problems in both the automated systems and manual processes.

Later, this software will also test whether the fixes really work. Like a new commercial product that must have high reliability, we will not allow the real life CMS services to begin until all their processes pass a minimum threshold of testing certification. The decision will be between you, Mr. President, and the Congress to determine what those minimum standards should be. I will refer to this step as acceptance testing. The CMS will not consider itself ready until it passes a threshold of testing as defined by its Board. At that time the CMS will make a presentation to you and your congressional peers regarding the results of their formal testing. The Board will then either accept those results or ask the CMS to go back and try again, armed with some detailed reasons why the Board rejected their readiness plan. Once the CMS gains Board acceptance, they will have the green light to proceed with offering services to the public.

Here is the good news. This is a proven approach. We take the 'untested' part of our weakness and we erase it. We even encourage skeptics to participate in setting the standards for testing acceptance. The argument now shifts completely. The focus becomes a matter of how well the system must pass simulation tests before we allow it to function in the real world. Incidentally, we can expect that during simulated testing we will learn many important lessons. The result will be improvements in both the automated and human operations of the CMS before any real money changes hands. And that is the point. We take the complaint of the Capital Magnification Service being both untested and new seriously. We turn it around by testing situations more extreme than those likely to occur. We should carefully document the lessons we learn in simulation along with the improvements we make to address them. In this way, we will capture important strategies for future consideration as the CMS matures in years to come.

I must admit I am tempted to stop here. The risk mitigation strategy of aggressive simulation testing is so strong that we need say nothing more about this weakness. However, I promised a counterargument that does not require any risk mitigation. So here it is.

Consider that experienced professionals will set up the CMS. They already know how to make sure an organization responsible for managing money does not produce any net loss. In the rare case that bad years occur, they make up for it in the good years. Regardless, anyone estimating a 50% loss is way out of bounds. Such a dramatic loss would only be possible if incompetent bureaucrats set up the system. We are specifically requiring otherwise. A badly-performing investment firm set up by experienced money managers should still experience no net loss. Rather, a bad year at such a firm would be one in which the gains were well below targets set by management. An example would be a venture capital firm that expects a minimum average annual return of 10%. In a very bad year a well-run firm may net something like a 4% return. A less well-run venture capitalist organization may even have a small loss, but that would be disastrous. Such a bad year would result in process changes, layoffs and some firings. The next year would be better.

The point is this: We need to make sure skilled professionals with the right experience set up and run the CMS. This step was an original part of the proposal. Another original assumption was to have the CMS set up similar to a commercial company. The pressure to move in that direction has built up so strong that I have modified this point. This proposal now calls on the CMS to be a citizen company, a new variation of a commercial company. We must hire an experienced commercial fund manager to run the CMS, and organize this company using solid commercial practices. We will not need to tell our new CEO how to make it all work. This person will know what to do already, or else they will not have been properly selected. The leadership and the commercial structure of the CMS, working together, will ensure that the money this organization borrows will not produce any significant loss, even in the first year.

Notice that the argument I just made further supports the case that we need an implementation as soon as possible. An earlier start date will allow the newly-created CMS more room to get things right the first time, before the economy gets any worse. Mr. President, you may find this time pressure to be a particularly important political motivator. Consider a doctor whose patient is dying on the operating table. He has a brand new tool that could save the patient's life if it works. How much testing should be done before he uses the tool? There is a tradeoff of one risk versus another.

The good news is that now our plan will succeed regardless of which choice we make. We can leave the decision for the politicians to negotiate. The best answer may be a compromise simply because that may afford the soonest start date. I expect that to be more important than whether CMS procedures are 85% optimized versus 98% optimized, for example. We could implement limited CMS operations very quickly while doing aggressive testing in parallel. Such testing could involve several stages with progressively higher thresholds releasing ever-higher levels of funding.

Alternately, we could just hire the best money managers in the world to run the CMS. We would pay them well if they succeed. If they fail, we should fire them and perhaps even require them to pay penalties. After all, if they are so good, they should also be rich already. We might just hire those who are willing to back up their performance claims with their own dollars. That is a capitalist mentality for solving a problem. Put the right people in place. Empower them. Do not restrict them more than necessary. Then put in place incentives for performance and penalties for failure. I personally like this approach for a fast track. Ironically, I would expect such people to establish a serious acceptance testing system or something very similar. A competent team of capitalists should solve this problem using some method they know of. How else would they have become successful enough to be considered for CMS management?

So take your pick. We can specify exactly how we want to address testing through heavy simulations or we can just hire people who already know how to solve this problem and are willing to put their money where their mouth is.

Weakness #2: Expanded Government with a Real Budget Impact
Even though we intend to set up the CMS as a commercial venture that reports to a government Board, our organization still has an operations budget to contend with. We have argued that the CMS will provide profitable returns on its investment fund even in the early years, but there is a footnote. These profits are deferred. That is, the government will hold the average investment collateral for about four years, within a range from as low as 24 months to a maximum of six years. That means the CMS will not realize the full profitability of the first year's investment for six years. This is also true for any given year of CMS operations going forward. In our total accounting, this is not a problem. The cost of running the CMS is included in calculating profit. So after six years, the profit from that first year's investment must account for the cost of running the CMS in that first year. Further, we must also include the cost of managing each investment during subsequent years when computing profit. These costs carry over year to year until they are cashed in or otherwise closed out, such as with a loss or writeoff.

Here is the rub: Put aside the huge investment fund that the CMS is managing for the moment. Perhaps we can all agree that this money is collateralized so it does not count as regular debt. However, we can contend that the cost of running the CMS falls in the same category of expense as running any other government agency. That means the cost of running the CMS adds to government debt. Those who are opposed to expanding government can therefore try to argue two points. First, Magnified Capitalism expands the size and scope of government. Second, running the CMS significantly adds to the national budget requirements, particularly in the first two years because of the cost of developing the new computer systems and testing arrangements. These are largely one-time costs, but they are significant ones. Since full return on investment takes six years to collect, we could only claim this plan adds to the national debt in the meantime. This increase in debt would be highest in the first few years.

This sounds bad. We are making bigger government while increasing national debt due to the costs of setup and ongoing operation. It is not a false problem, at least not technically. It deserves an answer. In the spirit of all our weaknesses we want to provide this answer in two forms, risk mitigation and a counterargument that does not require the risk mitigation. This time we will make the counterargument first.

The criticism of this weakness has two parts. The first is the idea of making government bigger. The second part is the concern about increasing our national debt. Let's first consider the issue about making government bigger. I have already pointed out that the general complaint of making government bigger usually regards non-revenue-producing agencies, or alternately, government inefficiency. The CMS is a new revenue-producing agency, therefore it is not the kind of bigger government people should be so concerned about. Furthermore, we have now determined that it will be legally operated as a commercial organization with government oversight from its Board of Directors. This citizen company strategy will help insure that the CMS's size is kept to a minimum, unlike typical government organizations. Therefore, we have addressed the first part of the weakness. That the CMS represents bigger government is essentially a misapplication of this kind of criticism. This organization is a commercial venture providing the government with services that make money for us all. In addition, those who complain about a growing government should embrace the benefits that the citizen company structure provides.

Establishing the CMS as a citizen company has a secondary impact with regard to keeping down the size of government. We have chosen this path precisely because our commercial goals require the extreme efficiency of a commercial company. More specifically, in a commercial venture, management is highly accountable. Low productivity is not well tolerated. The motivation tends towards smart business practices that favor high customer satisfaction and efficient use of automation. It would not surprise me to find that this model of governance works so well that it is later copied by other government departments.

Those who argue for smaller government would be well served by adopting this same kind of strategy as a means toward their goal. Perhaps one day we will convert many government agencies into citizen companies. Imagine if such companies ran more of our government. The management would be rewarded for higher efficiency and more effective results. The CMS would become a model of how to achieve smaller government that is also more effective for the money. Those who want smaller government might think twice before complaining. This plan might be their opportunity to prove government can be made smaller without losing any services. Perhaps there would even be possibilities for generating government revenue down this track, as long as it was through ancillary means.

A final point on the issue of bigger government is this: If an organization is legally a commercial one that just has government oversight, does its size even count towards the size of government? Is that not the same as counting a government contractor as part of the government? We do not generally count contractors today. Why would we make an exception for the CMS?

Now for the second part of the criticism, that the budget of the CMS increases national debt. There are two ways to answer this objection. In some sense these two answers are alternative versions of the same retort. Here is the first version: We should total the cost of setup and operations and combine them into a single budget for Magnified Capitalism. Call it the overhead cost for the overall investment, not unlike a mutual fund management fee. This moves the costs for both operations and setup into the same category as the investment fund itself. In other words, we do not separate the money the CMS invests from the money the CMS needs to operate. We combine it all into a single collateralized loan that is to be repaid with interest. Therefore, it no longer counts as national debt. The CMS is responsible for getting all the money back, no problem. We will design the program from the beginning to repay all its costs, including those higher one-time costs needed for CMS set up.

Perhaps some politicians will refuse to accept this approach and insist that we carry CMS operations and setup costs on our books just like any other agency's costs. In that case there is another solution. This alternative is mathematically equivalent to the previous answer but less elegant from an accountant's perspective. Essentially, the CMS will still be responsible for repaying its past operation and setup costs, only instead of carrying these costs on its own books, it will repay the government debt incurred over time. In other words, the real national debt increase caused by the CMS will be temporary. Within 12 to 18 years, the CMS will repay all its debt from CMS revenues. This includes the setup costs of this complaint as well as the total amount borrowed for the Fund and any interest due on all of it. From that point forward, ongoing CMS revenue will cover its own operational costs and Fund reloading. Not only will the government will stop carrying operational costs, but a couple of years later CMS business generates a new government revenue stream.

So whether we account for it one way or another, the problem entirely disappears in a certain number of years. The old debt disappears. Ongoing costs stop accruing. The Capital Magnification Service pays its debts, becomes self-sufficient, and then revenue-generating. Did our detractors forget the last part? Only the most shortsighted, budget-conscious politicians are likely to be against this strategy. The rest should be fighting to implement it as soon as possible. Magnified Capitalism starts paying off national debt after less than 20 years of operations. That is a big deal. In the meantime unemployment drops super low and business activity flies through the roof. We hit three birds with one stone. The only pause is that we hit one of the birds years later than the first two. Admittedly, this bird metaphor is a bit odd, but it illustrates the point.

Having completed the counterargument, I could take the position that there is little need for risk mitigation on this issue. However, we are generally wiser to attack on both sides. In the counterargument I placed particular emphasis on setting up the CMS as a citizen company. It should be clear that our plan shifted in the course of our analysis on this matter. The original idea was merely that we should operate the CMS differently from most government agencies so that it would resemble a commercial organization. I later offered setting up the CMS as a legal business entity as a consideration, and then I put forward the citizen company variation. However, the discussion over this weakness puts a sharper point on the issue. The risk mitigation strategy I am adopting is that the legal status of the CMS is no longer flexible. It is increasingly obvious that forming the CMS as a commercial company provides too many needed advantages. I am therefore including some additional details to elaborate on what it means to be a citizen company. This is the lowest-risk solution for structuring an efficient and effective CMS organization.

As the first citizen company, the CMS is legally a commercial business whose stock is wholly owned equally by every living citizen of the United States. To insure that the company follows the interests of its stockholders, the CMS Board of Directors will be composed of democratically-selected members of the federal government. The Chief Executive Officer (CEO) of the CMS, who is the top managing executive, will report directly to the Board of Directors. The Board's Chair should be the current President of the United States, with the balance of the Board comprised of a Senate subcommittee whose members are assigned and changed from time to time.

Furthermore, I would require the accounting books of the CMS and all meeting notes be publicly posted in electronic format without exception. Remember, the government may be responsible for overseeing high-level operations, but it is the people who really own the CMS. Regardless, to return to the main point of this section, true commercialization best addresses this weakness. It presents a clean form of accounting that takes all CMS operations and setup costs off U.S. budget books and moves them into a giant collateralized investment. The CMS will repay this investment in short order. After this point the government can expect perpetual profitable returns. This setup even supports the argument for a smaller government. The new citizen company known as the CMS could serve as a model for other government reorganizations in the future. Finally, there is something poetic about a free democratic society applying a new kind of capitalist-based business model to improve its own efficiency. Those who like beauty in their solutions might find something special here.

Weakness #3: All Plan Analysis Is Unqualified and Theoretical

The word "theoretical" in this weakness represents the idea that every claim in this strategy is not only subject to significant error, but might be plain wrong. Adding a concern about qualification gives the complaint two angles. Taken together, this suggests the possibility that we cannot trust the accuracy of anything in this proposal. Furthermore, these concerns cast doubt on the plan's fundamental conclusions.

This lack of trust has two angles. First, these criticisms highlight the fact that Magnified Capitalism is so new that no one anywhere has ever tried it, or even independently analyzed the idea. Second, they cast doubt on the author. I imagine statements like, "Does he think he is actually qualified to propose anything so grand or fundamental?" We can pick alternate words to finish that sentence; some might sound more insulting or sarcastic than others. I am bracing myself for the colorful variants that critics put forward. If I handle it right I should congratulate my detractors for their creativity and then remind myself of a key tenet in politics: When someone attacks another personally, they are probably both threatened and having difficulty making a counterargument through substance. But I should not disqualify the concern. The weakness itself deserves a proper treatment.

The logic of this weakness predicts an attack on my qualifications and similar attacks that Magnified Capitalism comes from a lone voice who is neither published in some peer-reviewed economic journal, nor arisen from some well-respected think-tank of economists.

One obvious answer might be to defensively summarize my resume. I could talk about my real-life experience running businesses as an entrepreneur. I could round it out by reviewing my work at larger companies as a product manager, or my experience and certification in formal project management. Perhaps readers would receive more insight from an understanding of my university studies and hobbies, or my father's influence on me in economics. His doctorate was in this field.

Somehow, even taken together, these pieces of information feel like exactly the sort of distraction a detractor would want to hear. It would mean they have successfully shifted the dialog away from the issue of whether or not Magnified Capitalism is a good idea.

Alternately, I could try a strategy that points to a long list of great concepts that were put forward by people with unlikely resumes. Einstein was a file clerk when he published his biggest ideas. Steve Jobs, one of my favorite visionaries, was a college dropout. But I think all of this is a waste of energy. Not only do I not need to defend my qualifications, the matter is moot. Just engaging on this front, even successfully, is a tactical loss in a political game because doing so allows the topic to shift from what matters, like taking the bait from a trap just because I think I can escape with it.

No, I choose not to go down that road. In fact, I prefer to flip the whole question around. It is better to just assume I have zero qualifications. I do not have a personal agenda here anyway. I have achieved my goal just by putting the plan into the public discourse. I need nothing further. The best defense against a personal attack is not to care one way or another.

So what is the counterargument if someone wants to focus on questioning the source of this plan? Here it is:

This is not about me. If the issue of Magnified Capitalism becomes a battle about me then we are way off topic. Forget about me. Look at the plan. Try to punch a hole in it. Take this strategy to someone whose resume you admire and ask him or her. I want my readers to do exactly that. Why else am I openly publishing this whole effort? I hope many other people run with the idea, analyze it, simulate variations on computers, and publish independent economic analysis for peer review.

I promise that even if we fast-track Magnified Capitalism into a speedy implementation, dozens of economists and other analysts will have plenty of time to weigh in with their professional opinions before we spend a penny. Thus the idea of my being "unqualified" is perhaps technically true at the time of this plan's initial publication, but from a practical perspective it is nonsense. In fact, I expect such attacks to come primarily from those who have something to lose if we implement the plan. When we detect an attack on the messenger instead of the message, we should assume money or politics is in play.

That leaves the more legitimate part of this weakness to address, the idea that Magnified Capitalism is theoretical. Of course anything new and untested is theoretical. Therefore it is not entirely off base to suppose that some conclusions written here will contain errors when compared to any real-life implementation. More astute observers might be chomping at the bit to point out that I have already addressed the issue of the program being untested in the section about the first weakness. There we determined to apply a dose of heavy simulation testing before we allow the Capital Magnification Service to manage any real money. Incidentally, such a serious effort to model and test the actual implementation before going live should trump all other types of lighter analysis by any economist, no matter their resume.

That is my answer. Many good people will analyze this plan before it gets anywhere close to receiving funding. The plan itself calls for heavy simulation testing before the CMS manages any funds. And as for me, I am not the issue. Consider that I might have just been lucky enough to be graced with a good idea, and the means and opportunity to present it to you. I leave it to my readers to use their own minds and methods to validate it. I certainly encourage them to do so.

The impact of this weakness on the plan is simple. We have already discussed simulation testing and acceptance before CMS can go live. This is most important. We must reapply it to address this weakness. The other impact is not so much on the plan itself as it is on you, Mr. President. That is the idea that you have been handed a goose. Take this goose to your team of advisors and professionals. You do not need to trust me. If this goose lays golden eggs you can easily validate that without any other input from me. Regardless, I would like to point out that the girl's webbed feet do have some gold flakes around them. I'm just saying...

Weakness #4: The Tuning Problem

This weakness is a serious one, but it is a bit complicated. It is the sort of weakness that economic analysts are likely to focus on. The explanation goes something like this: The Capital Magnification Service makes its income by offering a product line of different services, standardized business deals offered to capitalists. For each such service, there will be a set of fixed rules, qualifications, terms and conditions. In order for this plan to work, the services offered by the CMS must accomplish a series of goals. The first of these goals is this: The deals offered to all four capitalist types (venture capitalists, bankers, businesses and private investors) must be compelling enough that they will usually want to take them. Capitalists will need to agree it is usually advantageous to take the CMS's offers.

There is some complexity in arriving at such a collection of business decisions. The capitalists will have to conclude that they like CMS services. Taking these deals must make them more money than turning them down. Their own cost of complying with the government's standard terms and conditions, such as for reporting and other paper work, has to be small enough not to negatively impact this decision. . And finally, these services must make enough money that the CMS produces its required profit after taking into account the cost of running the CMS and repayment of its own startup costs. I have yet to detail any of this. I have essentially asked for a leap of faith that such a balance exists between business requirements, standard deal-based services, and CMS profitability.

Why have I not yet detailed these aspects of the program? A complete answer may be like asking to see the full tax code when first learning about the IRS. Fortunately, there is a more summary solution. I have delivered the key elements of these details in the context of this plan. A fair portion of this presentation, beginning right after this SWOT analysis, addresses various processes, rules, enforcements, incentives, terms and conditions. I will detail each subject when I reach the point in the proposal at which it applies to the overall strategy. Even so, while I will outline most of the big points, I am not presenting a complete CMS rulebook. This is an executive's strategic proposal only. A detailed rulebook for CMS would not be appropriate here. Rather, those who implement the CMS organization and its processes will complete the rulebook at that time.

For their benefit and for others curious about the higher-level answers, I have some good news. By carefully combing through this presentation readers will develop an understanding of the CMS service goals and principles. From this, a solid first draft of the CMS rulebook should be a straightforward exercise. Therefore we need but read on. Afterward we should have a strong sense of most of the elements that this weakness demands to see.

My response so far does not address the weakness itself. Assuming the CMS implementers study this executive summary, and even others' subsequent analysis, they will then draft a CMS rulebook. This rulebook will include all the terms and conditions for the standard business offers and the processes required to navigate them. Even still, what this weakness really suggests is that there may be some trouble finding a balance between the CMS's requirements and those of its capitalist customers. Perhaps the standard offers would not be as attractive to capitalists as we need for the magnification to take off. This would be the case if a lower percentage of capitalists take the deals than needed. Or perhaps CMS profits in a standard offering would be watered down too much for the deals to meet revenue goals. That might result in CMS income that is lower than needed. If the CMS's return on investment is too low, it will fail to deliver key financial milestones.

We can imagine many other types of practical problems, such as undesirable amounts of customer arbitration, terms that encourage high levels of customer fraud, or service aspects that favor one type of capitalist unfairly over others. We can summarize all of these matters as a "tuning problem". The issue is not that that the strategy does not work. It is that there exists a collection of undesirable drawbacks, defects, imbalances, and other detailed problems. These problems do not stop Magnified Capitalism from functioning. Instead they reduce the overall effectiveness or efficiency of the plan.

The tuning term refers to our fallback metaphor of the entire economic system being like a racecar. When introducing a major engine upgrade such as the rockets provided by Magnified Capitalism, we may notice that our engine now needs to be retuned to deal with the new fuel type that rockets use as well as the new top speeds of travel. The point is that although the new car works, it still has issues that may keep it from winning a race. These may be just small issues, but they can combine to create a complex and serious problem. The tuning problem suggests that the implementation of the CMS and its services will not proceed so very smoothly, especially until some real-life experience teaches us how to adjust the details appropriately.

I want to underscore that the tuning problem is most likely a short to mid-term issue. However, it also deserves respect for a variety of reasons. First of all, it is a serious political problem. If we find the system to be under-performing shortly after launch, the detractors who fought against it are sure to pounce. If the problems take too long to repair then they could assassinate and dismantle the entire plan. In some sense, such a result would be worse than a political fight that delays the whole proposal. After all, if Magnified Capitalism is tried but then killed, it will certainly be labeled a "grand disaster". The strategy that should propel the U.S. into a new era of prosperity and success would be castigated and dumped onto the scrap heap of history.

Even if we save the program from cancelation in the face of tuning problems, we still would be dealing with some troubling side effects. Most importantly, Magnified Capitalism may end up having a delayed reaction in the marketplace. This translates to delays in the benefits we seek and lower levels of benefits as we continue fixing the system. These are the kinds of effects we would expect from having too few capitalists being attracted to the CMS's standard deals. Such problems may arise from too many restrictive rules or terms that do not result in enough customer profits to offset the cost of participating. It could also come about from too many disincentives to conducting normal business. For example, there may be too strong a penalty for using offshore resources and not enough of a counterincentive for made-in-the-U.S.A. resources to balance the business decision. The result could be that we get far fewer takers than we projected. We would need to adjust the incentive-disincentive figures to produce the impact we originally sought. Remember, we cannot force businesses to conduct their activity in a way that will not be profitable. What we can do is make it more attractive for them to make the kind of decisions we would prefer to see more of. This is a good example of why I previously warned against overuse of restrictions and disincentives. Incentives by themselves, on the other hand, are far less likely to cause problems.

Alternately, the tuning problem could go the other way. We may find that standard terms are more disadvantageous to the government's side of the economic equation. This would result in a different set of negative impacts. In such a case we would expect plenty of capitalists to take the deals offered by the CMS, but the government's resulting profitability would end up lower than we need it to be. If we could choose between this class of tuning problem and the previous one, we should pick this one.

This point is easy to understand if we call upon our racecar metaphor again. One class of tuning problem tends to result in too few CMS customers, in other words, not enough capitalists are interested in using CMS services. For our racecar, this is like our engine is wrongly set to excessively restrict gasoline intake. The result is that our engine runs slower than we need it to. Our rocket car runs badly because the engine is sputtering, always starving for more gas. In our second class of tuning problem, plenty of customers sign up but the CMS does not make enough profit. In our racecar metaphor we find our engine is now mistuned with too rich a gasoline mixture. Now we are wasting gas but at least the engine is running fast enough. Driving this car we would still find it to be competitively fast. The engine might even sound OK, but the car's efficiency would be very low.

If we had to drive one of these two badly-tuned racecars, which class of tuning problem would we choose? To have any chance of winning the race we would pick the second choice, naturally. We would also work with our pit crew to fix the tuning every time we made a pit stop. This way we would fix many of the tuning issues before the race ended.

The moral of this story is this: There is likely to be more tolerance and patience with a program that produces the desired impact on jobs and economy, but has the government profiting at a disappointing level. That is the result of burning too much fuel. The plan still works, just like our racecar still races. Our racecar will have to pull over more often than we want to fill up on gas. If the car is fast enough, it can still win. For the CMS, this translates to having plenty of customers but not making enough money to meet our financial goals. If we create lots of jobs, but our profits are low, we still have a problem to fix, but we get to continue the race while we work on it.

We could go through many other possible "tuning problem" scenarios, but I think I have said enough to capture the essence of the matter. If it strikes the reader that this is a likely kind of problem to have, I am inclined to agree. That is why the matter deserves a particularly good risk mitigation response. However, there is also a reasonable counterpoint that I will discuss first.

If we started our Magnified Capitalism program without proper planning, the tuning problem would be a near certain issue. This is why this weakness should strike most of us as intuitive. However, we would have to ignore important plan elements that we have already discussed. There are at least two of these elements that attack this problem head-on. The first is the use of experienced business managers in the setup of the CMS. We can be fairly sure they would avoid setting up funding services that would either be unattractive to their capitalist customers, or produce very low rates of profitability. After all, we have gone out of our way to establish the CMS as a commercial entity specifically to address these types of real world issues. If the CMS falls short on any major measure, those setting everything up will be held responsible and should be fired. So we can say that we have already implicitly addressed the responsibility for risk mitigation by putting the right people in place to set the system up, and then putting them in a position where they must succeed for their own good.

We have another, even better plan element that helps us relax regarding the tuning problem. After studying the previous weakness regarding borrowing against the untested program, we determined to modify this plan in a very important way. Our strategy now includes a thorough testing and acceptance phase. In practice this is a huge adjustment. A second contractor (or team) who is not the one designing the automated CMS systems drives the testing. Their motivation will be to make the CMS processes break. This is a simplification, because 'break' implies that things either work or they do not. The reality is that it will be much easier for such testing to reveal tuning problems than it will be to totally break the system. The result will be obvious to you, the President, and Congress. After all, you are the parties responsible for declaring the CMS ready in the testing acceptance phase. You will see the results of various simulation testing and be able to decide for yourselves if the tuning problem exists based on actual data. If the problem is there, it should be evident from the thorough testing. Therefore, we have already addressed this matter from these two different angles – experienced management and thorough acceptance testing.

As with some other weaknesses, I find that the counterargument to this one is strong enough to stand on its own. But once again I say we can do better than that. There is enough real risk here to warrant plan adjustments. Therefore, we will now talk about how our effort to understand this tuning problem has helped us address what to do about it. The risk mitigation strategy here will address three different subjects: acceptance testing, terms and conditions design, and congressional authority. I will deal with these in the same order.

In our counterargument we leaned heavily on acceptance testing as the key part of our plan that will weed out issues related to tuning. However, what we might notice is that the acceptance testing that we added originally did not specifically attack tuning issues. So the first of our plan adjustments is to make a change so that our simulation testing is required to attack the tuning problem directly and with heavy emphasis. Recall that successful acceptance testing concludes with a report to the Board, that is you, Mr. President, and members from Congress. This report will include analysis regarding how market penetration (a measure of customer attractiveness) and CMS profits are impacted by various options for standard terms, processes, and standard incentive-penalty levels. In other words, everyone will get to see how the process of simulation testing addressed the issue of tuning.

Those with particular business experience might notice that our original testing program is missing a key element with regards to tuning. This is the matter of whether or not businesspeople will find the standard terms and conditions attractive enough that they take the government deal. In other words, we can simulate the impact of what would happen if businesses did not take the deal, but how are we checking whether or not that will actually happen? I now propose that we institute a new category of testing in our plan: focus group testing by real members of each of the four target capitalist groups.

In a focus group, we assemble a moderate number of people (typically 8 to 16 at a time) in a room. We expose them to the material we want to test. After they have had a chance to consider this material, a moderator asks the group questions about what they have just seen. In our case, we would assemble many such groups made up of real venture capitalists, bankers, businesspeople and investors. We would then expose them to the prototype service offerings. They would have a chance to see both a complete service offer and that deal's process, including its terms and conditions. The idea is to expose them to the kind of capital magnification services we hope they will be attracted to. Then our moderators would ask them what they liked and did not like and whether they would consider taking such a deal.

By running many such focus groups we could gather enough real-world data to determine if our CMS deals are terrible or more attractive than necessary, and we may even discover other useful information that will help improve the standard offers. The focus group interview would include questions like whether the wording was too complicated, whether the process requirements were too onerous, or whether the group participants felt comfortable recommending such a CMS deal to their management. We would learn a lot of practical information from focus groups to make the whole program better. Most of this data would be the kind that we would use to reduce the impact of a tuning problem. We can also enter focus group information into the testing systems to improve market simulations. In other words, by learning from these sorts of human tests, we can improve the automated tests.

One of the most useful aspects of addressing the tuning problem during the testing phase has to do with awareness. Being aware of the problem insures that we will not accept the program without first making a reasonable effort to address the tuning in testing. In order to prove that is accomplished, testers must execute many special measures. This includes running through a range of economic scenarios, from the extreme to the more typical ones. Thus we will collect a fair body of data and analyze it to prove the agility of the entire system. Finally, by doing such analysis, we can adjust (or tune) draft CMS processes using the feedback from both automated simulations and human focus groups. We have created an environment during the setup phase that insures we learn important lessons. We will understand tuning issues in great detail before any service goes live.

This brings us to the second aspect we are adjusting in our plan – terms and conditions design. "Terms and conditions" is a common phrase used by lawyers and businesspeople to refer to the legal structure of a deal. In the case of Magnified Capitalism, there will be at least four different types of standard deals the government offers to our four types of capitalists. These deals will offer the capitalists a large chunk of money in return for a piece of the business they are backing. The terms and conditions, commonly abbreviated as the Ts & Cs, will describe all the requirements and limitations the capitalists must accept if they take the deal. The Ts & Cs will also describe exactly what the capitalists will receive in return from the government. The Ts & Cs are essentially a standard contract for a business offer.

A key question that the tuning problem brings up is whether or not these four different standard business offers, or services, are high enough quality that most capitalists will take the deal. We must also consider whether or not each one is a good enough deal for the CMS. The devil can even be in the details. For example, maybe one of the standard deals seems appealing to customers until they start having problems. Then maybe the process trips when they try to get questions answered or resolved. Or perhaps it gets really bad when someone looks like they are cheating. Then we would need a legal investigation and some determination of what to do about it.

The whole matter of Ts & Cs can be quite complicated. Even though I am confident we can create standard Ts & Cs that are good enough to avoid a major tuning problem, there are two important points to consider on this matter. First, the fact that the tuning problem is made small enough not to trip us up, does not mean it will not exist at all. I expect there will always be some ongoing need to improve standard Ts & Cs. Like the engine that is tuned well enough to win a specific race, we can always do some retuning to make the car run even better for subsequent races.

Second, there is a more actionable point to make. We learned an important lesson in raising this weakness, which was this: If we are going to have a tuning problem, we prefer to have the kind that favors the capitalists rather than the kind that favors the CMS. The reason is that it is better to have the CMS falling short on profit than it is to have too few capitalists taking our standard deal. This observation should greatly affect the drafting of the Ts & Cs. There will be many occasions when those responsible for this drafting will argue over the details. In such arguments, one side will typically favor the CMS and the other will favor the potential capitalist customer.

We now have a new rule as follows: When in doubt, favor the capitalist. We shall in all cases of uncertainty try to keep the deal attractive. That means the CMS should err towards providing more customer support. It should reduce the number of rules. It should make the wording of Ts & Cs as simple as possible. It should keep the process requirements on the capitalist to a minimum. When deciding what the CMS cut of a deal is, the result should tend towards a sweeter capitalist deal. That is it. This plan change is about the philosophy of designing the contracts and other legalese. Hopefully, the early focus group testing will validate this approach. If we accidently make the services too good, focus group testing should reveal this as well. I expect it will always be easy to make the deals less attractive to capitalists and more favorable to the government, later, if we decide we really need to go that way.

The third and final plan area I want to adjust in response to this tuning problem is a touchy one. This adjustment regards congressional authority over the CMS program. Recall the warning that it will be easy for Congress to pass changes to the rules governing the Capital Magnification Service that could render CMS deals suddenly unattractive. In other words, the steering wheel that Congress has over Magnified Capitalism is so touchy that if we allow Congress too much power over the system we will run into problems. The kinds of problems we will run into will most often fall into this category of a tuning problem. Ironically, we can implement a beautifully tested and smooth running Magnified Capitalism program, but still get totally tripped up with one new change Congress passes later. In fact, to a lesser degree, the same thing can probably occur with a presidential edict that affects CMS processes or deal incentives. So when I talk about congressional limits, I expect any such limits to also apply to presidential power, or any other source of governmental oversight.

In order to prevent unintended consequences of the kind raised by the tuning problem, I am therefore requiring a new restriction as follows: Congress with the President can freely introduce incentive-based changes to CMS programs, including reducing or eliminating incentives already in force. However, any program alterations that call for rule changes, process changes, disincentives or penalties would fall into the category of "subject to acceptance testing". That means that we would have to test all such changes in the same manner as the original Magnified Capitalism program. Furthermore, if Congress passes changes which require testing, then their legislation must include funding to pay for such testing. CMS senior management would need to provide an official estimate for the funding required.

I have included this provision because we might have tested similar changes in the market simulator before, or the proposed alteration could be some other well-understood class of item. There will be other kinds of proposed changes that involve very expensive testing requirements. This pay-for-the-testing-up-front rule is like saying we have to pay for our lawyer before we can sue. In law, such a rule tends to reduce lawsuits to just those with real merit. We are applying a similar principle here. If we have to pay for the acceptance testing as part of making a change, we must have a bit more confidence that the change is a good idea and that it has gone through thorough preliminary analysis. By the way, if the change does not result in successful acceptance testing, we must discard it. So Congress will have some egg on its face if it passes such a piece of legislation that then fails to pass muster. However, that is the point. Better to have it fail in a simulation than to have it bring down the real CMS system.

Finally, any proposed changes that require testing must pass that testing with the same sort of standards of acceptance that the original program had to pass. CMS senior management would be responsible for presenting the test results, including a pass or fail conclusion on any changes subject to acceptance. If a change request does result in testing failure, the management report to Congress and the President (or just the Board) should include recommendations for adjustment. These recommendations would seek to keep the spirit of the original change, but improve the probability of its passing the acceptance testing. We will need to examine this entire topic more fully to develop detailed processes to optimize the constructive feedback between the government and the CMS with regards to such change proposals. I do not need to elaborate the entire plan for acceptance testing of congressional changes. It should be sufficient for now to leave this as an area to be developed more later. Detailing change acceptance processes should largely be a matter of straightforward planning and negotiations anyway.

Even with the requirement to pay for the testing, Congress will likely be tempted to make significant changes to the CMS rules over time. Such changes are bound to be problematic regardless of the details. We can reach this conclusion by viewing the history of the tax code. We often hear how onerous the tax code is, largely because there are such a large number of special rules. This volume comes to us courtesy of the lack of congressional restrictions or procedures that would discourage rampant rule additions and changes. Once Congress imposes a new tax exemption or special rule, it can become nearly impossible to later eliminate it.

The CMS processes and rules are subject to similar dangers. Even though our added requirement for acceptance testing should reduce the temptation to make a large number of changes, we can predict that we will still collect an unacceptable number of them over time. Therefore, I am installing two additional plan adjustments to address the risk of congressional micromanagement. The first requires that all rule changes have a built-in expiration date, until and unless they achieve an 80% congressional override approval. The second is that all rule changes require 60% congressional approval. In other words, let us try not to make changes once the system gets going unless those changes are compelling. Even then, we should err towards temporary adjustments in response to specific issues of the day. I imagine rule changes would typically gain permanent status with an 80% override once they were both proven to work for a certain length of time and shown to be widely popular. Thus, these additional measures to limit both temporary and permanent rule changes should not prevent truly worthy actions of these types.

We can now consider the matter of the tuning problem to be fully addressed.

Weakness #5: Congressional Seizure

It seems a sad consequence of today's politics that one party's desires inevitably become the target of the other side's mudslinging. There are many cases in which the political positions of a person or even an entire party have flipped around in a matter of a few years. The healthcare issue is the focus for some of the most dramatic turn-arounds of this type, although we can find similar examples with regards to national defense, right-to-life, budget strategies, and taxes, among others. Many politicians ignore the facts of history when they become inconvenient to the political strategy of the day. They treat such facts as gnats flying about that few will really notice. It seems to many of us Congress often considers politics more important than the work of the people. As I am sure you know, Mr. President, your opponents say the same about you.

This problem is particularly noticeable when it comes to negotiations on the national budget. It has been many years since the Congress approved anything resembling the President's budget proposal. We would need to go back to the Bush era for that. Of course, there is also this recent odd case of a President not even bothering to submit a budget. Presumably that was justified this year because you knew Congress would shoot it down and use it against you. That was a difficult decision. I understand why you did it, but I must say I found this to be a poorly-advised approach. I can only presume you might agree, with the benefit of hindsight. Regardless, this weakness that I am now raising deals with exactly the same sort of problem.

Since I brought up the recent Bush administration, we might recall that even then there were great struggles and disagreements. The Bush era is hardly a beaming example of how to produce wonderful political results, either from the view of debt management or in its attempt to produce lasting economic prosperity using tax breaks. Budget management or lack thereof is a fundamental problem within our government. There is a high probability that any attempt to propose a Magnified Capitalism bill will lead to a political battle. Even if the concept itself is miraculously supported by both parties, which it should be, there is still bound to be a large battle over the issue of budgeting. One side will certainly pursue a smaller or more careful approach. The other side will take the more aggressive tack by pursuing a shorter timeline with a higher initial budget allocation.

My personal view is that the Magnified Capitalism strategy is worthy of implementation independent of party affiliation. Furthermore, while I am inclined towards a more aggressive and accelerated plan, the far more important thing is to pass some sort of bill under any reasonable implementation. The weakness I am raising here may be an ironic one. Regardless of the reason, we can imagine that this plan could become a political hot potato. The sad fact is that agreeing on a principle is not the same as passing a specific bill.

Magnified Capitalism is an aggressive strategy in general. I could insist that there is only one right answer as to how large its budget should be. I could claim that acceptance testing should occur within a specific timeline. But it would be wrong to mandate such details. I am trying to insist only on those points upon which success truly depends. It is OK if well-intended political representatives who seek real solutions negotiate any of the plan issues that lie outside my firmly-stated requirements.

The weakness of congressional seizure gives us a reality check. Congress does not often function as a group of well-intended people seeking real solutions. Instead it usually behaves as a group of people who seek benefit from blaming and contradicting each other. Therefore Congress often appears stalled in multi-lane gridlock. This issue is arguably a consequence of having an aged political system that itself needs a tune-up. This makes the matter a candidate for some type of United States 3.0 strategy, after we have implemented our United States 2.0 plan. But for now we need to steer Magnified Capitalism through the political waters facing us if we are to deliver the potential of prosperity it promises.

What is the argument against this weakness? Is there any technique that can break through gridlock? And what of a risk mitigation strategy? How can we hope to pass this novel, aggressive plan through a congressional process that prefers to agree on nothing?

I will address the weakness' counterargument first. It is tempting to laugh, kick the dirt, and say, "There is no counterargument. Congress will never pass anything like this unless we put a gun to their collective heads."

But historically that is not entirely true. There are some cases in which Congress has come together to do something aggressive and expensive. The latest example occurred in October 2008 when President Bush signed the $700 billion financial emergency bill ("The Emergency Economic Stabilization Act of 2008"). In one of many examples of revisionist political history, many Republicans now call this the "Obama bailout". Regardless, the moral of this story is that both parties negotiated the bill in short order, and passed it with something resembling bi-partisan support by healthy margins in both the House and Senate. Why? How did that happen? Looking back at it through today's rhetoric we would be forgiven for thinking everyone was against it, especially Republicans. But the reality would be almost shocking if we were not talking about politicians.

What really happened was truly the opposite of what people commonly claim today. It was the Republicans who drafted the original idea and then were the main champions of this bill. The current (Obama) administration was handed the program in mid-implementation when it took office, and then with a gun to its temple, was strongly advised to follow through promptly. Since you did so, Mr. President, and the program was subsequently widely criticized, Republicans were quick to start calling it the Obama bailout from then on. To be fair, some of their complaints that focus on the bailout's implementation have some merit. However, that gets me off topic. None of these subsequent details relates to the issue before us. The interesting fact is that the bailout bill passed in the first place.

This recent history serves as an illustration of what it takes to get Congress to pass a bold move. To understand how the bailout bill made it through passage we need to recall the situation. There was near panic in the country over our economic state in the second half of 2008, and into 2009 when the administration changed. The economy was visibly crumbing. Real estate was already in a full collapse and still heading sharply downward. The stock market was also dropping fast and at risk of a total free fall. Business confidence was declining at an alarming rate. Most important of all, unemployment was heading down a similar path. It seemed that no one was hiring anymore. All the news regarding jobs was about layoffs and more layoffs. Other business news centered around one major corporation after another facing failure. Most banks were in trouble. Even our flagship American car company, GM, was going bankrupt. Americans felt that our government better do something big, and do it fast, or else the sky would certainly fall.

Incidentally, those fears were correct. While there is no shortage of problems with this bill, it is far better that it passed than that Congress did nothing. We would not want to experience that time period again without any government action. Our situation today would certainly be far worse. However, this is my personal opinion and not relevant to the point. The real point is to observe the kind of motivation, or atmosphere, that produced a major congressional movement.

This leads me to the tip of the counterargument. Our troubles are not repaired today. We may have avoided sudden death, but we are still on the cliff's ledge. No one has yet put forward the long-term solution. Magnified Capitalism is an opportunity for Congress to agree on something that benefits both parties but does not come from either. This program will greatly reduce unemployment. It will restore our economic leadership. Business activity will explode. Virtually every constituency will benefit - those who want to lower taxes, those who wonder how we will pay for Medicare in twenty years, and many others. The key to producing political action in Congress is to underscore both the urgency of solving our systemic unemployment problem and dealing with a large list of other shared benefits. We have both of these factors here. The urgency is underscored not just by our own need, but also by the certainty that other countries competing with us will implement this program before us if we do not act quickly enough.

This argument for action seeks to highlight a fine aspect of American character, the idea that when we realize there is a truly big problem, we can find a way to come together to fight it. It is a shame we cannot remember to put aside our minor differences and political squabbling during other times, too. Perhaps we can address that issue another day. The key here and now is to make the "we are still in urgent big trouble" argument. So let us put aside our infighting for this one good idea and make it work. Then we will be able to get back to our regularly scheduled political hostility. At least we will be doing so in a healthy economic environment. Maybe we can even fight about who did more to make the plan work so well.

Of course there is still a problem with this suggested counterargument. This plan needs to be heard. It needs to be shared. It needs a champion, a lot of political money, or the voice of the masses behind it. This brings me to the mitigation strategy. The counterargument is logical, but it can easily be beaten by the silence of ignorance, lack of enthusiasm, or louder voices already on a different path. Therefore, the primary mitigation tactic is to create a loud political imperative for prompt implementation of Magnified Capitalism. In other words, our mitigation strategy is to fight the gridlock with a political hot poker.

Not being particularly fond of politics, I am almost ashamed of this recommendation. Almost. I am not fond of guns, either. But then I imagine how I would feel about packing a gun if someone started running at me with a loaded rifle. The matter would become crisp if they appeared crazed with anger and rushed me with their finger reaching for the trigger. It is just one of many examples that warn against staking out any position without having room for some exceptions.

Magnified Capitalism is a real solution for American prosperity. It is here right in front of us. If it takes a political strategy to make sure it happens, so be it. What would such a strategy look like? The inroad can come from any one of three paths. First, we could sign up one or more political champions who wield considerable influence. Next, we could seek to acquire political action funding in order to mount a lobbying campaign and/or motivate the people to voice their support. Or finally, we could go directly to the masses in an attempt to create an active grass roots campaign.

For a political champion I nominate you, Mr. President. All you need to do is make an announcement from the White House that you are launching an initiative for Magnified Capitalism. I am sure that would garner a great deal of attention by itself. But that might not be the most leveraged line of attack. A better approach could be to privately consult with members of Congress and form a coalition from both parties with as many leaders as possible. Make it clear to your opponents that you are being generous in wanting to share the credit for this if they join promptly and in good faith. Admit that we should limit the fighting to the details of the plan, and even try to limit the time spent doing that. Otherwise, if they resist, advise them they will be left out. The people will find out who supported American prosperity and who preferred political maneuvers.

Make it tough. Play it hard and follow through. Make no vacant threats, just promises. This is the kind of bet that will define you and all those who join the Magnified Capitalism team. It should supersede the politics of parties in the same way the people's other historic needs have. You can assure your rivals and detractors that they can return to battles on other grounds after this. But on this point, we should rise up and come together.

After you have collected the biggest and broadest team of powerful supporters you can muster, then make your public announcement. Make that declaration with this impressive team of powerful supporters at your side. Pump up the other party for its ability to come together with you as true Americans. Cast shame on laggards without naming them. This will give them a chance to quickly change their minds after the speech. Do the political dance like the country's future depends on it. There could hardly be a better way to spend your political capital. To the degree it matters, the payoff will be far greater than just the country's success. I will resist developing an extended political strategy for you, however. I have made the point sufficiently to hand the details over to someone more focused on such things. You must have existing staff who can handle designing a plan that takes advantage of such a historic move.

Incidentally, Mr. President, if you hesitate too long in signing up as this plan's champion, there is an obvious political risk. That is that some rival, or worse, members of the other party will decide to take up this cause. Whoever does it first gains the most from its eventual success. It might as well be you.

Whether or not prominent champions volunteer, the next path that we should use to promote our strategy is to create an organization for that purpose. In other words, create an institution that collects contributions to pay for a more formal political battle. I have taken the liberty of seeding this effort myself. Anyone who is interested in donating time or money to the cause can visit the website: www.magnifiedcapitalism.com. This website seeks to establish enough support to start a formal Political Action Committee (PAC) to promote this plan. It also seeks to organize related efforts, such as rallies (see the grass roots description below), and distribute associated information.

If we can raise enough money, the PAC will then lobby Congress accordingly. Hopefully, we will collect sufficient resources to also run advertisements that help gain popular awareness and support. It might not be that hard to find the donations. Almost everyone will benefit from the fruits of Magnified Capitalism. This includes those out of work, those seeking funding for various businesses, average Americans who just want us to succeed, and especially the capitalists themselves. Bankers, venture capitalists, investors, and anyone with resources should be highly motivated to help us win this political battle.

While virtually everyone wins under this plan, the capitalists win hardest and fastest. There is some cause for optimism since these are the same folks who historically have contributed the most to political causes. It seems to me that this particular cause will have a big double benefit for professional capitalists. It will help related capital sources grow dramatically at lower risk and it will benefit the whole country. Here will be a political donation that the wealthy can truly brag about to anyone. How often does that happen?

The last of the three political paths I recommend pursuing is the one seeking a grass roots upswell. Through this tactic we would endeavor to generate enough popular support for Magnified Capitalism that Congress and you could not ignore it even if you wanted to. The main strategy here is the open distribution of this plan. I have already taken steps to publish this entire proposal and make it as widely available as possible. In turn, it is my sincere hope that some readers will become excited enough to tell others about it.

I want to encourage all good citizens to tell their friends and coworkers. Maybe they can just tweet about it. Some may choose to post their thoughts in emails, blogs or on their Facebook pages. Some might write their representatives, asking them to consider the matter. Others might propose that their favorite local organization contemplate some formal support. We can seek economists to conduct independent analysis, or try to get media attention. We want Magnified Capitalism to make its way into the national dialog. We should encourage people to discuss it everywhere from websites and television networks to private talks between friends. Such an achievement would be a sign that success is pending. If each reader of this plan took just one or two actions, the impact could become profound. The www.magnifiedcapitalism.com website will also serve to assist and track any momentum that develops on this front.

Opportunities

One distinction that can leave people scratching their heads is this: What is the difference between a strength and an opportunity? After all, an opportunity is a strength, right? And is it not a strength to have an opportunity? Clearly, there is some overlap. However, the main difference is that a strength speaks to some definite advantage of the current situation, whereas an opportunity is a potential that is less than certain.

Strengths include advantages that help the plan succeed. A strength can also speak to a fundamental, or inherent, plan benefit. In other words, a strength is an advantage we can count on. An opportunity, on the other hand, is some advantage that is probable, or at least possible, if we move forward with our plan. Opportunities are not entirely in the basket, but we can consider them as low-hanging fruit. Therefore, when we are aware of an opportunity, the important thing is to make an extra effort to grab it and secure it. This is how opportunities affect our planning. We list them so that we can be sure to include some extra planning to capture and secure as many as possible.

Once we have addressed an opportunity directly in our plan, we could argue it has been promoted to a plan strength. That is how the division overlaps. Also, there might be cases where we are convinced that an opportunity is so easy to obtain that we do not need to do anything more to achieve it. In such a case we might say that the opportunity is mislabeled. To you, Mr. President, such an opportunity is actually already a strength. Therefore we must use our judgment when deciding whether to call something a strength or an opportunity. Even brilliant people can disagree. The best way to deal with this type of ambiguity is to accept that we are applying the author's discretion to the division between the two choices. Disagreement is acceptable, for it usually does not matter that much one way or another. The focus, after all, is on what to do about the subject, not how to label it.

Opportunity #1: Total Repair of Employment & Economy

We start with the biggest opportunity of all. This plan is designed to repair both the unemployment problem specifically and the economy in general. After just hearing the difference between strengths and opportunities we can be forgiven for asking why this one is not listed under strengths. The reason is simple. It is possible to follow the main tenets of this plan and yet fail to repair the economy. What? Is this not the goal of the whole effort? How can I admit now that it is possible for us to follow this plan yet still fail?

The answer is simple. This plan will work under two primary conditions. First, it needs a lot of money behind it. I have already indicated that we will have to put up roughly one trillion dollars per year to achieve the sort of impact we seek. I have provided this estimate without the benefit of independent analysis. I would not be entirely surprised to find various economists suggesting that we need a bit more money. It also would not surprise me to find out that many think this number is higher than necessary. To me, that makes it a pretty good opening estimate for a single number; the better answer would be to provide a range, but at this time that would just sound evasive.

Regardless, this plan will only work if we provide enough funding for it to have the required impact. We can think of this funding level as a magic number. If we implement the plan with a figure lower than the magic number, then we should still see some benefits. However, these benefits will fall short of the stated goals. If we fund the plan with an amount higher than the magic number, then I have good news. The plan should succeed anyway. We do not need to predict exactly what the magic number is. We just have to make sure we do not aim so low that our budget is below it.

The second thing that must happen for this plan to succeed is a bit trickier. The most straightforward way to put it is this: We cannot compromise any factor out of the plan. In other words, it is not enough to enact most of it. I have considered every single point carefully. If an item is optional, I have said so. Most of these items are not optional. The reality is that people will try to change the plan. Too many politicians, economists and others will insert their opinions between the time I write these details to you, Mr. President, and the day the project becomes real. The good news is that we can probably get away with some changes, especially if they are true improvements resulting from even more careful analysis. But we all know human desires and weaknesses are prone to make people push for other types of changes, especially if motivated by political compromise. The fact is that the plan could even succeed with some minor degree of these types of changes. The problem is that it is also possible that just one poorly considered compromise could undermine the whole strategy.

For example, in this SWOT analysis we concluded that pre-acceptance testing is critical to making sure we have a minimum of tuning problems before the program goes live. What if Congress decided they did not want to pay for the cost of pre-acceptance testing after hearing an expensive estimate from the contractor? Or what if such testing "caused" an unacceptable delay in the implementation? Regardless of why it might be justified, I can predict removing the pre-acceptance testing would be a disastrous deviation from the plan, even though some might argue it is only a minor deviation. After all, politicians might correctly point out that we added pre-acceptance testing only after considering a specific threat. It is almost as if testing was an afterthought. How important can it be then?

My response to this attempt to minimize the importance of pre-acceptance testing is this: This plan walks through my thought processes in detail so that you, Mr. President, can see the discipline used to shape it. I did not divine a perfect plan. I had a pretty good idea in which I expected to find holes. Then I applied well-accepted techniques to refine it into an effective plan that we can still improve with care. The threat of the tuning problem, in this example, is real and serious. The plan modification to address it is therefore necessary and not optional. If it were optional, I would have said so. But I did not. And so it is with most of the other plan modifications and details you have read, and will read as we go forward. This will be a hard thing for some to accept. The only justified plan changes are ones that use similarly proven techniques based on real analysis of consequences. Otherwise, I expect the push for alterations will be about people wanting to save time or money, or promoting some political agenda. We need to guard against all such improperly motivated changes.

Therefore, the grand success of a robust economy with an ultra-low unemployment rate is actually an opportunity and properly belongs in this section of the executive summary. We have the plan. We need only follow it to the letter and feed it plenty of money. This is easily said but not so easily done. Can we make any additional plan modification to address this opportunity? You bet.

You may laugh at how simple this modification is. We need make only two new rules. First, we must make sure we aim high on funding. I have hinted at this in previous discussion but now the matter becomes more concrete. This plan depends on major funding. We must leverage capital sources by exactly the amount of money we are willing to put up. We will look at figures a bit more closely in *Chapter VII: Financials*. If we do not put up enough money, this plan will not work. If we put up enough, it will work.

At least, that is, if we also adhere to our second new rule which is this: We should not consider any deviation from this plan unless it includes a proper analysis that weighs all the consequences of the proposed change. In business terms, that means we will apply a strict form of change management to our plan. To change anything, we must generate a formal proposal called a "change request". The change request includes the impact analysis I referred to above. A change review board votes upon all change requests. This board could be the same people as the Board of Directors, or more likely, experts whom the Board designates combined with CMS management. There is room to negotiate the details of such processes. The point is merely to forbid changes unless a fair-minded group considers the matter formally and with discipline.

That is it. Otherwise, we might consider the repaired employment situation and economy a done deal. If we stick to the new rules this opportunity becomes a strength. I listed it as an opportunity to underscore the need to follow this plan very carefully, funding it with plenty of money.

Opportunity #2: Lower Taxes / Solve Budget Problems
We receive two big benefits by following this plan. In the shorter term, we experience the big economic surge. This is a bundle of positive effects that includes a significant increase in employment, production, business starts, capitalization of business expansion, and related goodies. As I stated in the previous section, we need only follow this plan with a precise discipline to nail this most important benefit. However, there is another huge impact that follows, too.

In the strengths section we touched on it by referring to a long-term windfall and steering. We called this a strength because we know that implementing the plan will produce a windfall. So why bother addressing a similar point as an opportunity? It comes down to two subtleties. First, there is the matter of managing the Capital Magnification Service in such a way as to ensure a regular return on investment, not just spikes of cash flow from time to time. Second, there is the question of what to do with the new government income. In other words, the opportunity here is to manage the CMS in such a way as to make sure its income levels grow steadily so we can count on this new investment money each year as a part of the national budget. The CMS needs to eventually make enough money that we can lower tax rates and solve other budget-related problems.

Here is something that may surprise you regarding that magic number we just talked about. This number is the minimum funding level at which Magnified Capitalism will solve our economic problems. The magic number becomes higher if we want to have a bigger impact on the national budget sooner. In previous discussions I suggested we could even eventually eliminate income taxes with this strategy. That is true. But it will not happen with the same magic number that just minimally fixes the economy, at least not very quickly.

Here is some good news. We can start the program with just enough money to repair the economy. This is our original magic number. Then, if we want to grow the CMS into an income tax replacement strategy, we would change how quickly it repays the money we borrowed to fund it. Want to offset income taxes even faster? Then we need to raise the CMS budget even higher. Politicians will be more likely to support such a move once the program has been up and running for a few years. The point is that the CMS will become a revenue-generating engine. If we feed it just enough gas to do the economic repair job, it will do that job and produce some minor budget-helping surpluses down the road. If we want this engine to do more work, we will need to feed it more gas over the long term.

In *Chapter VII: Financials* I will show an analysis that suggests how we might reach for different magic numbers and different CMS repayment plans. Turning these dials can have a dramatic effect on the level of income the CMS will produce for our government. But for our discussion here we can keep the point simple. We will first decide how much money we need to launch our program, bearing in mind the minimum level necessary to be sure of economic repair. The budget levels will then change in subsequent years.

No matter what the numbers are, we have an opportunity to earn steady new revenues for government use. And we also have an opportunity to use this stable new income in a manner that helps fix national budget issues. We can use this new money to help balance the budget, pay down national debt, lower taxes, improve funding to programs that are in trouble, or any combination of these things. The question before us is this: What plan adjustments must we make to ensure we bag these two related opportunities - steady investment returns and sufficient profits to make a positive budget impact?

Let us examine the issue of a steady income first. By this we mean we want our CMS investments to produce as steady a return as is feasible. As most professional investors know, this is a problem of balancing how risky the investments are with how diversified they are. So there are two types of investment strategies that produce a steady profit. The diversification approach simply means we spread our money out into many investments. There is good news here. The CMS program does this by the very nature of its business. But we will add a few new rules to keep it that way. The second approach is to balance risk versus reward carefully. In other words, the less risky an investment is, the lower percentage return we should demand. The more risky it is, the more reward we should ask for. In the case of the CMS this problem is extremely complicated and detailed. However, we can make a plan change to help ensure we manage the entire complexity in a way that produces steadier returns.

To keep diversification levels high, we need to encourage the CMS to make a large number of deals overall, and strictly limit the number of deals that use a big chunk of CMS money. Here we take advantage of the fact that we are setting up the CMS as a commercial company. We will include in the foundational rules of the CMS (the Articles of Incorporation) a requirement that CMS report quarterly to the Board of Directors. This report will include an account of what percentage of CMS funding has been allocated, and the distribution of these funds to each category of capitalist. The Board will judge CMS executives not just on overall profitable returns, but also on the equality of fund distribution among different categories of investment. This will include an overall risk assessment. In other words, if the executives want to keep their jobs they need to show they are managing the government's money in a diversified manner that does not over-invest in any one deal or any one category of deals.

To avoid truly significant investment errors, we must add one more rule. No single investment should involve more money than the CMS Investment Ceiling (CIC). The CIC is a cap. I expect its value to be roughly one-twentieth of one percent of the CMS investment fund, or 0.05%. If the CMS Fund is one trillion dollars and the CIC is 0.05% of that amount, then the maximum CMS investment in any one deal would be five hundred million dollars. That should be enough money to make the CMS the majority equity holder in most any new business idea if the situation calls for that. Of course there will be cases where that is not enough money, such as a startup idea for building space planes. But even then, this should be enough funding to encourage other capitalists to put up the difference. Regardless, we can model the actual CIC value in the pre-acceptance testing simulators to see what works best. The point here is that we must have a CIC cap so that we do not risk too much money on any one investment.

Now that we have insured that our CMS portfolio is diversified, what can we do to reduce investment risk? One approach is to make sure riskier categories of investment have lower caps, while less risky ones can qualify for up to the full CIC amount. I expect inexperienced capitalists new to the CMS program would have the lowest qualifying caps. They would also have to put up a higher percentage of their own funds. Until an entrepreneur can show a good track record, they will only qualify for a smaller government contribution to their project. Remember, this is the capitalist's track record we are talking about. It means if we are looking to fund a big business idea, we might prefer to talk to a more established venture capitalist. These more established and proven capitalists will qualify for higher caps, up to the maximum allowed CIC for those with the best records of performance.

I will provide some more details for how to manage this aspect of the program in *Chapter V: CMS Operational Plan Overview*. Investment risk management is an important aspect of CMS operations. Over time, the system will track different capitalists and score them based on how well they have managed government funds in their deals. The best capitalists will not only have the highest caps, but they will also receive higher total funding levels. This kind of approach will use market forces to produce the best investment partners. The system will also include processes to deal with poor performers in order to minimize their negative impact on the CMS.

We now have plan improvements to encourage steady CMS investments. But what are we going to do to raise our CMS profits high enough to make an impact on our big budget issues? That depends on how much revenue we think the government should bring in through CMS activity. Put another way, how much do we all want to collectively put into the CMS investment pool?

Let's consider the highest version of this goal first. We will scale down from this top goal afterward to see how that impacts the numbers. Our top goal is one where, eventually, the revenue from the Capital Magnification Service is enough to pay for the entire national budget. I do not want to focus too much on numbers in this section. We will look more closely at the figures in Chapter *VII: Financials*. However, we cannot avoid touching on them here. Let us say that the annual federal budget is roughly $3.5 trillion today. We could imagine the actual target to go up a bit if we do not trim our appetite for spending. Alternately, we could learn to reduce government expenses in order to bring that figure down. This would certainly help our particular challenge, but for now, we will not count on it.

If the CMS did as well as we could imagine, the return on its investments would be around 15% per year. More likely, it will be about two-thirds of that, or 10%, especially at first. This means the CMS will need to have an active investment fund of around $35 trillion to cover the entire federal budget out of its profits. That is a lot of money. Even if we distributed that out over a six-year cycle so that it represents around a $6 trillion annual Fund, this is still six times the original proposal amount.

I do not suggest we borrow anywhere near that much in any one year. Even if we maxed out our borrowing power it would take over ten years, likely a bit longer, to bring the CMS investment budget to such levels. So you see, Mr. President, the CMS will not replace all our federal taxes anytime soon. Even with an aggressive program, we should really expect it to take closer to forty years to accomplish this goal. *Chapter VII: Financials* will show us how that might look. For now, we might just think about this. If we were determined to get to such a point as fast as reasonably possible, what would we have to modify in this plan to get there?

Now here is more bad news. The key to achieving such high investment returns is for the CMS to acquire and manage a huge investment fund. Let us keep to simplified math for now. Let us say the CMS will need to manage an annual investment Fund of $6 trillion to meet our income tax replacement goal. However, the CMS takes a total of six years to receive all its investment returns from any one year's deals, so that makes the problem even tougher. Therefore the total CMS six-year set-aside must be about $35 trillion (rounded down) in order to build a revenue machine that replaces federal income taxes. This will cover six years of CMS investments until these investments bring back and refuel the set-aside fund. Anyone experienced in such analysis will know that the real figure is quite a bit lower since some investment returns will begin early, but these are just rough figures to give us an idea of the scale of funding necessary. The detailed analysis comes later anyway. The lesson of this quick examination is this: Although it would be possible to build such a huge CMS investment Fund in about forty years under a slightly optimistic scenario, what it would take to do that is probably not going to happen...probably.

Just for fun, what would that look like? What would we need to do if we decided we wanted to get out of the habit of collecting any more income taxes, and the CMS was the key replacement? Here are the three main points for such a dream. First, we would need to initially borrow as much as we possibly could for the CMS investment. In reality, I would not expect this to happen in the first year because this is too big a bet to make on a new program. However, it is easy to imagine such an effort gaining popularity after three or four years of CMS operations. This would be enough time to prove three things. First, it would be enough time to show the CMS was working to fix the economy. Second, we could see the CMS was making a profit. And third, we should then have proof that the capital markets could absorb a lot more money from CMS funding programs.

After pouring maximum borrowed money into the system, the second thing we would need to do to replace federal income tax would be this: We would need to let the CMS keep most of its profits for a few decades. My financial analysis shows we could replace income taxes in as little as 41 years if we let the CMS keep about 3/4ths of its profit for reinvestment so that it could accumulate the $35 trillion monster Fund we need to achieve this goal. Once that happens, we can stop paying taxes. The fastest track means we need to return most of the profits right back into the Fund.

Here again, I expect reality to be different from these projections. After all, why bother to make money if all we are doing is stashing it away? We can expect some short-term cash flow benefits from this program and we may even find them to be strategically desirable. So I do not expect we will accomplish this goal in an absolute sense. But we can try to return an ever-growing amount back to the CMS, especially as the Fund itself keeps getting bigger. In other words, the more money the CMS accumulates for investing, the easier it will be for us to reinvest more of the profits it makes. If we keep the CMS Fund smallish, then the result will be the opposite. We will be constantly tempted to put most of the investment profits to use in the federal budget. This method is very similar to any wealth-building strategy. If we know we want to get so rich that we never need to work again, we have to put aside increasingly more money from our investments until we get there. If we are too scared to do that, that is OK. But we will never reach the goal, either.

The third thing we need to do to achieve income tax replacement is this: We cannot forget that the CMS must repay the original loans we used to fund it. If we are borrowing a lot for the Fund, we might be tripped by an outlandish jump in debt. In other words, when we do the math, it will be the CMS that pays for its loans, not the people's taxes. In no way should we allow the CMS to avoid this important obligation. What this means is interesting. Once we reach a certain high level of CMS funding we have to make sure we do not increase the borrowing too significantly from one year to the next. That is because the CMS Fund will become so very large that we could not easily cover any big additional jump in borrowing with the next year's investment returns.

This situation is a bit complicated to describe without at the aid of a real-world example. I do not think we need to do this here. The point can be easy to understand, though. It simply means that if we continue to borrow money to feed a growing CMS Fund, then we should make sure any increases are steady ones. We should avoid sharp spikes in borrowing lest we cause some problems in covering interest payments. By the way, this strategy also means we make a plan to stop borrowing completely once the Fund gets big enough to keep growing without borrowing any more funds. This is when the CMS really starts paying back its loans and then generating true income.

That is pretty much it. There are other actions that would help also. We could reduce government spending. That would make our targets smaller and therefore easier to reach. We could do much more work on improving the Capital Magnification Service rate of investment return. In other words, we could focus over the years on making the CMS into a more efficient investor. This would improve the percentages that in turn would lower the investment fund total that the CMS had to reach. It would also impact how fast we reach our goal and/or how much we have to borrow. I am not counting on these points, though.

The issue of government spending levels seems like an independent problem. The CMS factor should influence the argument to reduce spending, but I do not expect it to drive the argument by itself. As for CMS investment returns, I do not think this goal will drive an improvement greater than would happen anyway. I think the CMS management will continuously seek improvements in investment returns no matter what the Fund size is. Some practical political pressures might pop up to push the investment strategy slightly this way or that, but I am left largely with the same opinion. A commercial CMS agency will continually improve its returns anyway, with a few burps along the way that are natural, too.

If we want to replace income taxes entirely with CMS revenue, then there are three main issues to focus on. To review: borrow as much as we can for the CMS Fund over a prolonged period, insure any increases in borrowing are steady ones followed by a planned drop-off, and allow the CMS to increasingly keep most of the profits it makes. If we did all these things we could eliminate federal taxes. I said it would take a minimum of forty years. To be fair this is really a best-case timeframe. The stars would need to all line up and everything would have to go our way for that to happen. If we make more conservative or realistic assumptions, the expectation would grow to something closer to fifty years, perhaps more. It is a nice legacy to consider for our children or theirs. Complete income tax replacement was never a real goal, anyway. The point is just that Magnified Capitalism is so powerful we could use it to create such a roadmap. Our brief analysis shows us what it would take if we really tried to go there, and now we know. Anyway, I feel just a little smarter for imagining what it would take.

I should mention that pursuing a fat CMS Fund on the road to income tax replacement has an impressive side effect. By the time we got to the goal, our government would have created a cash investment stash worth about $35 trillion. It would use this as an investment fund for perpetually raising all the money it needs, as we have discussed. In a crisis, however, that amount of money could fix most any problem we could imagine. We could think of the CMS Fund as an investment fund under normal circumstances. We could also use it lightly as an emergency fund for occasional big problems. These might be the sorts of bad things that happen every fifty years or so. But it would also be a super emergency fund for the odd 1000-year disaster event. This is the type of disaster reserve that could make a huge impact in the case of such rare national or global emergencies. That is a cool side effect. I think of it as government-stability insurance. No government has ever done that before.

What happens if we are not focused on income tax replacement? Do we ever get there anyway? We will probably never reach the goal of replacing all taxes if we never go for it. But choosing not to aim for that goal is not an intrinsically bad option. The CMS revenue would still produce money that offsets some portion of income taxes, or otherwise allows us to have more budget money to work with. As we might guess, though, there is a good reason to consider the most extreme case first. By seeing what we have to do to go all out towards the goal, we can also immediately appreciate what might happen if we do something less. So it is here. There is no obvious urgency towards building the CMS Fund for income tax replacement, so we could reasonably argue that we should not stretch ourselves thin by trying so hard. But that is not the same as not trying at all. We could, for example, choose a more modest goal. We could say that we want the CMS to pay for 50% of the government's budget in 50 years, for example. We could reach this goal with much less risk and still receive many of the same benefits. This would still be enough money to provide a major disaster relief fund as long as we did not have that disaster too early in our effort.

We could even make the goal more modest. We could just determine to continuously increase the CMS Fund year after year, except in extreme disaster years. That would insure our emergency fund grew along with our tax offset. How long it took to replace income taxes completely would not be the point. The point would be to simply improve every year. This is the tactic I recommend we start with. We take the same three plan modifications necessary to reach income tax replacement, and we just implement them in small measure, in other words, only worry about increasing the CMS Fund every year by an amount we can comfortably handle. Later on, some future President and Congress could decide to become more aggressive. But for us right now, simply starting the car down the racetrack with a good acceleration is a fine beginning.

I should make one last point about this whole idea of an ever-increasing CMS investment Fund. I mentioned that this Fund could double as an emergency or disaster relief fund. Obviously, the more we grow the Fund, the bigger a disaster we can address. But also, we do not have to limit our targets to natural or manmade disasters. We could even think of the CMS Fund as a type of rainy day fund, although I am a bit reluctant to use this label. Regardless, the CMS Fund is money the government builds in reserve for its own investment purposes, including some sort of stability insurance. Who is to say we cannot use that money to address any kind of rare problem such as an economic disaster, an unexpected war, or a global threat that no one has ever experienced before? My only hesitation is that I worry about overtapping the CMS Fund.

I suggest, for example, that we treat any use of this Fund as a capital loan. In other words, we should avoid just stealing the money from the CMS Fund. We should instead borrow what we need at favorable rates. We should only do that when we have trouble borrowing from other sources. This way, we will rarely reduce the Fund. When the government does use it, the money is repaid. The Fund recovers to go on. Otherwise, we risk destroying a new pillar of national stabilization and strength. Remember, if we reduce the CMS Fund or otherwise divert its money for government purposes, we can no longer use that money to spur economic development. In time our continued economic growth will depend on this Fund. We should avoid letting off the gas of our economic engine as much as possible. We should restrict the use of its money to dire circumstances that warrant a short-term economic hit. This is why I hesitate calling it a "rainy day fund". It is not so much for rainy days as it is for floods. But when we have a flood we will be happy to have the Fund's resources.

Opportunity #3: Steering National Strategy
Magnified Capitalism works through offering attractive business partnership deals to help capitalists with funding or loans. These capitalists receive government funds to magnify their business power in return for adhering to standard terms and conditions (Ts & Cs). Embedded in these Ts & Cs are optional conditions that can further increase how much money the capitalist gets, reduce the percentage of profits they owe later, or increase how much their government CMS rating will go up. These optional conditions are rooted in the various CMS incentives we have touched on previously. We can consider many CMS incentive types. Regardless, incentives encourage desired behavior with rewards, but do not require such behavior. There is never a penalty to the capitalist for deciding not to follow the incentive. An example would be a deal in which a venture capitalist was offered a payback discount for backing a deal involving the production of clean energy. Another example would be a cash bonus for an investor who backs a start-up committed to 100% made-in-America production. Of course these examples assume Congress puts in place such incentives for green energy and American production.

The program also includes disincentives or penalties. Penalties are typically standard terms that make a deal much less attractive, if not unprofitable, if the capitalist pursues an undesirable business behavior. We should limit most penalties to ethical, legal or accounting issues. For example, if a capitalist files an inaccurate quarterly report on the status of their business deal, they might have to pay a fine. I have already stated that we should avoid penalties for valid ethical business choices, with perhaps rare exceptions.

Then there are rules. Rules are not choices. They are requirements. In order to qualify for CMS funds, a capitalist must follow the rules. If they do not they may forfeit the funding for the deal, owe large penalties, have their CMS rating reduced, become blacklisted from any future funding (receive a CMS rating of zero), or even be subject to legal arbitration or prosecution. Rules are tough. We want to set up standard rules and almost never change them. Of course some changes will occur but we should limit these to very rare cases, such as to address unforeseen problematic legal issues.

I have reviewed these three types of lines in the sand for a reason. Once the CMS is involved with a significant number of business dealings, the government may decide to change incentives, penalties, and rules with profound effect. Some of these consequences may show that the change was a mistake on the government's part. For example, consider a rule that requires some percentage of production to be U.S.-based for any CMS-backed deal. Notice this is different from the similar incentive in the example a few paragraphs back. Such a rule might say something like this: Any product backed by the CMS must include at least 25% of its production in the United States. That sounds reasonable, right? It is a big mistake.

Rules like this are usually mistakes even if we cannot predict why. In this example it is a bit easier to foresee the error. Some types of business may not lend themselves to U.S. production at all. Especially today, the United States is not necessarily competitive or even able to produce a substantial volume of every kind of product or resource. That means there will be some businesses that cannot possibly accommodate such a rule. Other businesses could try but be so severely disadvantaged as to take them out of serious consideration.

By making this sort of rule, we are artificially excluding many capitalists from becoming involved with otherwise smart business deals that just happen to trip over an apparently reasonable requirement. If we start generating these kinds of rules, we will create a situation where the government is picking winners and losers, even if that was not our intention. This is a fundamental error for governments in general. We should not allow our new program to make any habit of such things. If we want to encourage a certain behavior, we must create an incentive. If that is not enough to produce the effect we wanted, we must improve the incentive. If we still cannot achieve our goal, there is probably something wrong with trying to twist the arm of business in this direction. A rule would have killed business where the strong incentive would simply have gone unused.

The problem is similar, although perhaps not as bad when we create penalties. Penalties can ruin a business plan even if they do not appear to be that strong. We should use them to make sure the government's capitalist partners behave in a normal, expected business manner. If we use them as a behavioral penalty towards otherwise fair business, then we may create a similar problem as trying to use a rule to determine behavior. For example, we could create a cash penalty for backing businesses that do not produce at least 25% of their product in the

U.S. This is a substitute for the bad rule from the previous paragraph. Unless this penalty was very slight, it might have the same negative effect as the corresponding rule we tried to replace. If the penalty is strong enough, it could kill entire categories of legitimate business as easily as the bad rule did. The touchiness with penalties, if we must use them, is to make sure they are applied with very careful measure. In fact, the enforcement used against those breaking rules is itself largely formed from stern penalties.

We might notice that we are left with the incentive as the preferred way for government to cause business to behave in the manner it desires. These incentives collectively form our racecar's new steering wheel. They are what Congress and the President should be constantly debating most about. What kind of incentives should the CMS put in place to encourage business growth in a specific direction aligned with our national strategy? Do we want to encourage inner city improvements? Then we must consider incentives for related real estate development loans and new business start-ups that employ inner city residents. Do we want to have more choices for non-lethal weapons in law enforcement or the military? We could try a business incentive for expanding or starting these kinds of ventures. The possibilities are truly extensive. The impact should be deep, especially as we learn what types of incentives work better than others. The net result will be profound for any government. The U.S.A. will have a clear way to encourage business to further the people's goals. This method will be market-driven, but steered gently through the optional incentives of the Capital Magnification Service. Not only that, but the impact on markets ought to be nearly immediate. Once Congress passes a new incentive, if it is a viable one, there should be some rush to meet its terms in the available CMS offerings. Our government will have a policy steering wheel like it has never had before. One change from Congress will produce a nearly instant market reaction, as long as the businesses affected by it see the incentive as sufficiently attractive.

Here are some general examples of where we can apply CMS incentives to guide national policy:

> *Business Technology Vision.* Strategic policy is all about steering toward a future vision. The Magnified Capitalism approach replaces the idea that government can pick market winners and losers with a more reasonable alternative. Now the government will partner with the capitalists who favor strategic categories of business growth based on associated incentives. The kinds of business growth we want to encourage are those in which leadership is particularly important. Today, such strategic industries include energy production, nanotechnology, robotics, aviation and space flight-related tech, and green technologies. We might consider specific national security interests related to defense or international positioning. We could then provide incentives for a variety of defense-related businesses, security

and policing technology, or intelligence-related businesses. I suggest that we not make technology-related incentives too broad, and avoid unlimited time frames. It would be wise to understand that encouraging markets toward the future is a matter for short-term policy adjustments that change frequently. As we learn to drive this racecar, we should keep a light touch on the wheel. This new car moves very fast, after all. Next year's great new strategy for defense or energy is likely to go in a different direction than we thought it would last year. Let us not put incentives in place that accidently force us to keep going down a path no one really wants to continue along anymore. All market-guiding incentives should carry very short-term expirations. By this I mean one to two years. If we still want the incentive after that, we just need to vote for an extension. If policymakers are worried that they will not gain that extension, maybe it is better for the people that we not try to.

Encouraging Businesses with Social Benefits. We can target funding toward business and personal efforts that include social benefits such as aid to the poor, elderly, children or the disabled. We could also include any kind of improvement in education, vocational training, or university programs. An example of a qualifying business concept would be a company seeking startup capital for a new service that provides K-thru-12 tutoring online. A business expansion example would include a new factory designed to employ physically and mentally handicapped personnel in a maximum appropriate capacity. An individual might qualify for a CMS-supplemented student loan by committing to spending their first three years out of college in a qualifying social position, such as working at an inner city shelter or school.

Increasing U.S.-Based Business. Policy control could include encouraging businesses to use U.S.-sourced raw materials, suppliers, contractors, partners, employees, production facilities, operations, distribution, sales, customer support, training, design, or any combination of these. The idea is that the more a company keeps its jobs and suppliers in the U.S., the more favorable the terms for CMS-provided funds will be. We would let businesses decide what works best for them; however, the hope is that such incentives would be strong enough to affect a significant portion of such decisions. Let us consider the following examples. Most big businesses today outsource some or all of their production and services overseas or simply use overseas facilities they own. Incentives in this category represent an effort to bring some portion of this business activity back to America. I would like to point out that in the event of a future national security emergency, having significant production ability within the U.S. could be critical. The vast U.S. production capabilities the government leveraged during both

World War I and II proved vital in those times. It might be difficult to repeat such a task today. This problem would become profound if a large portion of our manufacturing facilities were located in one of the countries we were having problems with, like China. Even if the situation did not escalate to all-out war, what would we do if China decided to suddenly withhold all manufacturing bound for the U.S.? Or what if our enemy just targeted exposed inter-Asian shipping, a strategy similar to the one that Germany used on Britain in WWII? The supply of most computers and other technologies, as well as a number of other types of goods, would be crippled. No one would be able to buy an iPhone once stock on hand ran out. We also would have trouble obtaining any device that used a flat screen, many children's toys, and a large percentage of shoes. The examples go on and on. In reality, most manufactured goods' supply would become throttled. Therefore, there is more at stake than just jobs. Keeping a fair percentage of self-reliance in place is a legitimate national security strategy. It is a topic worthy of careful analysis and monitoring by the military. We should make sure we can always manufacture some amount of any significant product within our own borders.

Repairing Regional Misfortune. We could apply national policy control using CMS incentives to mend regional economic activity crippled from a catastrophic event or sequence of misfortunes. We would likely apply such incentives under a limited time frame just to initiate some type of economic repair. These sorts of cases might include towns that lost a major military base, a region hit hard by a natural disaster, areas beaten down by a string of plant closures, or similar sorts of business development problems. We could even imagine that state governments might want to make CMS contributions towards such incentives or provide other kinds of participation in return for elevated assistance to address local issues. Thus, state governments could to some degree share the ability to steer national policy as a method of steering local policy, too.

Repairing Situational Misfortune. Just as we could use short-term incentives to address regional problems, we could embrace the same sorts of incentives to help repair the misfortune of targeted people nationwide. As an example imagine if there were another major fraud case of the same scope as Enron. Most of the ex-employees of such a large business were innocent, hard-working people. In the case of Enron, many employees lost not only their jobs but their retirement saving, too. We could use CMS incentives to give some short-term benefits to those unfairly tied to such a gross corporate failing. I would like to note here that most of the CMS benefits we have talked about are oriented towards corporations. However, there are many examples of benefits that help individuals. *Chapter VI: Use Cases* will go over the whole menu in its many applications. In general, though, citizens benefit directly in four ways. The first three include the ability to obtain most types of loans, obtain funding towards starting a business, and file a patent for a great idea without a big money backer. The fourth benefit will be a new kind of way to join a start-up business called the Prototype Development Network (PDN). There are also many secondary effects for individuals. These include more job opportunities from new companies and expansions (a better job market in general), the ability to form special arrangements or partnership businesses to leverage CMS terms, improved real estate and stock markets (more investment opportunities in favorable markets), better government services and/or lower taxes, and easier access to training and higher education (more schools open to take advantage of related incentives).

Redressing the Difficult Life. Some people have permanent disadvantages through no fault of their own. We can put CMS incentives in place to help offset such misfortunes. I already mentioned the handicapped under social benefits. But here we cast a slightly different kind of net that includes not only the physically or mentally handicapped, but also ex-military especially if injured, others who have served the people in any capacity but suffered some life-changing injury, those wronged by unforeseen environmental contaminations, and those who have suffered from a gross governmental oversight. In this redressing, we add incentives that are targeted more directly at those with such permanent problems. They may qualify for fast-track investor programs and investor collectives (groups of smaller investors), or start out with higher CMS ratings, allowing them to be favored entrepreneurs and favored loan recipients.

After saying all of this there is one exception I would consider with respect to making rules versus incentives. That would be basic participation in CMS funding. I mentioned it briefly before, but I want to revisit the matter with additional analysis. As I previously noted, I think only U.S. companies should qualify for CMS-funded deals. A U.S. company is one that is at least 51%[3] U.S.-citizen-owned. We will want more detailed rules to keep foreign companies from gaming this requirement. Regardless, we might look at this rule and rightly conclude I am being a bit hypocritical. This is not really a legal or process matter, as my own rule guidelines suggested, but a national policy type rule. What gives? Did I not say we should use incentives and not rules for such matters?

---

[3] As before, the 51% figure is a minimum example. I would expect the actual percentage to change over time in some range between this and 80%.

There will occasionally be situations in which a rule or penalty is appropriate for a policy control. I would argue that this is the first and most important example of such a case. Why is it an exception? Because this rule states that the Magnified Capitalism program, run by U.S. government funds, is intended to help U.S. companies and citizens only. Foreign companies or non-citizens can benefit in three ways. First, they can participate directly by backing a U.S. majority partner who qualifies for CMS-enhanced capital deals. Second, they can partner with a qualifying U.S. capitalist on the funding side of a deal. And finally, foreign entities can purchase shares in U.S. companies or make deals with citizens who qualify for CMS funding. The only limitation is that a business should not be able to switch to being less than 51% U.S.-owned while the CMS funded deal is still outstanding. I say we make this a rule because otherwise the CMS would become an international program. Maybe one day we can experiment with that. I can imagine a future CMS that wants to keep growing but is having trouble finding enough partners in the U.S. Its Fund would have to be huge for this to happen, though. Then perhaps we could go there, carefully. Until then, Magnified Capitalism is primarily a U.S. plan. A rule is appropriate for that because I want to kill consideration of non-U.S. funding.

Now we have a good idea of how Magnified Capitalism delivers a myriad of ways for us to guide our future. How does all of this potential to steer the country affect our plan? In two ways. The first is the easier and more obvious point. When you, our President, propose the related legislation for implementing Magnified Capitalism, you must make sure you include an important addendum: the package of initial policy incentives you want to include. For each policy issue you want to address, you must keep the priority level general. I suggest categorizing each priority on a scale from zero to four, like a grade point average from high school. A zero means you do not think it needs addressing today. A four carries the highest priority.

Using such a simple approach gains us two benefits. First, we can let the pre-acceptance testing determine the exact kinds of Ts & Cs that will best result in higher-priority incentives versus mild ones. This testing will produce a specific set of standard incentives for each level of priority so they are uniform and well understood. Second, this approach allows us to simplify the political battle so everyone can appreciate it. We will not be debating difficult-to-understand contract terms. Instead, we will debate which level of importance is appropriate for different kinds of policy matters.

The second way preparing for a policy steering wheel affects the plan is as follows: The CMS should design the standard Ts & Cs for ease-of-change with respect to policy incentives. In fact, we can key the entire program off of the same grading system that we just discussed for Congress to use, the four-point system that I recommended above. This would allow the CMS's Ts & Cs to remain the same regardless of the policy incentives of the day. The Ts & Cs would simply refer to an incentive guide that Congress updates separately in concert with the President. This guide would list all possible incentives along with their current priority (zero through four). Note that if we prefer, we can replace the zero through four scale with the five standard grades, A (as four) through E (as zero). Regardless, this approach encourages Congress to avoid changing the Ts & Cs themselves, a previous plan modification we determined was critical. But it does allow quick and easy-to-understand annual changes in national policy.

For example, this year's incentive for a new production facility in an inner city zone might be a grade C incentive (level two). Startups that are 100% located in the U.S.A. might get a grade A incentive (level four), and so on. The CMS, not Congress will, over time, optimize the actual incentive figures that define a grade A (level four) incentive. Similarly the CMS will set the different terms for grade B, C, D and E incentives, as well as what to do if funding qualifies for multiple incentives. This is appropriate as the CMS is responsible for both service testing and its own profit levels. But politics will still determine the direction of policy priorities.

Congress will also set the definition of a qualifying incentive. For example, if a business receives an incentive for being 100% located in the U.S.A., Congress will write any additional rules to clarify what this means. Will there be an exception for overseas sales offices? What about overseas customer support? Congress, usually working with the President, can therefore have exactly the sort of policy controls they should be focusing on. What they will stay away from is the inner workings of the CMS and related processes. That will be left to CMS business management, as it should. If CMS management does a bad job, the Board should replace them. But CMS processes should not otherwise be politicized, when possible at least. I am sure there will be the odd exception. As long as it stays a rarity our plan should remain intact.

Opportunity #4: Huge Secondary Benefits

When we recover from some sickness, we get more out of it than just the symptoms stopping. We become healthy. So it is when we get our government budget under control at the same time that the economy explodes and unemployment falls. All our pistons are firing. The rockets are working. The steering wheel is keeping us on track. We start to become a challenger in our race. What does this mean for our country? It is almost sad that we have to imagine it. Here I will list just some of the secondary benefits of implementing Magnified Capitalism.

Technological Surge. Many new business ideas are based on emerging technology. Along with the encouragement of fresh venture capital and investor funding for these kinds of startups and expansions will come a boom of related research, development, and productization. It is not just about new knowledge, but also about using that knowledge in products that become available to the public. This in turn leads to even more such development. We can predict some benefits, but many others are unknown. Usually, technology benefits are incremental and small, although as a large collection these should become profoundly important. We must also bear in mind the occasional technology breakouts that produce a big impact all by themselves. Many fields are ripe for such superstar breakouts, from biotech and nanotech to green energy. The most interesting cases to me will be the ones that most of us would never have guessed at all. Regardless, this kind of business surge is one of the best secondary benefits we could hope for. We want the United States to be the country that, above all, is where the new leading edge technology is invented and produced more than anywhere else.

Factory Production Jump. Even without incentives to produce in the U.S.A., a boom in overall business activity will produce a boom in factory production within our country. Since I also expect the program to include some incentives for U.S.-sourced goods, this jump in factory production should be even greater still. Combined with the fact that more and more automation requires fewer workers than in past decades, there should be a strong move back towards made-in-U.S.A goods. This will in turn improve domestic sales of support services and raw materials.

Rising Value of U.S. Goods. When everyone knows you make the best stuff, they want it, too. U.S. goods have enjoyed some degree of this benefit for much of recent history. However, with a resurgence of factory production under a technological boom, this effect should also magnify. As we start deciding to bring production home again, international markets will begin to demand these goods and services in growing numbers.

Tax Bounty. When the economy falls, government budgets shrink proportionately. But when the economy improves, government revenues go up in equal measure. So in a booming economy, all tax revenues will zoom up right along with private sector prosperity. No tax increase is required. More business means government revenues of all types increase. State budgets get fatter and easier to balance, as does the federal one.

Personal Value and Work Benefits – for Americans. What happens when there are so many companies trying to hire new people that they have trouble filling their openings? Salaries go up. Then benefits go up. Then perks such as stock options, improved health insurance, and retirement matching start becoming common. We saw a bit of this in the late 1990's. New and otherwise young companies in particular often offered new employees stock options. When such companies succeeded, everyone who worked there became fairly wealthy, or at least gained a nice retirement fund. The point is that when we solve the employment problem using Magnified Capitalism, we will end up with very high demand for most workers. Some kinds of people will be particularly valuable. Most everyone will be able to find a good job with decent benefits. It should become very common for companies try to lure us to the next job with an even better offer. That can mean more pay, but in good times these offers become more creative. Look for improvements in many personal benefits, from the quality of healthcare and retirement plans to standard vacation policies.

Real Estate Rebound. When the economy improves to the degree that unemployment becomes very low, all markets benefit. Real estate will be no exception. This is particularly true when there is high demand for skilled workers, because people end up getting paid more and increasingly relocate. How does that help real estate? Real estate stays depressed when people are reluctant to move because they feel stuck in their overpriced homes. But as more and more people find a better job somewhere else, they will need a place to live in their new location. Demand rises from people who now are making more money. We do not need or want real estate to skyrocket lest we begin heading toward a new bubble. Nevertheless, a healthy recovery is overdue and this will strategy surely spur it on.

Intellectual Property Explosion. When technology development surges, so do many supporting elements including strategic plans, new business proposals, copyrighted writings and designs, as well as patents. We refer to all of these items collectively as intellectual property. It is the collection of good ideas, American ones in particular. If we can make money from an idea, we will have less trouble starting a business based on it – or at least selling the idea to someone else who will. In fact, I can predict that there will be a hot new market in the buying and selling of intellectual property. Such a market exists today, but it is a struggle to make much from just an idea. In United States 2.0 a growing number of people will be able to make a living as pure inventors who sell their designs and business concepts in online markets.

Better Healthcare and Other Benefit Standards. Today, there is a certain mediocrity in the healthcare and benefits packages we can expect from the companies we work for. As I mentioned above, when demand for employees increases, then benefits offers improve attraction for new hires. The improvement does not end there, though. Existing employees benefit because their employers must quickly offer them similar benefits upgrades to improve company retention rates. In this environment what can we expect will happen to the de facto standard for benefits packages? It will necessarily increase. The providers of benefits will respond with better and better offerings to meet this demand. The de facto standard will become elevated for everyone. Voila! Widespread improvement in standard healthcare, retirement plans, and other benefits just from market demand. This alone should be enough to convince everyone we should hurry up and implement Magnified Capitalism.

Improved Funding of Entitlements. There is a problem that few politicians want to talk about, although it comes up now and then: the funding of Social Security, Medicare, unemployment insurance, commercial retirement plans, and even the investments that fuel private retirement plans. These entitlements and similar instruments come under stress when the economy goes south. However, when the economy takes off, especially if it is led by high employment, the opposite happens. In United States 2.0 older workers, the handicapped, the disabled, and others who have historically been underemployed will gain ever-improving prospects. Sure, we can retire for 60% of our old income, but what if someone is offering us more money than we ever made with the best benefits we have ever heard of? That is enough to make the energetic elderly decide to work a few more years even if they do not have to. Thus all of these retirement-based programs receive a stress reduction while the underlying investments do better than ever.

International Influence. This one is hard to measure, but it has to do with political power of all types – from governmental to business to personal. If we travel abroad and we are from Somalia, people will probably have some sympathy for us. Why? Because most people will see us as coming from a poor nation that is struggling in many ways. We can also look forward to little more than minimum attention by way of low expectations. If we are from the United States, we might anticipate the opposite, that we will receive something close to the best attention. With United States 2.0, this level of default respect worldwide should go up another several steps. For a vacationer this may not matter much, although it can make a real difference in the fun we experience. If we are travelling on business, though, this benefit will become increasingly valuable. If the United States is experiencing an economic breakout while the rest of the world limps along the recovery on our coattails, U.S. companies will find it increasingly easy to make favorable deals overseas. Not only that, but all our international partners will know our businesses have very little trouble finding funding for a smart business plan or expansion. Finally, there is the diplomatic effect. The threat of reducing business, such as with a sanction, with a country that matters less and less is not much of a threat. The same threat coming from United States 2.0 is going to be much scarier. Those who have the best relationships with us will benefit the most economically. Those who do not will be increasingly left behind. That is politically dangerous for any country in this increasingly interconnected world. From the seat of the President, all of a sudden the United States' prestige and influence will climb with everyone. We know we have real power when we can make friends and influence people without having to threaten to kill them. When our ability to do this climbs worldwide, it becomes easier to do great things. By contrast, today, even the like of North Korea thinks little of threatening us from time to time. Iran justifies testing us with naval probes and foot-dragging negotiations regarding nuclear issues. We can expect these kinds of provocations to become rare in United States 2.0.

Emergency Cushion. In our discussion regarding income tax replacement, I mentioned that the total CMS Fund would need to grow to an enormous level (about $35 trillion) to reach that goal. However, no matter the size of the CMS Fund, it will likely remain substantial, some trillions of dollars even in its first years. Even the basic CMS starter kit calls for about $3.8 trillion (see *Chapter VII: Financials* for details), as this is roughly enough to handle $1 trillion of new investments per year perpetually (we borrow enough for a $1 trillion annual Fund each year and then use the returns to pay it back). I also mentioned that we could use the Fund to address major emergencies, even before it reaches the target size. A variation of this same point is reiterated here. No matter how large or small the CMS Fund is, it will certainly be large enough to help address a major national or regional disaster to some degree. But instead of just doling out the money the way we might in the most extreme kind of emergency, we could have an emergency plan that fell just short of that. It would be like offering a cushion rather than a parachute in those cases when a cushion will do. We would achieve this by designing a special ultra-high-level incentive to be applied in those years when Congress wants to make a call for business-induced repairs. That way, we would still largely repay the Fund in the course of its normal business. I put it this way because with an ultra-high-level incentive we might be making a CMS funding service so attractive that it does not meet its own risk-reward goals. In other words, as an investment these incentives turn CMS deals into something close to a wash for the government (the CMS gains no net profit). Or perhaps we can design them to be slightly more profitable than that, but the point is the same. These are deals we only offer every once in a while when some situation really needs redressing. An ultra-high-level incentive might mean CMS deals include special bonuses for the capitalists involved, very low contribution requirements, or attractively lower requirements for carving out the CMS share of business equity, for example. Such special incentives would only apply to businesses and people who propose projects that would help repair the disaster situation, naturally. We could work out the details in advance, even update them annually, as a part of emergency planning. They would depend on the amount of funds available and the rough scope of the emergency that the deal was intended to address. Working such incentives out in advance would allow the CMS to perform the pre-acceptance testing of the related rules and incentive levels to be sure that we gain the intended effect without destroying the Fund itself. It would also mean we would become armed with a new emergency trigger ready at a moment's notice, yet we would have carefully considered the numbers long before we knew about the emergency.

This is a substantial list of secondary benefits. Each of these is an opportunity by itself. A more complete plan might make some adjustments specifically for each of these. I will not do that here. Rather, I will make a few points related to this entire category. All of these benefits are secondary because they represent specific kinds of economic and political success. It is sort of like saying, "Everything is going to get better, grow faster, get more funding, and spread our influence." How do we adjust the plan in anticipation of this? For help, let me refer to our racecar metaphor for a moment. We have installed our new steering wheel and rocket engines. Now we expect to win our next race. Are we ready for the success? Not really. It would be a good idea to go over the whole car and make some basic improvements. We probably need new tires and shocks, and maybe an upgraded battery or electrical system. Checking the old frame for cracks or stress points might be smart. How does this metaphor work for preparing the United States for all our secondary benefits?

We should prepare a plan to tighten our infrastructure. Just like our metaphorical racecar, our whole country cannot be expected to zoom ahead indefinitely unless we improve the support systems. So we should prepare some plans for what to do when this strategy begins to work. It may be critical that we address some of these plans sooner than others. Perhaps we can address some infrastructure improvement by adding CMS incentives towards these ends. We should prioritize addressing improvements in: the power system (and power grid), roadways, bridges, trains, automobile and truck standards, aerospace, fuel methods (switching to new fuels like hydrogen), international patent and copyright laws, and education options and standards. These are supporting elements that a roaring economy can trip over if they break down from an overload. We should make advanced plans for improving national infrastructure for each of these categories, and probably a few more. We should prepare for success by making sure we can handle it when it comes. The last thing we want is to turn on our racecar's rockets, start zooming way into the lead, and then have the tires fall off.

Threats

Not unlike the fuzzy line between strengths and opportunities, weaknesses and threats have some commonality. The differences between the first pair are comparable to the differences between the second two. For instance, a weakness is a problem that is clearly in place, whereas a threat is not so certain. Whether we classify a given problem as one versus the other is also subject to the author's analysis and opinion. So I am not overly concerned if my readers disagree with my decision to call something a threat rather than a weakness. I am merely applying a process tool to make sure we capture these items in one net or the other. There is some difference between the two pairs, though. We sought plan changes to capture opportunities and turn each into a strength. For threats, we want the opposite. We seek plan changes to keep each from becoming a weakness, thus preventing these matters from inhibiting our path towards success. With such clarification established, let us now review the threat list.

Threat #1: Rampant Inflation

I nearly classified this number one threat as a weakness. If we were to call it simply "inflation" the argument would change. Inflation and economic success often go hand in hand. We can also experience inflation under other circumstances, but if we have success we can expect some degree of regular price increases in most markets. We have lived with inflation most of our lives, even when times were economically flawed, as has been the case most of my life. Actually, it is quite historically unusual to have zero inflation, or even deflation. Deflation, a situation in which prices decline, is usually a terrible economic sign. We had a brief bout of deflation during the recent recession of 2009. Deflation shows a certain degree of market desperation. We expect to see deflation during a recession or depression. We also see it in a specific market when that market is collapsing, such as what happened with real estate over the last six years. There is no avoiding this point. The implementation of Magnified Capitalism will create an increase in the inflation rate. When things are selling well, when people are widely employed, prices do not go down much. The question we must address regarding this threat is not whether there will be inflation, however. The real question is how much inflation is too much? What rate of inflation is "rampant" or otherwise high enough to cause economic problems? And then we will ask, "How can we avoid those levels?"

How much inflation is too much? I could talk about numbers, although we could argue about whatever I picked. For example, inflation has been below 7% annually for the last twenty years. So maybe anything over 10% is terrible. That is actually about right, but this issue is not that simple even if we agree. The problem is that 9.9% is not great, and 10.1% is not much worse. Thus the matter is a bit fuzzy. Regardless, I think we can call our inflation-fighting plan moderately successful if we keep inflation below a 10% annual rate most of the time. The only caveat I would add is to consider excluding the effect of rising energy costs, which is arguably independent of any economic plan. Maybe that is cheating though, so we will try not to exclude any category.

Why worry about an inflation rate over 10% annually? Most economists think that high inflation depresses prosperity. My own opinion is that this rate does not automatically depress any segment of the economy, especially if every other economic sign remains healthy. So if we had nearly zero unemployment, and production and average income were all rising faster than inflation, then our situation would still be improving. There is a problem with even this case, however. At some point, inflation can bring about more inflation. It is a momentum problem. Some prefer to compare it to a spiral. Regardless, the real danger occurs when inflation gets a headwind and starts to pick up on its own. Then we should really worry.

There have been some examples in which a country's inflation just kept growing into what is called hyperinflation - inflation so out of control that the price of consumer goods becomes almost useless, and so does money. It takes an inflation rate of about 100% per month to reach such a level. That is way higher than the level I am talking about. We should never come close to this. Hyperinflation is a hallmark of government failure. Not only is it a government killer, it is an economy killer, and a creator of long-term recession (which is by definition a depression). Such a depression is different from most because observers can usually blame the problem on faulty government policies – like printing way too much money and not repaying debts. We are not talking about doing that, so I do not see this happening. However, the fear with high inflation is that people will start to freak out about how close we are to staring down the hyperinflation path. It is better to avoid going there at all rather than debate how close we can get without being in danger.

I mentioned I would prefer to have an exclusion for energy costs when measuring inflation. I raise this point again now so that I might discuss the causes of inflation. For a single type of product, the fundamental cause of inflation is its supply not keeping up with demand. Put another way, if we have an increasing number of people and their money chasing a steady amount of some product, then the price for that product goes up. Similarly, if demand stays the same but those who produce the goods are having trouble making the same amount they did last month, then prices for that product will also go up. This is a supply versus demand issue. That is the problem with energy lately, and gasoline (or oil) in particular.

The whole world, especially outside the United States, is using more and more gas and oil as economic development spreads. Interestingly, this is occurring even as we in the U.S. are actually learning to conserve and reduce our own demand. Regardless, oil supply is holding steady yet worldwide demand for it is increasing. So even if we in the U.S. continue to do a good job moving away from reliance on oil, worldwide demand will continue to push gas and oil prices higher. When these prices climb, all energy prices follow. When energy prices go up, the prices of many goods and services go up as well. Bingo! We get instant inflation that has nothing to do with anyone's economic policy, simply due to the fact that the world demand for oil is going up while supplies remain stable.

The government's economic policy can also produce inflation. The government promotes inflation by borrowing more money than it takes in, especially if that borrowed money is unsecured (pure budget deficit). Why, then, do we not have rampant inflation today? Because our Federal Reserve System is playing an interesting money game to artificially push the inflation level down. The U.S. government (via the Fed) loans money to banks at near zero percent interest so the banks can help buy our federal debt at around 3% and still make a profit. It is a nice shell game propped up by the fact that we hold the world currency. If we were any other country, we would not be able to get away with this tactic. Some economists are even surprised that it is still working.

Regardless, this method is not free. It produces more debt, but it is probably worth it as long as it continues to work. Probably. Some also argue that the Fed is overdoing it. I do not want to get involved in the details of that debate. My point is only that the government's policies directly affect inflation rates. This is primarily a matter of how much the federal government is borrowing versus how easy it is for banks to get their loans. Note that this also means we would experience much higher inflation today if the Fed raised its own lending rates to banks. It cannot lower them, by the way, because that rate is nearly zero already.

What can the government do to make inflation go down? Lowering debt from government borrowing and lowering Fed bank loan rates would have that effect. We already have super-low Fed bank loan rates, so there is no wiggle room there. If we develop a new risk of inflation, the only thing the government could do about it is to try to balance the national budget.

Now that we have a fair understanding of the problem, we can attack it. First, we will consider a plan modification. After the above discussion, the answer should be pretty clear. If Magnified Capitalism produces inflation pressures, then the only means left to counter them is to reduce the kind of borrowing that produces real debt. We need to include a long-term plan to reduce government deficits. Good news here. A greatly improved economy will increase government revenues enough to make up much of this difference. Later we can plan to use a portion of Capital Magnification Service profits for deficit reduction, too. And finally, we should be working on this problem anyway. What are we waiting for? Deficit spending is a poor long-term policy independent of this strategy. This plan just makes the job easier to tackle. So we should work to cut spending. I have my own ideas on where to focus, but any suggestion from me would be unqualified. This is an area that is controversial and deserving of its own plan. It is enough to say that this proposal provides a new motivation to do this important work.

Of course I will now introduce a counterargument to the threat of rampant inflation. Its main point is this: There should be no unusually high inflationary pressure in United States 2.0. How is that? Will there not be great demand for employees? Will this demand not produce rising salaries, rising benefits, and other effects that generally lead to increased business costs? Why, yes. Will there not also be an increased national and worldwide demand for U.S. products? Will there not also be more money everywhere from the global trickle-down? Of course there will. But there are also balancing factors.

Under Magnified Capitalism there will be a rising supply of nearly all types of products and services from the many new competitors that will pop up everywhere. There will also be a great advance in productivity, because that has been the long-term trend motivated by increases in automation, education, and improved business processes. There will also be more inclination to source locally in U.S. 2.0, which will eventually help limit supply costs due to the continuous price rise in long-range shipping. The improved U.S. infrastructure that this plan calls for will also add productivity to local sourcing and services. But the main factor is the competition.

It will be so easy to start a business in U.S. 2.0, we better be careful about upsetting our customer base through any means, including overly-aggressive price increases. Competitors that do not even exist yet will smell the customer pain and pounce into our market because we handed them a good business plan. There is nothing like miffed customers to motivate a sudden consumer shift to an upstart. Customers are typically reluctant to try a product or service from a start-up company, especially when they like their current supplier. The main exception is when we upset a customer for any reason.

No. I would say that capital magnification produces unusual business conditions that benefit consumers and smart businesses. Put another way, we will prune out a lot of business dead wood because consumer markets will not tolerate much abuse from anyone. Overall, this effect will be healthy. Most businesses will learn quickly that improving the quality of products and services will keep them strong. But there is no hiding the fact that those who do not accept this new rule will get burned by the many new contenders waiting to jump in. The corollary to the new business rule will be this: Businesses that last in United States 2.0 will be slow and careful to raise their prices. I think inflation will eventually stabilize to very comfortable levels well under 10% annually. If we do not believe this argument will hold up, reduce the deficit. That is a good idea anyway.

Threat #2: Holes, Odd Events, Deviations and Mistakes
Some project managers call this the risk of "unknown unknowns". In other words, we know that we have not thought of everything, even though we gave it our best shot. This kind of threat includes weird things that no one would have bothered to plan for even if someone had mentioned them in advance, like a possible meteor strike. That does not mean it could not happen. Then what do we do? We also include in this threat the probability that the plan will change before it is implemented. Not knowing what changes we will make means it is hard to judge whether they are good ideas or not. I worry most about changes that come about through political compromise, or worse, deal-making. We must also throw in the possibility that along the way someone's error will trip up a perfectly decent plan. A testing oversight would be ripe for big fallout, for example. Of course there is even the most unimaginable problem of all. Without meaning to, I might have forgotten to address a critical issue. This implies, naturally, that no one else catches the hole either. But that is beside the point. Every once in a while the emperor has no clothes but nobody who can effect change manages to do anything about it. Smirking in the crowd might not do the trick.

For this broadly unspecific threat I will offer my counterargument first. Hogwash! This plan is not secret. For goodness sake, not only have I presented it to you, Mr. President, but I will also publish it openly for anyone to read. There is hardly a better way to vet a strategy and its underlying plan than to let the entire country pick it apart piece by piece. By the time this strategy goes before any kind of vote there will not be a person of relevance who has not tried to add their voice, analysis, input, and conclusion. If there is a hole in the plan, the world would have to collectively miss it. If there is an odd event that trips us, then it would have to be one of apocalyptic proportion to overcome the safety measures installed here. By the way, if such an event were to occur, we might want to implement this plan as a means to fast-track our recovery. If we cannot muster the resources, then the disaster is so grand it is all a moot point anyway.

As far as plan deviations go, we can control those. We do not have to allow any deviation that we have not properly analyzed and justified. The public can demand this, and should. But even without this finger wagging, I do not really believe any politician would propose a change so dangerous that it would undermine the strategy. After all, if the deviation ruined the plan, then it would be the fault of those who pushed it through. So due to the political danger involved, I do not expect such carelessness from our lawmakers.

Finally we must look at the possibility of human error. It is not that I do not expect people to make mistakes. It is that there will be so many people working on this project, so much money at stake, so much invested in the system's various parts, and so many brilliant people overseeing the implementation (by necessity), that we will catch these mistakes. We will catch them because there will be processes and double checks to do so. That is why it is so important to make a solid plan. This plan includes such processes, and where they are missing, we should correct that error.

What can we change in the plan to make double sure such issues do not trip us? Let us take on each of the four items, one at a time in the order listed in this section's title. We will start with holes.

I would be the first to admit that there might be holes in the strategy, maybe huge ones. Obviously, I do not know what they are or I would have addressed them already. But there are many brilliant people who should be able to find all the holes that might exist. I want to invite everyone to search for them. The website I mentioned earlier, www.magnifiedcapitalism.com, will collect all such input, regardless of who it is from. We will also use this website to collect ideas for improving this plan in any way, including addressing holes that people may find. Furthermore, I am sure that before we implement Magnified Capitalism qualified people will conduct independent analysis. I would like to post copies of such reports and articles or otherwise refer to the sources of these at the same website. In such a manner I hope to show how we can constructively use transparent sharing of information and an invitation for criticism and related input. The main thing we will avoid is rhetoric and substanceless criticism (as in name calling). Otherwise, all voices are welcome to collectively improve the plan. Now we go on to the second item.

Preparing a plan for addressing odd events is a challenging topic in general. It reminds me of a soldier going into battle with little advance idea of the nature of the fray. What should the soldier do to prepare? Good training to maximum physical condition would help. Perhaps some body armor would be a good idea. How about extra equipment like night vision goggles, rifles that shoot around corners, a bazooka, grenades, a medic kit, mountain gear, snow shoes, a coat, a water breather, skis, rope .... Hold on. That is already too much. At some point we need to stop ourselves and realize there is a better solution. The soldier should ask his commander for more information about where he is going and what he can expect to encounter. Maybe all the information is not available just yet. OK. Then he should find out when it will be. Whatever he can know, he should find out in advance. If he knows some information will be last minute, then he should prepare for that, too.

The same method works for us in our situation. The plan effect is not that we should prepare for the oddest things, but that we should be prepared to make last-minute changes if weird things happen before we get started. The change management process needs to include allowance for responding to new information and situations at any point in the implementation, including after approval. That is our main adjustment to address weird issues.

What of our third item, handling plan deviations? Some parties might institute deviations even before the plan is approved, such as by congressional negotiations. Or these changes can come into play later, such as by presidential declaration, congressional amendments, or even by the processes established through CMS management and personnel. In any case, solving this problem comes down to using a disciplined change management process. If we institute a deviation before the CMS is established, then this change management process is implicit. In such cases the public, you, Mr. President, and Congress should all insist that proposed changes be accompanied by well-considered written analysis that is published openly for any to review. The proposal for change should include a formal impact analysis, along the lines of this SWOT analysis.

Once the CMS is established, there are additional impacts that we have brought up before when considering the risk of changes from Congress or the President. Such changes would require a 60% majority vote to adopt a temporary change, or 80% for a permanent one. In addition, the proposal would need to undergo formal acceptance testing, where it might need to be modified in order to pass. This would be done with some congressional oversight. If the CMS institutes changes from its own motivations to improve efficiencies, investment returns, and the like, then it, too, will need to go through a formal change management process.

All such changes must be submitted in writing (by internal personnel) subject to review by an internal change review board. If these changes are approved, they must then be simulated and pass the same sort of acceptance testing. Whether or not these changes can go live at this point is a negotiable question. If the impact of the modification is to remove bugs in the system, or to make changes that are demonstrated to improve service somehow, then I do not believe a congressional approval should be necessary. The Board should hold CMS management responsible for insuring that the changes they make in such a situation indeed meet the criteria stated above, and any other reasonable criteria they might add later. However, if the change has some possible or likely downside to weigh against its benefits, I suggest the Board bring this sort of change before a congressional oversight committee for approval. This committee would be one specifically organized to approve CMS change requests of sufficient impact.

There we have it. The new changes needed to address this threat are mostly incremental over ones we have already made in this SWOT analysis. Forexample, the last modification we just made was merely one that added details to a change management process we already included previously. This is a good sign. It shows us that the plan is tightening up to the point where less and less dramatic adjustment is needed as we go. Let us see if this trend holds up as we go on to the next threat.

Threat #3: Abuse, Cons, and Criminal Acts
Where there is money to be made legally, there will be those who are tempted to gain their piece by cheating somehow. I will consider three related categories here. Abusers are people who appear legitimate on the surface. They can be the customers of capitalists, the capitalists themselves, or even CMS or government employees, associates, or contractors. We are talking about anyone who is involved in the chain of the Magnified Capitalism process. If they have access to money, information, and systems, or if they touch the process somehow, those same people have the potential to abuse the system. In most every such case we would not need a new law to make the abuse illegal, although we might consider new ones anyway to treat specific risks with appropriate judgments.

A con is a bit different from an abuse, although its result could be very nearly the same. With a con, the people committing the wrongful act have planned to do it. A con more likely involves a group of people working together, although that is not necessarily so with a particularly skilled con person. Regardless, the main difference is that abuse tends to occur in situations involving opportunistic temptation, whereas a con is more like a criminal plan from its beginning.

I have added a third category of generic criminal acts with the recognition that there are bound to be attempts at illegal use of the system that fit neither of the first two categories cleanly. For example, what if a capitalist submits fraudulent reports on their deals in order to cover up mistakes or improve their CMS rating? Another example would be a rival business bribing a CMS employee to sabotage the funding of a business deal. I am sure we could think of many other examples. Most of them involve the motivation to contort the outcome of normal CMS processes towards a different end. Regardless, we might just consider all three of these categories as variations of the third one. They are all really just different kinds of criminal acts, which is a fair point. I divided them into three categories because of the differences in handling them.

This threat requires a slightly different nature of response. We can address most of this problem within the CMS. However, I have yet to give much detail about what the CMS actually does. So I can argue, as I explain what the effect of this threat on the plan would be, that there is no change. Instead, what I will discuss is details we have not heard before because we have not gotten to that part of the plan yet. However, because of the order of presentation here, an observer might note that the SWOT analysis insures the CMS processes are designed to handle criminal activity because the issue of criminal activity is raised early on. It is a chicken and egg problem. And like chickens versus eggs, the answer to that part is more philosophical than it is practical. The impact is the same. We have chickens and eggs. And so for this plan, I will present first the mitigation part of the answer. Our plan addresses criminal activity in CMS processes because that issue is part of the CMS charter. Whether these details came from SWOT analysis does not really matter, but I have provided some here regardless.

I mentioned the CMS charter. I will detail it more later on. However, a significant part of it focuses on enforcement. Enforcement is the part of the CMS that is similar to a policing function. It is also comparable to the IRS's auditing division. The CMS will not actually have police on staff. Rather they will have investigators, auditors, process managers, caseworkers, arbitrators, customer support staff and many related automated systems. These automated systems will include tools to help the CMS personnel do their jobs well. We can expect these tools to improve over time. Regardless, when we find problems, we will resolve these problems through written and tested processes. When these processes point to potential criminal activity, a CMS investigator will examine the matter through a formal investigation. If the investigator collects sufficient evidence to support a claim of criminal activity, the CMS will contact either the FBI or local police as determined by the nature of the suspected crime. The CMS investigator will work with law enforcement to follow through on any investigation. This investigator will be responsible for closing the case expeditiously. They should have some management incentive for correct resolution in a timely manner.

The other CMS personnel I mentioned should receive similar incentives for supporting investigations and audits. Note that audits are not considered criminal investigations. Rather, they relate to proper filing and tracking of the deals made by capitalists. When filing errors occur, they are usually handled directly by auditors, including the application of processes that result in penalties. However, there will be cases where an auditor discovers evidence of true criminal intent, or at least the possibility of it. In these cases, the auditor will call in an investigator to handle this aspect of the matter.

All CMS employees, especially those listed above, will have similar responsibilities. Anyone, such as a caseworker or customer support person, can run across evidence that some sort of criminal activity may be in play. There will be incentive for all CMS personnel to contact the investigation department for follow-up. We should also note that the fact that a criminal act is suspected does not mean that it exists. We may resolve these matters in various ways, including handing the issue to an auditor for correction, submitting a process change request (internal screw-ups), forwarding a warning to the customer from a process manager (mild abuses or mistakes), or even little or no action (as in a misunderstanding by a CMS employee).

Certainly, this description is very high-level. CMS management will insure the exact reporting structure is designed with written processes to handle policing and auditing matters. In the end this management will be held responsible for ensuring the CMS catches all types of abuse and handles them both fairly and quickly. Management will also be responsible for insuring mistaken suspicions of abuse are discharged fairly and quickly, with appropriate consideration to anyone harmed by wrongful claims. Those making wrongful claims should be flagged to ensure they are not the source of some patterned behavior, whether directly or indirectly.

Now we can consider whether or not CMS processes have resolved our threat. It appears that various personnel, especially auditors, process managers, and caseworkers, are likely to notice abuses. In any case, the automated systems should include tools for these same people to flag suspected abusive activity. In fact, this is the primary sort of computerized tool that triggers audits. Investigators should have similar tools that flag activities more likely to be criminal, or sourced from internal personnel.

Cons may be more complicated to detect only because they may be more carefully planned. But the same systems and processes that flag abuse should apply here as well. The one additional consideration here is a special kind of investigator's tool, a piece of software that correlates different kinds of suspect activity across the entire system to common subsystems and people. It falls under a new category of automation commonly called "data mining". For example, our special system might flag a caseworker because they consistently dismiss process problems from the same set of customers, but not for other customers. Or it might flag an auditor for failure to catch a class of problems at the same statistical rate that most auditors do.

When a data mining tool flags a problem it does not automatically mean that something is wrong. The flagging only provides evidence to an investigator of the possibility something is wrong. The investigator should then look at that case or person more closely to be sure. Once the investigator has examined the situation, the system should track the investigation even if it is dismissed. If the investigator does not launch an inquiry when a problem is raised, the system should track that, too. Policing by automation should become a large bowl of noodles carefully tracked by CMS computer systems perpetually. That way no person has to untangle the whole bowl, but there will always be those who are looking at one strand of noodle or another.

Finally, we can ask whether we have covered all criminal activity. I think the answer is "yes" inasmuch as the solution is broad and bound to have some holes. The implementation of CMS systems will evolve continuously to improve. There will certainly be cases of one type of criminal activity or another that sadly succeed in the short term. Hopefully the automated systems and people processes for policing will give very high priority to cases involving the most money. In this way, we can limit the most serious problems to one-off situations, or at least those involving smaller total dollars.

As we make mistakes, we will learn to fix the holes they illuminate. But there is no doubt that some abuse will be perpetual. We should track the total estimate of losses due to abuse, report on activities to improve the situation, and reward those who work to stop the abuse. The real goal is to manage the problem so that it represents a total loss so small that it can be easily recovered by legitimate gains. We should also reward CMS management for maintaining a judicious balance between strong enforcement of rules and law, and the fair and considerate treatment of its law-abiding customers and employees.

As a final commentary on this subject I want to add this one point: If there was ever an excuse to elevate the value of whistleblowers, then it would be for the support of CMS policing. For too long we have tolerated a social stigma against those who follow their conscience and try to right wrongs at their own risk. There is too much money at stake in the CMS to support such an errant inclination. I support large bonuses and automatic promotions for any successful CMS whistleblowers and their management (if the management is not involved in the problem). More importantly, I support the automatic dismissal of any senior management who pursue policies to the contrary, even if they themselves did not otherwise do any wrong. The CMS needs to be different. This agency should celebrate its own moral and social righteousness, but it needs to continuously earn such celebration. This one disposition may do more to limit abuse and criminal activity than any other plan element. From this one pillar we might assume the rest will follow.

Threat #4: Debilitating Legal Issues
In 1895 by a vote of 5 to 4 the Supreme Court ruled as unconstitutional the then-new income tax levied by Congress in 1894. And so for some time there was no national income tax and no IRS. Arguably the court overturned this tax law on a technicality, but that did not matter. It took fourteen years until Congress managed to send the 16th Amendment to the states for ratification. Four years later, in 1913, Delaware was the 36th state to ratify the amendment. With that the U.S. formally legalized federal income tax. The IRS was formed. We have had income taxes ever since. The total time from Congress' initial passage of the law to a practical enactment was about 18 years.

The moral of this story is to watch out for lawyers; they can delay almost anything. We might have rooted for them to keep fighting in 1913. But the reality is that we, as a country, needed the money. The United States would never have risen to its current position of power and prosperity had it not been for income taxes. That is not to say income taxes are the only way to collect such revenue. But we needed to collect that revenue by some means. This was just the demon we picked to do the job. But most of this is a sidebar. The main point is about the power of lawyers to derail and delay, not the virtue of the issue they might fight about.

We face a similar possibility in the matter of this program. Somebody is sure to feel like this plan steps on their toes. That person or organization is going to hire some expensive lawyers who are going to try to find a way to trip the plan. They might use a general attack on the whole idea of Magnified Capitalism and the Capital Magnification Service, or, more likely, some detail of it. I say a detail is more likely because details are easier to pick on. Why fight a principled argument when a technicality will do? Lawyers live off such things. They might choose the structure of the CMS as a private corporation controlled by politicians but owned by the citizens. They might pick on the ability of a private firm to impose or trigger legal actions on behalf of the government. Or perhaps they will choose to dismantle the many standard contracts we will have to negotiate and write in order to implement a proper CMS offering.

Another approach would be to attack various effects of CMS function, like the favoring of four specific capitalist types, or the fairness of enforcement rules. Perhaps the lawyers would pounce on the inequity of ever-changing incentives. Even after the CMS is up and running we can be pretty sure there will be legal challenges along these or other lines. Furthermore, in order to streamline processes and reduce costs, most CMS legal matters will be adjudicated with some type of arbitration. There are sure to be narrow challenges of the results from some of these cases. What about when we catch the real criminals trying to game the system? These people will still have a right to defend themselves, as they should, in a real court of law before facing any legal penalties. In the meantime some people will make attempts to countersue or take other action. The fact that the CMS is not actually a government agency may make this situation less complicated.

It is easy to predict that legal battles are part of the nature of this proposal. The threat here is not whether we will have legal issues, but whether we will be so overwhelmed by legal problems that they will trip us. Alternately, the difficulty may not be so much about the volume, but the nature of a very few issues that could threaten the plan. This was the disposition of our opening concern. What do we do if some opponent manages to successfully claim that the whole plan is illegal or unconstitutional?

Once again I will address this point by discussing details I have not yet revealed. Here is my opening axiom for consideration: The best way to confound a team of lawyers is with a better and bigger team of lawyers. This plan must, by necessity, employ a sports team of lawyers both during its planning stages and during its implementation. They will earn their keep, as there will be plenty to do. During the setup and planning stages they will challenge and defend every aspect of this plan. I say challenge in the same way a football team must practice against its own backup players. One team of lawyers will take on the task of trying to poke at the plan with legal maneuvers. These are the lawyers on offense. They will do the challenging. The other team will prepare the responses and countermeasures. This is the defensive team.

Everyone will learn from this exercise and we may need to make plan adjustments to address the issues raised. The legal team will perfect the contract language. They will fine-tune the legal structure of the CMS. They will carefully design the relationship between the CMS and government officials to meet the spirit of our plan without accidently doing anything that requires new constitutional changes. And finally, to the degree they may be helpful or empowering, our team of lawyers may introduce a batch of plan change requests for us all to consider. This preparatory work might even include a proposal for a new constitutional amendment to make the system work more smoothly in the long run. I hope not, but they will be a very good group of lawyers. Where there is a team of good, motivated lawyers, constitutional amendment dreams are often nearby. As long as we do not have to wait for the amendment's passage to get the plan going I might even be convinced of it merits, whatever those might be.

Threat #5: Bad Timing
Wait for cover fire before you jump out of the foxhole to throw the grenade. Only throw the long pass when your receiver is open. Do not kick your political opponent when he is already down. When the yellow light turns red, it is too late to hit the gas. Sometimes a well-considered plan can be triggered at the wrong time or under the wrong circumstances. Certainly there might be some circumstances under which starting Magnified Capitalism would be considered bad timing. What about acts of God or a global catastrophe? How about a world war or a terrorist attack? Does it make sense to start this program during the onset of a depression, unexpected energy crisis, or pandemic?

Here is the real answer: If this system were already in place, it would help us greatly to recover from all of these difficulties. However, I do believe that in the midst of a problem that stifles all economic activity, we should put the program on hold for a while. This includes both new and existing programs. That is right. I do not have a well-considered counterproposal for starting the plan anyway, or even triggering incentives in an established program. It simply makes more sense to pause, wait for the economic engine to restart, then follow through only after the smoke clears. Even if we already had a ton of money stashed away in a well-established CMS Fund, we would likely wait for the worst of a disaster to play out before beginning the economic recovery phase.

For goodness sake, address the people emergency first. Clean everything up. Get back on our feet. No one is going to start a business or give out a loan when they are hiding scared in their basement. We have to get past that part first. We rebuild the economy after everyone decides it is OK to go outside again. So we should do what is necessary to make that happen first. This has little to do with business. Disaster management is a unique kind of problem. Magnified Capitalism requires a working economy, whether it is one that is in a downturn or even just trying to improve. But anything that causes economic seizure is out of scope for this plan. That is when the timing is bad. The good news is that as long as most of us make it through, there should be a strategy waiting to aid us in the economic healing.

If I have a counterpoint at all it is this: We must distinguish between real bad timing and false bad timing. Real bad timing is what I described above. That would involve a situation so terrible that most, or all, economic activity stops for some time. A war probably would not do it unless it got so bad that nukes were used, or the enemy invaded U.S. soil. A terrorist attack would also not likely do it, except for perhaps a small delay to make sure that the matter was respectfully addressed. So if people start complaining that the timing is bad for triggering this plan, I am inclined to disagree on one primary principle. If we have the communications systems in place so that we can complain, and the assembly in place to complain to, then we probably do not have the sort of social seizure that it takes to justify a delaying action. If the argument is that the economy is already improving, that is not bad timing. That is perfect timing. If the argument is that we cannot afford the new debt at this time, then we need to reread the relevant counterpoint. If we think we cannot afford it, then the reality is that we cannot afford not to. I could go on but I risk being redundant. The point is merely to look for the signs of a false claim of bad timing. It would take quite a disaster to really have a timing problem.

SWOT Conclusions

That is it for the Strengths, Weaknesses, Opportunities, and Threats analysis. Perhaps I should have warned you, Mr. President, that this is no minor part of the plan. It has been an exercise similar to a thought experiment. In this sense it produces new perspectives and new conclusions, or at least plan adjustments. Mr. President, if you were not sure whether Magnified Capitalism was a good idea before, then I hope the SWOT analysis has helped to convince you otherwise. A bad idea would have trouble holding up against a detailed SWOT analysis. That is one of the values of the SWOT – to vet the strategy against likely problems and weigh it against the possibility of benefits. I trust you can see that most of the benefits are reachable and most of the weaknesses and threats are either defendable or addressable.

Actually, my goal is a bit loftier than just convincing you that this program is a good idea. I want you to get excited that we can really make this happen in short order. My real hope is that you cannot wait to get started. We will soon be ready to transform our wonderful United States into a country that gains the benefits of Magnified Capitalism.

III. SWOT Analysis

Before we launch United States 2.0 we need to learn more about what this means. This information will empower you, Mr. President, as a proponent, and embolden a deeper understanding of how the strategy will work and impact others. The next chapter will begin this part of the presentation. You should now be familiar with the strategy, the high-level plan, and the political argument. Coming next we will examine this proposal's real, direct impact on businesses and people.

Want to know if an idea is likely to work? Understand the footsteps of those you expect to do the deed. Take account based on your own view of the breadth of the issue. Do not accept a summary provided by an 'expert' who must necessarily inject a conclusion if only by their choice of editing. Learn the details so that you become one to whom others must defer. The more we all adopt these routines, the more we confound political experts who assume we only know what they tell us. Such habits will not merely open more of our collective eyes; they will help steer us toward success by turning lemmings into soldiers of righteousness.

IV. Solution Walkthrough

Now that we have made it this far into the presentation I must offer my congratulations. Hopefully we have agreed on the principle that the capitalist infrastructure of our country can be magnified, thereby increasing business growth and job creation. We can create a program that does this to whatever degree we have the appetite for. If we put enough money into it, we can solve most of our country's financial issues and make ourselves supremely competitive. Hooray.

But before we go off and make it all happen, it is time to understand what it is we are really taking about. What does the Capital Magnification Service actually do? If we were venture capitalists in United States 2.0, how would we obtain money from the government to help us start more businesses? Why would we want to do that, exactly? What would we need to do if we wanted to acquire even more money? What if we were among the other types of capitalists - the bankers, businesses and private investors? What would we need to do to receive our share of the CMS money? If we were any of these capitalists would we be excited about Magnified Capitalism? What would we worry about even if we were interested?

Let us imagine that we have gained congressional approval for this plan. Then we hired the impressive CMS management. Their team of lawyers worked with Congress and you, Mr. President, to structure the CMS as a citizen company. The CMS then hired their staff, completed their organization, developed their automated systems, tested their processes against a third-party testing system, and gained pre-acceptance approval from both you and Congress. Let us imagine that Congress put the money in the CMS bank yesterday, and the operations begin today. Whew! Now, how do we create jobs?

VC Walkthrough

Let us begin with the venture capitalist, or VC. The VC is my favorite type of capitalist because they embody the purest form of capitalism, but they do it formally as a business entity. A venture capitalist is typically a business formed by a team of wealthy people who made their money from some other business, usually one that they sold off years ago. They are often referred to as the partners, much like the main partners of a law firm. This team of partners was experienced at running businesses even before they joined or started the VC firm. By the time a new or emerging business approaches a VC for money, the partners have usually been running their firm for years, so their experience is pretty impressive. Through the years they will have reviewed countless business plan proposals, rejected most of them, and invested millions of their own dollars into the ones they did like.

The style of VC firms varies a lot. Some will insist on becoming deeply involved in the operation of the companies they invest in. Others will be more flexible. Some VCs prefer to invest in established businesses that need money to break out. Other VCs will consider startup ideas at the prototype stage. A very few will even entertain a totally green business proposal, as long as it is very well conceived and comes from a team of people well qualified to pull it off. Many of the most successful companies in the United States were at some point funded by money from a venture capitalist. Modern examples include Apple Computer, Federal Express, Electronic Arts, and Domino's Pizza, to name just a few of the well-recognized ones.

Of the two million new businesses started in the United States every year, currently only about 750 receive venture capital funding. Yet the National Venture Capital Association estimates that a full 11% of private sector jobs come from companies backed by VCs. They further estimate that 21% of the U.S. GDP comes from companies who at one time received VC funding. Notice that this includes companies that are still around, regardless of how long ago they received that money. What this means is important. It tells us that the professional venture capitalists are really good at what they do. They tend to back winners that grow to become important, make an impact, and survive. These facts help verify our strategy. One of the best ways to magnify the growth of young businesses is to ride the coattails of the VCs. Also, remember that if we pump more money into this kind of activity, we will increase the number of deals that VCs can make. This is the very heart of our strategy.

We can imagine looking over the shoulder of a VC firm on the first day of United States 2.0. They are aware of the new funds they can access since Magnified Capitalism is major news for their business sector. Let's invent a fictional firm called ABCD Ventures. We will call their designated CMS interface Ms. Smith, a senior partner at ABCD. She has studied the new government program and followed its progress through the news. Her firm has asked her to make sure they line up as much funding from the CMS as makes sense for ABCD. Here is what happens.

Ms. Smith signs onto the Capital Magnification Service website. There she finds a description of the CMS charter, new releases, frequently asked questions, services available and other helpful information. She learns that her first step is to register ABCD as a Professional U.S. Venture Capitalist with a verifiable multi-year history. A few clicks later Ms. Smith is filling out a lengthy online registration form, but she will only need to complete it once. She knows that the more information she includes to support the firm's expertise and successful track record, the higher ABCD's ranking will be as a newly registered VC. This ranking will be split into two ratings. One rating will address the size of ABCD's funding deals. This is called the VC Magnitude Rating. The other rating will be a measure of how successful ABCD tends to be versus how risky they are. This rating is formed from a pair of numbers called the Return Times Risk Ratio. The return is a measure of ABCD's overall profitability, while the risk ratio measures the percentage of deals they make that are losers within six years. With these two ratings the government, or more precisely, the CMS, will have a fair measure of what kind of terms they can offer ABCD, and how much total funding ABCD can qualify for per year.

Ms. Smith also copies the rules from the CMS website regarding how ABCD can maintain and improve their ranking as a VC. She then prepares a presentation to the other partners outlining what they need to do to qualify for higher limits and more deals in subsequent years. The bottom line is this: The more success ABCD brings to the CMS, the more their ranking will rise. Ms. Smith also learns that her company should not use government money for just their weaker deals. If there is a great difference between the success of the company's existing deals, and the deals that they use CMS funds for, ABCD could be subject to fines and even criminal investigations. The rules are clear. ABCD must apply CMS funds to the premium deals, or at least average deals, otherwise the program may not be profitable in the long run.

The next day, Ms. Smith receives a confirmation email from the Capital Magnification Service. ABCD has been approved as a registered Professional U.S. Venture Capitalist. Furthermore, ABCD"s ranking begins with a Magnitude Rating of $10 Million and a Return Times Risk Ratio of 8%. Ms. Smith knows these are excellent ratings that give ABCD a strong starting point. It also means that ABCD can now make a public announcement of their approval and ranking. Their new status as 'CMS registered' will also appear on the company's website as well as in their marketing materials. The other partners will be pleased as they expect this new CMS program to attract the best venture opportunities.

The following week the partners are ready to test the water with their first deal. They want to back a small mobile app developer who has a new concept for using mobile phones as a remote control for other devices. The developer has a prototype and some existing revenue from other software sales, but they need $20 million to manufacture and market the small device customers will need to buy to complete the new product offering. ABCD thinks this app is a winner. They have already spent months checking out this client and the business plan behind the concept. They were expecting to back the mobile app company anyway, but with the new CMS plan, they are now hoping they can do it without risking as much of the company's own money. In other words, they will have enough cash left over to enter into more deals with other clients.

The partners ask Ms. Smith to prepare a presentation comparing the consequences of using CMS funds versus not using them. Here is a summary of what she found: If ABCD makes the deal alone, they will have to put up all of the $20 million. If the mobile app company's plan succeeds, ABCD will make their $20 million back plus another $80 million in three years. The partners call this the "best" case. One of ABCD's other partners who is assigned to this deal has already made a more conservative estimate of $40 million profit in four years. He calls this result the "expected" case. If the plan fails, then ABCD would end up losing approximately $10 million of their original investment. They would not lose all $20 million because they have negotiated terms with the client to completely take over and liquidate them as soon as it becomes clear the company's plans are going to fail. This emergency clause, as tough as it may sound, limits ABCD's risk exposure. There is also some possibility that the plan will succeed just enough that everyone gets their money back. They call this the "break even" case. Now Ms. Smith compares these possibilities to what happens if ABCD signs up this deal for the CMS Venture Capital Funding service.

ABCD's CMS rating allows them to ask for up to $10 million per deal, for a maximum of 8 deals per year. If they make one deal using CMS funds, they are expected to use CMS funds for at least three more in the next year to avoid "non-diversification penalties", unless the company can show it cannot reasonably comply. In other words, to make one deal means committing to making several. So when ABCD decides to make the first CMS-funded deal of the year, they are committing to making more deals with CMS funds.

In the case of the mobile app developer, the government will back up to 50% of the deal. So ABCD could ask for their maximum $10 million government backing. The program would require ABCD to cash out within six years, which is fine since they are looking to be out in four. The government expects to be paid back at a rate that is only 60% of whatever ABCD makes on the share of the deal. However, if ABCD loses money, the government will accept a loss that is no more than 50% of ABCD's loss. This means there is a penalty for ABCD if the deal loses, but a bonus if it succeeds.

So what is the conclusion? I will talk it through, however, some people do like numbers laid out. I will try not to present columns of figures too often, but this table captures the whole scenario:

Small Mobile App Company Deal			by ABCD Ventures		(Gov't's Take)	
	Without CMS		With CMS		CMS Part	
Investment	$20,000,000		$10,000,000		$10,000,000	
	Profit in $	%	Profit in $	%	Profit in $	%
Best Case	$80,000,000	400%	$64,000,000	640%	$16,000,000	160%
Expected Case	$40,000,000	200%	$32,000,000	320%	$8,000,000	80%
Break Even	$0	0%	$0	0%	$0	0%
Worst Case	($10,000,000)	-50%	($7,500,000)	-75%	($2,500,000)	-25%

If the small mobile app company meets their optimistic goal, the best case scenario, ABCD would make a 400% profit of $80 million if they funded the project entirely with their own money. Using CMS funds for half of this deal, their profit margin would jump to 640% because they would risk half as much of their own money, but still make nearly as much in total dollars ($64 million).

Even if the deal is a loser, ABCD would lose less under the CMS funding plan than they would have using just their own money. Admittedly, ABCD would take a higher percentage loss under the CMS funding plan than they would going it alone, but the hard number cash loss is smaller if they work with CMS since less of ABCD's funds were involved in the first place. This higher percentage is part of the penalty for using the government for riskier deals. If ABCD loses, they take a hit with a higher percentage responsibility for that loss. But if they win, their win includes a bonus that makes up for that.

Ms. Smith's recommendation is simple. It makes sense to take the government funding on all the better deals, and none of the riskier ones. This determination will do two things. First, it will boost ABCD's profit margins on the good deals, while allowing them to make more deals with the same amount of cash on hand. Second, it will improve ABCD's rating with the CMS since Ms. Smith will be able to communicate this favorable bias in her CMS reports. That means ABCD's CMS terms and limits will get better and better if they can keep up a solid performance. Now we can understand the business decision clearly. The more ABCD uses CMS money, the more total profits they will make. ABCD just has to be careful not to use CMS money on bad bets, lest they risk eroding their rating and thus their benefit. This is exactly the kind of incentive we want.

There is a side detail to this situation as well. ABCD will need to obtain an independent assessment, or appraisal, of the mobile app deal. It will not cost that much; the process is similar to having a home appraised in preparation for applying for a mortgage. This assessment is called a Certified Business Valuation. We will discuss these CBVs more later on.

The government side of the deal appears shaded in the far right column of the table above. We can see that the government could make as much as a 160%

profit over three years, or a more likely profit of 80% in four years. While both of these results are a fine return on investment in excess of CMS goals, the second is fair but not amazing. Why is that? An 80% return on investment over four years represents a compounded annual interest of just 16%. That is OK, but probably just barely above the level required for the business plan to qualify for the deal. Regardless, if the deal goes south, the government would still get most, if not all of its original money back. That is because in most real world cases this deal would create some sales, so there should still be some profits in the bank, although I have not shown this situation specifically in the table. If it were there, this case would appear slightly better than the break-even case.

I want to mention an important disclaimer before I go on. The exact percentages, ratings, and figures I have shown in this example are rough estimates only. The real system the CMS uses has to be tested and adjusted as we have discussed. I expect the end result to resemble the sample here, though. It certainly should retain all of the main strategic points I have illustrated. Venture capitalists will conclude they should use government money for the better deals, and not so much for riskier ones. The VCs' profits will increase with their ability to back more business deals, thereby creating more jobs. How is that? When a VC backs a small company, that company expands, hires people, buys equipment, and opens new factories, testing labs or whatever their plan calls for. That is where the new jobs come from. Then, when the VC uses CMS money, they are left with enough funds to make more deals than they could have without using CMS services. So they make those extra deals and generate more jobs than they would have without the CMS. The CMS will make a profit, sometimes handsomely, other times less so. But in total, the CMS will receive a reasonable return for its risk.

Let's look at two more points that this example illustrates. First, venture capital firms should try hard to spend all the government money they possibly can. There is every reason for them to do that. This pressure has two interesting effects. First, it means they will be inclined to spend more of their own money then they may have otherwise done, because every deal requires some amount of matching money. Second, it means that there is a potentially high ceiling to how much money the CMS could manage. How is that? By adjusting the VCs' limits and ratings, the CMS could magnify potentially trillions of dollars per year just through the venture capitalist part of the program. It is kind of beautiful, if such a thing can be.

Now let's look at the second point that this example illustrates. Thanks to CMS funding, being a professional venture capitalist just became way more attractive. This shift will cause a sudden boom in the venture capital market itself. There is still good news for the existing VCs, though. Notice that having a long history of experience improves your rating with the CMS. This means the established VCs will receive by far the best terms and highest limits. However, there will be enough attraction for newcomers to make this an exciting time. Within a few years, some of those new VCs will prove to be excellent investors, and their ratings will climb along with their deal limits. This, too, is exactly what we want. More private companies will form to invest their own money in starting and expanding businesses just so they can take a bite of the CMS profit pie. OK, I admit I find that kind of beautiful, too.

Did I mention that many professional venture capitalist partners were once business owners who sold their businesses and became rich? There is an interesting effect that comes into play here, more so in the later years of our strategy. By accelerating the launch and expansion of more businesses we create more situations where the business owners succeed, too. These are the people who may have originally approached a VC for funding but not received it in the days before United States 2.0. In the example above we would be talking about the people who founded the small mobile app company. If their plan succeeded even moderately, that company's founders would become wealthy, especially once they sold out. In United States 2.0 there is a newly attractive enterprise for wealthy former business owners to take part in. They can either start new venture capital companies, or join with an existing one as contributing partners. So the money engine revs faster even with our foot at the same spot on the gas pedal.

Bank Walkthrough

The banking system is a fundamental part of any capitalist infrastructure. Most every adult who earns an income in the U.S. has a bank account of some type. Similarly, most of us take advantage of various bank services from credit cards to car and home loans at one time or another in our lives. Of course banks offer many other services, but they all reduce down to two categories. The first includes services for holding the customer's money, like checking accounts and CDs. The second category comprises services related to loaning money to customers. The complete list of these is quite a menu of loan types.

For businesses, the lending menu is particularly complex and includes services that help companies turn equity into cash. For example, an investment bank may help a private company go public. This means the bank provides a package of services that turns this privately-owned company into a public one by taking all the required actions to allow the company's stock to be traded on one of the popular stock exchanges. The process typically leaves the original private owners wealthy since they often sell a large portion of their stock holdings to accomplish the task, but that is not the only reason to go public. Doing so can also provide a cash infusion to the company itself, allowing it to implement new product plans and expansions. In other words, when a company goes public, new jobs are likely to result.

IV. Solution Walkthrough

For the purposes of this part of the presentation we need to understand two things. First, the banking examples I will give here are merely representative of our strategy. The actual CMS portfolio of bank services would likely be much more encompassing of available bank loan services. Second, Magnified Capitalism only deals with the side of banking that provides money, in other words, loans. We do not touch services having to do with holding money, like savings accounts. On the loan side, CMS services include investment-banking, since these activities end up providing money to expanding businesses. However, that topic is more complicated than we need to get into here. The point I am trying to make is that I do not need to describe every kind of bank scenario that CMS will participate in. It is enough to give a simpler banking example. Once we see how the program works in such a case, we can then imagine that the many other more complex banking cases would be comparable.

There is a notable contrast between the way banks make their money and the way a VC, business, or private investor does. In a typical investment, the investor risks some money and that money is locked away until they cash out their investment. This is basically the same whether they are buying stock in a company, real estate, or a valuable painting. We may add the caveat that it is common to borrow part of the money needed to make such investments. Regardless, in general, banking works differently from business investment in an important way.

When a bank provides a customer with money in the form of a loan, the bank is not loaning out its money. It is loaning out the money that it holds from other people and businesses – all those savings and checking accounts, for instance. It is not the bank's money. The bank is a middleman shuffling capital from a pool of customers who want a depositing service (those bank accounts) to a pool of customers who need loans. The government only requires the bank to keep a portion of deposits on hand. They are allowed to loan the rest to others at a far higher interest rate than they pay to their depositors. So banking is more like an exchange service than it is like a private investor. One part of the bank promises to hold the customers' money in return for interest and services. The other part of the bank uses most of that money to generate a profit (usually) from conservative loan-based transactions. On top of that, most banks are insured by the government so that if they mess up so much that they go under, the bank's depositors will still be able to get most of their money back out.

Notice that a bank gains an advantage when it can muster more depositors. This gives the bank a greater ability to provide more loan services. Finally, the Fed (Federal Reserve of the United States) also provides loan services to banks at special rates. This allows banks to borrow money at rates that are generally even lower today than the rate they pay their depositors. This complicates the banking system tremendously, but we are only noting it here for completeness.

So what does Magnified Capitalism do for banks? It provides government-amplified loans to banks, not that different from the way VCs receive amplified investment options in their deals. A bank can bring in the CMS as a partner in a portion of their loans. The CMS will put up some part of the loan in return for a smaller part of the profit than the bank gets. However, the CMS still makes a fair profit. It is as if the bank has a richer partner that does not need to make as much money but also does not want to manage the account nor take quite as much risk.

We can imagine a specific example of a fictitious institution called WXYZ Bank. Managers in the bank's headquarters have registered WXYZ as an approved CMS loan provider and received their CMS ratings. The same sorts of issues that applied to VCs and their ratings apply here, too. The longer a bank is in business and the more money it holds, the higher the limits it qualifies for. Also, the better the bank manages the profitability of its deposits, the better the comparable CMS risk ratings. The main difference is that with a bank, the CMS will generally be willing to put up a larger share of the money because the risk is lower, though the return is as well. Because of this factor, I will argue that we should treat the CMS as a bank, allowing it to amplify its contribution to bank loans with Fed funds. Without this modification, CMS banking activity would provide very low profitability. However, we could sustain a plan that leaves the Fed out of things to start with and then justify that element later. It is admittedly an advanced topic.

When we talked about our VC example, I omitted the topic of congressional incentives on purpose. It was sufficient at that point to look at a simple example that did not qualify for any government incentives. However, when we talk about loans from banks, we will probably need to focus on incentives of one type or another in most cases. Recall from the SWOT analysis that we decided on a standardized, multi-tiered incentive system. Some incentives might be tier grade "A", the highest incentive. Others would be lower, down to "E" grade, which simply means that the loan qualifies for no extra incentive. A student loan for a pre-med student who agrees to serve in a rural or poor urban area after college might qualify for an "A" incentive. A business loan for expanding a local factory might qualify for a "B" grade incentive. A personal loan for stock investments might qualify for a "D" grade incentive. The levels and types of incentives will vary from year to year depending on current economic policy as negotiated between the White House and Congress. What will not vary are the rules for how a bank applies the standard incentive levels available through the CMS program.

The system will work like this: A banking customer will come to WXYZ bank and ask for a loan. WXYZ will verify whether that kind of loan qualifies for a CMS contribution, and if so, what the current incentive grade is for that type of loan. The bank loan officer will probably offer detailed advice to the potential customer. For example, if the customer is seeking a student loan, the loan officer may suggest this customer consider making the kinds of commitments needed to qualify for higher incentives.

I will not be making a detailed calculation of specific examples in this section. I trust the example I used for the VC Walkthrough was enough to convey the point of the math. For banks the math would be far more complicated and would not add much more to our general understanding of how the program works. The general technique is the same as in the VC case. The point to understand is this: CMS services amplify the funds of every participating bank so they can make more loans. The result is that banks will have a new motivation to conduct a maximum of loan activity. Finally, the system will encourage participating banks to focus CMS funds on their better loans, similar to the way the system encouraged VCs to use CMS funds on the best deals. Thus, once again the CMS tends to participate in only the highest quality banking loan investments.

The main difference between the way a VC will experience the CMS system and the way a bank will experience it, other than the complexity of the math, has to do with the use of the incentive program. I expect that CMS banking deals will be peppered with such incentives, especially in the long run. This is not a bad thing since we are setting up a system designed to handle exactly that situation. We can make the incentives strong enough to promote policy-effecting changes in student loans, car loans, home loans, personal loans and business loans. Even when a loan does not qualify for a specific incentive, CMS participation alone makes the bank more motivated to approve loans. But the addition of the incentive program nudges various markets and individuals towards the policy direction of the day. The incentives should directly impact everyone. We can set up a system that gives the President the direct means to make it easier to buy an electric car, to buy property in an urban zone, to obtain most business loans, or to go to school if the prospective student has good grades and is willing to do some community service after college.

Business Walkthrough

It is tempting to say that because bank loans will be easier to obtain, we have done enough to assist the expansion of existing businesses. But I do not believe this would be true. There is a large class of potential business expansion that would be left on the table. Even with Magnified Capitalism's loan-easing effect, banks will only approve loans for relatively low-risk situations. Typically this would require the business to provide either tangible collateral or a well-established credit history that covers an amount close to the loan total. This leaves a lot of business opportunities out of the equation. We can view this discrepancy as a money-gap between the venture capitalist and the bank. If a business goes to a venture capitalist for funding, the VC will usually want a lot in return for their money, including a significant portion of company stock and likely some degree of management influence or even direct business control.

That is asking an awful lot from an existing company that just wants to expand its business, especially if it is otherwise successful.

In contrast, banks will offer loans only for certain kinds of expansions that are cut-and-dried. If the expansion involves a complicated business plan then the odds of getting a bank loan drop low. The bank will suddenly focus more on collateral or credit rating in such a case. If these are not sufficient, the bank may choose not to offer the loan even in the United States 2.0. That is why we have identified existing businesses as a third target for CMS participation. With Magnified Capitalism, any decent plan to expand business from an established company should receive funding. If needed, the CMS will provide that funding directly to the company in question through the service called *Business Expansion Participation*. Let us explore a fictional example of what that might look like.

We will imagine a fictional company called Micro Widgets, Inc. They make accessories for cell phones and tablet computers. Micro Widgets has been working on a cool new product, a WiFi booster so thin and small it will fit in your wallet or pocket. They call it the Micro Booster. It will make portable devices that use WiFi work from up to 5 times farther away, or in areas that suffer from interference. Marketing has a business plan with good data to show they will be able to sell millions of these devices at a great profit. The engineering department has even filed patents on some of the technical design aspects. The whole plan has been presented to the President and other senior management at Micro Widgets and received complete approval from all the executives except for one, the Chief Financial Officer. The CFO loves the financial projections and believes in the strategy but he cannot shake the main problem: They do not have enough money to implement the plan because Micro Widgets does not have the kind of manufacturing facility they need to make the devices. Furthermore, the only way to make the plan work is for Micro Widgets to build the devices themselves. They need $30 million to launch the product if they build the factory in the U.S., or $25 million if they build the same factory in Mexico (they ruled out China because a key parts supplier is located in North America).

Either way, they are facing the same problem. They do not have the cash, and the banks have already said that the largest loan Micro Widgets qualifies for is $10 million. Part of the problem is that the recession has kept Micro Widgets' sales modest and their growth slow. The company has little debt, only light credit, and only a few million in the bank after payroll and other regular costs are covered. Micro Widgets is a private company, but because their performance has only been passable in recent years, they are not in a great position to go public. They would probably have to sell half of the company to raise the cash they need if they went down this road, or if they approached a VC firm.

IV. Solution Walkthrough

This type of situation is ripe for help from the new CMS. Just like our previous examples, the company must first register itself with the CMS by filling out an extensive questionnaire. Essentially they are filling out a loan application, except this one specifically allows for two new possibilities that most banks would not be eager to accept. First, the loan can be used for a business plan that involves new or expanded products, sales, or services. Second, the collateral for the loan can be some portion of the shares in the company even if the company is a private one. In other words, rather than giving up part of the company to obtain the money, the company puts up that part of the company as collateral against the loan. Furthermore, the terms of the loan are more like the terms of funding from a business partner or VC, not a bank. So in that sense, it is not really a loan; it is a deal.

In the CMS online application, Micro Widgets must provide a formal estimate of how much the company is worth, how much of their company they are putting up for collateral, and how much profit they expect to make from the business plan. This makes the application different from a bank loan as well. The CMS will consider the fact that the loan money is going to produce new sales. Like with a deal from a VC, a Certified Business Valuator must provide an independent assessment. The CBV is a key new type of independent service that the CMS will be using for many kinds of deals. The CBVs help keep businesses and VCs honest, and can even provide helpful advice similar to the way a tax preparer can give a consumer advice on filing their taxes. These inspectors are special accountants who double-check a company's claims for estimated worth of the company and value of the business plan. The inspectors receive a modest fee up front for their work, a bigger bonus later if they were close to correct, and a rating reduction or loss of certification if they keep getting it wrong. We will describe them more in later sections.

Once again, I will not insert a table of numbers. As was the case with the banks, numerical details do not really matter since the final program will be reworked and fine-tuned through computer simulations and testing. But the goal is the same as the results we got in the VC Walkthrough and Bank Walkthrough. The business provides a profit share to the CMS, and the contract requires complete repayment of the loan within five years. The company can repay late within six years with minor penalties; otherwise, on the six-year anniversary the CMS will own and then quickly sell the collateralized stock of the company.

The CMS would use a network of special investors for this sort of stock sales if they had to. This would be similar to the kind of special investors who buy foreclosed real estate. So the penalty for failure is high. We would put many other details in place to reduce fraud and abuse, too. For example, I mentioned that the deal needed a certified business valuation before it can be approved. In some cases the CMS may decide to require two or three independent CBVs to validate the company's financial claims, such as a borderline case involving a maximum of money. Just as the CBV's ratings improve if the deal works out, a similar consequence happens to the business, Micro Widgets in this example. Once they have successfully completed their first CMS deal their CMS rating will improve. This will empower them to make bigger deals in the future. So it pays for everyone to get it right every time.

Notice the company cannot receive the loan without taking a big risk. They could still lose much or all of the company by getting it wrong. This is as it should be. The CMS is not intended to provide money for high-risk business deals. But they do want to make sure that all the good business deals get the funding they deserve. The key is if the company is willing to bet their own stock on their success. The CMS will then only need to have one or more CBV inspectors validate that the claims being made are real. Then the business receives 100% of the money they need from the CMS. What I did not mention above is the detailed terms. The value of the collateralized stock, for example, will likely need to be much higher than the total dollar amount the CMS puts up, as much as double the CMS funding amount. If the company is not worth that much, then they may not qualify for this deal.

In our example, Micro Widgets was asking for $30 million. The total stock of the company would probably have to be worth $60 million for them to qualify in this example. That represents risking 100% of the company. If they had good financials, their risk rating might be lowered. That could reduce how much their stock would need to be worth for collateral.

Also, we are assuming they are building their manufacturing facility in the U.S. Why? Because there will almost certainly be some strong incentives in any CMS deal for them to keep the factory here. Maybe we reduce the collateral, or reduce the amount of profits they have to share, or even offer a cash bonus if they succeed. We will design and test the actual incentives to be sure they work as we need them to. But the point is that this company now has a new avenue for expanding their business. They would be wise to be careful. But if they have a great idea and a good business plan, they will now have a way to achieve their business goals that was not previously available.

Actually, I admit I designed the Micro Widgets situation to show a company that was stuck. They could not implement their plan without this new kind of help. The reality will usually be a bit different. With the *Business Expansion Participation* service, business-funded expansion will become so much more attractive that many businesses will begin looking for ways they can grow just so they can qualify for this funding. The reason will be similar to the reason the VCs will try to use CMS funding even though they have their own money. Profit margins are designed to be higher if they use CMS money. Also, their business power will go up if they use CMS money. Therefore, even companies that would not have otherwise needed it will start applying for such business expansion deals. The Micro Widgets example shows the CMS as a logjam breaker. The real world will see far more businesses taking advantage than just this type of case.

Businesses will be expanding left and right just to flex their power, improve their CMS ratings, and raise their total profits. Most businesses will want to take advantage of favorable loan terms and related government incentives. Just as there are tax specialists, books and seminars today, in United States 2.0 a new specialty will develop. This new area will teach businesses to improve their outlook by leveraging CMS-based services and incentives. The capital magnification will occur on a wider scale than the original target intended. Notice that this race for businesses to acquire CMS funds will still require that they expand. The result is another beautiful thing. Existing businesses will go on an expansion spree, which naturally translates to a hiring spree.

Private Investor Walkthrough

Why do we need to include more services? After all, the three CMS services I already described will spur the economy. The reason is simple: our strategy calls for it. I think a key tenet of business planning is to design a great strategy and then follow it 100%. Stopping now would be wrong because there is one more target to hit. I said we can trace new jobs to four sources of money, four types of capitalist. We cannot forget this last one. Ironically, it may even be the most important of them all.

The private investor is the most American of capitalists. They take the most risk. Now, we might think that makes them the worst candidate for capital magnification. After all, the CMS already favors lower-risk opportunities from all the other capitalists. Why even bother with the wildcat version? The private investor is most apt to make a series of bad mistakes and high-risk investments, and even arguably be the largest source of abuse and fraud. I would not disagree with any of these points. But there is an important issue to consider. Most angel investors are private investors. The angel investor is the one who backs a brand new idea from nothing. If we have a great business plan but no team to help us build the business case, we probably need to see an angel investor. If we have a patent concept but no business plan, we might want to find an angel investor. If we go to our rich uncle to borrow money to start a retail business and he provides that money, that uncle is our angel investor. Anyone who backs a business that does not yet exist in any form is essentially an angel investor. These are the types of private investors I am particularly interested in.

There is more to the private sector than just the angel investors. Magnified Capitalism can help a variety of private investors, even those we would not have called "investors" before. There are even two different CMS services that can help people with no money and no business plan. I am not talking about gifts here. Everyone who plays with the CMS must make a deal where they take a risk in order to gain anything. Then they have to work hard. This is capitalism, but extended to a deeper level than previously possible. The CMS has to offer a range of different services to cover all private investors, but it goes so deep that absolutely anyone can participate. I will get to all of these services shortly. For now, let me focus on the easiest and most obvious target. I will start with the angel investor, and then the others will follow. I must make one more aside about the private investor, or private entrepreneur, before I go there, however.

For those who might still prefer to focus only on the "professional" capitalist, here is a rub to consider. To have a purring economy with this new system, every part of the engine needs to be working in a new, higher gear. So far we have made sure the business pipeline is well fed with capital in three of our four strategic targets. Banks will be spurred into helping businesses and individuals who need loans. Established businesses with great new ideas will have access to a new source of capital for their expansion plans. Venture capitalists will have their abilities magnified. The VCs can help either fledgling businesses on the verge of success or very professional start-ups. But where do the fledglings come from? How do we feed that pipeline?

There is an entrepreneur behind most every fledgling business. These true capitalists work on new business ideas, take risks and approach angel investors. They work hard for high risk until they are either ready for the big bucks, make it on their own, or fail. If we do not support this part of our economic pipeline, then we are ignoring the part of the car where the gas first enters the engine. We need to upgrade every part of the racecar or we take a risk. Do we want to create a choke-point on purpose?

Even though private entrepreneurs are the kind of capitalists that make the most mistakes, United States 2.0 needs them to step it up, too. Especially once the system really gets going, we may need these kinds of investors most of all. The question is not whether we help them, but how we do it without getting burned by all the risk. After all, as I suggested, this is also the field where we might expect to find the people who are most unconventional, least disciplined, most prone to error, most needing of help, and even most inclined to be criminals. The bottom line is interesting. The private investor group is the trickiest of our four targets, but they could be the most important.

There is a special reason why private investors are a particularly important group of capitalists to support. Perhaps it is not so critical to point out this reason since I have already justified the matter. However, this may be a point that appeals to all of us on an intuitive level. Therefore this is also a political point. Here we go. The private investor is the largest and least privileged group of the four types of capitalists. All a person needs to join it is an entrepreneurial spirit. As we will see, a private investor can have money, or they can have a great idea, or they can just be willing to bet on themselves. A private investor is anyone with a dream to succeed and a willingness to turn that into action. In other words, of our four capitalist targets, this is the group that most Americans can hope to join directly themselves.

For the first time in the history of any country, America will truly deliver on its own rhetoric. Everyone can go for it if they are willing to try. To me this is a way of saying that in United States 2.0 we are going to bring the American dream within reach of anyone and everyone. Including this fourth type of capitalist broaden's our strategy's reach. We are not just saying we want to help businesses and rich people. We are saying we want to help everyone who is motivated to start a new business. That is absolutely everyone, no matter their situation. This is the part of the strategy that makes Magnified Capitalism both fair and attractive to every citizen, even if they do not see how they will benefit from the rest of it.

Now that we are excited to help individual citizens become entrepreneurs, we are ready to explain how to do it. Remember that the key to addressing this segment effectively is to provide services in such a way as to minimize the government's exposure to both failure and fraud.

I have designed four different magnification programs to help our private investor segment. I call them Private Venture Funding, Cash Flow Assistance, Patent Funding Program, and the Prototype Development Network. These four programs are intended to solve the different types of hurdles that a small company or fledgling startup faces due to insufficient funding. The first, Private Venture Funding, is a general solution. With this service an investor can greatly improve their access to available funds. They can further improve their terms if they can find qualified partners and/or mentors to join their effort. Cash Flow Assistance allows an existing small business to borrow a small part of their business equity. The Patent Funding Program is a new way to patent a great idea without having the $30,000 to $100,000 it takes to push through that process today. And finally, the Prototype Development Network (PDN) is a way to have foundational business development done for free in return for a share of the success. The PDN will allow any good business concept to be prototyped with no upfront investment. Once prototyped, a business idea becomes a much better candidate for formal venture capital funding or angel investment. Perhaps just as importantly, the PDN is a new way for the out-of-work or underemployed to build their resumes, become productive, and perhaps even make a living. Each of these four programs is separate so we can combine them in any mix needed. Here is some detail on each.

Private Venture Funding

On the surface this program is similar to the program described for professional venture capitalists. We can imagine creating a new lower grade of venture capitalist that therefore has the highest risk level, so receives less advantageous terms and conditions. This is enough to allow anyone to obtain some CMS funding. They just have to put up some part of their business as collateral and have that portion professionally judged by at least two different Certified Business Valuators. This program will also measure private investors for risk and rating, just like any VC. Their age, experience, past dealings with CMS, and legal records will come into play. Some investors may be turned down, but in practice we should try not to do that for anyone but proven criminals. Rather, the CMS should just keep reducing the amount of the loan (or deal) they are willing to make, proportional to the project's risk and the individual's past experience.

We should not discourage microloans. Very small business, taken in bulk, can have a profound impact on local economies. This is a recently proven phenomenon that many people have used effectively in other parts of the world more than in the U.S. The Private Venture Funding program can be a means for us to participate in the success of microfinancing. But this same program scales up, too. If someone has a good background and a moderate amount to invest, the government should be willing to help them at somewhat higher limits. And so these limits should continue to increase as the applicants' qualifications improve further.

The key is this: When we say that the terms are not as attractive for private investors as they are for a professional VC, we are generally referring to two different aspects of the lending situation: the terms for success and the terms for failure. Less attractive terms for success means the government receives a bit more of the pie when an investor succeeds. Less attractive terms for failure means the government expects to be exposed to a decreasing percentage of any losses. With a large pool of such deals, the government covers its higher risks and maintenance costs by making the offered deals somewhat less attractive than similar deals made to professional venture capitalists. We will have to work out the exact balance in testing and simulations however, because this is an economic needle-threading. We still want these capital deals to be attractive enough that most who qualify will take the deal. However, we cannot go so far in that direction that the abusers and higher rates of failure make the numbers bad for the CMS. The private investor part of the program should not be significantly less profitable than any of the other three capitalist targets. We will have a similar testing and tuning requirement for all Capital Magnification Service programs and standard deals. However, the need to get this just right is strongest for the private investor segment.

It may strike some people that this program is particularly weak for an average person of ordinary means. That is not entirely an accident. This program should not expose the government to such an abnormal risk of failure due to lack of business experience, for example, that it is forced to make too many large deals that fail to become profitable. However, there is a path for the person who thinks they have a great business strategy but not the means to qualify for the private funding deal they need. They can sign up with one or more partners who can share the financial burden. If that is not sufficient, they can try to get one or more mentors to take them on. Let me explain this interesting incentive that is built into private venture funding.

The government needs to minimize exposure to risk so it rates the applicants for a deal according to various factors like their history, collateral, and experience. The resulting rating determines the terms of the deal the CMS is willing to offer, including the all-important maximum funding amount. If an applicant does not qualify for a high enough maximum to execute their business plan, they can still do something about it in short order. They can try to get partners to sign up with them. Everyone who signs up as a partner will contribute to reducing the risk of the deal. That should create an increase in the maximum funded cash amount. Of course if things go south, the failure will impact all the partners' debt and ratings. But this is a way to allow the market to self-regulate.

If the original applicant has a truly great business plan, they should have no trouble signing up enough partners to take the risk with them. If they cannot do that then perhaps they need to improve their original plan. And that is exactly the point. Alternately, or even in addition, a business idea may need so much money that a small team of partners is not enough to provide the money that the plan calls for. Then the people involved would have two more options left. The original partners could try to build a huge collection of partnerships that resembles a cooperative, or perhaps more accurately, an employee-owned business. This is a fascinating effect of Capital Magnification that I hope becomes very popular.

The other road the entrepreneur could consider is to approach a business mentor. This is similar to approaching a professional venture capitalist, except the mentor is a bit smaller and perhaps less vested. In other words, the person with the idea can try to find a senior investor with some means and good credit. They would be called a mentor because they will probably receive a larger share of the business success than the original entrepreneur does for their money. But if the idea is so big that the entrepreneur needs a mentor, then that should not matter. A smaller piece of a big pie is still a big piece of pie. Besides, the entrepreneur will not receive just money from such an arrangement. Most mentors will have good experience, detailed guidance and advice to offer. Most likely their participation will drive many business plan modifications that should improve the odds of success. The mentor may even want to have an active role in running the business.

The improvement of the odds of success should be evident when the Certified Business Valuations are conducted. The entrepreneur, the regular partners, and the mentor would work out the details together, not unlike a deal worked out with a professional venture capitalist. Usually, the mentor will put up some of their own money and offer some of their other resources as collateral. But the main purpose of including the mentor is to partner with a pro who really knows what they are doing. Their experience and background should go a long way to improve the whole business team's ability to obtain CMS funding. I expect that a new capitalist service will emerge to help address the need for mentors, the professional CMS business mentor. They will be like mini-venture capitalists whose emphasis is on helping upstarts improve their business planning.

Real professional venture capitalists or collections of wealthy people who want to move in that direction will probably even offer mentoring programs. We could spawn a new market for such micro venture capitalists. They would seek to leverage the CMS program for inexperienced entrepreneurs who have good ideas and motivation. This would truly open up capitalism to every level of society, bringing the American dream closer to reality for anyone with the guts to go for it. By offering such services to people of lesser means, the micro venture capitalist will do exactly what the CMS wants to see happen. The market will insure that good ideas are nurtured and adjusted so they are more likely to succeed. Bad ideas will either be filtered out, or transformed into good ones that have a chance for success. Risk lowers. Rates of CMS profitability go up. Capital magnification touches more new businesses. Our plan reaches an important yet most difficult goal.

Cash Flow Assistance

Private venture funding is great for helping new businesses get started, but that is not the whole answer to supporting private investors through the CMS. We certainly do not want to ignore small businesses that have already been launched but are hitting some bumps. That is why we add the Cash Flow Assistance program to the private investor portfolio. In this case the need we are addressing is the situation in which an existing small business gets stuck due to cash flow problems. It is a very common problem.

Imagine we started a dry cleaning business in one location. We invested all our money, borrowed everything we could, worked hard to set the business up, and now we are one year down the line. The business is working pretty well. The number of regular customers is increasing over time. But we have a problem. To handle our increasing traffic we need more equipment. That will result in a much higher profit since we will not have to hire too many more people to handle it. With the equipment we have today, we are having trouble keeping up with business demand. This problem stops us from growing and that in turn keeps our profits just barely positive. Our bank credit is tapped out. We have no spare cash to buy the equipment we need. This is a very ironic situation. We can see what we need to do to make our business profitable and healthy, but we are short of the means to get what we need to do it. This is the cash flow problem. Our money is all tied up in the cash cycle of the business.

The key to this kind of deal is that we have an existing business with well-established cash flow. We ought to be able to borrow an amount of money roughly equal to two or three months' worth of operating costs. If that is enough to make an investment in equipment that will measurably improve our cash flow or total monthly business, this is not a bad risk. The CMS should offer such a loan (or deal) if the business meets all the criteria I just described. This is not a loan for trying to save a drowning business. It is a loan for a business that is on its way up if except for that one obstacle they need to overcome. The applicant has to be able to show that this is the case. A Certified Business Valuator will need to sign off on the claims as part of such a CMS application. This service will act like a high-interest loan with both business and equipment as collateral. It is intended to be a short-term loan but could be converted to a longer-term one if there is a good explanation for why the profits were delayed.

Patent Funding Program

Another gap we can fill is one many people may not be aware exists. This is the problem of filing a patent. While anyone can technically file a patent for under $200, if that is our total budget and we are not ourselves patent attorneys, we can expect the effort to be a complete waste of time. Without professional assistance almost all patent filings are rejected on technical grounds. There is a reason why patent attorneys exist, and why a regular attorney will refer to the specialist patent attorney whenever they have a client with a patent claim. It is really hard to get a patent approved. I will not go into the very deep and complex reasons why. It is enough to say that the effort is nearly impossible without specialized legal help. Not only that, but a successful patent process can take about three years from the first filing to the date the patent office finally grants the patent.

Since we need the patent attorney in order to have a ghost of a chance, we can expect the total cost of our patent to range from $30,000 to as much as $100,000 or more. These costs are 99% attorney fees. We will owe this amount whether the patent office issues the patent or not. The amount it costs varies according to how complex the matter is and the luck of our timeline. That is, if things go quicker, the cost tends toward the lower side. Lest patent attorneys misunderstand my position, let me be clear about another thing. These high fees are not generally a rip-off. Doing this legal work is difficult and requires specialized education. Patent attorneys earn their money, especially if they manage to get the patent to go through.

If we want to be the most competitive nation in the world we need to recognize that the patent issue is a big problem. It means that only medium-sized and larger corporations can afford to file patents regularly. The average person with modest means cannot even afford to think about filing a patent today. Yet, this is where most of the great new ideas come from. There is one more key matter to consider. If we have a patent issued to us, we can sell it to an investor (or a company). Alternately, we can build a complete business plan around the patent and try to obtain venture capital funding. With a patent in hand, the odds of a professional VC seriously considering our plan go way up. Having a patent is very strong evidence that the idea is unique enough to legally fend off some amount of competition. It also differentiates our business strategy from all the others out there.

Before I go on to offer a solution, I want to highlight an issue that high patent costs enable. This is the fact that existing businesses tend to offer relatively tiny rewards, if any, when their own employees produce patentable ideas for them. The employer has the employee locked up in two ways. First, thanks to the employee agreement that they probably signed when they took the job, the employer owns all the employee's ideas, or at least the ones they invent that address the employer's business. Second, the employer knows that the cost of patenting is prohibitively high. It is so expensive that employers typically pursue patents for only a small percentage of their employees' ideas. It is hardly an option for anyone to quit their job just to file a patent on their own.

This last point creates little motivation for businesses to reward inventors who work for them. Some companies do offer patent bonuses. A few make it just barely worth the trouble, but most only offer token rewards to employees who produce patentable ideas. However, if we made it easier for a private individual to file for a patent, this situation would certainly change. Just to protect themselves from losing their smartest people to the enticement of going it alone, existing businesses would need to greatly increase their standard rewards for employee-produced patents. As far as United States 2.0 is concerned, this consequence is fabulous. With higher rewards will certainly come more motivation to invent within the company the employee works for. An easier patenting process will also create an increase in private patents. The result will be more patents from everywhere. Now we just need to solve the original problem.

How do we empower citizens with the ability to file for patents themselves? The answer is the CMS Patent Funding Program service. Recall that the main cost of the patent process is the price of hiring and maintaining a patent attorney. The government fees are a small fraction and should total under $1000 from start to end. The Patent Funding Program therefore focuses on deferring the cost of the lawyer's services. Here is how we can do that: Patent attorneys will become a special entity at the CMS. They will register themselves and be tracked, not unlike a Venture Capitalist or Bank. That means they will be rated for the quality and risk of the patents they file.

Here is what the CMS will do for them: They can receive payment three times from the CMS as part of the deal they make with the patent owner. The first time they get paid occurs with a valid and accepted patent filing. The second payment is a larger amount if the patent office approves the patent. The third payment is the largest of all, occurring when the entrepreneur obtains funding or sells the rights to the patent. In other words, the big payoff happens when the CMS gets its money back, with interest, as part of the third step.

This is a bet on the attorney more than the inventor. A better rating for the attorney will improve their terms (and hence, payments). As part of the first step, a Certified Business Valuator is also required to provide an estimate of what the patent is worth, as well as any business plan that leverages the patent. This will help both the lawyer and the CMS determine if this effort is worth the trouble. From the inventor's point of view, the goal of filing a patent becomes greatly simplified. Now, instead of trying to come up with a huge amount of cash to gamble on the patent filing, an inventor only needs to do a far simpler thing. He or she need only convince a CMS registered patent attorney that his or her patent is good enough to be converted into a business, or be marketable, once it is accepted.

An experienced patent attorney together with a Certified Business Valuator should have little trouble picking out the good ideas from the more risky ones. The attorney will barely make a living if they regularly choose patent applications that are rejected. If they continue filing bad patents they can be suspended or removed from the CMS program. A good attorney should be able to run a fine practice by supporting mostly strong patents through the CMS service. Incidentally, this will also have the effect of encouraging more new lawyers to become patent specialists, because there will be a new and straightforward business model for making a living through the Patent Funding Program. A few years down the line, the better attorneys, even the younger ones, will make a windfall from their more successful patent filings and the bigger payments that come with those. More attorneys working on these patent filings will result in even more competition to find inventors who want to file.

Once again we have used the technique of magnifying market pressures to produce desirable economic effects. In this case, we have made it more attractive to become a patent attorney and easier to for patent filers to fund the process. The result is more patents, more businesses from those patents, and more success for everyone involved. Incidentally, although the purpose is to help individuals file patents, businesses can use the same program to file patents, too.

The main caveat is that a business may choose not to use the Patent Funding Program due to three main downsides. First, a sufficiently successful business will usually guarantee a patent buyout, or repayment plan, once the patent is granted. In other words, they would expect to be the buyers of their own patent, so there are only two attorney payment stages instead of three. The business only has to make the big second payment, however, once the patent is granted. The second problem is that failed patent efforts would affect an individual's or business' CMS rating. For a person, this is arguably a minor penalty. That is why the CMS focuses more on the attorney's rating for this service. For a business, however, risking lowering their CMS rating is likely to be a more serious consideration. The final disadvantage for a business to use this service is the cost. The total cost of filing a patent this way is expected to be higher than if they completed the filing conventionally. Why? Because the CMS gets a cut and the CBV must be paid. I expect participation in the Patent Funding Program to add as much as 100% to their total costs. But the business will only pay this amount if the patent is granted. Thus it is a deferred payment. It is a business decision whether it is better to pay $50,000 now for an unknown result, or $100,000 for an approved patent in a few years. In many cases businesses will be glad to have the option.

From the CMS's perspective, the return on investment for the patent program is similar to the model we used for VCs. That is, the money paid to the lawyers is not really a loan. Rather, it is a business deal. The CMS expects to get a cut of the money made from the successful patents. This includes minimums and an equity stake. In other words, by participating in the CMS program, the inventor is essentially selling a part of their future patent to the CMS in return for the money they need to see the patent through. The exact share depends on the official business valuation and the rating of the attorney that the inventor signs up. Notice the effect of a better lawyer here and throughout the program. Inventors will be encouraged to shop their patent ideas around to find the best lawyer they can. By this I mean one with the highest CMS rating. A higher rating will improve the terms of their CMS-based deal. From the government's perspective this produces a fine market effect. The highest-quality lawyers will claim the bulk of the good patent ideas. This is exactly what we want, as we can afford to pay better terms to the lawyers who produce the most winners.

Prototype Development Network

The fourth program we want to establish for supporting the private investors has to do with turning an idea into a functional device, sample product, or demonstrable service. Those of us who have tried to obtain venture capital funding for a new business are very familiar with this problem. It is classically a chicken and egg problem for the entrepreneur with a great business idea. If we take our great idea to a VC to try to get funding they will ask for two things. First, do we have a patent? We addressed this problem in the previous program. The second thing they will ask is, "Do you have a working prototype?" Alternately, they may ask a similar question for other types of businesses: "Have you tested your business model in the marketplace?" This second version is like a prototype but for services. Regardless, the punch line is similar. If we expect someone to put up a bunch of money for our business idea, they will usually expect to see evidence that the idea will work. If the business involves a product we want to manufacture, then they will want to see a version of that product in action. If it centers around a service concept, they will want to see how far we have been able to go in simulating or testing that service with real people. If we cannot do one of these things, we may have trouble convincing even a private angel investor to help us.

The Prototype Development Network (PDN) is the CMS service designed to address this problem. It is a new way for someone with a good business idea, but insufficient funding, to take their concept to the prototype stage. I am using the term prototype broadly here. It can mean setting up a test for a new service, building a few devices by hand that will later be manufactured, testing a special device, designing or architecting a new product, testing a new product, writing functional software or an app, or testing software. By prototyping I mean doing work to advance a business concept so we get closer to proving it will work. It can even mean limited sales of a product or service to provide evidence of market viability. Any work short of a full-blown production-scale business can be called prototype development.

Here is how the PDN service works: The CMS will organize an online cooperative of people whose skills can support product prototyping and service testing. These people will be rated and tracked similar to the way patent attorneys are in the Patent Funding Program. The main difference is that the workers (a.k.a. "prototypers") will receive either low or no immediate payments on initial completion of their work. Actually, only the best and most experienced prototypers will receive any immediate payment. The reason is that there are bound to be too many volunteers here. These people should preferably do the prototyping work based on the likelihood of business success. Therefore, the prototype developers will obtain most or all of their income from deals only after the business they helped receives investor funding. Once a business gets off the ground based on these people's work, prototypers will become prime candidates for regular jobs working on the commercial versions of the product they helped to launch.

The highest-rated prototypers will receive some money from the CMS up front, and even better terms later on. As in our other programs, the original entrepreneur is essentially offering a share of their business to the Prototype Developer Network in return for the work. The CMS will retain a small percentage of any profit for its effort, advanced payments, and coordination. The bulk of the equity, however, will be split among the prototype developers. Who gets chosen as a prototype developer and what share of the business they receive is a bit complicated. Essentially, the business owner(s) will choose people with different skills from online menus and make them offers that fit into simplified categories, or packages, that the CMS designs for this purpose. This system will make it far less risky for all sides of the deal, as the terms and conditions will be based on tested standards. The entrepreneur will only need to negotiate standard grades.

For the prototyper's part, they can expect to receive offers that include business presentations or summaries from a variety of hopeful entrepreneurs. Such summaries will include a Certified Business Valuation, so the potential worker can have a formal assessment of what this deal might be worth if it succeeds. In the end, prototype development will result from teams formed online and governed by the Capital Magnification Service. The prototypers will come from a broad range of professions: electrical engineers, programmers, mechanical engineers, contract manufacturers (for low-volume production of prototypes), marketers, web designers, and even product testers. By signing up for the Prototype Development Network almost anyone can take a shot at participating in a new venture. These prototyping activities will often be part time, although that could be negotiated as well.

If the prototyper has no experience or skills, they would likely have trouble getting any job other than some type of testing role. They would also likely be offered only the minimum standard level of compensation. But when a business prototyped in this way succeeds, even these participants could receive a handsome payment for their efforts. The more interesting case, however, is the prototyper with informal or self-taught skills. That can still mean most everyone because nearly anyone can teach themselves a new skill or convert an existing hobby into one. A budget-conscious entrepreneur might choose a motivated person like this to do interesting work that they otherwise would not qualify for.

The PDN has a powerful side effect. It produces a new way for anyone to gain experience in whatever type of profession they are interested in. It lowers the bar for people who want to change professions because it takes less formal training and experience than they would need to switch careers in the usual way. To participate in a new career in the Prototype Development Network we just have to do two things. First, we must make a good case that we can do the work. This can be as simple as an explanation of a hobby, or some reading we have done, or a class we took online. For some it might even be a case of willingness to study or be guided by the managers of the startup. The second thing we will need is flexibility in terms of payment. We probably will not be paid at all for about a year, perhaps longer. If the argument for our skill set is weak, our payment level may also be on the low side. Remember, these are business deals that only pay off if the business obtains funding or otherwise succeeds.

But even if prototypers do not end up making any money on a specific project, those who do prototype work will build real world experience and references. We will improve our entire population's skill set and their resumes just through the efforts of those motivated enough to try. This is what I meant by an entrepreneurial offer for anyone and everyone. A prototyper will gain real experience for sure. They might also get paid later on, and if they are lucky, they may even be paid well. But the most valuable aspect is the work experience.

Once someone has worked on a PDN deal, if they did a good job, they will be able to sign onto another project with an easier argument and better terms. Eventually their resume will improve to the point that they could qualify for a regular job with their new skill set, that is, if they do not receive an offer for a job from one of the companies they helped get started.

We may notice that the PDN service has a particularly low risk exposure for the government. CMS payments are designated for a minority of prototypers with very high ratings. Otherwise they only need to cover the cost of running the program. Therefore, PDN deals do not need to secure a very large portion of the business equity. The entrepreneur should therefore find this service highly attractive since they give so little to the government in exchange for all this volunteer work.

We may also notice that this program produces a means for almost anyone to make a living, even if such work is part time and payment-deferred. I want to be careful not to mislead anyone, however. There will be many people who do work as prototypers without any compensation. Part of the problem with being an entrepreneur, whether at this level or a higher one, is that a person can work very hard and end up with little to show for it. This is a matter that we should consider carefully. Although anyone can make the attempt, it may not be the best solution for everyone. However, as I promised, the offer allows anyone to share in the capitalist dream. This dream is an opportunity for success, not the promise of it. I do expect that most people who are persistent should eventually find some degree of success as prototypers.

This brings me to a caveat. In simulation testing for the entire CMS program we may find that we achieve better (or similar) results if most prototypers receive at least a token payment for their participation. By "most" I mean those who meet some minimum standard, such as verified and accepted results from the entrepreneur (i.e., they actually fulfilled their duties and their work was approved). It is not critical to decide this issue now. It will likely be easier to make the non-guarantee of payment attractive and profitable to both business and government. It will also weed out poorly-performing prototypers, such as those trying to scam unsuspecting entrepreneurs. However, if such scams can be limited by other means, a minimum payment to anyone who does a reasonable job will make the Prototype Development Network a more attractive forum for the masses.

The PDN could ultimately become a way to elevate our collective productivity. Those who can work multiple part time jobs could do so. Those who have trouble finding work any other way may be able to make a living through the PDN. And those who want to switch professions or otherwise need to beef up their resume with fresh experience in some field will now have a fighting chance to do that. If nearly everyone is sure to get paid something, even if the project fails, the PDN becomes a far more popular means for addressing such workforce improvements. Therefore I strongly recommend that we carefully consider and test the minimum payment option.

Workforce improvement was not my original goal in this strategy, so I did not require the minimum payment. However, workforce improvement is a worthy goal in itself. It is possible that simulation testing will support somewhat less attractive standard offers to the entrepreneur in return for minimum payments to even the lowest-rated prototypers. I would encourage such an alternate implementation if we could still maintain a highly attractive solution to the original problem. Remember, we want to make it easy for new business ideas to get off the ground. If the PDN provides a smaller pool of workers because prototypers must be willing to gamble on their ability to pick successful projects, then smaller is OK. If the network is huge because so many people find part time work this way, that would be fantastic. I do not need to predict which outcome will occur to meet the plan goal. It is sufficient to know that the Prototype Development Network will meet the primary goal under any variation. It would be a dream come true if this network was the final step that brought unemployment to historic lows, and raised national productivity to levels above those we previously thought possible. This kind of possibility is just gravy.

I have an extra observation to add before we go on. It is not really that critical to our plan, but it is both unexpectedly interesting and slightly helpful to the big picture. We did not spend too much time discussing the kind of deals the PDN could offer to prototypers. The main compensation is a small piece of the business equity. We can think of it as getting paid with some stock from a startup company. It is a lottery ticket of sorts. Most people will cash in the equity with the very first investor offer. In fact, I expect that this will be a government-required option. In other words, if a private investor or VC funds a business that previously used the Prototype Development Network, then that funding must include enough money to minimally pay off the prototyper's efforts. This will insure closure and payment to both the government, and to those who gambled on providing their personal services. It is possible, if the prototype concept is wildly attractive and the entrepreneur very shrewd, that this initial equity would turn out to be worth far more than the minimum required. In these cases, the prototype workers will share in the success proportionally with the entrepreneur. So prototypers can have an upside surprise. Occasionally, some will even become wealthy this way, but we should expect this to be a rare and limited occurrence.

Regardless, part of the standard terms for prototypers will be the option to defer part or all of their payment, depending on how much of the company they want to hold onto. Imagine we are paid 10,000 shares of a nascent company to do some work to help them get off the ground. Ten months later they offer us 50 cents per share for that work we did. We could cash it all in and get $5,000, or we could keep some or all of those shares instead. If the prototyper really believes that the underlying business will take off, holding those shares for a few years might be a brilliant move. I imagine many more prototypers will become wealthy this way than by selling out in the initial offer. Some prototypers will hold large portions of their earned equity in the companies they helped start. Once some of these businesses become publicly traded, the prototypers who held most of their stock payments will collect big.

Of course, like many business decisions and investments, this is the gambler's move of a capitalist. It is also another way capitalism will be magnified under United States 2.0. We will not only produce more ways to make a living; we will produce more pathways to earned wealth. Notice there is no gift here. When wealth happens it still comes from good work, smart decisions, and even some risk taking. It just becomes easier for more people to participate in the kind of processes that can produce wealth. That is a cool thing. It also helps the whole strategy when wealth becomes increasingly common. So here is another way that will happen.

Solution Walkthrough - Conclusions

The more we flesh out the details of our strategy, the more concrete the impact becomes. For me, Magnified Capitalism becomes authentic when we see what it does for actual businesses and people. It will spur each of our four strategic targets to a higher level of business activity. It will amplify and proliferate the professional venture capitalist segment. Their rise will generate more new businesses and jobs, along with an emphasis on growth in areas of strategic national importance. Bankers will be awash with new motivations to lend more money for all types of purposes, especially those with CMS-provided sweeteners.

These sweeteners are just a reflection of national policy embodied in CMS incentives. Existing businesses will start mining their own organizations for new growth strategies, because any good growth strategy will provide them with an excuse for CMS funding under favorable terms. We should watch out for unprecedented growth in previously conservative business circles. In fact, growth should become the new standard for existing businesses. Business growth means more jobs, naturally.

And then there is the private investor. Sitting on a large bank account has never been as interesting as it will be in United States 2.0. It is going to be attractive to fund startups and build our CMS rating. We can dive in heavy or take the more careful route of becoming a mentor. Entrepreneurs will have new methods to develop their ideas, whether they get together with friends in an investor partnership, or just take that patentable idea directly to an attorney.

There will be options for everyone. By everyone, I mean even those who are not wealthy or those who previously considered themselves neither inventive nor entrepreneurs. We will make it far easier for these people to join up with others who have vision but few resources. Anyone with a brilliant idea or much-needed product plan will have a shot. There will be new ways to find needed funding, new ways to pay for key patents, and new ways to prove to investors that a business concept is viable. We will raise improving national competitiveness to an art form. Those who are not at the center of an organization can still throw their hats in the ring to help. There will be new pathways for professional growth by participating in the establishment of other people's new business efforts. For one thing, we should notice a large increase in the demand for everyone's services, whatever they may be. The demand for workers will be on a rocket ride. United States 2.0 will be a beautiful place for those who only need an opportunity to prove themselves. There are no handouts here. But we will be awash with opportunities to get a hand up.

"The Capital Magnification Service manages the largest investment fund on earth. Our customers are also our stockholders; that would be the body of all United States citizens. Under government supervision, I see our primary role as erecting and fortifying a new pillar for America. This pillar represents survivable success. We enable an exciting environment of opportunity for every citizen willing to put forth a fair effort today. In the process the CMS becomes the steward of an accumulated fortune for this great country. We have found a formula that both benefits us now and also pays a piece of today's success forward. With this approach we will insure every subsequent generation is more stable, prosperous, and stress resistant then the one that came before it."

- Future quote of a CMS CEO regarding his vision -

V. CMS Operational Plan Overview

What is the point of discussing an Operational Plan at this stage? Is it not enough to just consider whether or not we should implement the program? Once we receive approval for the formation of the Capital Magnification Service and its funding, can we not just leave organizational details to the new management?

No.

This proposal is incomplete without a description of the organization we intend to form. The discussion of the Operational Plan is arguably the ultimate purpose of this whole writing. My presentation is really just a proposal to form an organization. Everything we have talked about up to now has led us to the conclusion that we need a new branch of government, although we will operate it as a commercial organization to gain necessary efficiencies. This organization is the Capital Magnification Service.

Simply stating a strategy is not a complete solution. A detailed argument by itself is not a complete proposal. Painting a picture of the positive effects that result from a great move does not tell us what that great move is. Hopefully, Mr. President, you are convinced we need to build our new racecar. We know now that it will have rocket engines and a special steering wheel as key strategic elements. But before you decide to buy this racecar we have not built yet, you should know how we plan to do it, how it will work, and what the measure of success will be. By now you might think you will like your new car no matter what these details are. It would be wise to learn about them anyway, if only to better prepare yourself for delivery.

We will address the Operational Plan in this proposal as an overview. That means we focus on a strategic picture of what the Capital Magnification Service is, how it should be organized, and what it will take to create it. I will take a top-down approach. This means discussing the organization's vision, charter, scope and strategic goals. After that we will examine the main functions that the CMS will fulfill. In the last portion of this Plan Overview, I will provide an estimated timeline showing the steps needed to go from today's executive summary to a fully functional CMS. As a student of business planning yourself, Mr. President, you may notice that our CMS Operational Plan Overview parallels current methods for commercial project management. This is aligned with your original instruction to me.

Before I proceed with the discussion I want to address what may seem to be an obvious omission. This chapter is called an overview precisely because it is not a complete operational plan. If it were, I would also discuss CMS process flows. These concern processes that the CMS will execute in the course of conducting its business. A description of process flows involves describing exactly what each department of the CMS does as it implements services. For instance, it would answer questions about how customer registrations are handled and what processes a new service application goes through before it is approved.

There are obvious problems with trying to include such descriptions here, however. First, they involve too much detail for an executive proposal. The second problem is a bigger one. As you read this overview, Mr. President, you will see that I have purposely listed detailing CMS operations as a later step in the plan! We want a provisional CMS crew to design these details precisely because the processes themselves are subject to testing and adjustment. In contrast, our focus today is to structure a strategic, goal-oriented plan. With this approach one related point does come through. Much of the CMS process design is implied by the strategy anyway. This is because the strategy drives the intended outcomes of CMS processes.

Here is a final observation before I begin the Operational Plan Overview. Mr. President, this chapter is designed to meet your requirement that this executive proposal follow formal plan methods. It is much more than that, though. The elements we are about to address represent some key punch lines for the whole strategy. Most of the remainder of this presentation, before and after, concerns justifications and impact. But in the discussion that is about to begin, we see the animal standing clearly for what it is, stripped of most of the interpretation and analysis found elsewhere in our discussion.

Vision Statement

A vision is a view of the future that encompasses a broad goal. A good vision should be compelling and memorable, even exciting or inspirational. In the faux quote italicized at the beginning of this chapter, you read what a future CMS CEO might say about this vision. That quote captured the idea pretty well. I will extract and paraphrase this same vision here:

The CMS shall first erect and then fortify a new pillar for America. This pillar will provide ***survivable success.***

You need only remember two words from this vision: "survivable success". It might also help to imagine these words carved into a metaphorical pillar that keeps our country from falling over a cliff. Regardless, the faux quote at the beginning of the chapter explains this two-word description of our new pillar. Here is an equivalent explanation that provides a deeper elaboration.

Until just a few hundred years ago, every government that ever existed has eventually lost power or been forced to fundamentally change into a new form. Interestingly, the United States actually has one of the oldest intact governments in existence, especially if we only consider the major players. People are naively complacent when it comes to the risk of revolution, disasters and wars. Yet history teaches us that these are inevitable. There is good reason why no government or single empire of great size has ever survived more than about six hundred years (624 years for the Ottoman Empire, followed by the Romans at 503 years; the Mayan records are incomplete but they may have lasted over 700 years). None of these governments bothered to protect itself with a pillar of strength that could withstand the rare upheavals that eventually do come around. Aside from such a long-term vision it also helps to have a good measure of tolerance, freedom and justice for all, as well as avoiding too much warring and bad governance decisions. But I digress.

If we all agree that the United States is worth maintaining indefinitely, then we should do something about that. By the way, the moment when there is a big problem on the horizon is way too late. The whole purpose of a survivability strategy is to build it into the way we work every day, never stop improving it, and hope we never need it. That way, by the time we do need it, the resources we built will be thick and strong. Your challenge to me, Mr. President, was to design a strategic plan that fixes the unemployment problem. My answer is that we should build a new function the government oversees that is responsible for delivering enhanced business opportunities to everyone. That is the CMS. In the process of running the CMS we should allow some profits to continually accumulate.

The CMS Fund will never stop growing until that terrible day when we really need it, the moment a great disaster of the rarest type either hits us or looms ahead. Then we will be able to draw on the resources of many generations to make it through our terrible problem. It will be a gift from the past to help insure the future. Think of it as country-grade health and life insurance. That is why there are two words to the vision. "Success" means the opportunities and jobs offered to all citizens today and in the future. We add "survivable" in front to remind us that we will try to set the new record for a lasting government, or at least make it through the next big problem. Anyway, that is the vision I am proposing to you. We should build a new pillar of survivable success.

In my proposed vision I suggested that "survivable" be the main partner to "success". We could consider an alternative vision that produces the same result. Here we will once again produce a new American pillar, but this time we will emblazon these words on it:

Growing Prosperity from Accumulated Success

This version of our vision might have a broader appeal in that the emphasis is on continued growth. By accumulating an ever-growing CMS Fund we maintain a sort of country-insurance, as the previous wording of our vision emphasizes. Such insurance is ultimately more important than anything else to me because it means we have a new kind of resistance to major troubles. But I also suspect that some people may have difficulty getting excited about that kind of message. This alternate message about "Growing Prosperity from Accumulated Success", in contrast, allows us to emphasize a different benefit: The larger the CMS Fund grows, the more economic benefits of Magnified Capitalism we gain. Also, the larger the Fund, the more the CMS can contribute to the national budget, thereby reducing the tax burden.

As we accumulate a bigger and bigger Fund towards some rainy day, that growing Fund drives our economic racecar faster and faster. We can expect our risk of huge disasters will decline just because our population will grow so prosperous and wealthy. After all, keeping the people productively happy and rich with resources greatly reduces the risk of any sort of revolution. It also minimizes the negative impact of occasional bad governance decisions. To a slightly lesser degree a successful CMS reduces other major risks, too. More economic development should allow improved security, military, and technological development. In other words, we can position this version of the vision with a more preemptive emphasis. It is sort of like saying, "The CMS will encourage such strong economic development that we will become major-disaster-resistant." So this second vision is somewhat happier and may play better. But since I know there is no such thing as totally eliminating risk, I still prefer the idea that our strategy provides some real insurance. Take your pick. Each vision leads us down the same path.

CMS Charter

Vision represents the slice of nirvana we are striving for. The Charter represents our approach to getting there. We want the Charter to be as concise as possible because it represents a big picture view. That should keep our Charter easy to remember, or at least easy to understand. Here is my attempt at it. The Capital Magnification Service Charter contains these eight points:

1. **Citizen-Owned Company.** The CMS is a special investment fund management corporation owned equally by each U.S. citizen as a new right.

2. **Government Oversight.** The President of the United States and the Senate (or Congress) share management oversight through their seats on the Board of Directors.

3. **Magnified Capitalism Implementation Only.** The Fund managed by the CMS shall only be used to implement the principles of Magnified Capitalism, whose details can be modified by written agreement with the Board of Directors.

4. **Top Priority Is Jobs from Collateralized Deal Funding.** Management's top priority is to spur new business opportunities with deal-based investments, thereby creating jobs and commercial activity. Investments will take the form of non-controlling deals offered in partnership with existing commercial sources of capital, or deals for funds and services offered directly to private citizens. These deals will be collateralized by equity in businesses, patents, reserved assets, or by contractual agreement. Deals shall be set to cash-in or expire after no more than five years, or up to six years with some penalty.

5. **2nd Priority is to Accumulate Profits.** The second priority is for the CMS to make a maximum profit from effective and efficient deal management and accumulate those profits back into the Fund perpetually.

6. **CMS Fund Seeded by and Available to Government.** The Board of Directors will arrange for financing of the CMS Fund and startup costs. They will also determine any subsequent Fund increase, payback schedule, and subsequent drawdown that would provide revenue to the U.S. Treasury.

7. **Limited Government Controls.** Other than the administration of Fund levels, the Board of Directors management control will be limited to changes in deal incentives, penalties, legal rules, and the assignment of the CMS Chief Executive Officer (CEO) position (including compensation package). Deal incentives will utilize preset incentive grades built into CMS services. The CMS will collect detailed statistics that aid the study of its services' impact upon the economy, with the goal of better predicting the effects expected from future changes in government controls and CMS Fund levels. The CMS management will set the target budgetary impact for the sum of all deal incentives in

order to manage its profit targets; however, topic may be subject to negotiation with the Board.

8. **Transparency, Customer Service, and Careful Enforcement.** The CMS will be managed under a banner of maximum transparency in all matters feasible. This includes the publishing of details regarding processes, organizations, finances, deals and registered partners. Customer interfaces, including most customer service, will be conducted primarily by electronic means (e.g., the internet). However, management must keep customer satisfaction levels high by whatever means necessary when standard electronic interfaces fall short. Enforcement of CMS rules will allow standard processes for second opinions, escalation to higher management, and settlement through arbitration (in that order). In both commercial complaints and those that could result in criminal prosecution, all parties involved will have access to all evidence for and against, and the opportunity to provide counterevidence and question CMS employees involved in related processes.

The Charter tells us what we are forming, where the money comes from, and what the CMS will do with that money. It also makes clear what power the government has over the CMS Fund, management and rules. By understanding each part of the Charter we develop a complete comprehension of the organization responsible for implementing Magnified Capitalism.

Why Citizen-Owned?

There are a few nuances that are worth exploring deeper as an aside to the Charter. Beginning with the first point in the Charter, notice that the CMS is citizen-owned *as a new right*. This is the first time I have raised this point, so it may be a surprise. Why is it important to put it this way? The answer has to do with whose money is in the CMS Fund. By making it clear this is a citizen-owned company we accomplish two very important goals with one statement.

First, we are making it clear that the CMS is a financial extension of every U.S. citizen. Essentially, any living person who is a U.S. citizen implicitly holds one share of the Capital Magnification Service company stock. Incidentally, these shares are non-transferable. A citizen cannot buy or sell these shares. If a person stops being a citizen or dies, their particular virtual share of CMS stock disappears. But otherwise, while we are alive and in good standing, the company belongs to us all in equal measure. More importantly, so does the money in the Fund.

Herein lays the second implication of treating CMS ownership as a shared citizen-right. We are saying that the CMS is not government *owned*. It is only government *managed*. Why does that matter? Because governments can change, fall and otherwise become non-responsive to the people. If the U.S. government should ever go down any of these roads then the people will have a legal footing to keep the CMS Fund off the deck of a sinking ship. In other words, the government only manages the CMS as a representative of the U.S. citizens. This is legally the same as saying that a board of directors only oversees the management of a company as long as they represent the wishes of the stockholders. Stockholders can replace the board of directors by a proxy vote when this is no longer true. The same condition is true for the CMS. If the U.S. government fails to represent the interests of the citizens for any reason, then that government is no longer in charge of the CMS money, either.

This deals us a double protection. First, it protects us from a future situation in which the representatives of a failing U.S. government might steal from the CMS stockpile. This would most likely be a temptation just before a government collapse. By saying the CMS is a citizen-owned company, we should have more legal options for protection. The CMS is designed to survive outside any particular government. We could reasonably expect that a new U.S. government would form pretty quickly in such a situation. I am sure that having an intact CMS Fund would be most helpful for the ensuing recovery.

The second protection is even more important than the first, in my view. Having the citizens legally own the Fund removes the temptation to try any trick that redirects money away from the people's interests. This protection covers the downfall of the current U.S. government but it guards the Fund in less extreme situations as well. Consider a case where power tempts a sufficient number of Board members. Whether they are weak, or outright con artists, citizen ownership provides legal obstacles to wayward members of the CMS Board of Directors. Now any such bad guys should have far more difficulty diverting CMS funds for nefarious purposes. Whether the government is in trouble, or just some key people running it are, citizen ownership makes it more difficult for anyone to steal from our national investment fund.

Oversight Shared

I want to point out an issue in the second Charter item that I purposefully did not clarify. The Board of Directors oversees CMS management, handles Fund allocations, and can modify rules like the deal incentives. Earlier I stated that the President of the United States should be the Chair of this Board. What I did not say is how exactly the power is split between this Chair, you, Mr. President, and the other Board members. Also, I did not define exactly who populates the Board membership, how many seats there are, and what that process is like. Presumably the Board members are all U.S. Senators assigned like they would be to any Senate Committee. Alternately, the assignment of Board seats could involve a more complex process that includes participation from House members.

I cannot bring myself to set a hard rule for this process that is justified by this plan's requirements or the strategy. It only matters that both (or all) political parties are represented in roughly equally proportion to the population, and that the Chair has as much effective power as several other Board members combined. This extra power should fall short of about 40% because we do not want to make the rest of the Board irrelevant. We can negotiate this matter of managing Board membership and related power and even change it over time without affecting this plan in any way. The only issue that really matters is that the people view the Board as fairly representing their collective interests.

The Principles of Magnified Capitalism

The third Charter item states the CMS will only be used to implement the principles of Magnified Capitalism. As of this writing, these principles are all contained in the proposal before you, Mr. President. However, subsequently this situation will change. I expect to volunteer as the keeper of accepted changes to this strategy for some time to come. Please visit the previously mentioned website, www.magnifiedcapitalism.com, for the latest news on such events. I understand that at various times people will disagree with me about a range of topics, or I may become incapacitated or otherwise stop performing in this role. My hope is that eventually we will establish a formal organization that becomes the official keeper of the underlying principles of Magnified Capitalism. I suppose it could become like any other philosophy of economics. There will be the original version, the accepted modifications, and those still being proposed and fought over. Few things remain crisp and unchanging. Hopefully the arguments will keep largely to the edges.

Jobs versus Profits

I could have combined Charter items four and five since they both describe the CMS's two top priorities, that is, except for one large concern. Charter item four concerns the use of CMS services to spur the country's economic engine, thus producing jobs. Item five involves making a profit from these deals. If we stated them together we could have called them "The CMS Business Model". But I split them up because it is important that the profits be clearly subservient to the economic impact. Why? Jobs are number one because it is this priority that spawned the CMS in the first place. It was your objective, Mr. President, for me to address the issue of jobs.

The profits will be there. We should recognize and reward CMS management for achieving high profit margins. But the bigger management reward should go to those who drive a huge increase in job creation. In time I expect many people will mistakenly try to flip the priority around and push the CMS towards more profit above all else. It does not take much of a prognosticator to see that one coming. It is a mistake to do that, though. I hope most future CMS CEOs and Boards will keep a close eye on how well the CMS encourages economic growth and the related effectiveness of service incentives (the policy steering wheel).

We should always be better served by keeping the priority on economic impact. Why is that? The people will benefit most when the nation's economic racecar is running in the highest possible gear. We should also benefit significantly if we are effectively steering our economy towards policy goals that won politicians their elections. That is the main job of the CMS. The people also benefit from a CMS that turns increasingly healthy profits. But this benefit is more indirect and therefore secondary. A more profitable CMS simply means the CMS Fund grows a bit fatter that year. But if fewer jobs are created because of decisions that favor an increase in CMS profits, then we must be careful. Such decisions should only be justified if the CMS is in danger of failing to generate sufficient profits to meet minimum financial goals. The profit must be high enough to repay debts and grow the Fund. Anything more is gravy. This gravy is not worth broad economic sacrifice.

No Government Micromanagement

Charter items six and seven deal with the role of the government as represented by the Board. Item six concerns deposits and withdrawals to the Fund. Item seven involves the other functions the Board is allowed to have. This item is purposefully limiting. The Board can fire the CMS CEO, but it cannot and should not try to tell that person how to run the company. If they fire the CEO it should be mainly for failing to meet economic impact or profitability goals, and perhaps a combination of lesser goals specified in the Charter. These should be traceable to management mistakes or negligence. The only exceptions would involve serious legal or ethical violations.

Item seven mentions that the CMS, not Congress or the President, determines the total amount of money devoted to deal incentives. Why is that? There are two reasons. First, the CMS is responsible for determining the details of each incentive grade. It will decide how a level 4 (or "A" grade) incentive translates to a standard deal's terms and conditions. This includes how much this incentive grade improves a customer's profits, raises a prototyper's rating, adds bonuses, or whatever change is needed to have the appropriate impact. The same is true for all the incentive levels applied to each CMS service. That is a complicated system we will probably have to adjust each year. Why must we adjust it? That answer is the second reason the CMS is responsible for all the funds used by incentives. We will adjust incentive details to address both effectiveness as an incentive, and impact on CMS profitability.

Remember, an incentive makes CMS services more attractive to qualifying candidates. That means it also reduces the CMS profit for those qualifying deals. What if Congress went on an incentive spree and decided to create one thousand new grade "A" incentives some year? Might that not ruin the ability for the CMS to meet its profit goals? Yes, it might if we also allowed Congress to determine how to implement a grade "A" incentive. But this Charter provision says that the CMS will decide how much to invest in each incentive grade. So the effect of Congress' incentive spree would be to water down all incentives because that would be the way the CMS would have to deal with the matter.

As an example, CMS management might tell Congress in advance, "This year we have allocated 2% of our profit margin to the incentives package. We estimate this package will support 6 A-grade incentives, 10 at B-grade, 15 C's and 20 D's." They would probably also provide a dollar figure, but Congress would then know that if they can keep the total list of incentives close to the guidance amount, then all incentives will work as intended. If Congress goes nuts and tries to create too many incentives, the CMS will have no choice but to adjust the incentive terms downward so they do not lose more money than they allocated for this purpose. If Congress wants to avoid that consequence, then they can negotiate with CMS management for a higher total incentive allocation. That is OK, but everyone will be on the same page this way. If Congress needs an extraordinary package of incentives in a particular year, maybe they can do something special for the CMS team to account for that. By the way, I have said this issue involves making a deal with Congress because it is Congress that allocates the money. In practice I would expect most of the negotiations to occur at the Board level, which naturally includes the President.

I raised an important point previously but I want to emphasize it here. The original reason we set up the CMS as a corporation rather than as a government agency is that commercial organizations tend to be much more efficient. We really need that efficiency. It will translate into the CMS generating both more jobs and more Fund profits. The efficiency of a capitalist society is based largely on the competence of commercial businesses. Bad businesses fail, or at least their boards tend to fire their CEOs. Good businesses find ways to prosper. A company must be nimble, run by an experienced senior executive to do that consistently.

Government organizations are usually run very differently from commercial businesses. Federal agencies are slow to reward performance and tend instead to favor personal entrenchment and organizational politics. Such an inclination spawns these types of problems:

- Inefficient procedures as a consequence of generations of political compromise

- Difficulty proposing and adopting changes that improve efficiency and effectiveness. Instead there is political cover for those who seek minimalist solutions and a continuation of the status quo.

- Very low degree of personal responsibility. Poor performance rarely results in dismissal, especially at any level below the agency heads. Government unions (whose members are about one third of government employees) and all levels of management emphasize tenure over performance. The nature of government management tends in this direction anyway. The reward for personal performance is buried below the reward for not causing any trouble. This is a formula for empowering the political bureaucrat.

The way we run most of the functional part of our government represents a contradiction to me. The democratic election of the President, governors and legislatures provides for our collective representation. Thank God we do that pretty well. This results in the political assignment of government agency heads. These people are usually at least loosely responsible for their performance toward policy goals. But we run the rest of our government under a totally different management philosophy. This second philosophy is effectively identical to that used by most governments around the world, even the socialist and communist ones of the past. In other words, the guts of most agencies are composed of bureaucracies. If we allow that type of organization to creep into the CMS we will all be sorry, no matter the justification. That is why we need a clean division between the ability of the Board of Directors to steer policies and their temptation to trip up the workings of a commercially-modeled organization.

I also mentioned a secondary goal earlier, the idea that a successful CMS could serve as a new model for government efficiency. We can view this proposal as an experiment to prove the value of moving towards capitalist management methods of governance. The United States, a proudly capitalist country, may finally learn to leverage capitalism towards its own government function. Once we demonstrate how to do this well with the CMS, then maybe we can begin converting some other government agencies into citizen companies, too. Someday most government management may be modeled on the CMS approach. These would be commercial organizations owned by the citizens but managed by the political body in very limited ways towards key goals.

I am fully aware that some will claim we already use capitalism in government whenever we outsource a government function or hire government contractors. For instance, it is becoming quite popular for states to outsource prison operations to private companies that specialize in prison management. Most politicians agree that there are benefits to outsourcing and contracting because of the efficiencies inherent in capitalist management principles. However, the model I propose for operating the Capital Magnification Service is very different from either outsourcing or contracting. In the CMS approach, a government agency is really a citizen-owned corporation managed with limited government oversight.

V. CMS Operational Plan Overview

I have called the CMS a "citizen company" many times now but put off justifying the reasoning behind this term. Now I will explain. The citizen company approach establishes a different perspective and priority for senior management compared to commercial outsourcing or contracting companies, because the citizen company's primary goal can be anything we desire it to be. It can be primarily altruistic instead of just profit-driven. By this I mean we can place public interest at a higher level than pure profits. In the case of the CMS, we placed a higher priority on generating jobs than on making a profit. Then we simply apply capitalist management techniques to these alternate priorities.

This gives us another perspective for understanding why government should not micromanage a citizen company. If we allow government to do that, we ruin the capitalist structures we need. Politically-based management, in contrast, destroys the motivation for goal-oriented performance. These obsolete methods produce the bureaucratic structures found in most other government organizations. It is amazing that the same management methods extinct socialist and communist governments used still exist. These methods are used by many of the government agencies around the world, even in a democratic country like ours. The contradiction is that we have proven the outstanding benefit of democratic capitalism, yet our government relies on an ancient socialist bureaucracy to oversee much of its own function.

The citizen company approach allows the CMS to employ management techniques we know are superior. We set it up as a commercial company but modify the profit-only motivation to include performance metrics toward a package of other goals. That is why the CMS is a hybrid organization. The citizen company is commercially run, but answers to the people. The government participates only to represent the people, thereby making sure the CMS is living up to its Charter. The profit motivation is still present, but the main purpose of this profit is to maintain a healthy degree of self-reliance. Otherwise, the citizen company exists to serve a needed, shared goal.

On top of that, we have purposefully defined exactly which issues the government is allowed to steer in the course of conducting its oversight. In the case of CMS, oversight is primarily limited to the adjustment of CMS rules and service incentives. The government can modify high-level features of CMS deal-making services to align with the citizens' current priorities. Otherwise, CMS management must determine the best ways to achieve their goals. The Board will reward CMS management well if they achieve the goals in the Charter. The Board will be replace them if they do not. The result is a new kind of company that provides a service (or product) that the citizens need. The citizen company uses capitalist methods to achieve strategic goals that are more important than profits alone. Furthermore, the stockholder's representatives (a government-sourced Board of Directors) can steer the high-level product strategy as well.

By the People, For the People

The last Charter point is a triple play. It specifies the need for "Transparency, Customer Service, and Careful Enforcement". These three issues go together because as a set they constitute a sort of philosophy of operations. These are not subjects commonly addressed in most company bylaws, so they are not implied by capitalism alone. This Charter item represents the recognition that this organizations, the CMS, is set up by the citizens to serve its people above all else.

Most public companies in an open market are incented to increase shareholder value. That often means they aim to maximize short-term profits above all else. But our citizen company has a Board of Directors that cares about more than just profits. This attitude reflects the will of the people who own the company. The Board wants to see economic impact above all else. Especially in the beginning this means job creation. We should watch as CMS management focuses on that issue. However, we add the eighth Charter item as a new kind of citizen company goal. The management must practice a high level of respect for all citizens. Secrecy is bad. Customer happiness is very important. Rule enforcement must be considerate and careful.

Transparency keeps all activities above board, easy to inspect, and hard to scam or slough. It empowers all citizens to challenge, question, and provide detailed input. This Charter item says that the citizen is both our stockholder and our valued customer. Therefore everyone is able to see what the CMS is doing, how the CMS is doing, and why the CMS is doing it.

We will automate Customer Service as much as possible for efficiency. That is fine for most situations. But when a problem arises in which the automation it is not sufficient, we need alternatives that include the option of talking to real people. This is the same customer-is-the-owner philosophy applied to customer support. I imagine a TV commercial with an announcer saying, "At the CMS, when you do business with us, we treat you like our owner, because...you are." The CMS should provide the kind of service quality that we want for ourselves.

Now I understand that there is a lot of optimism built into this statement. The Charter merely sets the goals to strive towards. We will assess CMS management based on how far it can go in reaching towards these goals. When they fall short, they will have to answer for their actions. When they succeed, we should be prepared to give them appropriate bonuses or similar performance rewards. That is how capitalism works. We need to keep that part of the equation in place to get the results we want.

By the way, when senior management receives strong performance rewards they are inclined to do the same for their staff, and so on down the line. In fact, if management does not 'trickle down' their own good fortune, I suggest this is evidence of negligence. Rewarding goal-based performance is key to using capitalist methods in a citizen company. We should never assume that CMS management will be altruistic in meeting goals and gaining performance bonuses. I can accept that they may be greedy for gaining monetary rewards as long as they act within ethical guidelines. After all, the Board will only likely consider hiring a CMS CEO who has experience running an investment fund, or some similar financial firm. This is a person who made it to the top at least in part motivated by monetary incentives. They figured out how to succeed at their job so they could earn money. We want that person. The altruism will come from the goals we give to management. Let us pay them well when they deliver on those goals. It will be worth it.

Careful enforcement represents the third leg of the customer-is-the-owner philosophy. It is a tricky balance. With so much money at stake we will certainly encounter plenty of problems. These problems will range from misunderstandings and honest mistakes to blatant attempts to scam the CMS with fraudulent deals. The CMS needs to approach this entire subject with the attitude of a parent working with their child on a problem. We will assume the least ill-will first. We will do our best to treat problems openly and with the same consideration we would want for ourselves. Borrowing a standout Christian teaching just for its philosophical wisdom, you might recognize this as an application of the Golden Rule.

That does not mean it is OK to be a criminal, or even to simply break the rules. There are still consequences to doing things wrong. But we will handle them with an assumption of minimal guilt and maximum consideration. If after all that we determine someone is breaking rules or worse, then they must pay the appropriate penalty. But the guilty party should not be able to make a fair complaint about the process that led to their conviction on the matter. The point is to make double sure the CMS does not accidently railroad the innocent and to assure that we treat the guilty with an ample degree of fairness and a little more respect than they may deserve.

Incidentally, I should make it clear that the CMS will not actually prosecute anyone directly. We may assign serious problems to a formal investigation. If that process concludes that an illegal act probably occurred, then we will forward the entire case to the FBI for law enforcement proceedings. We are not creating a new law enforcement agency. Also, we will forward copies of the entire case, including evidence and procedural records, to the accused parties in parallel.

CMS Scope

In a formal project plan it is very important to talk about scope, in other words, the limits and boundaries of the plan. Some planners do not bother with this since the scope is implied from other parts of the plan, such as the Charter. But this is misleading because it is only partially true. It is exactly this blurry impression that makes scope a problem worth discussing. Let us briefly consider how we might apply our racecar metaphor to clarify the subject.

The strategy is to upgrade our racecar with rockets and a steering wheel. Our Charter states who is buying the car parts, what kind of parts we are using, and that the whole car needs to be checked over once we complete the upgrade. Here is a question: Do we buy new tires? One mechanic could argue that we must. What about the following other issues: Do we need new shock absorbers, a new carburetor, a new exhaust system, or rebuilt brakes? We could say our upgrade project needs all these things. When we install the new tires, should they be the same type as the old ones or a newer kind better suited to rocket speeds? Will the tire size be the same or should it change? Will such changes affect the tire rims? Given the higher speeds, do we need a new kind of axle or steering system?

Project managers call this natural tendency for a plan to keep growing "scope-creep". It is what happens when a project grows and grows until it develops a number of possible problems. The obvious one is that of trying to do too much given the available time and resources. Then the project team ends up behind schedule, over budget, unhappy, and over-worked. A worse possibility is being forced to stop the project before it is completed due to running out of time and money. The team has now fallen short of its goals. The project is now a failure, or it may just perform badly because the team did not finish some key parts of it well enough.

Finally, by talking about scope up front we are communicating important information to the project sponsors, the ones who have asked for the plan and will pay for it if it goes forward. In this case, you, Mr. President, are the main sponsor of this plan. Later we will add Congress and arguably the whole country, since we all will have to approve and finance the program. Regardless, scope tells the sponsors what will actually happen if we enact the plan – no less and no more.

Here is the scope for the Magnified Capitalism plan we are discussing:

Magnified Capitalism Strategic Plan – Scope List

Included:

1. **Congressional Legal Team** – This small group of lawyers is responsible for addressing the legal requirements of preparing the initial congressional bill. They will make sure this bill includes any necessary legal changes to form the CMS as we have described it.

2. **CMS Bill Approval** – Congress OK's the plan without determining how much money to put into the initial CMS Fund. A modest operating budget is included in the bill to pay for startup. This budget covers the cost of hiring key people, including a full legal team and CMS management. It also pays for all the other preparations needed to generate a formal request for the full CMS funding (#6 below).

3. **CMS CEO** - We should hire executive management early. This person will be responsible for building the rest of the management team as well as the crew that executes most of this plan.

4. **Full Legal Team** – Here is the short list that this team must accomplish: Form the corporation, draft all standard deal agreements and registration forms, compose the Board of Directors' rights with written limits negotiated, and set up a complete legal framework for all CMS deals. This framework will act as a legal rulebook for CMS operations. It will address issues such as the processing of penalties, arbitrations, and escalations to law enforcement. Later when we test CMS processes, we are sure to find problems that impact legal issues. The standard terms and conditions and legal rules are all bound to require regular adjustments. A portion of this team will remain full-time to provide legal maintenance and related counsel.

5. **Formation of the Capital Magnification Service** (as described by the Charter) – In conjunction with the legal team, the organization forms and hiring begins. After the CMS CEO, hiring will proceed with the executive staff, then the people reporting to them and so on (top down). At some point, however, the focus will shift towards hiring critical path functions – like process planners, business analysts, and testing personnel. Many regular staff will initially have only a skeleton crew suitable for documenting and fine-tuning processes in simulation testing. Once the CMS gains congressional acceptance testing approval, we will announce a service launch date and the balance of the CMS staff will need to be hired and trained in preparation.

6. **CMS Fund Financing and Operating Budget** – With a comprehensive plan created by the skeleton CMS crew, the CEO will go before the Board and then Congress to request a specific Fund allocation for the first two years, and a corresponding budget to run the company. The bill for this budget should include a congressional commitment for unspecified funding over the following five years, with specific funding after year two to be determined in annual requests. The initial financing of the CMS Fund itself can be made subject to successful acceptance testing.

7. **Setup and Acceptance Testing Costs** - One-time funding is needed to pay for the development of automated systems to run many of the CMS processes and a separate but comprehensive testing system. The testing system will include a market simulator that will challenge both CMS automated and human processes in various ways under different economic conditions. Testing will produce simulated performance measurements (metrics) to help judge whether CMS processes are ready to handle real market activity. This funding includes the operating costs for up to three rounds of application for congressional acceptance. The budget for this item can be included with the request for an initial operating budget (#6 above), but I have shown its cost as a separate line item for discussion.

8. **CMS Services** - The CMS will test and then offer the menu of products (standard deals) as described in *Solution Walkthrough* and subsequent sections. These include specific standard offers to venture capitalists, banks, and existing businesses. They also include a package of four private investor services that help create opportunities for entrepreneurs and other citizens directly. All services include some variation of a registered customer list and a related rating system. The system will track the ratings of all participating capitalists and citizens in such a way as to affect their qualification levels for subsequent CMS offerings. The CMS will openly maintain the rules and processes that govern ratings, and the system will include procedures to redress citizen complaints.

9. **CMS Operational Plan** - After the program passes acceptance testing but before we launch public services, the CMS will publish a full documentation of all its processes. Prior to acceptance this documentation should be made publicly available in draft form. CMS staff will then electronically maintain and publicly post this document indefinitely, as the processes will change from time to time.

10. **CMS Web Disclosures** - The CMS website will include up-to-date disclosures of personnel, active and pending deals, registered customers (e.g., capitalists) and their current ratings, financial statements, company performance metrics, and pending investigations, in addition to providing a service interface for products and support.

11. **Acceptance Testing Platform** - The CMS will keep and maintain the original market simulation testing system for use in considering future changes proposed by Congress, and for the testing of internal process changes or other predictive reporting. Note that future CMS changes put forward by Congress should include the cost of any upgrades to this system or additional labor needed to test such considerations.

12. **External Recruitment and Training** – The CMS will depend on two types of services, but will not directly control them. These are Certified Business Valuators (CBVs) and CMS Registered Patent Attorneys. The CBVs are key to almost every CMS service. We will need to plan and launch a program to insure that an ample supply of CBVs are in place before the first day CMS services are offered. This activity will include training, certification, and probably some initial compensation for the first CBVs, since their business will not begin until the CMS launches. Patent attorneys are not as critical to the breadth of CMS services, but nonetheless need to be prepared in advance to handle the customer demand that is sure to hit them as soon as the *Patent Funding Program* service becomes available.

Not Included:

1. **Detailed Board of Directors Plan** – This plan describes the power of the Chair vs. other Board members as well as the method used to populate the rest of the Board. The President and Congress will negotiate this issue. We will define some non-negotiable key elements of this plan in advance, including the Board's legal limits of power over CMS operations. Also recall that any change the Board submits (through congressional action) that affects rules or processes, or imposes penalties, has special requirements and restrictions. Such changes require 60% congressional approval for temporary effect, and 80% approval for permanent implementation. Also, these changes must include additional budget amounts to cover the cost of new acceptance testing and possible simulation upgrades (see also #6 below).

2. **Initial Package of Standard Deal Incentives and Penalties** – We want to keep the policy-of-the-day as a political argument separate from the setup and funding of the CMS. This is reflected in a standard deal incentives and penalties package. The actual package of incentives can change as often as yearly. If there is no agreement initially, then the CMS will operate with only the baseline of penalties prepared by the legal team and included in all simulation tests. These would be basic penalties for failing to follow processes or breaking laws. The penalties subject to congressional change are those that may discourage certain business decisions, for example, a penalty for a deal that supports offshore production, or any bank loan deals whose purpose is commodity investments. As I discussed previously, I encourage all future leaders to favor using incentives to drive national policy, as they are more tolerant of errors than penalties are.

3. **Cost of Acceptance Testing Beyond 3 Rounds** – The intent is to gain acceptance from the Board within three rounds of market simulation testing. After each test, the CMS will present the results to the Board. If the Board approves the results, the acceptance testing is considered to have passed. Otherwise, the testing department must provide detailed feedback

to CMS management so they can improve processes and retest with adjustments in subsequent months. If the CMS still cannot gain acceptance after three rounds of testing, that might suggest a political problem. This three-round limit will highlight such a roadblock, as the full Congress will need to allocate more money for subsequent testing. Put another way, we should be able to achieve acceptable simulation testing within the first three rounds. Setting the limit to three rounds encourages Congress to meet this target if that is reasonably feasible.

4. **CMS Fund Allocation and Incentives for Year 3 and After** - Every year Congress should pass a new bill that allocates CMS funding for the year after next, as well as any updates to the incentives. This timing is the reason we start with a two-year commitment. This approach forces an annual formal progress report from the CMS CEO to the U.S. President and Congress, as well as an updated budget recommendation and request. It also gives all parties plenty of time to debate the Fund allocation and incentive strategy every year. We may have to separate these two items– Fund management and policy-based incentives - if Congress gets hung up on one or the other.

5. **New CMS Services** - People will undoubtedly propose new CMS services not already described here. If these services are of a customer support nature in that they do not directly produce revenue or result in a new type of financing deal, then it is possible for the CMS to implement them within normal budgets and timelines. An example of such a service (if it did not already exist) would be if the CMS added an online locator for the nearest registered CMS bank, CBV, or CMS-Registered Patent Attorney. But if anyone proposed a new type of deal-based service, that would require a separate plan, justification, testing, and approval from the Board of Directors, then the full Congress. In addition, proposals for new deal-based services require that we modify the rules as well. This means Congress would have to approve these changes by a 60% majority for temporary (trial) offerings, and 80% to make the offering permanent.

6. **Acceptance Testing of Congressional Changes (Cost)** - As I mentioned in the "included" list, the CMS will maintain the original market simulation testing platform perpetually. However, congressional proposals that change rules or processes or impose penalties will require additional funding just to cover the acceptance testing for such a proposal. This money will pay for the programming modifications and personnel needed to run the new testing as well as conducting the required analysis. Note that national policies produced through changes in incentives do not carry the requirement for acceptance testing or its cost, because a general incentive system is built into CMS processes and was tested when we set up the program. The incentive goals and grade level are otherwise flexible and can

change from year to year. But flawed changes to processes, rules, and penalties are not so easily dealt with. A mistake in any of these areas could derail large portions of the CMS by suddenly rendering entire deal offerings unattractive or unprofitable. The acceptance-testing requirement addresses this risk in two ways. First, it encourages policymakers to use incentives as their main control mechanism because they can meet their policy objectives without incurring retesting costs or testing-induced delays. Second, it protects the CMS from inadvertently destroying its working business model. The testing of riskier types of proposals in a market simulation allows the CMS to estimate the actual business impact of such changes. The CMS will report the results of this testing back to the Board (and therefore Congress) for acceptance, fine-tuning or reconsideration.

Before we close the matter of scope I want to point out an important caveat to this whole proposal. We expect that we will make changes to this plan between now and the time a Magnified Capitalism bill finally goes before Congress. By changes, I mean the addition of more detailed analysis and planning. I do not expect the information I am presenting here to mutate into something else entirely. In fact, I am confident that most everything I am presenting is solid and should survive, except for the instances I have pointed out otherwise. But when it comes to subjects like the CMS Scope List, it would be easy for follow-up planners to fill this list out with many more entries. The effort above is therefore just a high-level starting point suitable for executive consideration. A final CMS plan would cut the edges of scope with a much sharper knife.

CMS Strategic Goals

It should be clear by now that we will implement our strategy with one key move, that is, the establishment of the Capital Magnification Service. Therefore, when I talk about the details of how we will set up and run the CMS, it is the same as addressing how we execute our overall plan. Since we are about to discuss the strategic goals for the CMS, it may be helpful to equate this to the strategic goals for Magnified Capitalism in general.

What exactly are strategic goals? What distinguishes a goal as strategic? First, strategic goals are high-level ones. Second, they should apply directly to solving the original problem the plan was created to address. A nearly equivalent approach is to ask whether achieving the goal indicates progress towards achieving the Vision Statement. In our case the primary goal is to reduce unemployment, or equivalently, to instigate a marked increase in job creation. Our vision was to create a new American pillar of survivable success. We might notice that the vision here is broader than the original strategic goal that you, Mr. President, set forth in launching this undertaking. That is OK. The targeted employment objective represents the core of our most important strategic goal. In order to meet the full vision, however, we will need to achieve some additional goals. I will present a complete list shortly.

Goals with Metrics

Before I do that I want to inject a hot topic in the matter of professional management: the use of metrics. When planners use the word metrics they are talking about measuring business progress by calculating a number to represent that progress. Essentially this means that we find a way to keep score of how we are doing, only the score we get might not have been very obvious until we went out of our way to create it. This subject reminds me a bit of comparing competitive gymnastics to baseball. In baseball, we do not typically need a judge to calculate the score. Umpires make sure players follow the rules but it is unmistakable when a baseball team's score increases and by how much. At any point in the game there is little question who is winning. The scoreboard presents the current tally for convenience. The most important metric is obvious here. I will not mention the less critical metrics that some baseball fans like to get into, like hitting averages and error rates. Here we are focused just on the metric that determines who wins the competition. The baseball score is this metric. That score tallies the total runs for each team in the current game.

Scoring in gymnastics (and figure skating and some other sports) requires far more extraction. Judges must follow detailed rules and guidelines when they assign their scores to gymnastic performances. But the casual observer can be forgiven for wondering how one competitor beat another, especially when the numerical difference is a narrow one. After all, the score itself can strike the some of us as a mysterious entity. Yet, most would agree that these judging systems work well enough to be useful for purposes of comparison. We could hardly have a competition in the sports that use judge-based-scoring like gymnastics without some kind of judging process. Thus their judges produce metrics in unobvious ways yet they have a practical result.

Metrics have been used in business and management from the beginning of the written record. In fact, linguists think the earliest human writing is a form of numerical accounting (like how much grain was put in the storehouse). So metrics are not new. Financial bookkeeping represents the most typical way people and businesses use metrics. Keeping track of units sold or the number of customers are also common business metrics. So what is the hot part of metrics? How many customers we have this month, or the amount of money in our bank account, these are like baseball. More complex methods for determining metrics are more like gymnastics. Advanced metrics score the performance of something that does not have an obvious number associated with it. Yet management can find this information very useful once it does have a number. This number can tell us not only if business is good or bad, but whether it is improving and by how much. To find this out we need to come up with a way to judge a business process that produces a meaningful number. A good metric represents a fair and consistent measure of the subject we want to keep track of.

Here is a practical example: Imagine a cable TV company is losing customers because it is receiving too many service complaints. There are many problems but it is not clear which ones the company should work to solve first. So the V.P. of Customer Service introduces a new tracking system for sorting out the complaints. Now the cable company employees ask all customers who call with a service problem a few standard questions to rate how happy or frustrated they are with different aspects of their cable service. The employees input this information into a computer that generates numerical ratings for the following: quality of installation, service wait times, quality of the TV picture, support of HDTV, and overall service value. Within a few weeks the system has collected enough data to show the most serious culprit. In this example perhaps the V.P. finds that customers are most unhappy about the low number of HDTV channels available.

But the result is not what matters. The point is that the company identified the problem clearly by designing a new set of metrics. Not only that, but once the new metrics are in place, they are useful for continued management of the business. In the future, this cable company will be able to produce charts that show in plain numbers how much they are improving in every aspect of their business that they have a metric for. The impact of changes in services and processes will become measurable. They will be able to check their customer satisfaction rating after adding five more HDTV channels. Then they can verify it again after adding twelve more. By comparing the scores they can make good business decisions. Later, when they decide to add more field personnel to reduce service wait times, they will be able to see if they added enough people to meet quality objectives. Management will even be alerted when they later find an unexpected drop in satisfaction with picture quality.

Business results that can be expressed with numerical metrics help to justify the effort of fixing a problem. Without the metrics, we may not know whether the fix was effective, or whether a new process even works. With the metrics we can even keep track of how well an aspect of business continues to improve or worsen over time. Of course, the metrics in the cable TV example were pretty simple. If later on the company's customer satisfaction numbers go up due to some change, there will be little doubt that improvement actually occurred. These are solid metrics. In many cases, the metrics we want are just hanging there waiting to be collected. In this case, management needed to add a new standard customer service questionnaire. The point is simply that metrics are not hard to create or find. We just need to decide what we want to track and then pick the easiest way we can think of to score it consistently.

There is one more important factor about metrics. When designed correctly, they are not easily colored by interpretation. If we want to track how well the CMS is doing over time, we could just wait for the annual report from the CEO and ask them again every year. But without any metrics we would have trouble tracking any aspect of the business except the financials. Of course we will insist on looking at the financial figures. These are very important metrics. They will tell us if the CMS is profitable, for example. But the best way to keep our fingers on the pulse of the CMS is to require them to keep track of a set of metrics that measure every issue we care about. We do not need to leave this up to CMS management. Metrics do not affect how we run a company. But forcing management to provide detailed metrics does produce a useful degree of transparency. It is hard to hide from numerical measures.

Finally, there is the real punch line. We could state our strategic goals in some nebulous way, for instance, "Achieve important improvements in the national unemployment rate." Or we could express our goal in terms of hard numbers. That is what I am proposing. We should continuously track all strategic goals in the form of metrics. That is why I am adding the following new strategic goal: The CMS will maintain a comprehensive set of performance metrics so that everyone can transparently observe subtleties in management changes. Now we are ready to review the full list as a menu.

List of CMS Strategic Goals and Supporting Metrics

Shown in order of priority

1. **Keep National Unemployment Rate Below 5%** - The government already tracks and publishes the unemployment rate. CMS's efforts seek to keep unemployment below 5% at all times. This target level is commonly considered to be a healthy one. However, we also want to know the portion of national employment that CMS programs have provided directly. The following supporting metrics allow us to attain a fair notion of how effective the CMS is in motivating job creation. These, and all CMS metrics, should be updated and posted to the public at least quarterly:

- **Service Volume** - Number of deals participated in by service (deal) type. Tracking this information shows us if the total business of the CMS is picking up steam and how balanced it is among all services.

- **Partner Network Size** - Number of registered CMS capitalists by capitalist category. This measure gives an idea of how attracted the capitalists are to participate and whether this interest is going up or down. Partners also include CBVs and Registered Patent Attorneys.

- **Service Magnitude** - Average deal size (dollars) per service type, and dollar totals. Are we making a few big deals, a bunch of little ones, or some mix? This metric gives us an idea of the nature of the deals most capitalists are favoring.

- **Capital Magnified** – Average and total dollar contributions from the capitalist side of CMS deals. This is the private commercial money that the program magnifies. This strategy is about using one CMS dollar to generate an economic impact of more than a dollar. This metric tells us what part of that "more" is coming from the capitalists. The terms of each deal should make the per-deal answer obvious.

- **Gross CMS Jobs** – Total number of jobs created through CMS deals. This includes business deals that probably would have happened even without CMS services. Here we learn how many jobs the CMS has a role in supporting. We collect this metric because it is an obvious one. We simply add up the total number of jobs that each CMS deal produces. However, to do this we will need to make sure that every deal application form includes the question, "How many (U.S.) jobs is this deal expected to produce?"

- **Net CMS Jobs** – Total number of new jobs attributed to CMS participation. This metric calculates new jobs created solely due to CMS services. This is, therefore, the most important metric of all. Net Jobs is a bit trickier to track than Gross Jobs. We will probably need to include another question on each deal application form that asks, "Would you expect to engage in this business even if the CMS did not participate?" Net Jobs would focus on those jobs associated with applications that answer "no" to this question. When Net Jobs goes up, we know the CMS is making a growing impact towards its number one goal. When this number goes down, management has some explaining to do.

2. **Track and Improve Competitiveness** – Competitiveness has not historically been measured by a consistent standard. We should change that by coming to some agreement on such a measure and then tracking it. Recall that improved competitiveness equates to greater ease in establishing and running a business. So this metric considers all the sources of money Magnified Capitalism is designed to address, plus taxes, business regulations, cost and access to workers, cost and access to production facilities, shipping expense, and even the overall buying appetite of the broad market. This is such a complicated concept that it is no wonder there is no standard metric already. However, when faced with a situation like this economists commonly replace detailed calculations with a survey. We can just sample the opinion of a few hundred random businesspeople and ask them to rate the current economic environment for competitiveness from one to ten. The metric would be their average score. Competitiveness is our number two strategic priority because the primary means by which we are creating jobs is improving competitiveness. In other words, competitiveness represents the core of the CMS strategy. With that in mind, let us consider some future time when the job figures do not improve as expected. It will be then be very helpful to see if competitiveness also failed to advance in the

same period. The results will help us better understand what is going on and why.

- **CMS Deal Penetration** – For every service type offered, the CMS should calculate the percentage of qualifying deals that use CMS funds. This calculation only applies to registered capitalists. The resulting metric will tell us two things. Mainly, it shows how attractive each CMS service is. It can also provide clues when we run into problems such as having too many CMS rule-based restrictions, or if a wide range of capitalists are using up most of their available CMS funds. In other words, measuring and tracking penetration helps us understand how attractive the CMS offerings are at the current time. If the number goes down, something may be starting to go wrong. Deal penetration is directly related to competitiveness because increasing penetration should increase competitiveness. Yet, competitiveness is a soft qualitative measure that includes many factors outside CMS control. But penetration can be computed precisely and is directly related to CMS activity.

- **Competitiveness Quotient** – This is the main metric that tracks competitiveness through a survey of businesspeople. Such opinion polls, while admittedly qualitative, are especially useful if the main goal is to understand whether the overall national environment is getting better or worse.

3. **Exceed Target Return on Investment** – Return on Investment (ROI) is a common calculation for business managers. It is simply a computation of how much money the business made or lost. When stated in total dollars this is just called profit. However, this metric is often more useful for calculating the rate at which the business earned the profit. We find the rate by dividing our profit by the amount we invested. The answer is ROI, usually expressed as a percentage. When we invest in a mutual fund, the fund usually reports its quarterly performance as a percentage returned. The interest on a loan is also essentially an ROI measure for the party providing the loan (e.g., the bank). There are some caveats. Interest on a loan is often expressed as an annual rate. By contrast, the ROI for business planning might be shown as the total profit over the course of the whole project, regardless of the time involved. To make these numbers easier to compare, we will set a standard that all CMS ROIs be reported as annual rates. The other metrics shown here provide some supporting role to CMS profitability. In other words, ROI measures how profitably the CMS is managing the money in the Fund. The other metrics help us understand why we are ending up with this particular ROI. I have explained the special case of Target ROI last.

- **Financial Summary & ROI** – Like a summary of an accountant's ledger, we should generate reports on payables (costs) and receivables (income). Payables include operating costs and one-time costs. Receivables are the money collected from deals, sales and services. Virtually every company has some version of this setup. We just need a summary here. The report shows the total profit as a bottom line (receivables less payables). Finally, the summary gives the overall CMS quarterly and annual ROI. We should also calculate ROI for each service type. That way we can see which services are the better CMS investments, and which ones are bringing the numbers down.

- **Closed Deal Profitability Rate** – Every year (and each quarter) some of the CMS deals will close. Closed deals are those that the parties entered into some time ago but that are now finished. Deals close when the terms of closing were met, such as when a venture capitalist sells a startup company's stock or when the final payment of a loan is collected. However, the CMS could also close a deal for special reasons, such as legal action, or the deal timed-out and was processed for immediate collection (similar to foreclosure). Regardless, once a deal is closed the CMS will know how much it made or lost on that deal. We want to keep track of the percentage of CMS deals that make money. This percentage should be better than 90%, nearly all the time. We also want to look at deal profitability rates for each type of service the CMS offers. That gives us another way to see which CMS services need management attention.

- **Risk versus ROI** – The CMS has the task of standardizing a rating system for its capitalists. This system includes assigning a risk score that considers the history of the capitalist and their track record with CMS deals. That information will enable us to generate a Risk versus ROI metric. This metric will show the amount of profit (or ROI) the different risk groups contributed. A simple example involves dividing the capitalists into three groups – high, normal, and low risk capitalists. Now we calculate ROI for each of these three groups separately. The low risk capitalists should have the best ROI. If the high risk ones have a negative ROI, for example, then we probably need to adjust their service terms to account for this.

- **Deal Loss Rate(s)** – The CMS should not just report the overall loss rate (the opposite of the deal profitability rate). More importantly, we should have metrics that show losses due to specific categories of problems, such as illegal activities (suspected and under investigation), contract problems (including misunderstandings), and poorly understood/executed processes. Of course, for those losing deals where none of these apply there are two more categories: losses due to underperforming business deals, and losses due to business failure.

- **Target ROI** - This is the special ROI number that we are most interested in. It represents the rate of profit that the CMS must minimally achieve in order to meet its Board-agreed financial goals. The Target ROI is therefore going to change every year depending on what the government management expects. There is an important subtlety about this CMS goal. Just meeting the Target ROI, or slightly exceeding it, is more important than making a far higher maximum ROI. Why is that? Because in order to earn a very high profit, we may have to compromise other priorities such as total number of jobs created or improved customer satisfaction (see below). That may not be the ideal combination for our shareholders, the U.S. citizens. The Target ROI is the number the CMS needs to achieve so that the whole program continues as expected and as needed. The CMS can try to reach a higher goal, and it should, but only with some care. Every priority on this list deserves its fair share of attention. To achieve that balance well will require some expense. The Target ROI lets us know when we have hit the profit rate we need and thus we can start putting some additional resources towards the other priorities. That said, there are bound to be times when the CMS vastly exceeds the Target ROI without necessarily compromising other priorities. This could be the case when all the CMS services are performing well with few problems in a strong economic recovery. Metrics like ROI are useful, but they need interpretation to complete the picture.

4. **Improving Customer Satisfaction** - The CMS should track a customer satisfaction index for both the capitalists and those who use the capitalist services with CMS backing. This metric should sample customer satisfaction at the setup of a deal, the closing of a deal, and after addressing any type of customer issue (i.e., a complaint or problem). CMS reporting should include satisfaction rates, complaint rates, and rates for those requesting second opinions and management escalations. For this goal we can likely assume that the earliest levels of customer satisfaction represent something near the worst levels. Therefore, the CMS should seek to continuously improve these metrics from that time forward. At some point the CMS will approach a threshold beyond which it will be particularly difficult to improve further. Metrics taken at this level can therefore define near-optimal performance in the area of customer satisfaction. Then this goal would shift towards one that merely works to keep customer satisfaction metrics hovering near these lofty highs.

5. **Improving CMS Deal Efficiency** - There is a value to keeping CMS employee efficiency high. Higher efficiency means lower costs. It also means that the same organization can handle an increased volume of business. From the perspective of seeking a fair profit, we should spend only as much on CMS operations as we really need to. We can measure worker efficiency by calculating the average number of deals made per CMS employee, including contractors. An even more important measure that we should

track is cost efficiency. This metric compares total CMS costs to CMS deal volume, giving us the average dollar amount to manage a deal. We should also calculate deal efficiency by service type, allowing us to compare the average cost of supporting one type of service versus another. Efficiency metrics allow everyone to see how effectively the CMS uses its resources. Changes in these metrics can provide useful information about CMS processes and related management decisions. Declines provide warnings, and increases suggest validations about recent process decisions. In any case, efficiency is the lowest of our main priorities for good reason. We should trade it only disproportionately against the more important priorities above, if at all. This metric has a special consideration, however. For those who hope the CMS model of government management produces a more efficient way to conduct the people's business, these metrics are paramount. The efficiency metrics described here could become the standard by which we judge regular government bureaucracies.

The Board of Directors should expect one more piece of information from CMS management along with all of the goal-related metrics listed above. For each goal, CMS management should receive an analysis of what the current metrics mean, in other words, a goal-by-goal self-evaluation. The evaluation report should state how closely the actual metrics match with earlier projections, and provide new projections for upcoming years. For each goal, if all the numbers are perfectly on track, then management can say that no action is required to improve further. Otherwise, the analysis of each goal should include a detailed root cause finding and an action plan towards progress.

When we consider the performance of the CMS it quickly becomes apparent that the matter is not as simple as asking, "What is the national unemployment rate?" For instance, in the earliest months of CMS operation, we should expect to see some ramping-up effect. Together with the national unemployment rate, the metrics above will better help all citizens understand the impact and performance of the CMS. We will see how much of the unemployment problem the CMS can claim to address. We will also discover whether the CMS is really improving and whether some types of services are producing unexpected results. In later years these metrics will have even more importance. In fact, I expect this strategy will be so successful that keeping unemployment rates below 5% will be easy. Therefore, in a booming economy with a well-established CMS program, people will view our most important goal as a low bar of success. If that was all we cared about, CMS management could become complacent because they would just have to make sure they did not mess anything up.

Our requirement for detailed metrics changes that. The people will see whether the CMS can still improve its performance and where improvements are needed most. More important, the transparency itself will motivate management to take appropriate actions. That is the main value of transparency in general and metrics in particular, by the way. It is not so much that we use details to beat someone up, but they cannot hide from them. This exposure tends to keep executives moving in the right direction. Transparency with detailed metrics provides a nearly self-correcting method of management. Those collecting the metrics will know they have to answer for the results they report. It is a strategy that keeps management on their toes. And when the metrics exceed expectations, management receives the rewards they deserve, and so do those who work for them. The result is profound in an important way. Metrics allow us to direct the power of capitalism towards goals that are not limited to profits alone. Without establishing metrics that enumerate progress towards multiple goals, this effect would be much harder to achieve.

Principal CMS Functions

I have spent much of this presentation talking about how the Capital Magnification Service will solve many problems. What does this organization actually do? Let me put it concisely here.

The role of the CMS is to manage a huge investment fund (the CMS Fund) on behalf of the citizens of the United States. It does this according to the new economic strategy called Magnified Capitalism. Under this strategy, the CMS is only allowed to make special kinds of investments. These investments are standard deals, or services, that it offers primarily to those who have some money to invest. Whether they are businesses or individual people, those with the money are called capitalists. The main purpose of the standard CMS services is to help capitalists conduct more business than they could, or would, otherwise. The CMS targets four categories of capitalists with its services: venture capitalists (VCs), bankers, established businesses, and private investors (including entrepreneurs and pretty much anyone else who wants to participate). This plan calls for the CMS to offer the following menu of services, which are each considered product offerings:

Capital Magnification Service Menu of Product Offerings:

1. **VC Funding** - A standard deal for partnering with venture capitalists in the co-funding of business startups, launches, and expansions.

2. **Bank Loan Participation** - A standard deal for partnering with banks in co-funding a wide range of loans, especially those for education and business.

3. **Business Expansion Funding** - A standard deal for partnering with existing businesses in good standing, providing co-funding of an expansion, new product development, or other type of growth plan.

4. **Private Investor Portfolio** – Four additional services targeted at private individuals who want to participate in economic development to a greater degree than they could otherwise. These are:

a. **Private Venture Funding** – A standard deal similar to the VC Funding product, except that it accommodates investors of any background and level of resources. It even supports what we might call micro-deals (similar to microloans). More importantly, it encourages those with greater aspirations to assemble into coalitions or partnerships in order to qualify for larger deals with better terms. The rating system also encourages partnerships to include mentors, investors whose expertise and experience greatly elevate the rating of the entire plan.

b. **Cash Flow Assistance** – A deal that is essentially a short-term high interest loan for very small businesses that qualify. It targets the common situation of a modestly successful business that would like to invest in a major improvement but is hampered by a cash flow problem.

c. **Patent Funding Program** – A deal offered to patent attorneys and their inventor clients. It allows the attorney to get paid for processing patents from private inventors who otherwise could not afford to hire them. This service encourages the attorney to focus on marketable inventions likely to be granted the patent, and therefore more likely to become valuable. The attorney is paid at three stages in increasing amounts – filing, approval, and cash-out (patent sale or investor backing of an underlying business).

d. **Prototype Development Network** – An online service that helps entrepreneurs get work done on a new business idea before they have the money to hire employees or contractors. The main goal is to prototype a new concept sufficiently to prove its business value and attract an investor. Entrepreneurs can also use the PDN to find major or minor business partners as well as to start a business with a very small investment. Workers are paid with equity (stock) in the startup company. The workers can convert their stock to cash as soon as the company reaches its cash-out goal. The business reaches this point when the startup either finds an investor or reaches a total preset revenue goal. The PDN service doubles as a special kind of job generator. It provides a new pipeline for full- or part-time work, and for building experience and references in a new career path. The workers, called prototypers, may receive some advance payment if they have sufficiently high CMS ratings. Regardless, most or all of the pay is both deferred and at significant risk. Prototypers must be offered the option to get paid when the business reaches the cash-out goal; however, they can also choose to hold on to some portion of their company stock on the bet that it will be worth more later on.

Notice that each service involves making a business deal. With some exceptions in the Prototype Development Network, these deals involve CMS money in addition to the capitalist's funds in order to execute a business plan. The detailed terms vary considerably. However, the favorability of the terms depends significantly on two inputs: the capitalist's CMS rating and the results of one or more Certified Business Valuations.

The entire activity of the CMS revolves around this service menu. Its focus is on making these deals over and over again. These deals become investments in American business. We can expect most every type of activity not just to generate jobs, but to do so by leveraging private capital. The CMS expects to make a profit on most of these deals, and an overall profit even when taking its losses into account. A typical investment fund faces this same problem. In this case, however, the CMS will tweak the terms and conditions of the service offerings in a market simulator to make sure it strikes a balance between two opposites. These opposites are the terms of attractive services that capitalists will want versus terms that insure a fair, profitable investment of the people's money.

CMS Functional Roles

Now that we have once again reviewed the business of the Capital Magnification Service we will consider some key mandatory organizational functions. The CMS will have much in common with many commercial businesses in that typical corporate functions will still be necessary. This includes executive management, legal counsel, human resources, finance, sales and marketing, and operations departments. We have already touched on some of these. I will focus on highlights.

The Executives

I do not need to add much regarding executive management. Here are a few thoughts that I did not previously emphasize. Recall that the Board of Directors hires the Chief Executive Officer (CEO) of the CMS. You, Mr. President, as Chair, will lead this board. Senators and/or Representatives will populate the rest of the Board. The details will depend on future negotiations. In any case, one of the Board's most important jobs will be to set up the CEO's incentive package. This pay package should be loaded with performance bonuses keyed off the metrics we discussed above. Some may find this unappealing since that means the CEO could make a lot of money from what is effectively a government assignment. I hope the CEO makes a bundle, and so should we all. That is why the design of the incentives is so important. We want the CEO position to be a desirable job for anyone with the right experience. This person should be an expert capitalist who comes from a background where they ran a similar business, such as an investment fund company or a venture capital firm. The base pay should be minimal, so if they do not meet the goals set by the Board, they have little to show for it. But the bonuses for performance should be very attractive.

Not only that, but the CEO should have few restrictions from percolating similar performance bonus incentives down to his staff, and theirs, and so on down to every CMS employee to a decreasing degree. Managers in the business world expect performance incentives; these bonuses are one of the key differences between the CMS and a regular government agency. They represent a method of shared capitalism. However, in our case, the incentives will be based on various metrics. Profit (as ROI) is one of these, but it is not the most important one. There are many other metrics that represent other kinds of company goals. For example, a CMS process manager might expect their bonus package to weigh heavily on efficiency metrics, while a market simulation programmer might receive more bonus incentive if their software helps deliver real job creation.

The point is that an employee's main incentive should match the ability of their job to have some impact on the appropriate metric. It will be a principle job of the CEO and the executive team to hire quality management and implement a performance-based incentive structure throughout the CMS that aligns well with the direction of the Board. If the CEO does this effectively, the whole company will progress in accordance with the Board's priorities. If not, the Board should be quick to replace the CEO. The worst thing the Board can do is to be tolerant of poor performance at the top. They should set a high standard and expect excellent performance at all times for this critical role.

The other issue that the executive team is directly responsible for is project management. These people own the timeline, the budget, and the deliverables for their parts of the CMS puzzle. In the beginning, this means setting up the company, designing detailed processes, hiring employees, and building the computer systems. The executive team should be held directly responsible for completing these actions. If they blame lower-level people for delays, cost overruns, or failures, then they should be fired. It is that simple. There is a reason executives get paid what they do: they are responsible for success, and they own the failures. Management that maintains this standard tends to succeed. If the organization allows excuses and blame at the highest levels, then others at lower levels will notice and follow suit.

Incidentally, notice I did not say we should automatically fire an executive who was responsible for some failure. They should be fired if they do not take responsibility for it. When something goes wrong, a good manager will raise their hand and say, "This is mine. I am on it." First they will figure out what broke and get it fixed. Then they will find out why it broke in the first place, and do whatever it takes to make sure it does not happen again. They must take both actions, not just the fix. Finally, when the matter goes before the Board something impressive can happen. The CEO can explain to the people's representatives how management owned the problem and dealt with it.

Legal
The Legal Department will probably be a bit larger than it is in most other companies due to the extensive contract issues involved with all CMS services and the special relationship the CMS has with government. Furthermore, many companies that conduct investigations and related enforcements carry out this part of their business under the management of their Legal Department. These investigations and enforcements are a major function at the CMS, whether they are done through the Legal Department or under some other structure. For purposes of discussion, I will assume these matters fall under the umbrella of Legal. These activities include both the investigative function and arbitration. In addition, there is a need for formal change control, which we could also include under Legal. Here is a brief on each.

Investigation is essentially a form of rule enforcement, but not technically a policing action. The CMS will have neither actual police nor the power to arrest anyone. However, its processes will include penalties for improper, incorrect, or erroneous execution of terms and conditions. Also, although the CMS will not arrest those suspected of committing illegal acts, they still must take action about these matters. Some of these responsibilities will be spread throughout the company. Auditors will catch financial problems. Deal managers will track customer reports and adherence to processes. There are many other touch points. However, if a CMS employee does find an issue that may have been produced by either a process problem or a criminal act, then they must take the proper steps. Those who notice a problem should not generally have the responsibility of following up. But they are responsible for handing the matter over to a CMS investigator. Furthermore, if a customer is eventually accused of an illegality, they should have the right to a second opinion. This means a senior investigator will independently review the case and give their analysis. If these investigations determine that the matter may be criminal, then the investigators will work with the FBI for enforcement. Otherwise, the investigators will work with process managers and customers to enforce penalties.

If there is a contract disagreement between the CMS and a customer, the primary course of action is to take the matter to arbitration. This is similar to taking a lawsuit court, except that the court is a private one designed to handle such matters. In particular, the arbitrator, who replaces a judge, is already highly knowledgeable with regard to CMS contracts, laws and processes. Also, the processes are streamlined and therefore the matter is settled more quickly and with less cost to everyone. Customer defendants are not required to have a lawyer represent them and will be guided through their options by those running the arbitration. In extreme cases, customers can still escalate grievances to a formal court of law, but arbitration greatly reduces the volume of such cases. Legal is the obvious department to set up and run arbitration processes.

The last responsibility I want to mention that we could assign to Legal is that of change control - the formal method by which companies manage modifications to their business practices. In other words, there will be times when someone at the CMS figures out how to do something better, or how to fix a problem. If that fix changes any kind of standard process, we need to be careful. The fact that a change fixes one thing does not automatically mean it will not cause a bigger problem somewhere else. Fortunately, we can apply well-established methods in such a case. The person who came up with the idea or to whom it was assigned will need to fill out a proposal form. These proposals can involve changes to the terms and conditions in a service, a software program, a manual process, a customer form, or similar alterations to the CMS's business practices.

Called a change request, this proposal form will detail what the change is, how it works, why it should be made, the steps necessary to implement the change, the estimated cost in money and time, and who will be affected at the CMS. Then, representatives of every major department at the CMS will need to consider the change request, with emphasis on those who may see some effect. Then all these people will meet at regularly-scheduled change control meetings. There they will discuss all the latest change requests, going over the upsides and the downsides of each. Finally, they will vote on each change request to approve it, send it back for enhancement, or reject it.

Those who manage change control must make sure the appropriate people take all the right steps and record the results. If a proposal is approved, the change control group ensures such changes are implemented exactly as intended. They may do this by assigning a project manager to each approved change. More importantly, the change control group makes sure this is the only way anyone can change working systems. In a small company change control would seem an absurdly unnecessary overhead. Even many larger organizations do not do formal change control. These are often the same companies that are constantly fighting fires. Change control keeps a working system working well.

It should be difficult to change a carefully-designed system. Millions of dollars and years of work could be at stake. This formal process prevents a single person from throwing a wrench into the machinery. A purposeful troublemaker is far more likely to be both stopped and caught when change control is on guard. Finally, those people who do the work to put through a positive change will necessarily be recognized, as they should. Given the amount of money at stake, we definitely need to implement this sort of change control system.

Human Resources

I have listed Human Resources as a necessary department. They will manage personnel issues and benefits, just as the HR departments in most companies do. However, I can think of one arguably unique quality about the CMS version of HR. This department should have some special duties with respect to managing employee incentives, because we will use many formal performance metrics to determine related bonuses. We want the CMS to use performance bonuses liberally and strategically. HR is the likely group to have responsibility for this activity. They should assure alignment of appropriate incentives to the responsibilities of each job.

Another possible special responsibility for HR might be support of whistleblowers. Employees should feel free to contact at least three different channels if they find a serious problem occurring anywhere in the organization. These three channels are their own management, the Legal Department, and HR. There should be strong management penalties for refusing to support whistleblowers and follow up on their complaints. There should also be strong incentives to support whistleblowing that uncovers real problems. HR may own this enforcement equally with Legal, as a counterbalance.

Finance

The Finance Department at the CMS will be very important. Finance needs to generate, track and report on the wide range of metrics we discussed above in additional to normal responsibilities like accounts receivable (collecting money) and accounts payable (bills and paychecks). This group should also be responsible for functions like financial audits of deals and some deal management functions (financial approval of new deals, closing approval of finished deals, credit checks).

Sales & Marketing

Sales are a bit different at the CMS than in most service companies. Here a "sale" is made whenever a person or business is approved for the service they applied for. It is not a traditional sale because usually the customer receives some money from the CMS in accordance with the terms of their deal. However, eventually the customer will return this money to the CMS, usually with some added profit. In that sense a sale in this system somewhat like selling a loan. Regardless, even though almost all sales occur using online systems, there must still be salespeople behind those systems. Salespeople must be available to address complex situations and help customers make successful service applications. That is why the customer service function should fall within the Sales Department. That way, when a customer needs help of any kind, the same customer service group can address the problem. Sales will design the interface of the online sales function, track the results, and be responsible for any manual processes those systems cannot handle. Finally, any new customer application for service will include an approval from a salesperson, even if the application was filed electronically.

Marketing, which can be combined with Sales, is related but focuses more on the broader strategy and market communications, just as in many other companies. Marketing designs the business plans and product plans for the future. This is the product management aspect of Marketing. If a deal is going bad or has unusual problems, we might assign an investigator to check it out. If a whole service is experiencing issues such as not enough customers signing up or profits showing lower than expected, we can assign a product manager to analyze the situation. They would propose a strategy for repair, such as a new advertising approach or working with another department to fix processes.

Marketing is also responsible for public relations, advertising, and other promotions. Notably, this means Marketing runs the CMS website and manages its content. Website content includes product updates, press releases, news, and most other functions, except those specifically assigned to another group.

Operations

I will use Operations as the banner for the rest of what CMS does. In practice, this is an organizational structure that varies greatly. We should not be very concerned about the details of this department. This is not so much a proposal for the CMS structure as it is an outline for discussion. With that in mind, in this section I am going include the Information Technology (IT) function as a part of Operations. I will put Research and Development (R&D) and Testing into Operations, too. Finally, I will add a Process and Project Management group. Many companies do not even have such a group, especially the Process part. I will touch on the highlights of each of these.

IT handles the computer systems and all other automation and technology. Importantly for us, they run the computer farms, monitor them, and keep odd hours insuring these systems stay up and working even when things go wrong. Other departments may be responsible for the software and content that is loaded onto the computers, but IT keeps them physically operating 24 hours a day, seven days a week. IT should also include a high level customer service function. That is, when customers have a problem, they contact the normal Customer Service people I already mentioned. However, if the customer's problem ends up being due to a computer failure, Customer Service will bring in the special IT people assigned to address such issues.

Research and Development includes two different sets of responsibilities. Research involves prototyping new ideas to determine whether they have enough merit to be considered in future plans. Development involves implementing approved plans. At the CMS, Development will focus almost entirely on computer software. This includes the software that runs the website, the software that keeps track of the business activity (databases and network management), and the software that searches for interesting correlations (data mining, warehousing and reporting). In this last category I anticipate a particular focus on designing special tools, some of which will look for patterns that suggest illegal activity or other abuses. Other tools might flag deals that are in trouble. In these situations, the CMS might offer business consulting assistance to help solve problems. Development will also write software apps for use on customers' laptops, tablet computers, and smart phones. As with IT, Development also includes employees who are assigned to help Customer Service deal with special problems in CMS software.

Let me raise the issue of an observable trend in programming here, that is, the popular tendency to outsource software development. While CMS management should ultimately decide exactly how to conduct such activities, I want to point out a great disadvantage to outsourcing in this case. The CMS will need to constantly revisit and upgrade most of their software on a regular basis. That is exactly the situation in which we should hire the programmers directly and do the work in-house. That way most of the people who know the ins and outs work for us. The next version of that software will be cleaner and easier to revise and upgrade. When problems come up, a similar situation applies. The programming experts would already be CMS employees. This is just a tangential suggestion, however.

Testing is more important at the CMS than it is in many companies that produce less critical software. In our SWOT analysis I suggested that we hire another vendor to build the testing systems in order to set up a sort of competition in the initial acceptance testing. This suggestion also implies that the market simulation part of the testing system will be vigorous and thorough. In other words, the third-party testers are more likely to successfully break the CMS systems that they are testing. By conducting this function through another vendor, we can trust the results more.

While I recognize the value of this approach for initial testing, I also want to say that at some point the CMS needs to bring most of those people into the company, too. Otherwise, we need to hire them under a recurring testing contract that represents a permanent relationship with the CMS. Regardless, those who do the testing will be very valuable and will be needed again and again. Every change or addition to the CMS systems and processes must be tested. In practice we will usually do this testing in batches, often called new releases or version upgrades. Acceptance testing differs only slightly from regular testing in that acceptance testing is part of a formal analysis prepared for the Board of Directors. In other words, when the government must approve either the initial CMS readiness, or later releases that include government-mandated changes, then the kind of testing done is called acceptance testing. When the changes come from internal CMS changes, they are just a part of regular release testing. The two are actually almost the same. The main difference is primarily the way we prepare the results for external presentation.

There is a growing trend in management today to create a separate Project Management Group within each company. The idea here is that project management requires a special skill set to be done correctly. Increasingly, companies even require project managers to be certified. This subject comes into play at the CMS for two particular reasons.

The first is the nature of CMS services. They are almost all just business deals based on standard contracts. Once Sales approves a new deal, the CMS must provide its portion of the financial contribution to the commercial partner, or customer. Then the customer will regularly report on the deal's underlying business until the deal is closed and the money repaid. Someone at the CMS needs to receive these regular reports and track them. Even if reporting is largely automated, there must be real people behind the reporting processes to make sure the process is working smoothly. These people will step in when issues arise, and are responsible for improvements, problem-solving, and escalations. We can call these people project managers, but I think it is more accurate to call them process managers, because they are following standard processes that are already in place.

There is a second category of work that calls on advanced project management skills. Here we want to bring in the more highly-experienced project managers because these are matters that require plan creation, negotiation, and management. The project managers are the ones who designed the original standard CMS deal processes. We bring them back in to manage major changes to standard processes and to offer project management services for ongoing internal CMS projects like coordinating software release teams. That is why I chose to call this the Process and Project Management Group. The name distinguishes the two types of management roles.

That is it for the CMS functional roles. While I delivered this information a bit like an organizational overview, I want to underscore that I am not trying to do that here. The detailed design of an organization includes who reports to whom, and which group is responsible for one activity or another. At most companies these responsibilities shuffle around all the time. I have seen major changes occur as often as every six months in some organizations. The main thing I wanted to cover is not how we arrange the functions at the CMS, but to make sure all of these functions were described, whatever the organizational arrangement.

Proposal Timeline

Timelines are fun. No really, they are, because everybody always wants to know the answers they are supposed to provide. Of course, the question is always some variant of, "How quickly can we complete this proposal?" Then when we provide the answer to such a question, whether the asking party is passionately for or against, we can expect the fun to begin. We can easily distinguish plan supporters from detractors just by their response to a timeline's projected delivery date. Supporters will encourage us to make it happen faster. Detractors will challenge the assumptions we made in the timeline in an effort to show that we were unrealistically optimistic.

Later, when we actually implement the project, it often turns out that the original proposal timeline was wrong. It could have been too conservative, or more commonly, unaccounted-for difficulties may have delayed the matter. I say "unaccounted-for" rather than "unforeseen" on purpose. If our proposal timeline includes an extra three months to deal with two computer system crashes, a delay from a flooded facility, and the auto accident of a key system designer, we would encounter skepticism from both sides. Supporters would say that we cannot predict such things, so we must remove them from the plan. Detractors would just laugh, but not "with us".

In reality, project managers cannot know they will have these specific problems, but most understand they are likely to run into some unforeseen ones. We cannot usually get away with including a step in our timeline that says, "Unforeseen problems - approximately 3 months". The experienced project manager is left with three choices: First, they can make it clear that the timeline assumes nothing will go wrong. Incidentally, no one ever remembers that disclaimer when problems do turn up, so it is a bad choice. Second, the project manager can pad the timeline. This is the most common choice, although few admit it. Padding means "rounding up" time estimates for many items in the timeline, resulting in a total estimate that includes room for delays. Of course, the problem with padding is that it can be obvious and difficult to defend.

Then there is the third option. We can design the plan behind the timeline to include an inherent ability to manage delay. This is like designing a building to be earthquake-resistant. It costs a bit more to build than a regular version of the same building. After all, designing a skyscraper whose site is near a fault line is complicated. The building is likely to experience some earthquakes. How many and how strong the earthquakes will be is an unknown. Do we really want to construct an ordinary building there? And so it is that most tough plans will experience problems that risk delay. How many and how bad the problems will be is the unknown here. But before we happily declare the need for a special timeline in this case, I have to hit the brakes. There is a special problem with the fault-resistant timeline. This kind of timeline does not resemble a line at all. It might instead look like the branches on a tree, or worse, like a programmer's flow chart. These charts are typically littered with different shaped boxes and multiple arrows coming out of multiple decision points. These charts are ugly, inappropriately so for this kind of high-level initial presentation. I therefore recognize that a better timeline version exists and we can call it up in some later detailed project planning session.

That leaves me with what I find to be a humorous conclusion. The strategy I will follow resembles the first option. Recall that is the kind of timeline that assumes nothing will go wrong. For the benefit of my own sanity I will offer two variations of the best-case timeline. These variations produce a short-hand version of the self-repairing timeline by including alternate estimates for "expected case" and "worst case". The result will be a clear answer to the timeline question because it is both straightforward to follow and includes impact of potential delays. It is the kind of timeline that makes the most sense for this sort of introductory executive presentation. We could really implement Magnified Capitalism in the best-case timeframe. However, that would require heavy political pressure by both parties and the public. With a milder degree of consensus and fair support we should experience a timeline closer to the "expected" one. If there is a fight at every step of the process then the disappointing "worst-case" timeline will most closely represent what plays out.

Magnified Capitalism Timeline

Each column of numbers shows the passage of time in weeks for a different timeline variation. The steps shown are most closely aligned to the best case one:

Best Case	Expected Case	Worst Case	Step #: Completed Step description [# weeks taken to complete Best * Expected * Worst] [running subtotal of # weeks Best * Expected * Worst]
.... # Weeks from start ...			
6	10	40	
			Step 1: CMS Legislation Drafted [8 * 16 * 104][8 * 16 * 104]
12	20	80	Step 2: CMS Bill Passed and Signed [2 * 4 * 52][10 * 20 * 156]
			Step 3: Appoint CMS CEO [4 * 8 * 36][14 * 28 * 192]
18	30	120	
24	40	160	
30	50	200	Step 4: CMS Financing Proposal [16 * 26 * 52][30 * 54 * 244]
			Step 5: Full Funding [4 * 6 * 26][34 * 60 * 270]
36	60	240	
42	70	280	
			Step 6: Build + Acceptance Testing [12 * 16 * 40][46 * 76 * 310]
48	80	320 (318)	Step 7: CMS Starts - Services Offered [2 * 4 * 8][48 * 80 * 318]

The bottom line answers are: the best-case scenario will take 48 weeks, which is about 11 months; the expected case totals 80 weeks, or around one and a half years; and the worst case comes in at 318 weeks, which is just over six years. Please keep in mind that the differences among the three cases are largely determined by politics, which in turn is roughly driven by popular demand. As I mentioned, the expected case represents the outcome from a fairly strong political pressure. The best case could represent the insistence of public outcry, but it could also represent the effect of powerful political maneuvers. Such maneuvers are available to a sufficiently motivated and tactful chief executive. This means that you, Mr. President, have the greatest ability of anyone to drive a more aggressive timeline. Other types of political scenarios could also produce the pressure required to move quickly. For example, if enough citizens rallied to drive the process then the actual timeline would also trend closer to the best case scenario.

The following are expanded explanations of each of the seven steps shown in the timeline above.

Step 1: CMS Legislation Drafted [8 * 16 * 104]

> (As a reminder, the three numbers in brackets are an estimate of how many weeks this step will take according to three different cases - best case, expected case, and worst case. So while step 1 could take as little as 8 weeks, it is expected to take 16 and could be delayed to as long as 104, which is about two years.)

In this first step towards implementing Magnified Capitalism, congressional legal teams draft the initial bill(s) to launch the provisional CMS. Notice that we are using the previously described method (see the Scope List) that has Congress passing two bills to implement the CMS, rather than just one, plus a third annual bill that installs the initial batch of incentives. This approach addresses some perceived risks from skeptics because it involves conducting a detailed analysis before committing billions of dollars. This first bill commits primarily to the effort of this analysis. After receiving the analysis, Congress will have more confidence in the estimate for the full costs of running the CMS and the total funding required.

Having two bills rather than one also separates the argument over which service incentives we should implement in the first two years from the discussion about whether or not to implement the entire program. Full funding is therefore deferred. For this first step Congress is paying to set up a skeleton CMS crew (the provisional CMS). This crew will then work to establish a detailed financial proposal and many related details. Later Congress will be able to revisit the question of "Will it really work?" after these people produce comprehensive estimates and independent economic analysis. The people responsible for implementing Magnified Capitalism will be able to offer greater detail in answer to most questions and concerns. This procedure should elevate confidence to pass the funding for the rest of the plan (see step 4).

Step 2: CMS Bill Passed and Signed [2 * 4 * 52]
This step represents the time it takes to debate the provisional CMS Bill drafted in step 1, pass it in both the Senate and the House, and then gain a presidential signature. The bill itself is detailed above. Primarily, it provides for enough money to hire the skeleton crew. This crew will then prepare the detailed plan and financial analysis to be presented in step 4.

Step 3: Appoint CMS CEO [4 * 8 * 36]
Once the provisional CMS Bill passes, you, Mr. President, will need to nominate a CMS CEO. We can expect that Congress or the Board will confirm this person. As you know, such approvals can be either swift or greatly delayed depending on the controversial nature of the candidate and related factors. This is an important step, however, because the CEO's main role at this stage is to hire the executive staff that in turn will hire the rest of the skeleton CMS crew. This provisional CMS team will do the serious work needed to make it past the next step.

Step 4: CMS Financing Proposal [16 * 26 * 52]
We have hired the CMS skeleton crew. They have worked out a draft of the CMS Operations Handbook. The automated systems needed for CMS Operations and Approval Testing now have detailed designs. We have completed a detailed economic analysis to forecast CMS Fund requirements. All this work has helped produce complete cost estimates and a formal financing request. Much more legal work has also been completed. The provisional CMS organization is ready to provide a formal plan to Congress and testify if needed. This step is intended to help Congress create the second bill that commits to a full CMS implementation (see step 5). The analysis conducted during this step allows Congress to better understand how much money is needed, gain a more accurate estimate of the U.S. economic impact, and instill a higher confidence that the entire strategy will work. During the time this step is being prepared, you, Mr. President, will need to negotiate with Congress the details of how you will run the Board of Directors, if you did not already do this earlier.

Step 5: Full Funding [4 * 6 * 26]
Congress holds hearings and passes a complete funding package, as requested in the detailed analysis completed in the previous step. Note that the big commitment of financing the CMS Fund will be subject to a successful demonstration of functionality by the CMS. This demonstration, which we have formally titled acceptance testing, will seek to prove that the CMS plan will work down to the exact details of each CMS service.

Step 6: Build + Acceptance Testing [12 * 16 * 40]
During this period the CMS builds its automated systems and then tests its standard operations in a U.S. market simulator. Analyzing the simulator results allows the CMS to tune its processes and standard service Terms and Conditions until they are optimal. These are then finalized as the real standards that the CMS will use commercially. With good test results on the finalized standards, the CMS is ready to request formal acceptance testing from the Board. While this step is occurring, Congress passes the first two years' CMS service incentive package if they have not already done so.

Step 7: CMS Starts - Services Offered [2 * 4 * 8]
It will take just a little bit more time for CMS operations to begin after acceptance testing. In this brief period the CMS will prepare to launch all of its services at full capacity. There will be some additional hiring to handle the expected demand, as well as some technical preparations such as launching the public website. Also, the CMS will finish up preparing a nationwide network of independent Certified Business Valuators (CBVs), as well as insuring a group of CMS Registered Patent Attorneys is in place.

A Footnote on Process Flows
I mentioned that if this chapter were presenting a complete operational plan, rather than just an overview, I would have included CMS process flows. I have purposely left that kind of detail for the CMS skeleton crew to complete as a future step. However, I do have some related notes of interest.

The design of some CMS processes will be pretty apparent, while others may be less so. Those that are not so obvious should receive particular attention in follow-up analysis and planning. A short list of such processes includes the following:

Open CMS Processes of Interest

- **Standardized Service Incentive Tiers** - I pointed out earlier that the Board will manage all CMS service incentives on an annual basis. These incentives provide the government with a national policy steering wheel. However, we determined that we should implement these incentives in a standardized way, such as by using pre-established tiers. If Congress (or the Board) was allowed to set dollar amounts for incentives rather than using the standard tiers, they could easily create incentives that were either insufficient or overreaching. Using standardized tiers further allows us to pretest the incentives in the market simulator, insuring that the different levels have the intended effect. Finally, a change in tier grade for some services may even include a change in service terms. These may be necessary to avoid problems or improve attractiveness. This will be apparent in simulator testing, but would be nearly impossible to forecast from the perspective of a Board member.

Regardless, I have left the exact design of the standardized tiers as an open action. Alternate proposals for detailing the design should be very interesting to compare.

- **Board of Directors** – I specified that the Office of the President should have the duty of Chair of the Board. Furthermore, Congress should populate the rest of the Board. However, I left it open to negotiation as to how many seats the Board will have, how many seats are for Senators and how many (if any) are for House members, and how those people are assigned and rotated. I also left open the process for voting on various matters, how to implement bills enacted by the whole of Congress such as rule changes and annual incentives, and the distribution of power among the seats on the Board. The negotiation of these rules and processes between the President's office and the rest of Congress will be fascinating.

- **Congressional Incentives** – I suggested that the CMS create a menu of predefined categories subject to incentives. These might include activities like producing green products or establishing manufacturing facilities in disadvantaged areas. Not only do we need to complete such a menu, but we must carefully word the definitions of each incentive. Otherwise, we will find incentives with unintended loopholes or constraints. Furthermore, whatever the initial incentive menu is, we can be sure that Congress will want to add some that either do not yet exist, or that are modifications of existing ones. We should establish processes to make these kinds of changes relatively easy to implement. If this sandbox is easy to play in, Congress should be content to stay in it. If it is too difficult, then Congress will be motivated to change structural rules in order to get what it wants. We definitely do not want that. Therefore, the design of the processes involved in enacting congressional incentives is very important.

- **Congressional Rule Changes** – Recall that we have special tough requirements for Congress if they determine to enact both temporary and permanent changes to CMS rules. They will do this, regardless. There should be guidelines for how to implement the approval testing and the rules themselves. In the future, the CMS might even want to run some simulation tests or provide existing test analysis of rules that are known to fail testing in some subtle way, or that define some sort of threshold. More advanced planning on the implementation of rules changes should generate a smoother experience and better changes.

- **Customer Rating System(s)** – Every CMS service will utilize a customer rating system. We will use this system to help judge the risk and thresholds that the CMS is willing to consider on a given deal. In the walkthrough section I gave a simple example. Here, we imagined a two-number rating system. How exactly to formulate ratings is an open issue. It is also an open issue whether or not the rating system will need to be more involved than the two-number-rating that I described. There is naturally a tradeoff between complexity and ease-of-use. Getting this right will be important to profitability as well as service attractiveness.

- **Certified Business Valuators** - Virtually every service makes use of a new kind of professional, the Certified Business Valuator (CBV). These people create the Certified Business Valuations that are required to complete most every deal offered by the CMS. This new service is to the CMS what a property appraisal is to a mortgage bank. CBVs will formally predict the fair market value of a business proposal. We will need to create a standard for how to make this prediction, a recommended training regimen for the CBVs, and a certification test program so people can qualify to become CBVs. Then we will need a rating system for CBV's, as well as enforcement and oversight procedures. Finally, we need a special fast-track solution for establishing the initial nationwide team of CBVs. Otherwise the adoption of early CMS services will get hung up due to the fact that CBVs do not exist today.

- **Service (Deal) Tracking and Management** - One of the functions within the CMS will be the tracking of each and every deal customers make. These deals are the embodiment of CMS services and therefore its investments. We must track progress so that we can provide assistance, raise warnings, and learn effective lessons. Deal management includes the initial setup of a deal and the closing (see also next two bullets).

- **Service (Deal) Approval Criteria** -Specific processes must govern whether or not a customer's application for CMS service results in an approval. If the CMS rejects a deal, there needs to be consideration for providing an explanation and guidance for how the applicant can modify their proposal to repair it. If the CMS approves a deal, there will still be a series of steps for moving from gaining this approval to issuing a check and making sure the deal is now being tracked.

- **Service (Deal) Closing Process** - Recall that a deal closes when the customer repays the investment to the CMS along with the full profits called for by the service terms. Every deal will have an expected close date (target), an early close threshold (for possible bonus terms), and a late close threshold (for penalties and then forced closure). We will need to carefully define all of these processes and their repercussions and clearly communicated them to customers. Forced closure is very much like a real estate foreclosure on a property mortgage. The CMS will need to establish a process, like an online auction system, for the liquidation of delinquent deals. Here prospectors will buy the rights to deals that did not pay the CMS in full by their forced closure dates. Notice that the standard terms of CMS deals will specifically provide for this action. Therefore, when someone fails to pay off a deal they made, they are not necessarily off the hook with just a bad CMS rating. A new investor will take over the CMS rights for whatever extended period they may wish to pursue. There will also be criteria and processes for fully closing deals that no longer have any value, or that otherwise qualify for closing under some special circumstances. We will need processes for recovering losses from customers who provided other types of collateral as part of gaining deal approval. Closure of PDN agreements is different from the closure of other CMS services. Certainly we will need to clearly define processes to make sure prototypers get paid when the deal reaches its cash-out goal.

- **Problem Resolution & Escalation Procedures** – The CMS will have a cascade of processes to deal with customer service issues. These begin with the online system, where an abundance of help should be available. The interface should include the ability to post questions or conduct a live chat session with a customer service associate. The customer may need a caseworker or deal manager to handle contract issues over the phone or via other communications methods. Second opinions should be available for conflict resolution, followed by standardized processes for management escalation. Finally, we will need to provide guidelines and systems for conducting formal arbitration. We may even end up forwarding these, in rare circumstances, to a regular court.

- **Investigations and Tools** – The CMS will have both an investigative function and automated tools that aid in the warning of potential abuses, legal problems or contractual issues. The investigators will use such tools, as well as processes embedded throughout the CMS, to take up new cases. We will need to formally track these cases to ensure only one investigation is carried out per case, and to ensure the results of such work are preserved for future consideration. When an investigation leads to the conclusion that a customer is probably guilty of wrongful acts or negligence, then we must define processes to handle notifications and any necessary enforcement procedures. These processes must support the accused's ability to challenge witnesses, inspect evidence, settle the matter through arbitration, and even appeal. If law enforcement were ultimately required, these procedures would include handover and coordination with appropriate authorities. We cannot merely dictate these procedures. We must negotiate them with the those authorities.

"At first I thought, 'Citizen company? That sounds like communism! Like we need that.' Most of the other government agencies I've dealt with already act like they are part of a communist system. The people I've talked to who work at such places are often quick to blame their problems on some bureaucratic mess. Most people know this, so I don't expect that to be news. Anyway, when my restaurant business ran into a problem two years ago, someone suggested that I try using the CMS Cash Flow Assistance Program. Just thinking about applying for government assistance made me anxious. But I needed the help so I went ahead with it. Guess what I found out? I had it backwards. The CMS doesn't act like any other government agency. Working with them, I felt like a valued customer right away. But it wasn't the same as a bank, or a broker, or a store, either. I mean, I could tell they had to make money from our deal, but it was also obvious that other goals were just as important. The CMS guy I work with most is called a deal manager. He admitted to me that he will get a bonus when our deal successfully closes out. But then he said this, 'That will take a few years. In the meantime I can get bonuses just for keeping enough of my clients happy!' And the services they have are just amazing. I mean, their purpose is to make sure my business gets whatever extra support I need. It's almost like I have a super-rich friend who understands business management. OK, this friend won't just give me money for free. But they are eager to make a really fair deal. That makes it the next best thing. Now get this. The other day I finally asked my deal manager why they call the CMS a 'citizen company'. He said it was because he and I and the rest of us, we are all CMS stockholders. Besides, their CEO reports to a board of politicians that includes the President. Apparently, she'll only keep her job if she kicks butt."

[Committee members laugh]

- CMS customer testifying before Congress -

VI. Use Cases

This is my favorite chapter of the presentation. Here I get to tell stories about what real people will experience. I will step through many different benefactors and illustrate how the strategy affects them. This is where our proposal becomes personal. We see that capital magnification helps people who deserve it. We are not handing something to them. Instead they become empowered, with more ways to earn their way forward. An illustration unfolds that demonstrates the broad reach of Magnified Capitalism. It paints a stark contrast with other economic strategies.

Before we start...

Speaking of these other strategies, it should be useful to point those out first. This way we will appreciate what we are competing against. As we review the use cases, we might consider what would happen if instead we were to follow one of these other approaches. At least from a political perspective, there seem to be only two leading U.S. economic strategies out there today, that is, the Republican plan and the plan Democrats have put forward. I would like to warn you before I go on. Regardless of which philosophy you prefer, what follows may leave a bitter taste in your mouth. And if you think I am being too hard on one party, just keep reading. No one escapes unscathed from the harshness of the following analysis. Truthfully, I prefer to think of it as revealing our true reality. Of course, this revealing is exactly the point. Here we go.

The Republican vision is one of lower taxes and less regulation. It says that government is the problem, so reduce the size of it, reduce its power, and pay less for a smaller beast. There is a "new" variation occasionally credited as an attempt to advocate the Tea Party vote, that involves the inclusion of, or perhaps emphasis on, some long-term deficit reduction. This variation therefore includes both cutting taxes and reducing the deficit. Notice the implication of combining these two points into one strategy. Such a combination requires a more dramatic reduction in the size and cost of government than the version of Republican strategy that emphasizes tax cuts alone. Regardless, the Republican economic strategy is clear, consistent, and even intuitively appealing to many.

My first observation is that this promise to pursue deficit reduction is not actually a new variation of the party's strategy. The previous Republican President, George W. Bush, made vigorous claims to be a fiscal conservative before being elected. His campaign went so far as to promise to "pay the debt down to a historically low level." Of course we know that as far as budget management goes, the opposite happened once he was elected. His administration negated efforts to balance the budget and instead set historic records in the other direction.

When his father, George H. W. Bush, ran for President in 1988, he also beat the drum of fiscal conservatism. To his credit, he tried to follow through on this belief even to the point of famously agreeing to raise taxes while in office. This move was a principle political cause of his failed reelection attempt in 1992. When Reagan ran in 1980, he promised to balance the budget within three years. As with George W. Bush, what was implemented went totally the other way once he got in.

That leaves us with an important conclusion. There is nothing new about Republicans claiming to want to balance the budget. The strategy the Republicans support today, at least in their rhetoric, is essentially the same as the platform every Republican presidential candidate in recent history has run on. We can look even closer and observe another related detail. Today's Republican candidates' claims of deficit reduction are either suspiciously unspecific or based on proposals that would never gain passage into law. George W. Bush did exactly the same thing when he ran. Fool me once, shame on you. Fool me twice....

Let us put the deficit reduction question aside for a moment. We observe that today's Republican Campaign supports an economic strategy that is the same as one George W. Bush backed when he ran in 2000. His Republican economic strategy ruled the first eight years of the millennium. Congress cut taxes and reduced regulations. They did not take these actions lightly, but vigorously. Now recall the historical analysis I made in the first chapter. The enactment of these types of Republican policies produced record budget deficits, unleashed industry-wide banking abuses, and resulted in the worst recession most of us have ever experienced. What did we learn from that?

First, we can just ignore any President's claim to be both a fiscal conservative and a tax cutter. We should observe that balancing the budget while promising to cut taxes is a have-your-cake-and-eat-it-too kind of promise. The one arguable exception, George H.W. Bush, tried to take a step in this direction through compromise on the tax issue. He was politically assassinated for it. As he learned the hard way, cutting taxes and reducing the budget deficit are in fact opposing goals. If we are already having trouble making the government spending cuts we need to balance the budget, we will make the job nearly impossible if we also cut taxes.

Historically, the few times when we have made meaningful progress toward reducing deficits, the effort has not included tax cuts. Yet it seems that once in office, most Republicans have given a higher priority towards tax reduction than towards budget balancing efforts. So I find it somewhat ironic that the few large moves on deficit reduction in the past had a Democratic President behind them. Regardless, we must conclude that a Republican's promise to balance the budget is, at best, a well-intended impracticality. Thus, political candidates who promise both lower taxes and a lower deficit must be one of two things. Either they are lying as a political strategy, or they are naïve. Take your pick.

Note that there may someday be an exception to this rule, especially if a candidate offers a very specific proposal that accomplishes the task (cutting taxes and balancing the budget), and they win their campaign after proposing it. This would give them the political cover to do the dirty work required to accomplish such a goal. Dirty work? There is the rub. Cutting taxes and reducing the deficit requires seriously deep budget cutting. Even without the tax cuts, the budget cuts necessary to balance the budget are profoundly problematic. Now consider a proposal that does this while also cutting taxes. Such a strategy will be very ugly to multiple constituencies. That is the reason no one has done it yet.

We have seen that Republican presidential candidates typically claim they are of the new, fiscally conservative type. The wise will ignore this as pure rhetoric. They can label their claim "new" only because Republicans never actually do it. Curiously, they also never pay a political price for their failure to do so.

Regardless, that leaves us with the second leg of the Republican economic strategy, the part that they do not claim as new. Over the past fifty years, they have consistently represented, and implemented when elected, the general philosophy that government should get out of the way. This translates to less regulation and lower taxes. Democrats often point out that Republican efforts in such pursuits have consistently provided disproportional benefits towards corporations and the wealthy. In response, the Republican justification for this effect usually centers around the need to create jobs.

Please now cue the drum roll as I state the most important part of this brief recap. Each of the last few Republican Presidents has implemented this strategy of getting government out of the way. To his credit, George W. Bush was particularly aggressive and tested the theory behind this strategy very well. But there is no hiding that fact that in every case where the Republican strategy ruled government, it simply did not produce the intended long-term results. It does not matter how intuitively attractive the theory behind it is. We can even be excused for believing it should have worked, as many did and some still do.

But especially thanks to George W. Bush, we really tested cutting taxes and reducing regulations 100%. This Republican economic strategy simply does not work. We can even go back to Reagan's presidency and say pretty much the same thing, although his version was less severe. We may also notice that the Reagan era ended in a smaller recession. So why is the Republican Party not pursuing some major modification or a whole new strategy today? I admit it has taken me a while to understand. I now believe I get it. The reason Republicans are making no major changes to their economic strategy is twofold.

The first reason is essentially political. Those who originally believed in the Bush strategy do not accept its failure. They blame every other issue that they can. They believe that the Republican economic philosophy is too intuitively correct to be wrong. We still hear people repeating this reasoning. They have elevated this philosophy almost to the level of a religious faith. "Certainly, we cannot expect a business to hire more people if government is taxing them to death," goes the chant. "Now is not the time to raise taxes on job creators. We must find a way to lower taxes. That will produce more jobs and a better economy." And what of the budget troubles this creates? "We have economists who say we are overstating the budget problem. Once we recover, we will collect more taxes from the prosperity produced. That is how we'll pay the deficit down."

And what of all those times we implemented tax cuts but the jobs still dried up because the economy tanked? Believers will not admit it is the strategy's fault. Instead, Republicans blame the next President, the Democrats, the wars, Congress, or something else altogether. When pressed, some Republican economists have devised very creative excuses to explain how the economic disaster came about through no fault of the very policies the same people insisted would solve all our problems. Mostly though, Republicans try not to think too much about past failures at all. They seem to proceed forward with a sort of mid-term memory loss. Once they have justified the past and explained it away, they forget it.

Let me be clear. Although today I consider myself an independent, I have been a Republican. I have empathy with many of this party's pursuits. But how can a whole party refuse to recognize that this recession came at the very end of an eight-year stretch when they got almost everything they wanted? If the party cannot learn from that, what will it take? Experience should produce a growth, an evolution, even a total shift. So why does the Republican economic doctrine of 2012 sound the same as it did when George W. Bush ran in 2000? The first reason is this tendency towards stubborn myopia, which I just described. And then there is the second reason. This may stun you.

It is, with all due respect, your fault, Mr. President.

> (Note: This comment and some details that follow comprise one of just a few specific references to Barack Obama in 2012.)

Remember, I said the people have two choices for economic policy. The second choice is the Democrats' strategy. Herein lays a problem. Thus far, the Democrats have not supplied an economic policy that anyone can easily explain or understand. This administration's economic decisions all appear to be tactical ones. We can fairly observe that they take the direction of 'the opposite of what the other guys want'. Harsher critics call this situation class warfare because these positions have the flavor of being anti-wealthy, anti-business, or based on some other pitting of one group against another. Although most people do not agree with the more extreme criticism, that does not mean they give the administration good marks, either.

The way I read it, the real problem is that the Democratic economic policy is vague, reactionary, and ultimately impotent. To make matters worse, of the few specific proposals the Democrats have put forward, several have been transparently politically motivated. When the purpose of a proposal is just to force the other side to publicly respond, there is trouble. The people witness the illumination of an ideological difference, yet this effect comes at the cost of valuable resources, including political capital. All this time and effort ends up accomplishing nothing...on purpose. The two choices the politicians offer the people are therefore very frustrating regardless of which side we are on.

What does a voter considering the Democratic approach see? They might imagine a well-intended firefighter whose main economic principle appears to be fending off the wrongful ideas of his foes. They may like this President, but it is hard to see his administration's economic vision. It is even harder to imagine that such patchwork will actually lead to a repair. This approach leaves the impression that this President is just holding ground until the economy magically repairs itself.

Alternately, a voter can choose the opponent Republican. This is the guy who offers a familiar policy everyone understands. There is some peer pressure here because nearly 35% of the citizens still agree that cutting taxes represents some kind of cure. It also helps that the Republicans recite this mantra like a prayer every time they get in front of a camera or microphone. Is no one willing to contest the Republican premise?

Regardless, here is the real punch line that explains why so many still cling to the same unchanging Republican economic strategy: It is hard to make a counterargument if no one ever proposes a better solution. In other words, the Republican strategy still stands because no reasonable alternative has challenged it. This leaves me somewhat sympathetic with the Republican diehards. After all, if the other guys cannot offer us a better solution that we can understand, maybe the one we do understand is not that bad. Maybe the Bush strategy only failed because of… (pick from the list of naïve excuses I outlined three paragraphs above).

To your credit, Mr. President, I expect you are well aware of the missing economic strategy problem, otherwise you would not have asked me to put this proposal before you. I presume you are sincerely searching for a new policy that can really solve the big problems. I hope Magnified Capitalism encourages you. I hope Republicans will be encouraged, too. Everyone should be. This strategy is not intended for just one party, but for the good of the whole country.

Please accept my apologies for the political rant. I am finished with it. Not only do I feel much better now, but I thought I needed to say it in order to set the stage for what follows. We all need to collectively take our heads out of the sand. Neither of the two strategies before us produces solutions. Thinking that one of them might work just weakens the motivation for Magnified Capitalism, so I put a sharp point on the matter with my critique of both parties' economic positions. A clean contrast now forms when we consider the use cases that follow. These situations represent a reality we can own. If we pursue this plan, wonderful things will happen. If we do not, I honestly hope we choose some other new path.

In the rest of this chapter we get to see how Magnified Capitalism will make its impact. This part of the presentation is not about theory, or macroeconomics, or even the metrics I am admittedly so fond of. It is about people. We are going to see how this plan transforms the lives of real, hard-working Americans. No one will get a handout. But by offering a well-lit path based on achievement, we will deliver success over and over in many variations. What I really hope becomes obvious is this: When people feel hopeless or beaten, it is easy to stop trying, or more often, aim only for the minimum. But when people are surrounded by opportunity, the opposite happens. Motivations come to life. Full potential awakens. I believe there is a happy capitalist buried somewhere in most of us. Hard work is not a burden when we really want to do it. People who believe they have a fair shot usually go for it. And when people make it, when they achieve success, this success spills out to everyone around them.

Life in United States 2.0

For the following use cases it will be helpful to understand a few common points. Most importantly, these stories occur in the hypothetical future. We may assume they take place about ten years from now. Each use case begins by describing some fictional person's "situation". Next, I describe how that person will navigate their problems "before United States 2.0". That description assumes an economy only slightly improved from today, if at all. As a shortcut, I will often simply describe it as if it were today's economy. Why is that? It does not matter whether a primarily Republican or Democratic strategy comes into effect between now and then. As I argued above, neither approach represents a cure of any kind. This leaves us with an economy that still needs to heal. My simplified prediction is that our economy will limp along a near flat line, perhaps a little better. Therefore, the situation will be essentially identical to today.

After that, each case considers what will happen instead "in United States 2.0", in other words, when the Capital Magnification Service has been in place for around eight years (estimating the program starts in two years). Its Fund size has held at around one trillion dollars per year. The borrowing for the Fund, however, stopped after the sixth year, so the CMS has been totally self-sufficient and repaying its debt for the last two years. While the U.S. economy has long since recovered, the cases we will examine focus on those people who have yet to utilize CMS services themselves. We can assume that the unemployment rate has fallen to around 5%, and that quarterly GDP is tracking a growth rate near 6%.

This means the economy is not just healthy, but energized. The numbers could easily be better, but I do not want to assume that because these use cases emphasize the benefits the CMS provides. If I turn up the economy too much, the examples might become too murky. Even though we could attribute an even hotter economy to our strategy, the solution to each person's problem might appear both too easy and non-specific. For example, if the unemployment rate were to actually drop closer to 4%, I could solve many of the personal use cases with "... and then they got ten job offers." Although perhaps humorous, such a description dodges my goal here.

VI. Use Cases

For each use case, we will experience an individual's interesting situation vicariously. Some are positive and some are negative. The emphasis is on how the Magnified Capitalism environment offers new choices for dealing with challenges and opportunities compared with an environment largely unchanged from today. Each example represents a different microcosm of the real world. My first use case involves the most challenging personal situation in the set, a pregnant high school dropout. Subsequently, each next case proceeds roughly up the economic food chain. The ex-con is second, followed by a disaster victim, and a high school graduate. Along the way we will visit a laid-off accountant, those with families moving to the U.S., an inventor with a great idea, as well as others. After considering such personal stories, we will close out the discussion with a few use cases involving business owners. At the wrap-up I will provide some observations regarding common themes that we may not have expected.

A. Pregnant High School Dropout

Situation:

Amy is a 17-year-old who was about to become a high school senior when she found out she was pregnant. Amy is one of the 3.5% of women between the ages of 15 and 19 who will carry a baby to term in any given year (all stats here are from the CDC for 2010). Note that since one third of teen pregnancies are aborted, Amy had over a 5% chance of getting pregnant in each year starting at age 15. After doing the math, we may be surprised that she had over a 30% chance of getting pregnant by the time she reached the age of 20. These are the odds for all U.S. teenage women. At the time these young women become pregnant, 81% of them will be unmarried. Getting pregnant also drops their odds of graduating from high school from 90% down to around 50%.

Regardless of the stats, our Amy is not married and has decided to drop out of school so she can focus on her baby. Her motivation is financial. Amy's parents cannot afford to pay for the care she and her baby will need, especially in the long run. Furthermore, they were upset at her for getting pregnant in the first place. They told Amy that if she wanted to keep the baby, she would have two choices, either get the father of the baby to "help", or get a job herself. Presumably this was their strategy to try to convince Amy to marry the father. Otherwise they hoped to motivate her towards getting an abortion so she could finish her schooling before trying to raise a child.

It turns out that the father of her unborn child is neither particularly interested in the marriage option, nor is he a great candidate in other respects. Not only did he break up with Amy before he found out about the pregnancy, but he is still an unemployed high school student himself. This leaves Amy feeling like he is therefore a pathetic choice for a husband. Sadly, even from a pure cash-for-child-support perspective, this young man will be of little help to her, at least for a while. Since she is of a strong mind to keep the baby "no matter what", that leaves her with a single solution path. Amy needs to get a job and start some kind of career.

Choices before U.S. 2.0:

Under any economic circumstances, Amy has a pretty big problem. In an economic environment similar to today, it is a particularly tough one. Amy's main options include some kind of low-level work-from-home job; a position in retail, food service, or hospitality; or some type of work in a telephone call center. All of these will become problematic to some degree as her pregnancy gets closer to term. The work-at-home options tend to be marketing-oriented and commission-based, such as pay-per-lead or pay-per-hit jobs. This is better than nothing, but would not provide her any health insurance, which she really needs. It would also be very hard work for uncertain pay. A job at a retail shop, restaurant, or hotel would be nice, but Amy's physical state is a bigger issue for these choices, as is her lack of a high school diploma. It turns out that many of these establishments require a diploma, especially for the more appealing and less physical positions.

The call center work is probably her favorite target, but here the difficulty in obtaining an offer may be the highest of all. Call centers are often subcontracted to overseas firms. Those that are located in the U.S. often have requirements for experience and at least a high school diploma, sometimes even a college degree. Regardless of which industry or career Amy goes after, the competition for all the job targets is very tough. Given Amy's lack of experience and missing diploma, there is a fair likelihood Amy will remain unemployed for quite a while. When she does get a job, she should expect it to offer no insurance and pay either minimum wage or a very modest commission.

Choices in U.S. 2.0:

As I suggested in describing the overall U.S. 2.0 situation, Amy's outlook is substantially brighter just due to the fact that the unemployment rate is so much lower. That means all of the target positions she would have considered today are going to have more openings in this hypothetical future. The result should be that more employers have an active interest in hiring her. When the unemployment rate is high, employers know they can be picky. When unemployment is low, employers become more motivated to apply creativity when considering job applicants.

Maybe a high school diploma is not so critical for certain positions if Amy gives a good interview or has solid references. Alternately, some hiring managers will put more weight on her experience in clubs and afterschool activities than they would have before. In any case, these are soft (or mushy) benefits attributable to the generally improved economic climate.

However, as I mentioned in the introduction, I want to focus on the more concrete benefits Amy experiences that are specific to Magnified Capitalism.

The most important of these to Amy is the Prototype Development Network (PDN) service from the CMS. Recall that this is a special resource that helps startup companies, and some other small businesses, get work done with deferred pay. We call this pay "deferred" because the compensation for this type of work is a negotiated amount of stock shares in the young company. However, this stock will not be convertible to cash for some time (typically 8 to18 months). Therefore, prototypers work for deferred pay with some risk that they will not be paid at all. That means prototyping work via the PDN is a weak solution if immediate income is the priority. But before Amy dismisses this track, she will need to consider two big pluses the PDN offers her.

First, working as a prototyper will allow Amy to gain experience in better career paths than she would otherwise qualify for. For example, if Amy can use a mobile phone or a computer, she may be able to sign up for some kind of software testing work. Alternately, Amy can try to leverage any other strength she feels she has. If she is good at accounting, she could apply for some entry-level finance work. If she has skills in drawing, especially on a computer, she may find some opportunities in digital art. Amy can even try her hand at other self-taught disciplines wherever she is so motivated.

It is not unheard of to learn programming, technical writing, project management, and other valuable skills through such an approach. While some people pursue these avenues today, in U.S. 2.0 self-education will be far more common. I expect a cottage education-support industry to grow around the needs and desires of prototypers who are starting new career paths. That means new tools and certification programs will pop up to help self-teaching efforts become both more formalized and more legitimate. For Amy, the biggest value of the PDN will be that she can gain experience in a truly interesting career path of her choice.

The second big plus the PDN has for Amy is the fact that much, if not most, of such work is not only flexible part-time, but also remote (work-at-home). Many PDN jobs will allow her to set her own hours and conduct most of the work using her computer and an internet connection.

What could happen with such a gamble? If Amy does a decent job for the first startup she signs on with, she will earn new references and work experience to help her get the next job. The main gamble here is that Amy may be unable to deliver. Then such work might not just be unpaid, but also of limited value on a resume. Picking a subject she knows how to do or is comfortable learning is therefore very important. If her first project is for a company that successfully receives funding, then Amy's pay comes about a year later when she cashes in the stock that she earned. If she is lucky enough that her startup does really well in obtaining funding, then her pay might be substantially higher than anything she could have made at a regular job in today's environment.

Finally, her work to help a startup gain successful funding provides Amy with another career possibility. Such a company would have a strong motivation to hire Amy full-time. After all, they made it as far as they did at least in part due to Amy's work. Who would be better qualified to continue that same work? She has already proven herself and they know her. Amy's PDN strategy is more realistic if she counts on working with several startups, most of which will probably not pan out. But once any one of Amy's PDN companies receives full funding from their investors, she can expect them to offer her a regular job. That is the point of the PDN in general. When these startups obtain funding, and also later when they succeed in the marketplace, they will bring many of their prototypers, like Amy, with them. Of course, these companies will also hire many others as they grow.

Starting off as a low level prototyper is not Amy's only choice in U.S 2.0, but the other choices carry some further entrepreneurial risk. Essentially, Amy has two other kinds of options that may or may not work well for her. How well they work for her depends on what Amy is good at, what she is able to learn, and how much risk she is willing to take before getting paid. The first of these other choices is the Patent Funding Program, the system that allows inventors to file for patents based on their potential business value. This option would require Amy to have, or come up with, a great patentable idea.

While we could argue this is a long shot, I prefer to turn the matter around. I would say that if she did have a great patentable idea, she should go for it. This patent program would insure that all the Amy's in U.S. 2.0 could pursue such goals. She would have to do a lot of work, though. This might include hooking up with other inspiring entrepreneurs to fill out her management team. They would then build the business proposal to apply for startup funding. Alternately, she could use CMS resources to sell her patent idea while it is pending approval.

Amy also has a second advanced CMS-based option. If she does not have a great idea to patent, she can still sign up to work on the business side of someone else's startup. The CMS Prototype Development Network supports any kind of job role associated with prototype development. That means it also includes those startups that are looking for true partners. Perhaps Amy thinks she might be suited to be a minor (second tier) partner handling quality control. Of course, she would be challenged to make a good case for herself in such a role. But opportunities will arise, especially for those startups that are in a weaker business position. Many such businesses will not even take their first step because they will fail to fill all the management roles they need. That means some startups will consider anyone with the motivation and a half-decent claim that they can handle the work. In our case, Amy read a lot about quality control in school projects. Since then she has hoped to become more involved with that specialty.

Searching the PDN, Amy makes an interesting find. The not-yet-started Fuzzy-bot Company has an idea for marketing specialized toy robots for toddlers, but they need someone to oversee their quality control efforts. Amy is willing to tackle the project. Fuzzy-bot has said they will offer the quality control manager a guaranteed minor partnership and permanent job. Amy's first challenge will be to demonstrate her qualifications. Amy can explain her interest in the field, how she has studied the topic for a school project, worked on robotics in a high school class, and even written a paper on the importance of quality control standards. If she really wants to impress them, Amy can even draft a paper outlining how she would tackle Fuzzy-bot's particular quality control requirements.

We might guess she would need to do a lot of extra work to go for this job. She would need to do more research on quality control and on Fuzzy-bot's business in particular to have a realistic chance. Then, if the desperate Fuzzy-bot company agreed to take her on, she would have to work very hard to pull it off. Finally, to win big, not only would Amy have to do her job well, but Fuzzy-bot would need to succeed in obtaining their funding. But guess what? This is what entrepreneurs do all the time. Capitalism is about taking a risk, especially on yourself.

There will be many like Amy who are both motivated and able to take such risks. This is exactly the kind of person who often does the best work. In Amy's case, she gets the offer. She is going to work very hard to make up for her lack of diploma. Amy will learn all she can about what Fuzzy-bot needs her to do, and then work her tail off to make it happen. What a great result that is. If the Fuzzy-bot business ends up succeeding, suddenly Amy's gamble pays off big – she has a fair stake in the new company and a nice mid-management position. But even if everything does not work out, Amy still benefits. She will have made significant improvements to her resume as well as her references and personal knowledge. She will have learned a few skills that better prepare her to try again. Amy's next effort will leverage her Fuzzy-bot experience, perhaps qualifying her for a regular job at a more junior level of quality control. Or more likely she will try another PDN role, only this time she will have much better qualifications and a higher CMS rating. Whatever she does, her second opportunity should be one that has a far better chance to succeed.

We can add one more special job possibility for Amy, but this one involves issues beyond her control. She can search for incentives that target her situation. Recall that CMS incentives sweeten deals that help businesses expand and start up. Now consider that pregnant teens are a group that the government currently targets with various efforts, although today these are largely preventive or educational measures. Regardless, I would expect the pregnant teen group to be on the candidate list for CMS incentives, perhaps in the form of a hiring incentive.

Some companies receiving CMS funding will receive better deal terms if their proposal includes the intention of hiring qualifying people. Such people could be any subgroup imaginable that needs help finding work. The company would receive these deal bonuses only if they actually hired enough people who qualify for the incentives. Qualifying subgroups that apply to Amy could include pregnant teens or unwed mothers. Other examples of subgroups that might apply to Amy and her peers include the handicapped, those with special needs or victims of disasters. If there were CMS businesses in Amy's area, or she found CMS businesses with work-at-home openings, then we could expect Amy's prospects for finding a job to improve this way.

The subject of CMS incentives leads me to point out another improvement for Amy's situation, one relating to PDN incentives that apply directly to prototypers. Let me first explain an essential detail. Prototype workers receive a subtle but important benefit that I have only brushed upon. Prototypers who obtain high CMS ratings will qualify for a minimum guaranteed pay. This is money they receive from the CMS immediately after completing prototype work. I did not emphasize this earlier because I was focusing on offering opportunities to anyone who is willing to risk deferred pay on a successful venture.

Those prototypers who gain a lot of PDN experience with good job reviews will see their CMS rating rise. Not only does that make them more attractive to the next venture looking for PDN workers, but a high enough CMS rating qualifies prototypers for the minimum guaranteed pay I just mentioned. This pay is an advance against the pay the CMS expects this prototyper to make. The CMS is willing to front this money because the worker's high rating means they have a strong track record and provide quality work. Do keep in mind, though, that this minimum pay is only a fraction of the full deferred pay amount. But in some situations, such an advance may be very important, even critical.

Now consider this additional point: PDN incentives enacted by Congress will work by effectively raising the CMS ratings of targeted people. This increase would apply when considering whether the prototyper qualifies for minimum guaranteed pay. In other words, if pregnant teens were one of the groups targeted by a PDN incentive, Amy would qualify for minimum pay faster. She may even qualify for it on her first PDN job. Of course, Amy may also qualify for other PDN incentives. If any incentives applied to Amy's situation, working as a prototyper would become a significantly more attractive option for her. The higher her CMS rating grows, the bigger her guaranteed pay becomes. Incidentally, this is true even without any incentives. The difference is that, without an incentive, Amy would have to have much more PDN experience to qualify for the guaranteed pay.

Before I wrap up this discussion about Amy, I have to admit I left several options out on purpose. The most obvious is the possibility that Amy could get a job at a CMS-funded startup without qualifying for any special incentives. In United States 2.0, new companies should be popping up all over. Many of these will take advantage of CMS funds and related programs. Certainly, we can attribute Amy finding a job at such a company to Magnified Capitalism directly. However, this would make Amy's direct benefit a non-specific case. Although such a benefit is both realistic and likely, it suffers from the mushiness problem. Recall that Amy's benefit from an overall improved economy was similarly mushy.

Another example I could have mentioned was the possibility of Amy starting her own business. Some CMS services would certainly apply here. Instead I focused on Amy's goal of aiming for a minor partnership or mid-level management job at a startup using the PDN. That was asking a lot of Amy in her situation. Starting a venture entirely by herself would be far harder than this, so I left this one out with the footnote that I look forward to the exceptional pregnant teen who pulls off this even higher goal. In any case, I will dive into how CMS programs help startups directly when I examine the following use cases. I will bring up other issues I left out from Amy's choices in subsequent use cases. These include other services for which a pregnant high school dropout is not a likely target. But as with the possibility that she might start her own business, some impressive exceptions will occur from time to time.

B. Ex-con

Situation:

Before I relate the story of Bob, our newly-released convict, I will take this opportunity to highlight an open issue. I have not indicated whether or not released felons will qualify for any CMS services. I will assume in this story that while on parole, an ex-con can qualify for non-partnership-level Prototype Development Network jobs. Later, once an ex-con is released from parole, their rights should be upgraded to allow entry into minor-partnership-level PDN jobs. I am otherwise of the opinion that ex-cons should not qualify for the business-level services, except as the receiver of business services from other qualified capitalists. Even in this case, we should require an ex-con to fully disclose their record.

Why allow ex-convicts to qualify for any CMS services? I personally have two reasons, a moral one and a practical one. The moral reason is that I believe convicts are usually just people who found themselves in a more desperate or challenged life situation than they were equipped to handle. Put another way, I believe most people want to be good, but can be drawn towards bad decisions under difficult circumstances. I, for one, am glad that I was raised in decent neighborhoods, went to pretty good public schools, had hard-working, loving parents, and did not make too many bad decisions that I could not recover from. I expect most convicts, and here I mean those who are truly guilty, could not say the same. More often than not theirs is a sad story of bad fortune, bad parents (or lack of mentoring), bad environment, and schooling unsuited to handle their situation.

That does not mean they do not deserve the punishment they receive. And we still need to be careful of those who really are unable or unwilling to reform. But I also have a spiritual belief that guides me here, based on my personal interpretation of the New Testament. I think God will find it challenging to be any more tolerant of me than I am of others. Therefore, I tend be careful when called upon to make grand judgments. The result, when I am strong in my own character, is to err towards favoring no more punishment than is absolutely required. Regardless of each person's own view, a helpful effect of this philosophy is that it produces some clean logic. I can conclude that if someone has served their time then they have paid the high cost of their decisions. A civil society should consider such debt paid lest they disrespect their own justice system. We could also look at the situation from the other side. Unnecessary restrictions on ex-cons are arguably unfair. That leaves us only having to worry about which continued restrictions are truly necessary.

I also have a practical reason for offering at least limited CMS services to ex-cons. If we are inclined not to trust any felons, we should find the alternative of not providing any CMS assistance to be scarier. The prison system releases felons all the time. In fact, the United States has the highest rate of incarceration of any country in the world. Note that over 1% of adult Americans are in jail now. The figure rises to over 3% if we include those under probation or parole. Over 6% of our adult population has been convicted of a felony in their lifetime. That equates to over 12 million people. Since about two million of these are currently in jail, we can consider the other 10 million people to be ex-cons. What we are really talking about, then, is convicted felons who are no longer in prison.

Which situation should we all prefer, a society that makes it very difficult for anyone to hire an ex-con, or a society where with modest effort even an ex-con can easily find respectable employment? If we force convicts to suffer high unemployment rates after they are released, we are asking for trouble. I could make a good case for the opposite approach. We should offer released convicts lots of help getting jobs, if only to address our collective security. I suspect assisting ex-cons will end up costing society less than putting more of them into another desperate situation that they are ill-equipped to handle.

In this case, Bob served time for the most common category of felony people are arrested for in the United States - breaking drug enforcement law. Incidentally, felony DUI is the second most common. Only when we look at the third most common offense, property crime, do we see the kind of criminal actions most people presume of felons. Bob was no angel, though. He started out as a pot user in his early teens. His habit became too expensive for his part-time income from odd jobs to support. His solution was to start growing his own marijuana. As it turned out, growing extra required very little more work than growing just enough for himself. We can guess what happened next.

He started selling his surplus to other people, then growing more and more as sales improved. Doing this as a teenager in a state where marijuana is totally illegal was risky. Bob had trouble drawing a line beyond which he would stop. Being high most of the time certainly did not help his willpower. Then there was the money. Eventually he was making more this way than he could imagine earning at a regular job. As with most such situations, eventually his luck ran out when one of his "salespeople" was caught, arrested, and pled to a lesser sentence in return for testifying against the local kingpin. By then Bob was 22 years old and his pot business had been around for six years. He was the kingpin.

Fast-forward nine years. Bob is released on parole for good behavior, which he truly earned. He dealt no drugs in jail and otherwise caused little trouble. Did he learn his lesson? That is hard to say without a test of character. What is a thirty-one year old ex-con, ex-marijuana-kingpin supposed to do once he is out on parole? We can say this: Bob appears to be turning a new leaf. He certainly never wants to go to jail again but he is frightened at the slim prospects for supporting himself. He worries about his lack of job experience. Claiming his real experience on a resume strikes him as risky. "Does an employer really want to hear how I cleaned roads, sorted license plates, and ran laundry machines in jail? Would they prefer to know I ran a successful illegal drug manufacturing enterprise?" Bob often wondered about such issues as his parole date neared.

Choices before U.S. 2.0:

The government offers tax credits worth about $300 per year to every business that hires an ex-con. In the U.S. it is illegal to discriminate against non-violent ex-cons, although that seems like a difficult law to enforce. After all, nearly every job application asks whether the applicant has a felony record. One saving grace here is that if a person serves less than 30 months in jail, eventually their record will be expunged. This allows them to legally answer such questions as if they had never been arrested...unless that job is one of the many that qualifies as exempt from this rule. This category includes the military, security positions, financial management, and various types of personal caregivers, among others.

The Labor Department has a few small grant programs to help ex-cons. Goodwill, Inc. is well-known for welcoming released felons to its ranks. Other companies and non-profit organizations also regularly offer similar opportunities. Some prison systems provide skills training programs to help prepare their inmates for release. With all this support we might be excused for thinking Bob and his fellow parolees should be in good shape. Unfortunately, the opposite is true. While we lack a formal figure for the unemployment rate of former convicts, experts widely agree the number is many times that of the nationwide unemployment rate. The actual figure is therefore almost certainly higher than 35% today, perhaps closer to 50%. If a person has a felony record, they are a member of a subgroup in long-term economic depression.

Choices in U.S. 2.0:

It might not surprise us that Bob benefits from Magnified Capitalism in much the same way as Amy did. He experiences an overall improvement in opportunity due to a lower national unemployment rate. He is also likely to qualify for jobs from CMS-funded companies that seek incentive bonuses for hiring members of qualifying subgroups. Ex-cons would certainly be a logical subgroup for Congress to consider targeting for such incentives. Bob therefore shares in all the same mushy benefits, and perhaps also qualifies as a member of an incentive subgroup.

Unlike Amy, Bob will not qualify to become a minor partner in a startup through the Prototype Development Network. This right will only be restored later, when he is released from parole. Nor will he be a candidate for directly obtaining business-grade CMS services. That leaves Bob forever disadvantaged should he try to run his own venture capital firm, bank, or any other business, at least with respect to obtaining CMS services for his firm. However, these services are at the high end of those available. We did not even consider Amy for any of these except the minor partner one. What benefits does Bob receive either directly or indirectly through Magnified Capitalism other than having an easier time finding a regular job? He has one primary new avenue to consider. He can become a regular, non-partner prototyper using the PDN.

If Bob has trouble finding a regular job, or if he just wants to establish legitimate work experience in some field of interest, becoming a prototyper is the way to go. Hopefully, there will also be a qualifying incentive in place for ex-cons on the PDN. If so, that would help Bob receive some minimum guaranteed pay for his prototyping work. We should note, however, that whether Bob gets a regular job or finds work as a prototyper, he is still on parole. That means a parole officer will monitor his activities until the parole is satisfied.

Regardless, Bob is a great candidate for a number of positions other than blue-collar labor. Although he originally developed his skills in an illegal operation, he is more than competent at several useful disciplines. He knows the principles of organizing a distribution channel, such as for sales or manufacturing supply. He is skilled at running the operations of a cultivated farm, production greenhouse, or packaging facility. He even understands how to track and forecast financial figures, like production costs and sales. Finally, he understands sales and marketing principles, especially as they relate to multi-level marketing. He certainly has both interest and real world experience in all these matters.

Resources available online can help him learn more about the subjects he may be interested in pursuing. As was the case with Amy, Bob only needs to determine where he wants to focus, and then do the work required to break into that segment. I want to point out an important distinction between Bob's opportunities today versus in United States 2.0. Magnified Capitalism provides Bob with a formal way to turn interest and limited skill into useful experience and references. In today's world, interest and basic skill alone are not enough. Bob would probably be forced into some type of blue-collar labor work, if he found any work at all. So this is not just about getting a job. It is about pursuing a satisfying and productive life he can be proud of.

In this case, Bob has decided he enjoyed growing plants in a controlled environment for production purposes. This may seem amusing considering that he originally learned how to do it merely to sustain his pot habit. He did go to some trouble later to learn more refined growing methods that supported the volume of his marijuana business. Bob himself figured out how to do all of the indoor agriculture involved, including engineering his growing facilities. In prison he found he missed the botanical processes and the satisfaction he felt from seeing successful results. After searching the PDN for any related work, he found several startup companies whose business depended on establishing indoor greenhouses of various types. One calling itself Urban Canned Collectives (UCC) has an idea for selling greenhouse conversions of unoccupied office space. This model includes some new technical inventions. They need to take their idea from concept to working system, so they are seeking several prototypers to test working variations of their concept.

Bob is excited by their green approach to piping sunlight from the roofs of skyscrapers using fiber optics instead of installing costly artificial lights. He reads up on other peoples' work in related technology. Some similar efforts involve the use of hydroponics while others focus on new methods of optimizing CO^2 levels in a growing environment shared with people. Bob is bursting with ideas about how to make good use of limited office space for growing plants. He is sure he could set up a cost-effective mini-prototype farm that would help prove that UCC's concept can work commercially.

Bob decides to be honest on his resume when he applies. He will make no effort to hide what he used to do. "The business I had was a mistake for which I have paid the price. It did, however, leave me with a keen skill for engineering indoor greenhouses." Bob is hopeful that he can get this work. In his application to Urban Canned Collectives he attaches a paper he wrote just for them. In it he outlines why he thinks his prototype farm efforts would be successful for UCC. Whether he gets this particular job or not, Bob has become excited about his life for the first time. He knows he wants to do prototyping work as an urban farm engineer. This excitement is translating to self-motivation, self-education, and ultimately, creative work to break into his new field.

C. *Disaster Victim*

Situation:

In this use case we will discuss a young woman named Carmine. She is a resident of Beaumont, Texas, a city near the Gulf of Mexico and the Louisiana border. Until recently, Carmine worked as a waitress in a local restaurant for several years. The management there was so happy with her work that they began preparing her for a promotion to shift manager. Although Carmine had not planned this career direction, the opportunity excited her and would increase her pay. Regardless, all this became moot when the hurricane hit a few months earlier. This was a catastrophe for many gulf coast towns in the area, but Beaumont was hit hardest of all. The federal government declared affected surrounding counties in both Texas and Louisiana to be disaster zones. Many people lost their homes and businesses and were unable to return until just recently.

When Carmine finally got back home from the state-sponsored shelter, she was relieved to find her apartment and possessions were largely still intact. However, the restaurant she worked at was completely flooded and now out of business. Not only that, but most of the other businesses in town were either directly or indirectly affected. If they escaped physical damage, most still lost nearly all of their customers. Only now, after many months, were some people returning to the area and trying to restart their lives. Official estimates said that as many as 40% of the local residents would never return. Carmine had a little savings on hand and the government provided some additional disaster relief. That meant she could eat and pay the bills for at least a couple of months. However, she was not sure what to do with her life now.

Choices before U.S. 2.0:

I should emphasize that the issue we are addressing in Carmine's use case is not the short-term disaster relief problem, but the problem people face in such situations over the long term. We can assume that both state and federal governments have worked hard to insure basic safety, shelter and infrastructure repair appropriate for the fictional Beaumont hurricane described here. We even recognize that Carmine has received relief funds to help her get by for some time to come. We can further assume that Congress has passed a relief bill that includes tax breaks to help local businesses recover, low interest business loan guarantees, and extended funding of the National Guard and local agencies to complete additional infrastructure repairs. We have encountered such circumstances before and they will happen again. What the government does in such situations is both helpful and important; we could argue that they should do even more. Regardless, we have also seen that none of these measures ever produces a prompt, full recovery of the local economy.

Essentially, even with all the help described above, every major disaster area can count on being thrown into a local economic depression for years. Unemployment will remain high. Local businesses will be challenged by both costs and market reductions. Supplies will be more expensive, especially at first. The recovery will be incremental and painfully slow. Those who do not move out will need to be brave. Those who do leave cannot be faulted for seeking a better environment. To a significant degree, having a large portion of the population relocate elsewhere after a disaster provides some relief to the local infrastructure, including its economy. How is that possible? Because otherwise, the rate of local unemployment would be even higher, as would the demand and cost of goods and services needed for the recovery. When an area is stressed by disaster, it helps it for the population to be thinned initially, just to speed healing. Those who remain are either more anchored in the region or more stubborn in attitude. These are exactly the sorts of people who should stay.

Carmine is on the fence regarding relocation. She grew up in Beaumont and loves it here, or at least she did. Her parents retired and moved away a few years ago, but she has lots of friends and seems to know almost everyone.

Even though so many people are leaving town, she wants to find a way to remain. But Carmine is not naïve. She knows that to stay is to sign up for at least a few very tough years, and it may be close to a decade before the local economy is really strong again.

What choices does Carmine have today? There is a fair amount of waitressing work to be had if she leaves town. She cannot say the same about staying. The few jobs available are mostly related to construction and repair. These are not activities that Carmine is good at or interested in. As hard as waitressing is, construction and repair does not appeal to her at all. There is some non-paying volunteer relief work available in town. Although these volunteer positions are also mostly repair-oriented, not all of them are. For instance, there are some relief agencies in Beaumont that provide food and personal services, such as assistance for the elderly.

If Carmine stays, her main strategy would be to keep applying for waitress positions until she gets one. Today there is a lot of competition but almost no openings. However, she has strong references and was great at her job. It might take a while, but she is confident that local restaurants will start reopening soon. They would consider her a top candidate for their job openings. In the meantime, she could try some volunteer work at a soup kitchen. It is a gamble, though. What if her money runs out before she finds work? Then again, Carmine's parents have offered to let her move in with them in Orlando, Florida. They say plenty of restaurants in Orlando are hiring, and there are also jobs at the entertainment parks nearby. It seems the wiser strategy may be to just leave town. She can always come back in a few years when the local economy finally bounces back.

Choices in U.S. 2.0:

Of course, we will expect the improved economy under Magnified Capitalism to provide Carmine with more opportunities in general, but this improvement has a particular impact in a disaster situation. United States 2.0 experiences a higher rate of personal wealth at all levels, whether it is business owners, investors, or even those lucky prototypers who did startup work for a company that made it big. When a disaster hits, the government is not the only source of assistance. Many private individuals from all sectors help as well. If there are more wealthy people, then the benefit from private donations and other personal efforts goes up, too. Carmine gets double the mushy benefit here.

Another aid Carmine can count on is CMS incentives. In many other use cases, it is hard to predict whether or not someone qualifies for incentives. In fact, we can expect that Congress will change the CMS incentive schedule with great regularity. But in the case of a big enough disaster there is little doubt that Congress will come together in a bipartisan way to pass emergency incentives for every CMS service, probably to a maximum level for at least a year or two. That means venture capital deals, bank loans, business expansion, and all the CMS private investor services will suddenly become boosters for both the victims and the affected local businesses.

With these incentives other companies, even those not previously located in Beaumont, will have extra reason to set up some portion of their newest businesses there, or otherwise hire people who were affected by the hurricane. Banks will have the motivation to provide loans to businesses that support these affected residents. VCs will have incentives to include Beaumont in their plans for new ventures. Beaumont's displaced and remaining residents who sign on for prototyping work will typically qualify for minimum guaranteed pay. People from Beaumont who start businesses after the disaster will be similarly favored for all CMS services. The full force of CMS incentives will kick Beaumont forward. This will do what no other government program has ever done. It will produce a strong local economic surge to fast-track Beaumont's long-term economic recovery.

The question I have is not whether CMS incentives will work, but rather how fast a local economy will recover using them at a maximum level. This is our first use case example in which Magnified Capitalism cracks a problem whose solution is out of reach today. Carmine should see all of Beaumont bounce back to life much more quickly than she would have if the disaster had occurred before we implemented this plan. By the time the CMS incentives expire, her town could gain an economic vigor it never had before.

Today we might expect this type of disaster to depress the local economy for up to 8 years. I expect Magnified Capitalism to shorten that time frame to less than three years. Regardless, we should see a rush of new opportunities in the affected region. Not only will Beaumont spend less total time in depression, but the city will also experience a short-term advantage. Carmine will not need to wait long to see new and existing businesses opening up. Even if she sticks to the strategy of just looking for a regular waitressing job, her prospects should be much brighter much faster.

Alternately, as we saw with Amy and Bob, Carmine could consider becoming a prototyper, especially if she was interested in gaining experience in a new field. As I mentioned, it is a near certainty that Congress would enact incentives to allow Carmine to qualify for minimum guaranteed pay if she did go down that route, but we have already described two PDN examples. For Carmine, there are two other interesting services that the previous use cases did not address; Bank Loan Participation and Private Venture Funding.

Bank Loan Participation makes it more attractive for banks to offer loans that contribute toward many kinds of business, real estate sales, and education funding. Since Carmine is a resident of a disaster area, we can expect all possible bank loan incentives to apply to her. This should make it easy for Carmine to qualify for attractive terms on a student loan to go to college. She would also find it easier to purchase real estate, buy equipment or a car, or obtain a business loan. To qualify for the business loan with full incentives, Carmine would need to locate her business in the Beaumont area or hire the required number of local residents.

Any bank that makes such loans will receive similarly attractive terms from the CMS. They will want to make as many of these kinds of loans as possible. As a result, major banks will show up in town shortly after the disaster. They will offer residents a variety of prepackaged deals along with exceptional personal services. Ads will pop up everywhere urging residents to refinance their homes and vehicles, refinance their business assets, or even apply for a loan to start a new business (using collateral). Other ads will point out that the disaster makes it a great time to go to college because of favorable student loan deals. Carmine will be tempted into considering this last option in particular. However, another opportunity rises up and attracts her attention. This involves the other CMS service that I promised to discuss.

We may recall that Private Venture Funding (PVF) is essentially a scaled-down version of the Venture Capital Funding service. The main difference is that PVF encourages customers to form private investor teams or partnerships. The greater the number of people who combine to request PVF money, the higher their total CMS rating will be. A team of investors' collective rating also raises the total amount of funding they can apply for. What I did not mention is the impact of incentives on a team. We might assume that when an investor team proposes to locate a new business in Beaumont, or to hire people from Beaumont, their proposal would qualify for better terms due to disaster incentives.

But PVF incentives will also apply to the whole investor team's CMS rating in proportion to the shares of the new company assigned to qualifying members. If the investor team includes Beaumont residents, the whole team benefits from this. In other words, as soon as Congress enacts the disaster incentives, teams of private investors will form and seek Beaumont residents who want to join them. These teams will look first for people who have money to invest. But others will consider offering partnership seats to those who have the experience and motivation to run part of a business, especially if they can also put up at least a little money, too. These investor teams will post their interest on special websites, perhaps even using the CMS PDN site as a proxy.

Carmine finds such an investor team, a group of out-of-town investors who want to take advantage of the CMS disaster incentives in the PVF service. They are looking for applicants who are willing to live in Beaumont and run a new restaurant as their local partner-chief-manager. They have designed a special restaurant management strategy that they expect to work well in situations like Beaumont's. The chief manager will be required to put up a small cash investment, but in return they will get a fair share of the new company and can draw a salary as soon as the restaurant opens. By assigning a significant number of the restaurant company's shares to a local resident, the investor team is pumping up their benefit from CMS incentives. They will train their local chief manager in their proven restaurant and financial management techniques so they can be confident of making a strong profit within a few years.

This is the perfect kind of opportunity for Carmine. She has just enough money. She also has enough experience and good references to make her case. Although this opportunity is the first one of its type that she has seen, it is apparent that other investors are preparing similar offers. If this investor group does not pick her, Carmine will keep trying with others until one of them pans out. It occurs to her that if this strategy takes too long, she could just form an investor group herself, except in this case, she would start out with the local-restaurant-manager position. Her open task would be to find out-of-town investors interested in joining a team that wants to take advantage of the Beaumont disaster incentives. Carmine could even use the PDN to beef up her management team with minor partners who are also local. She will study the details of how to achieve this goal while she waits to hear back from the original investor group.

D. *High School Graduate and/or College Dropout (with No Money)*

Situation:

This use case will be about an average middle class young man named Derrick. He is a high school graduate who avoided trouble in school but was merely a fair student. We can imagine that Derrick may have attended college for some time, but did not have the right disposition to stick with it. Regardless, the same career options will apply whether or not he attended any college.

Derrick, now 20 years old, lives with his parents, who are both still working. They can afford to support him for many years if need be, but neither they nor Derrick wants this. He often laments to friends and family that if he could find the right job, he would be quick to move out on his own. What does Derrick do with most of his time? When he is not watching TV, playing on his computer or mobile phone, or socializing with friends, Derrick likes to work on his car. He has customized his late model used Camaro in many ways, from the stereo to the engine. Even its paint and body have been "pimped", although not by a professional shop. Derrick made most of the car modifications himself in order to afford them. Derrick spends much of his time fixing up his car, cleaning it, making some adjustment or other, or working on the latest modification. He spends much of his remaining free time reading about how to complete the next car mod.

To make money, Derrick has worked most of the last three summers picking fruits and vegetables at a farm owned by a friend's family. For this work Derrick earned minimum wage, enough to afford his old car and most of his expenses beyond room and board. Life often feels like drudgery to him, though. The best of his friends see him as a nice guy whose lack of regular work leaves him a bit poor and down. His lesser friends sometimes act annoyed with Derrick, as he can come across as a bit of a lazy leech. He never has money, but he also does not seem particularly motivated to work harder than he minimally needs to. Derrick's view is that he cannot find anything he likes, although he is hard pressed to name what that would be if he did find it.

It is tempting to look at Derrick and say, "Who cares?" From our vantage point, dismissing Derrick is easy since he appears to care little about himself. However, he represents lots of people, even those much older than him. Many people have trouble finding their spark of motivation, the interest that drives them forward. For those who get hung up, the difficulty can grow worse with time. Imagine if Derrick never breaks out and just sticks to his minimal, meaningless work pattern until the day his parents cannot, or will not, help him anymore.

That would be a tragedy because Derrick is not a bad person. He has neither evil intent nor the inclination towards immorality. Neither is he totally unskilled or fundamentally stupid. In fact, as long as money is not at issue, most people find him to be lightly humorous, fun-loving, and kind. We could argue that he is very unwise in his lack of life planning, but most of us could be accused of that to some degree. Derrick has just nurtured this defect too much. The tragic part is that he represents a potentially wasted life. Society, the government, his parents and even his friends have all invested effort into Derrick. Yet his returned contribution or output, even in the form of mere emotional happiness, is seriously low. This is not what he wants either, but no solution presents itself.

Derrick has motivation and intelligence, but it is buried. When forced into a desperate situation, he will do what it takes to solve his problem. So if Derrick's parents were to kick him out of their house, we can be sure he would find some kind of work. Fortunately for him, it does not take this kind of drama to get him moving. Social and practical pressures are building all around him – from his friends, his parents, his own desire for car modifications he cannot afford, and even girls he would like to date. Everything he likes, loves or wants to love expects him to find some kind of regular job and make some real money. This very morning Derrick wakes up with an epiphany. It is time to get his life moving. He has determined to find work. If it turns out to be something interesting, that would be great. But he has finally reached the point where he will take anything.

Choices before U.S. 2.0:

Derrick's basic options are pretty obvious. He can apply for almost any job that pays minimum wage. There are many careers to pick from here. The problem for Derrick is that most of these will strike him as boring and dead-end. He might have enough motivation to put up with that issue for now. After a few years, though, he is likely to have regrets.

Another path for Derrick to consider is to obtain some additional education so that he might qualify for a job he likes. For him, some type of trade school might be the best choice. A career as an engine mechanic, auto detailer or body work specialist are all obvious possibilities. If he asked, Derrick knows his parents would pay for as much of this kind of schooling as they could. Student aid based on need is out of reach, however, as his parents' income is too high for him to qualify. He is pretty sure that if they tried to pay for the entire cost of his trade school, it would ruin their retirement plans. This leaves him reluctant to ask for the money. The more considerate solution would be to save up for school himself. Derrick, tired of living at home, also wants to move out and be on his own as soon as he can. Earning only minimum wage makes it difficult to meet either goal anytime soon. He is not sure which goal is more important, the saving for school or the moving out.

Regardless, he decides to work extra hard at applying for any positions related to cars, including sales, repair and detailing. With time he hopes to find some sort of work, even if it is entry-level.

Choices in U.S. 2.0:

It is a shame I have already discussed the Prototype Development Network. In many ways, Derrick is an ideal candidate to become a prototyper. Even though the economy is generally better under Magnified Capitalism and therefore Derrick should have much less trouble finding the kinds of entry level positions I discussed above, doing PDN work instead is a much better strategy for his situation. The reason is that as a prototyper, Derrick can explore a wider range of interests.

Finding a career that motivates Derrick is arguably far more important than whether he makes much money right away. His parents will not mind if much of his income is deferred, especially if he is honestly trying out different career options. With the PDN Derrick could sample a variety of auto-related jobs, or even careers that he did not expect he would like until he read about them. For example, he might like to try software testing since he is very comfortable with computers and smart phones. We will just keep in mind that for other people in Derrick's position, United States 2.0 will deliver both the mushy benefits of an improved economy and the strong alternative strategy of working as a prototyper.

We could also have used Derrick as an example for Private Venture Funding. Remember how Carmine found an investor group that wanted to set up a restaurant in a disaster area? They were trying to take advantage of CMS incentives. That left them willing to offer attractive terms to an onsite manager. Now, imagine another investor group looking to set up a car pimping service or a similar customization shop. They might try to reduce startup costs by using the PDN to find employees. Their business plan might become even more attractive with a strategy that turns the initial shop managers into minor partners. In return for being hired as managers and receiving some company equity, these minor partners would have to agree to live in a qualifying area such as an urban development zone or economic recovery zone. That way the investors will qualify for extra CMS incentives when they apply for funding. Derrick might be willing to move to such a place in return for the career jump, especially if it was not too far away. He did teach himself particularly well in the area of car sound systems. He could easily modify his resume to emphasize this skill, perhaps qualifying him to manage that aspect of the shop's work. But Derrick is not going to go down this path, either.

In this case, the CMS service that most affects Derrick's ultimate career choice is Bank Loan Participation. This is a straightforward decision. In United States 2.0, loans for educational purposes are significantly easier to obtain and more attractive in their terms. This is true even if Derrick's loan does not qualify for any particular kind of special incentive. But he really wants the best possible loan terms, so Derrick decides to check out the list of trade-school degrees that qualify for incentives. He hopes to find a subject that interests him. During his search he notices that some loan incentives require graduates to commit to accepting a special job for a certain number of years.

He is a little disappointed to find no incentives for learning how to be a professional car stereo engineer. But he does find a different trade he likes that does qualify. In this version of United States 2.0, the CMS offers educational incentives for trade degrees in vehicle modification for security purposes. We can imagine Derrick could find incentives for other pursuits that would be more appropriate at other times, so this is just one possible example. Regardless, in this hypothetical future, to qualify for a vehicle security trade incentive, a student must commit to work for a military contractor for at least three years after graduation. Derrick decides adding armor and bullet-proofing to vehicles would be cool and fun. His mom and dad would hardly have to pay for any of his education. Finding a very good job would be almost automatic, and that would happen soon since it only takes eighteen months to complete the schooling. Finally, with the income he expects to receive at his new job, he will be able to repay the education loan within just a few years. Now excited, Derrick decides the three-year job commitment is no problem at all. This is a career he could stick with.

E. Laid-Off Accountant

Situation:

When Ella took the financial analyst position at the young Automated Apps Company, she thought it was a smart gamble. AAC was right in the middle of the new wave of smart phone apps. They had already achieved some success with both games and utilities. Her career outlook appeared bright and interesting. AAC really needed Ella, too. Her previous company was in a declining industry. Ella knew she had to find other work before the industry crumbled. The job offer from AAC saved her. She liked her work at her new company. AAC was rich in technical types, but few there understood how to manage their books or analyze the profits they expected to make from new projects. The company really needed her.

The company became even busier last year when AAC found out a much bigger software company, Electronic Parts, was looking closely at them. Ella's boss, AAC's Chief Financial Officer, was a brilliant financial expert herself. It had already been three years since the CFO hired Ella and they got along great. Just as Electronic Parts started making regular visits, the CFO began assigning Ella to special, secret projects involving forecasting future financial figures under different scenarios. It was obvious to Ella what was going on. The office soon started buzzing with rumors until it finally happened. Six months ago it became official. Electronic Parts bought out AAC. AAC was to be "integrated" into the bigger company.

At first it sounded like great news. Within two weeks, most everyone at AAC received some kind of bonus. Then the merger activities began. Ella stayed busy showing her new Electronic Parts merger managers the details of AAC books and related systems. Her old boss, the one-time AAC CFO, moved to a new job as the V.P. of Acquisition Finance. That left Ella worried since she did not follow her into that part of the bigger company. When Ella did reach her ex-boss on the phone, she received enthusiastic support but no real guidance. Two weeks ago, the finance managers Ella had been temporarily reporting to stopped asking her for new work. She could not get anyone to tell her what her regular assignment was going to be or who she should report to.

By the time she got the pink slip this morning, Ella was not surprised. Although she qualifies for some severance pay, Ella is now officially laid off. About 75% of the old AAC people found new jobs within Electronic Parts, but Ella was not one of them. Apparently they already had plenty of accountants and analysts. She has enough money to cover up to eight months of living expenses before she will need more funds, such as unemployment assistance. There is no time to waste, however. Ella knows this is her life savings she will be burning up. The sooner she finds a new job, the less of her hard-earned money she will lose.

Choices before U.S. 2.0:

There is some good news for Ella. Her performance at AAC was excellent. She has fine references and is in a career with a fair amount of demand. Odds are good for her to land another financial analyst position somewhere. Is there any bad news? The main problem is that her three years at AAC were partially wasted. One the one hand, she developed useful experience, tuned her skills, and has good references. On the other hand, she has been at the same career level for a long time. Ella is skilled enough to have been promoted and had been working hard towards this end. Now she will probably have to start over at nearly the career same level. Her next financial analyst position will likely leave her feeling like she is green for a third time. Her bad luck leaves her frustrated.

From Ella's own perspective she is now an expert in corporate finance. Some of the work she did at AAC was very advanced. It covered establishing new financial processes, supporting installation of automated solutions, conducting business sales and plan forecasting, and even doing analysis in support of a complex business buyout. Ella feels like she could even handle being a CFO herself, but she has never been promoted in her whole career. In this job market a laid-off worker is lucky to find a job at the same level they had before. Many people have to settle for something a little lower, especially if they are unemployed while they are looking. Even with all her experience, it is unlikely Ella will receive an offer for a higher-level position. It is a simple matter of competition. Given the choice between Ella and someone else who has already been a "senior analyst" (the next level higher for Ella), most prospective employers will pick the person who has previously held the higher title. As it is, Ella will be lucky to get a job at all in this market. Hopefully, she will not need to settle for too much of a pay cut.

Choices in U.S. 2.0:

Under Magnified Capitalism Ella has little to worry about. Not only can she find a job quickly, but in this hypothetical future job market the tables are turned. Employers with openings care far less about someone's previous title. They have to be flexible because it is too hard to find qualified people otherwise. Therefore, Ella's actual experience will determine the jobs she can go for. Given the kind of work Ella has proven she can handle, a very small tech company, particularly a startup, might even consider her for the position of CFO. She can surely expect to qualify for a mid-level financial position at a more established firm.

We could talk about Ella using the Prototype Development Network, although in her case this may be unnecessary. Certainly many startups will be looking for accountants willing to take deferred pay. However, no matter how sweet their offers, Ella would probably not have any interest in such companies. It is likely that such a startup would need to take on people far less established than Ella is. The PDN may also be a means to locate offers from startups looking for partners, both minor and major. This could include CFO positions or other jobs with management responsibilities. These opportunities might interest Ella a little more. However, Ella lives alone with no family support. She also does not have enough savings to feel comfortable taking the delay in pay that a new company would probably require. After all, she can probably find a decent job pretty fast. Even though it would be interesting, working for a startup is not the kind of bet Ella wants to take right now. If she does not receive any job offers in the next few months she might change her mind. Otherwise, such risks are better suited for those who either have a better backup plan, or are more desperate.

This same issue rules Ella out for starting a company herself, so there is no need to discuss Private Venture Funding. She certainly sees no need for any kind of loan, at least not yet. We begin to think that Ella's main benefit from U.S. 2.0 would be the mushy general one of an improved economy. However, Ella did a Google search for 'financial analyst jobs' and found something special I have not detailed before. It turns out that the CMS needs more Certified Business Valuators. In fact, CBVs are in huge demand. But CBVs do not work for the CMS directly. Being a CBV is like being a doctor, a photographer, or a real estate appraiser. Most CBVs have private practices. The problem is that such a practice is really a small business. However, there is good news for qualified people. The CMS offers them a package of services that helps set up their business almost automatically. Of course, as an experienced financial analyst, Ella qualifies for such a package.

What is included in the CMS Certified Business Valuator career package? Ella will receive free training and educational materials for two months. Existing CBVs say it is hard work if an applicant expects to pass the certification test on the first try. But accountants and analysts are well-positioned for passing the test. The career package includes the cost of taking the test up to three times. The applicant is limited to trying once a month, to encourage further study if they do fail. Finally, once they pass, they are offered a free two-week seminar and more training materials to guide them through setting up their own CBV private practice. This same class will also assist the applicant with the alternative strategy of trying to join one of the new CBV partnership firms. These companies are slammed with work and are always making offers to those who are well-qualified or who earn very high certification scores. The CMS will even prequalify an applicant for a small business loan if they need it, although it turns out that even new CBVs usually do not.

Why are Certified Business Valuators in such high demand? And why does the CMS provide such aggressive assistance to people who choose this career? It turns out that the CBV service is foundational to almost all of the CMS' own services. Virtually every CMS business service requires a formal, independent Certified Business Valuation. The CBV makes a formal estimate of the potential value of a business plan. They even estimate the odds that the plan will succeed. These formal estimates include evaluating a planned business expansion, or even a successful patent.

CMS processes usually require the services of a CBV precisely so that the CMS itself does not make judgments about whether or not some business is worth the amount the applicants claim. But the certification process for CBVs insures that all business evaluations are conducted with specific methods and standards established by the CMS. Thus the independent CBV helps insure the entire system is fair and market-driven. But because most CMS services require the services of a CBV, a bottleneck develops if not enough qualified CBVs are available. So the CMS has an aggressive program to encourage people to become CBVs. The CMS website even helps customers locate CBVs in their area. This is a convenience for customers, but also makes it easy for CBVs to find clients as soon as they begin work.

This employment situation becomes even more interesting if a valuator is very good at their job. Certainly, there is a quality difference among CBVs. How does the CMS favor the better ones?

CBVs receive a CMS rating for their work just as customers do. Their rating goes up and down with both volume and accuracy. A terrible CBV will make off-the-mark estimates and judgments that may lead to problematic deals or even business disasters. Skilled CBVs will produce highly accurate business valuations. Such valuations give a deal a higher confidence, qualifying the applicants better at lower risk. Valuations from green or weak CBVs receive lower deal scores, resulting in less attractive terms or even service rejection. In other words, every applicant to a CMS service will benefit by using the highest-rated CBV they can afford. Good CBVs develop a better CMS rating and will make more money. If they are smart, they will even offer advisory services to their clients before these clients file formal CMS service applications. Such advice will help applicants succeed. Incidentally, we might notice that everyone wins here. Bad CBVs obtain fewer jobs and smaller deals. Good CBVs receive more and bigger deals, make lots of money and help the CMS succeed where it matters most.

For Ella, this is the perfect opportunity. She is exactly the right kind of person to take advantage of this program. Since she expects to study hard and work hard, Ella will make a fine CBV. With the current demand for CBVs, she expects her income to double compared to last year, even as an independent worker. That is just for the first year of her new Certified Business Valuation practice. There is very little risk. With her background, she can take the class and become certified within three months. The CMS assures all new CBVs a useful minimum of clients within a week of passing the certification. If her certification score is as high as she expects, Ella might even find it easy to obtain an attractive offer from one of the new CBV partnership firms.

F. *Cannot Retire – Ex-Longshoreman*

Situation:

Frank started working at the docks when he was a young man. He loved loading and unloading cargo from the ships at the harbor. It was tough work intended only for the physically robust. It made him proud to say he was a longshoreman even as he continued working past his 54th birthday a few months ago. His union's retirement plan would take care of him in a few years, then he would finally spend the time with his wife and family that he had always promised.

However, shortly after that 54th birthday, Frank was rear-ended in a minor car accident. As soon as he got out of the car, he knew something was wrong. He could hardly stand up. Weeks later, after seeing several different doctors, Frank was finally able to walk again without pain. Now on short-term disability from his job, he had a serious problem, though. The doctor told him he would have to take it easy from now on or his back would not hold up. There was no way he could do his job anymore. Since his injury was not work-related, he did not qualify for longshoremen disability benefits. Yet, he had no choice but to quit his job when his short-term disability ran out. Nor was he old enough to receive Social Security benefits yet. By just missing the qualification age for his full retirement package, he will be a bit short on income even after his partial benefits kick in a few years from now.

Frank therefore has two problems, a short-term one and a long-term one. His short-term problem is that he needs to make some money pretty soon. He has been saving for retirement and still has a few more weeks on disability pay, but it isn't enough to last the five or six years until he begins receiving his partial retirement benefits. Also, although he could survive up to two years on the money he already has in the bank, doing this would ruin his future by draining his retirement savings.

That brings us to his second problem, a long-term issue about his retirement planning. Until his injury, his retirement plan was clear However, now that Frank does not qualify for the full benefits he planned on, his reduced retirement income will no longer be enough. Frank and his wife will either need to sell the house and find more a more affordable living solution or put off retiring until they solve the problem. In the worst case, Frank might eventually have to ask for help from his two sons. He is not going to do that without a fight. The battle has just begun. There must be something Frank can do to prevent such a fate.

Choices before U.S. 2.0:

Frank's best hope is to beg his current management to save him with some type of job change. Ideally, that would be a promotion to a low-level management position, like a crew chief or some type of coordinator. He could also see if there was a job for him in the union. There were times when such changes were likely in reach. Frank had the experience for sure. He even believed that he could perform such jobs better than the people he knew who did them. But he never really put forth any effort to go for it. It seemed simpler to just keep on doing what he knew and loved. Now desperate, he had little leverage for negotiations. As he approached each person who might help him, the problems of the economy kept hitting him in the face. "Sure," they would say, "You would be great in that role. But you know, we haven't had an opening like that in quite a while. Everyone is being careful right now. We are always worried about layoffs and budget cuts these days. If anything does come up, though, you'll be the first one I call."

Frank is now a little scared. His whole life he has relied on his physical strength to do what he loves. Now he must find a way to prove his worth based on other factors. He applies for any shipping industry openings he can find that will not stress his back. These jobs even include vehicle driver and machine operator positions, which are still a bit risky. He even tries for entry-level jobs in the back office, like clerking, sales and support. He has some chance as there are many back office managers who know him as a fine man and dedicated worker. However, he is not seen as a strong candidate for this type of work and jobs are scarce. Before his efforts are over, he will apply for minimum wage work outside of the shipping industry. His experience there will not be worth much, but Frank is proud. If that is what it takes, he will do it.

Choices in U.S. 2.0:

We are starting to reach the point where we have already discussed every kind of CMS program applicable to each new individual. Frank provides us with a good example of someone who could benefit from just about all of them. Therefore, we will quickly review his choices and consider this the last individual use case that receives a complete treatment.

We begin with the now-familiar mushy benefit, an improved general economy. This means Frank is much more likely to have the kinds of opportunities he most wishes for. In the other use cases, while it is still important, this general benefit seems vague and less interesting. But for Frank, it is far more concrete. He was surprised by unplanned circumstances. In his situation, he just wants to get a small but much-earned promotion that allows him to reach retirement with a bad back. This simple goal should really be easy for him to achieve in United States 2.0, even though it is nearly impossible otherwise.

Frank could also pursue work as a prototyper, or make other business connections using the Prototype Development Network service. He is a pretty good candidate for prototyping work. He knows a lot about shipping industry processes and equipment. Any sort of business involving this industry could benefit from his expertise, especially if it involved the design of new equipment or services related to longshoremen. From a financial perspective, Frank can also afford to take a few risks with deferred pay. He has the time to try several prototyping jobs so that if some do not pan out, he still should be OK with the income from those that do pay out.

Frank is also a candidate for more advanced use of the PDN, qualifying for a major or minor partnership at some level of management. We know that with a higher payoff there usually is more risk. The same is true here, but for Frank the tradeoff might be attractive. Using the PDN, he may find new startups in the shipping business that are risky enough to have trouble filling their management roles. In these cases, someone like Frank may be a reasonable choice. For example, he would be great at assembling a team of shipping equipment testers. He could even make a good case for handling sales or logistics. After all, he does have industry contacts.

The PDN might even expose Frank to offers of being a full partner in some new venture, especially if he can also qualify for some type of CMS incentive. Remember, he has some savings, so he can consider making the contributing investment expected from a partner. Also recall that one way to qualify for an incentive would be for him to be willing to relocate to a geographic area that meets the criteria. This could involve a new business in some part of the country recovering from disaster or a town recovering from some other economic issue that Congress decided to address. For instance, it could be as simple as relocating to a nearby port city that lost a Navy contract. The business would need to make sense for him, though. But it is not out of Frank's realm to consider running a small shipping services company, like one that leases unusual equipment or provides contract longshoremen support during peak periods. The latter might be a growth segment in United States 2.0, especially as exports grow dramatically.

Let us say that Frank does join up with a team of investors to form a company that will lease special-purpose shipping dollies and containers. They will call their startup Fragile Cargo Movers (FCM). Now that Frank is an FCM partner, he can benefit from other CMS services. The partners could use the Bank Loan Participation program to improve the working capital of the new startup, or to help purchase some necessary heavy equipment. Note that loans for equipment may make particular sense, since a startup will more easily qualify for collateralized loans than loans without collateral. Also, the total CMS score and capital invested by Frank's combined investor team will make a big difference for the CMS terms in any kind of loan.

The same factors will also improve the terms available to FCM if they decide to apply for CMS Private Venture Funding. The new company could even qualify for both this funding and bank loan services.

And finally, if FCM is a big enough idea, Frank and his partners may want to obtain commercial venture capital. We have not talked about that sort of funding yet, but the matter is not particularly complicated. This is the kind of funding FMC would apply for if their business plan projected many millions of dollars in profit in the near future. Frank and his partners would offer a venture capitalist firm a large piece of their company in return for a very large investment. The Capital Magnification Service would provide some degree of matching investment depending on the venture capital company's CMS score and the evaluation of one or more independent Certified Business Valuators. Of course, this would mean that the CMS would also become a shareholder in FCM. But in return, Frank and his partners would have the resources they need to execute their business plan, starting a new company that makes it easier and more cost-effective to ship fragile cargo.

It may occur to us to question whether or not Frank is the kind of person to take such a dramatic and risky step. First, we should realize that this situation may not actually be that risky for Frank. Ironically, the bigger the deal, the less personal risk. Why is that? Under the FCM business plan, Frank can reasonably draw a salary as soon as the new startup starts bringing in revenue. If Frank is the President, or perhaps ends up one step lower as the V.P. of Operations, his salary can easily be far more than he made before. It could still take several years before we find out how successful FCM will be. That is when the company's stock is sold to the market and all the investors receive their payback. These investors include Frank, who as a partner holds a nice chunk of company stock. If FCM succeeds moderately, Frank can expect to become wealthy. That should happen right around the time he was planning to retire anyway. In the meantime he will have a great job making enough money to keep building his retirement fund.

If his company is instead very successful, Frank will become a multi-millionaire when he retires. I do not need to elaborate. We might add that this case also produces many jobs for the U.S. economy, good jobs that range from blue-collar positions to sales and management. Finally, we should not overlook the fact that a successful Fragile Cargo Movers means FCM has succeeded in providing the kind of new shipping services that favor the competitiveness of U.S. companies.

What is the worst case scenario? The situation in which FCM fails to meet its financial goals after several years, or even goes under. Frank would still likely have earned some income during the effort, although his company stock would have little to no value at the end of it. He may or may not have improved his personal retirement fund in such a case. But even if he did not, Frank would still receive two benefits here. First, he would have made some income for a few years to stop his financial bleeding. Second, his management experience would be truly fantastic. If he could work a couple of years more, he should have no trouble qualifying for another management role at either an existing company or a startup with much better prospects. In this worst case scenario, Frank still has a better result than most of his likely outcomes from before United States 2.0. Perhaps most important, it is in Frank's hands to decide whether or not to go for it.

I feel it necessary to add an important observation when judging Frank's likelihood of success in participating in such a large startup. Most of us might imagine that Frank's odds of success would be less than 50%. After all, he has never held a management position before and now we are considering whether he could succeed as either the president or perhaps an executive vice president at a new company. Three important facts improve Frank's odds and reduce the risk of his inexperience in management. First, he is necessarily partnering with other investors. It is very likely that all of them have much more business experience than he does. That he convinced them to take him in as a partner means that they must know he needs support to address the holes in his experience. They can accomplish this support in many ways. His partners could provide direct or third-party training and seminars. They could team him up with one or more investor-partners who have the right experience in a sort of on-the-job mentorship.

They could also provide him with self-training tools and milestones that provide strong evidence he is learning what is required to succeed. Any of these steps in any combination would address Frank's experience issue.

Second, in order to obtain commercial venture capital, the FCM's investor team will need to convince at least one VC firm to provide funding. Even with CMS backing, no business will receive this kind of funding unless they can convince a VC firm to also put up its own money and undertake all the other work needed to support success.

So if we think Frank has long odds we should know that is only true before he and the rest of his investment team obtain VC funding. If they receive the funding, they have convinced another team of qualified investors to give up millions of dollars for their cause. We should recognize that accomplishing this aim requires lots of professional caliber work. Essentially, by getting their funding this way, Frank and the FCM team will have proven they have prepared themselves enough to actually run this company. We also know that the VC firm may have injected some hands-on help along the way, made adjustments to FCM plans, and even possibly installed their own people into FCM management. Whatever doubts we might have about Frank, he has already had to transform himself to get this far.

And finally, CMS has its own double-check. All CMS deals will require at least one Certified Business Valuator analysis in order to gain approval. The CBV analysis will use CMS standards to give the FCM business plan a score. This score will include estimates of the odds of success and the likely value of the business after four years (in this case). The analysis will also include information whose detail will be worked out by the CMS, but regardless the CBV analysis has one main goal. Using standards tested in both simulation and real world experience, an independent professional will judge the probability of this business succeeding. Finally, let us recall that the VC firm's application for CMS funding includes a collateralized backing of the deal against losses. The VC firm is insuring success by covering some of the risk with even more of their own money. Between this investment and the CBV's analysis, the CMS will have good reason to believe that FCM's plan will succeed. If FCM receives VC funding with CMS approval, Frank's confidence for success should be very high, and so should ours.

Format Shift -Use Case Summaries

The preceding use cases have illustrated and discussed all the Capital Magnification Service products. We should consider a few more situations, but elaborating on how the CMS will directly impact them would start becoming redundant going forward. Therefore, for the balance of the use cases I will be brief. The situation descriptions will be shorter. The solutions will no longer discuss "before U.S. 2.0". And I will simply refer to the CMS services that will apply, with perhaps a few special notes. We should assume that all of these cases will benefit from the mushy advantage of a better economy. I will otherwise not mention it unless special reasons apply.

G. *Poor Relatives from South America*

Situation in brief:

Gina, a U.S. citizen, has successfully sponsored her uncle Greg, his wife and their baby boy to legally immigrate to the United States from Brazil. Her uncle and his family are going to stay with her until he can get established. These relatives have little money and no special skills. Gina is of average means herself.

Choices in U.S. 2.0:

My discussion will focus on Greg, although we could either substitute his wife, or add her participation. Greg does not qualify for prototyping work as he is not a citizen (unless this provision changes). He also does not qualify directly for any of the other CMS services for the same reason. However, some companies that received CMS funding may have openings that are targeted for special incentives. Greg should research these to see if he meets the incentive requirements, or can do so by relocating. However, in some cases these openings may also be restricted to U.S. citizens. This use case illustrates an important principle of Magnified Capitalism. It is not intended to be an immigration magnet. Although the economic success our plan delivers to the U.S. will create attraction for immigrants, I am purposefully not proposing any direct service that will add to this appeal.

Indirectly, Greg will still benefit. In addition to the lower unemployment rate in general, many start-ups will be looking for cost-effective labor and skilled workers at various levels. Greg should have plenty of opportunities at the low end. We may also remember that U.S. 2.0 is rich in self-training and self-help solutions spawned by the flexibility of PDN work. Even though there is no direct CMS assistance for such endeavors, Greg can still take advantage of these solutions to educate himself in a field of interest. He might survey the market and pick a career with high demand that requires a minimum of training and cost for him to qualify or become certified. I imagine a range of possibilities from a position as a professional chef to various types of mechanic or technician jobs.

Finally, although not qualified for CMS services himself, Greg could offer his assistance to a U.S. citizen who is participating in a CMS program but is in distress. It is easy to imagine a market developing of unqualified people like Greg who offer their help in such matters. This market would act as a parachute for people struggling to reach their CMS-driven goals. An example would be a situation in which someone was responsible for testing a new food processing machine. However, perhaps this person became ill or was otherwise over-committed to a volume of work that they could not deliver in time. Rather than let their prototyping project fail, this person may seek people like Greg to help for a piece of the deferred pay. Greg would also then gain experience and references in exchange for this help.

H. *College Grad in Philosophy*

Situation in brief:

When Herbert went to college he did not know what he should major in. After taking a wide range of classes he decided that philosophy was his favorite topic. Ignoring the advice of others including his parents, Herbert followed his heart and finished his B.S. degree in this discipline. Now a graduate, he is facing the cold reality those other people tried to warn him about. There are few jobs available that require a philosophy degree, and not that many more that even consider it an advantage.

Choices in U.S. 2.0:

Herbert can always change focus through prototyping work. What would be more interesting, however, is if Herbert were to leverage his degree somehow. For instance, he might find a way to tie a specific philosophy to some business practice, perhaps in the field of marketing analysis or product design. Then he could legitimize this linkage with PDN experience, since this approach would be far less likely to succeed in the job market until then. In other words, Herbert could develop a work method or technique based on some philosophical strategy. Then he could take on prototyping jobs that would use his techniques and prove their efficacy. He could also try his hand at developing some special product, writing, or service process that comes from a philosophical perspective. In such a case, Herbert might benefit more from other CMS services that support patents, new businesses, or even bank loans.

J. *New App Idea*

Situation in brief:

Jane is in a quandary. She just thought of an awesome new idea for a mobile app. No one else does anything like it and she is sure there will be a big demand. However, she is a mid-level marketing manager with only modest savings. She is not a programmer and not particularly technical. She has enough excitement and optimism to organize the effort to sell her app, and perhaps a bit more. Looking into the matter further, she discovers that the app unfortunately cannot be patent-protected. What can Jane do?

Choices in U.S. 2.0:

This one is easy, perhaps even obvious. Jane can probably have the app prototyped, maybe even ready for market, essentially for free. The PDN's specific purpose is to enable entrepreneurs to receive whatever help they need to develop a concept to the point where it can be formally funded or commercially launched. In the case of a mobile app, there are often minor differences between a prototype and a commercial version. It can come down to an issue of testing, which can be addressed with PDN resources as well. Also, the cost of launching an app is very low since iTunes, Google and others provide startups with ready marketplaces for essentially no upfront cost.

Jane can probably build the business case and run this effort on the side until it takes off. It is up to her how to go about it. She can go it alone as the main investor, or if she prefers to have help, she can sign up a few partners using the PDN. These partners could be any mix of major or minor ones, depending on whether she needs some cash, a technical designer, experienced senior management, gap-filling management, or is having trouble finding qualified candidates for various roles. Notice that if she builds a management team first, her business will be more attractive to qualified prototypers. There is more than one way to build confidence, since prototypers must be convinced to take some risk before they sign on. Upping the offer to prototypers and updating the business plan with improved quality are other ways to attract good help. Regardless of her choices on the details, Jane only needs conviction and motivation to turn her app idea into a real business.

K. *Research Thesis – Biotech (or any large-scale business idea or invention, especially the patentable ones from qualified sources)*

Situation in brief:

Kevin recently completed his doctoral thesis in microbiology. Entitled "Arbitrary Length Nanotube Assembly via Hydra", his advisors considered it a great piece of work and it formally earned him his PhD. In his university lab, Kevin managed to create a training regimen for a common microscopic fresh water animal, the hydra. He taught several hydra to link small carbon nanotube fibers together, end-to end, resulting in a longer nanotube. To those not versed in the field of carbon nanotubes, this may sound like a curious or irrelevant activity. But those in the field understand that this is a really big deal. Carbon nanotubes are potentially one of the next big technologies.

These microfibers are far stronger than steel and even spider silk. They have many other useful characteristics, but they also suffer from a big practical problem: no one has yet figured out how to manufacture usefully long individual threads. Once we solve this problem, carbon nanotubes will eventually replace steel cables, nylon ropes, and even microelectronic wiring in many applications. We may also weave them into fabrics stronger and lighter than the Kevlar used in bulletproof vests.

One thing is clear: the first person to figure out how to cost-effectively produce a spool of carbon nanotube thread could become a billionaire. Kevin believes he can turn his university experiment into a large-scale manufacturing solution, but he has problems to deal with. He has no money and no business experience. He will need to undertake some additional experiments in order to prove his methods will work in a production environment. He also does not trust anyone to keep the details of his billion-dollar idea a secret.

Choices in U.S. 2.0:

Kevin represents a special potential that Magnified Capitalism has for multiplying our big economic successes. Today, Kevin would find himself in a much more difficult position. Without professional business advice his ideas may languish, because his most obvious path towards commercialization would be to take a research position at an existing biotech company. Researchers at such companies rarely receive anywhere near the kind of compensation their ideas are truly worth. Instead, the companies that hire people like Kevin pay a modest patent bonus, or a commercialization bonus, perhaps along with a raise and promotion. But this only happens at the more reasonable firms. While some might call such rewards fair, if it was our idea we would probably resent the millions our bosses made while we earned just enough to pay off our student loans.

Lots of people have similar, high-quality ideas today. Many will hand these ideas over to their employers in return for whatever they can get. But Kevin will not, and we can expect a lot of others to also keep their best gems in their pockets. In United States 2.0 Kevin receives all the help he needs to take his idea from concept to prototype to full-fledged startup biotech firm. And because other technology companies will know this, they will change their ways, too. In this future we can look for technology firms to start paying their geniuses something closer to a fair share of the profits for the next great advance. That, too, will tend to bring more of the best ideas to light quickly.

Do I need to list every CMS service that helps Kevin directly? Interestingly, that list would include most of them. Kevin will use the Prototype Development Network to find and build a professional team of business partners. He will need such help for business planning, organization, project management, and initial funding. This team will assemble the formal startup company. They can then use the PDN again to build the team of prototypers to test Kevin's advanced ideas. During the testing phase, or perhaps just beforehand, Kevin can use the Patent Funding Program to insure his ideas are formally protected. He should have no trouble qualifying for this program.

The new startup may try to gain Private Venture Funding at this stage to help them pay for some of the costs of prototyping the nanotube manufacturing process. Depending on the circumstances, they may alternately or additionally apply for Bank Loan Participation. At such an early stage, they would likely use this money for collateralized lab equipment. Later on, they may draw on such loans (or lease financing) for the machines used in actual manufacturing.

Finally, and perhaps most importantly, once Kevin and his new partners develop the proof-of-concept prototype, they will be ready to approach a venture capital firm for the big money. This is the kind of situation where he and his partners may be able to attract competition between multiple VC firms if their prototyping goes well. We must remember that once they receive this funding, they will be required to offer a commensurate payoff to the prototypers who helped them get here. They will then have the money, including the CMS Venture Capital Funding contribution, to turn the original idea into reality. Those keeping a checklist will note that the only CMS services I did not mention are Cash Flow Assistance and Business Expansion Funding. Those two CMS services could come into play later on, once Kevin's biotech business has been selling a product for some time.

L. *Ready to Retire (including those who have earned enough to retire early)*

Situation in brief:

Linda has had a successful career. She has worked hard and saved judiciously. By the time she reached 64 years of age, she had been a Director of Operations at a major communications company for over nine years. We can imagine that with consistent contributions to her IRA, strategic stock investments, or perhaps even a hobby of real estate investing, she has become financially independent. She is ready to retire.

Here is a dirty little secret: How much do people need to save in order to live off of their retirement savings? If we can live off of 80% of our current income, and we can maintain a 10% return on our investments, then we will need to accumulate a retirement investment fund of 8 times our annual salary before accounting for any Social Security or retirement plan payments, which will lower this number somewhat.

But we will ignore these entitlements for simplification purposes. If Linda was making close to $130,000 per year at the end of her career, she has just barely qualified to enter the millionaire's club by the time she retires. Incidentally, this use case can cover a range of the modestly wealthy, from those who become multimillionaires far earlier in life, to those slightly less well off than Linda by the time they retire.

The burning question before Linda is this: What does retirement mean? Will she spend 100% of her time in non-productive leisure activities? Or will she merely take a long vacation and then come back eager to do something new, if only as a part-time commitment? Most people in good health who have been productive their whole lives have trouble spending all of their time in leisure activity. Usually, they have at least a little desire to keep a toe in the game. For some, it is more than a toe. This becomes even more true for those who retire because they made a small fortune early in their lives. The better off a person is, the less likely they are to totally stop working upon retirement. For them, all retirement means is that they do not have to work. The ideal retirement is therefore one where we work as much as we feel like. What do people like Linda do now?

Choices in U.S. 2.0:

I am particularly fond of the impact Magnified Capitalism has on the retired. If they are also at least a little wealthy, their choices are seriously interesting. Our plan encourages continued participation from those who have the most experience to pass on. I will run through Linda's choices just briefly.

It is worth mentioning a special point about the improved economy here. A healthy economy tends to be an indicator of lower risk for investors in general. In other words, if Linda just wants to enjoy actively managing her investments, she should be in good shape for most investment choices. Real estate should be secure. Most stocks, especially the core industries and established firms, should be safe in a diversified portfolio. Even direct investments in various startups should be a better bet in a booming economy. Linda should be mindful to limit the portion of her savings that she is willing to put towards the riskier choices, just in case she bets wrong. Especially when managing a retirement fund, no single investment should use more than about 5% of the funds. Some would argue that even that portion is aggressive.

Looking at CMS services in particular, what new options does Linda have? For one thing, she might enjoy being a prototyper. She would be a great choice for that type of work. She has excellent qualifications so she should be in good demand. Her experience should also raise her CMS rating. And the prototyper's risk of deferred payment would be absolutely no problem for her. She already has a sufficient fixed income to live off of. Anything she made working on Prototype Development Network projects would be gravy. This point applies to all retirees, especially those who do not absolutely need extra money.

Initially, Linda may even prefer to take it up a notch. She could focus on PDN opportunities at the high end, the ones offering major or minor partnerships. Since Linda has the money and management expertise, she could certainly go for many full partnership opportunities. Not only that, but her work experience is of such a high caliber that any startup she works on would probably benefit greatly from her participation. Of course, once Linda becomes a partner in a startup using the PDN, she can, along with her new partners, participate in almost all the other CMS services. Bank loans, Private Venture Funding, Patent Funding, and even full-fledged Venture Capital Funding - all of these services are available for her company to use to assure success.

If Linda should participate in a successful startup as a partner, another interesting consequence occurs. Assuming she sells off much or all of her stake after a few years, Linda will have become much wealthier. In the next venture she could put herself in the driver's seat as the main investor. She might even eventually have enough spare money and business creation experience to become a partner in a commercial venture capital firm. Linda is exactly the kind of person we want in such a role. This use case illustrates how Magnified Capitalism does not waste success. Much of Linda's earned wealth and experience returns right back into the economy. She not only helps fuel business creation with her money, but she helps elevate its quality by continuing to inject her insight and experience.

M. *Rich Relatives from Overseas*

Situation in brief:

May was born to Chinese exchange student parents when they were enrolled at the University of Southern California. They all went back to China as a family after both parents graduated with engineering degrees, but May received a benefit from the timing of her birth. Born here, she was automatically a U.S. citizen. As soon as she was old enough, her parents sent her back to the United States to study. However, because May was a U.S. citizen, she needed no special visa. In fact, after she graduated, she decided to stay here.

During May's lifetime, her parents enjoyed continued success in the Chinese solar cell industry. China had become dominant in this segment with the combination of low-cost labor, access to special raw materials, high worldwide market growth, and government incentives. By the time May was 26 years old, her mom and dad had retired early with an accumulated wealth in excess of 4 million U.S. dollars. They missed their daughter and the United States that they fell in love with as students. Working through the paperwork with ease, they had arranged to immigrate to the U.S. They intended to stay with May for a little while until they worked out a plan. Even though she now has a good job as a web page designer, her dad is promising to help her do even better. May is not so sure she needs this help, but appreciates his attitude and is looking forward to seeing both her parents.

Choices in U.S. 2.0:

How is this scenario affected under Magnified Capitalism? We might recall that the program includes an exclusion preventing non-citizens from directly participating in most CMS services. However, May's dad is a smart man. Before planning his trip he read up on the details of CMS rules and the experience of other non-native businesspeople working in the U.S. He knows he has many of the same options that Linda had in the previous use case, as long as he does one thing differently. He must make sure May, or some other U.S. citizen, is the majority partner in any business he participates in. Also, he cannot directly use the PDN for making his contacts or having prototype work done. But if he joins with a citizen partner, like May, that person can make such contacts and develop business relationships on his behalf. In other words, he must back a U.S. citizen who will gain at least 51% of the financial benefits (assuming that is the agreed rule).

Whether this citizen is May, another friend or relative, or someone May finds for him, some American will be significantly elevated financially by this foreign investor's attempt to take advantage of CMS services. May's dad will also likely provide business advice in any venture he takes on, so his experience and input will still be leveraged. I will not go through the list. We can otherwise review the previous example regarding Linda to be reminded of specific CMS services.

N. *Business Trouble - Retail*

Situation in brief:

Nick's Sporting Goods used to do very well in its mall location. However, in recent years, a lot of shoppers have switched to online purchasing for their sports equipment. To his frustration, many of his customers now even use smartphone apps while in his store that tell them where to find his products online for less. Nick provides customers with a chance to see and touch clothing and sports accessories, but they increasingly buy the items from an online discounter after visiting his store.

It took a bit longer than it should have, but Nick finally fought back. His new strategy has two angles. First, his product line now includes specialization in two specific sports. He chose tennis and soccer because of local popularity. He has just started making team-based sales to local schools and community organizations in these sports. The store now carries many harder-to-find accessories and equipment options as well as customization services. The second part of his strategy is to start selling his products online. The only problem is money. He is not sure he has enough funds to pay for all the technical development and new staff he will need.

Choices in U.S. 2.0:

Clearly, Nick's store is a candidate for the CMS Cash Flow Assistance service because he has existing sales, even increasing sales. Also, the money he needs should only improve this cash flow. The Certified Business Valuation he will need should back him up as a good candidate in a lower-risk situation. If not, then this valuation should at least give him some detailed business feedback to allow him to improve his plan and qualify on a second try. Nick may also be a good candidate for Business Expansion Funding, which would carry a higher cash limit but also require him to put up more of the equity in his store as collateral.

If he chose a more conservative direction, Nick could qualify for CMS Bank Loan Participation. He should check with his banker on that. There could even be a special loan incentive for someone in his situation, such as one that covers online business conversion costs. If Nick were in a more desperate situation, he could even take on some investor partners and use Private Venture Funding. Here he would essentially be selling part of his business to new partners, who in return would provide cash and improve his CMS rating to qualify for funding with better terms.

O. *Expanding Manufacturer*

Situation in brief:

Opticrystal is the maker of various kinds of eye treatment chemicals, drops, contact lens cleaners, and eye medications. Their President, Olivia Osterman, has just left a presentation the Product Marketing division gave. They are projecting a dramatic rise in demand for one of their latest products, Lasik-eez. The data is clear. The market for people who have had Lasik eye surgery is growing at a rapid pace.

Opticrystal's Lasik-eez is designed specifically for these people in that it helps improve their vision while reducing an accumulation of associated eye mucus (a.k.a., rheum). However, due to the special process required to make Lasik-eez, Opticrystal has a big problem. They are already making the product at full capacity in their special Mexican production facility. Yet, not only are resellers complaining about short supplies of Lasik-eez today, but they expect the supply problem to become much worse. Olivia is facing a quandary.

Her people have just told her that the company can expect demand to rise to four times current production rates within five years. If Opticrystal cannot supply enough of the product, one of its competitors will surely step in to fill the gap. Yet the expansion costs required to keep up are not minor.

Opticrystal will need to put up about $25 million over the next two years in order to build a new, larger Mexican plant . It is very much worth doing because this product produces a great profit margin. But currently, the company has neither large cash reserves nor particularly good credit.

Choices in U.S. 2.0:

I might mention that Opticrystal could probably obtain the money it needs without Magnified Capitalism. The main problem is that the source of such money would probably have to be a venture capital firm, who in turn would expect a fair share of the company's equity. For an established company that might be a very hard pill to swallow. This decision could easily be difficult enough that it could delay the construction of a new plant. The company would probably first pursue every other possible source of financing. They would then try to get VCs to compete against each other to obtain the best possible terms. All that would take time, which is a big penalty in this situation.

Regardless, there is a CMS service designed specifically for such cases: Business Expansion Funding. Instead of selling part of the company to fund the expansion they need, Opticrystal only needs to use their stock as collateral for a funding deal with the CMS. They might have to pay some high interest rates over a short term, or alternately, provide some profit sharing over a slightly longer term. But in the end, they should be able to repay the funding without selling off a piece of themselves.

I should add an important point that we are probably expecting to see. There is a near certainty that this CMS service will include a strong incentive for building the manufacturing plant in the United States rather than in another country. The only reason Opticrystal is manufacturing in Mexico in the first place is to reduce labor and facility costs. If the terms for Business Expansion Funding were improved enough to favor a U.S.-based solution, we can be sure Olivia Osterman would make the decision to build the plant here instead. If there was an additional incentive to develop this new facility in some region that needed economic recovery, or if Opticrystal could qualify for other incentives without compromising their end strategy, they would probably make appropriate changes to qualify for those as well. Why would they choose not to, unless the incentives were too weak to justify the plan modifications? This example illustrates how incentives can shape major business decisions, with the only cost being a slight reduction in CMS profit.

P. *Company Founder Ready to Cash Out*

Situation in brief:

In business there is a common truism that company executives come in two flavors, the entrepreneurs who start new companies and the people who are good at running established ones. It is rare to find the founder of a company still running it more than five years after that company makes it big. So it is with Portable iEquipment, Incorporated (PiI). This company has made a fast name for itself building accessories for mobile phones, especially the latest smartphones. Their success comes from combining high quality with a customizable 'cool factor.' PiI's big seller is a phone docking station that has a digital picture frame for its skin, yet it also talks to TVs and stereo systems. The smartphone becomes an audio-video control system while putting on a display of its own. College kids use it as a party centerpiece to produce special effects while it performs a digital DJ function.

The founder, Paul Panache, is getting bored with his duties as President and CEO. Though he was once excited to be running the company by the seat of his pants, now the situation is different. He has teams of people demanding his attention, meetings all day long, financial pressures, new proposals to review and on and on. Yet, his company has been growing so quickly, it is just barely making a profit. Everyone thinks Paul must be rich, but he really is not. Nearly all of his financial resources are tied up in PiI. Tired and bored with his duties, he would like to sell out now and do something else. But he is worried he will need to run the company for a few more years before he can get most of the value of his stock.

Choices in U.S. 2.0:

No one needs to feel sorry for Paul. What Magnified Capitalism does for this situation is to improve his options, as well as to encourage him to make some business decisions in the direction of any applicable incentives. Paul has three main choices here: He can take his company public, he can find another company to buy PiI, or he can sell part of his stock to a venture capital firm or a private equity firm (which is similar but more specialized). These options do not change under Magnified Capitalism so much as they become either more practical or more attractive. In other words, in today's environment there is a higher chance that Paul would reject some or all of these choices, at least until a later time. In U.S. 2.0, Paul would have an easier time getting the kind of money that would allow him to move on.

He will probably want to take a nice vacation, buy a house filled with some new toys, then start another business. This is what everyone should want. This plan allows Paul to focus on what he is good at: launching innovative startups. It also ensures he has plenty of resources to do that well. As far as which CMS services apply, we can take our pick from the high-end ones. Venture Capital Funding is an obvious choice. This CMS service would make Paul's company more attractive in a partial or complete buyout from a wide range of investment firms. A competitor or compatible manufacturer might want to make Paul a buyout offer. Here he could trigger CMS Business Expansion Funding to improve the offer and widen the list of suitors.

An applicable CMS service that might not immediately come to mind is Bank Loan Participation. We might not think of it at first because it requires special banking services, and therefore financing, in order to take a company public. This CMS service could help make the go-public option more cost-effective and more attractive to any underwriter. Regardless of his choice, there are bound to be incentives in play here. Paul may make a few last-minute business adjustments to take advantage of them, regardless of his choice of strategy. That means PiI might modify where they build their products, who they hire, where they locate customer support services, or which suppliers they use. PiI would make these choices in order to qualify for better CMS terms in whatever exit strategy Paul chooses.

Use Case Wrap-up Observations

Only by going through this wide-ranging set of use cases can we really appreciate certain kinds of effects. I could try to claim these observations without discussing use cases, but now that you have read about so many people, Mr. President, your own view is richer. The following points now reveal themselves as evident.

- *Broad Economic Improvement*

  While I have consistently claimed that U.S. 2.0 will include the environment of a significantly improved economy, we should now see the reason this is true from a ground level perspective. Literally no one is left out. There is economic improvement for every kind of situation. The nature of this improvement can vary, but it is always present. Not only that, it is usually there in multiple flavors, both directly and indirectly.

- *Motivation through Choice*

  There are people who still ask why communism failed. The one-word reason is 'motivation', or lack thereof. Communism has the tendency to kill personal motivation. Capitalism works because it has exactly the opposite effect. Magnified Capitalism works because it broadens and expands on this same source of energy for each individual. This is important. Ultimately, a society is not a nameless mass. The United States is us...you, me, our neighbors, the rich, the poor, everyone. A plan that improves the economy should affect everyone. The use cases illustrate that effect most clearly.

  This program is not just for the downtrodden, either. Yes, for those facing difficulty, Magnified Capitalism helps motivate a stretching, a mobilization, and a risk-taking rather than an acceptance of defeat or complacency. Such an impact on the more beaten-down and disadvantaged people is apparent and useful. But this benefit does not end with the harsher situations. It is carried throughout the spectrum of use cases. At every level of success, this strategy motivates these same human characteristics to higher levels. Even the wildly successful are inspired to reach higher. Even those with a good excuse to retire are enticed by attractive new choices to stay engaged and remain productive to whatever degree and manner works for them. I would even dare to say that such engagement should generally elevate the twin sisters of life-happiness and life-satisfaction.

- *Economic Accelerator*
  The use cases show over and over that people's choices improve in United States 2.0. However, more than just that, the length of time it takes before they succeed tends to become shorter. In other words, not only does this system broaden success, it also delivers all manners of success in a speedier fashion.

- *Deep Impact of CMS Incentives*
  One of the more complicated aspects of Magnified Capitalism is its ability to steer national policy through the use of incentives. When we discuss the theory of incentives, we might find it easy to dismiss them as too complicated or uncertain. However, once we walk through the use cases, their applicability should be clear. In every case where they could be triggered, the incentives shaped business decisions. They will work. They will steer business and individuals in the very direction they are intended to. And they will do this without either unnatural force or high cost.

- *Importance of the CMS Rating System*
  This observation may strike us as a bit more subtle than some others. The CMS rates everyone it works with numerically, both with an initial rating and with an adjusted rating as individuals and businesses prove themselves in actual dealings. As we read the use cases we might notice that a poor rating is bad news, and a good one is helpful. This carrot and stick method not only encourages ethical and successful business dealings, it weeds out the bad apples very effectively. A person's or business's CMS rating may one day be almost as important as their credit score is.

- *New Safety Net Based on True Opportunity for All*
  Today we have a social safety net based on fundamental entitlements. However, this net is only intended to support basic survival. Magnified Capitalism adds a new kind of safety net. Its intention is to help people break out of economic stagnation or even depression. It is not based on an entitlement, though. It is a safety net based on extending the reach of opportunity. This powerful strategy makes investment money more accessible resulting in more opportunities, easier opportunities, and importantly, opportunities that were previously out of reach for many. Taking risks, starting a business, trying a new idea – these no longer need to

be reserved for the rich. Instead, we create a means for everyone to participate to the degree they are comfortable.

- *New Specialties, Business Models and Markets*
I have listed this last because it is arguably the narrowest observation. However, to those who take advantage, it is the most life-changing. United States 2.0 will have brand new types of professions, new ways to operate business ventures, and even new kinds of markets.

The big new profession will be the Certified Business Valuator. Part business advisor, part accountant, and part appraiser, this job will be an exciting and rewarding way to make a living for those so inclined. Not only will there be independent CBV practices, but there will certainly be new CBV firms organized around particular strengths and advantages.

We can make a case that the introduction of the Patent Funding Program will also fundamentally transform the nature of a patent attorney's job. We should certainly see a great expansion of the numbers of these lawyers as well as a new kind of law firm that caters to the related service.

The Prototype Development Network combined with Private Venture Funding will enable and encourage investors to form new kinds of partnerships, or investor groups. Although we only referred to these services a few times in the use cases, these investor coalitions will establish a new method for people to become major or minor players in a variety of innovative businesses. In many cases, the available partnerships would never have been formed without Magnified Capitalism. That some investor groups will form for the specific purpose of taking advantage of incentive programs is entirely new.

And finally there will be new markets, although to be fair I hardly mentioned them. What are they? One market should eventually form for the sole purpose of trading the startup stock that prototypers earn through conducting PDN work. That is, I expect a market to form that allows prototypers to sell the stock they earn earlier than their contract requires. Some people will therefore get paid much faster and with less risk simply by selling their earned shares to speculators in such a special stock market. Of course, no one will be required to participate. For people who have an immediate need for cash, however, this will be a welcome option.

Another new market will fulfill the need for self-help training and certification. While we could argue this exists today, I expect the nature of this market to transform so radically that we will not recognize it in United States 2.0. In short, there will be an abundance of formal testing we can take to certify our self-taught skills in some field, as well as related study packages to help us prepare. This will come about due to many people's need to provide better evidence that they are competent in some skill for which they otherwise have no evidence or work experience. These certification programs will be driven by the needs of people seeking prototyping work. Because such certifications will often require real additional learning, we collectively gain a national improvement in both skill and productivity.

Finally, it is important to add that all people's participation in the existing educational system will also be elevated in both numbers and priority for the same reasons. Specifically, we can expect many of those who obtain some PDN work based on less rigorous certifications to then be able to afford a more formal degree or training program. Improved access to bank loans for higher education and trade schools will contribute further to this effect. Finally, over time, with the widespread pervasiveness of better education comes competition at the individual level. It might be easier to find work and gain success with less a formal background; however, the best opportunities will still favor those who have a stronger resume. Only now those better opportunities will deliver a far higher payback through a combination of lower risk and fatter compensation. The value of all levels of education is magnified.

"If we found a way to make an absolutely guaranteed 10% annual profit on our investment, how much should we put into that investment if we had to borrow all the invested money at a 5% annual interest rate? Of course the answer is 'as much as we possibly can.' Then the only issue is this matter of an investment being absolutely guaranteed. No single investment is absolutely guaranteed. Some investments come pretty close though, especially if they are based on numerous smaller investments. For example, the business model of a bank is generally based on the above question, except their interest rates and profit rates vary over time. The answer is the same, however. A bank will take as much of our deposits as they can get because they have established a process for lending that consistently makes a profit at a far higher rate. Sometimes an individual loan will go bad, but they test their processes in a way that makes sure loss rates are fairly predictable and accounted for in their calculations. The more loans the bank offers, the more predictable and consistent its profits are. The goal of the Capital Magnification Service is comparable. The CMS establishes rules and processes to make its services effective. An effective service is one that is both attractive to the customer and profitable to the business. The profits from winning deals must then be fine-tuned to average higher than our costs. If you can do that over and over with thousands of deals, the results are essentially guaranteed. It works that way with a classic bank business model. It even works that way for a casino. If they work out the odds out properly, a casino gets pretty much exactly what it expects to make just because of the vast number of bets made in its favor. Interestingly, the bigger the casino, the more total bets there are, and therefore the more precisely they can predict and guarantee total profits. The same is true for a bank – advantage goes to the ones making the most deals, typically the bigger banks. Total risk declines with the volume of your investments."

- Future CMS CEO giving a financial lecture -

VII. Financials

As suggested by the above lecture quote, investment returns can approach a guaranteed rate of return with sufficient diversification. This is just a financial extrapolation of the saying, "Don't put all your eggs in one basket." The big question is not whether such a system can turn a profit, but rather how effective the entire solution will be. "Effective" means lots of things. I want all CMS services to be so attractive that almost everyone who can qualify will want to. That kind of effectiveness is focused on market appeal or customer value. But effective also means profitable. Especially for a financial service, profitability pulls in the opposite direction from customer value. That is why the Capital Magnification Service will need to establish and continuously run market simulations for all its services. Part of their ongoing responsibility will be to fine-tune service effectiveness and be the champions of understanding how effectiveness changes under evolving circumstances.

This brings me to the financials, a dangerous topic for some. Every business plan must include numerical analysis. That is a requirement. Unfortunately, a discussion of numbers can also serve as a remedy for insomnia. To make matters worse, any attempt to predict exactly what the numbers will be in a business plan generally turns out wrong. The prediction may be only a little off, or more commonly, it might be way off. But a business plan's financial analysis is almost never exactly right.

I offer you a solution to both issues. On the matter of potential eye-glazing, I will try to keep the discussion as short as possible, and focused on the interesting punch lines. Also, we should assume that before we enact Magnified, a team of financial analysts will examine these matters with great scrutiny. The analysis here, therefore, does not need to be elaborately detailed. It only needs to show enough specifics to illustrate that we have envisioned a real solution. If the actual figures turn out a bit different it should not matter much. For the benefit of those people who may be tasked with examining this plan more closely, I have also included a detailed spreadsheet in the appendix that provides the numerical details behind the analysis I have done in this chapter.

This brings me to the second complaint about financial projections, their famously poor accuracy. My solution to this problem is to cheat a bit. I do not try to make predictions with a single number. Rather, I use a different approach. First I consider the worst case scenario. This means I run the figures from the perspective of a pessimist. Then I consider the best case scenario and run the figures as an optimist. Finally, I present both answers. Guess what? The real answer will turn out to be somewhere in between. So I cheat by not predicting a specific number but instead mathematically bounding the problem. Being right all the time this way is therefore not too surprising. With this type of range-based analysis, the real answer often falls close to the middle of the two extremes. So if I am forced to narrow my projection to a single figure, I will typically give the average between best and worst case scenarios, perhaps less some amount to account for risk. But there is no need to do that in a strong business case. The argument is iron-clad if I can show that all the plan will work even in the worst case. Then we can be pretty comfortable that reality should turn out to be better than that, but it does not really matter by how much. Our optimistic number just becomes an upper limit of curiosity. It lets us see the range of how much better things can be.

Since I want to focus on the most interesting numbers, the obvious question then becomes, "What are those numbers?"

If this were a plan for a typical corporation, the answer would be obvious. The executives always want to know the "bottom line." Most people understand this to be a euphemism for "profit". The reality is a bit more complicated than the common definition of that word. A Chief Financial Officer who would prepare, or at least approve, the figures of a formal business case would be sure to show several versions of profit, including gross profit, net profit, ROI (return on investment), and EBIT (Earnings Before Income Tax), among others. He would express these variations of profit as both percentages (of revenue) and as fixed figures projected over different timespans. Some executives are more interested in profit margins while others are more interested in EBIT. A venture capitalist, in contrast, will be particularly focused on net profit at the end of the project term. So if we offer a four-year plan, they will want to know how much they can expect to make at the end of those four years for the money they put up. The truth is that these are all just different ways of looking at the same basic idea. My preference is to keep it simple. We will keep the emphasis on annual calculations of net profit and a stripped-down version of annual return on investment. This equates to total dollars earned and the interest gained on the investment, respectively.

Other than looking at profit in these two ways, what else should we care about? An investor, who in this case is the whole of the American people, always wants to know another figure: How much will it cost? Or more precisely, what is the required investment, how much are we borrowing, and how soon will the debt all be paid off?

The rest is details. The spreadsheet analysis I have provided in the appendix projects these figures year by year. It also shows some of the supporting numbers, such as different types of costs. I have provided these primarily for those readers who want to challenge the answers and create their own projections. Not only do I welcome such work, but it is necessary that many other people make this kind of calculation over and over in order to test this strategy. All anyone needs to do, however, is verify that my worst case scenario produces a workable plan. Actually, there is a bit more room for error than that. The plan is validated even if someone else's more pessimistic worst case scenario still works, although I expect most economists and analysts will find that my worst case scenario represents a reasonable, if not overly conservative, lower limit.

We might recall that I referred earlier to the total investment that Magnified Capitalism requires. At that time I used a round figure of one trillion dollars per year as the rough CMS annual investment total. This represents an amount sufficiently high to have a major impact on the economy. I labeled this figure the "annual investment Fund" because it is the amount of money that the CMS will manage each year to provide its financial services. This is similar to answering the question, "How much do the total deposits of a bank add up to?", or more precisely, "How many total dollars does this fund management company manage?" This figure is therefore not the total annual cost of running the CMS program. To calculate a total budget we also need to include the annual cost of running the company, paying back the costs of setting it up, and the cost of borrowing the money in the fund. The good news is that the adjusted answer is only a smallish increase over the original number. The investment Fund itself is by far the biggest part of the total required budget.

However, an obvious question does arise. Is a trillion dollars too much? Alternately, is that enough money to have the necessary impact to fix all the economic issues quickly? And finally, did I not say that the actual figure will be different from this? I did. So how are we supposed to navigate the issue of budgeting? The answer to that is interesting. First, consider the financial impact of this program using a one trillion dollar Fund. We will calculate the optimistic and pessimistic results promised under such an assumption. These results show how many jobs we create and how much the economy improves. They also show how much profit the CMS brings back to the government over time and at what cost. Now consider this: Was this level of investment too much? Did it have enough economic impact? Roughly, we can cut the costs but should expect the benefit to be reduced by the same percentage. Or conversely, we can increase the investment and expect a comparable increase in benefits. This program scales both up and down depending on how much we borrow for the total CMS Fund. With minor deviation, it is just that simple. I will discuss the impact of choosing to invest less versus investing more after the financial projection. Finally, since I promised earlier, I will discuss generating enough CMS profit to eliminate income taxes completely. This will help us see what kind of decisions would be necessary to achieve such a goal over time.

Financial Summary

Now let us review some details regarding my actual projection. Please refer to the appendix for all the tables I have produced to back up this summary.

I have called my version of the Magnified Capitalism projection the "Trillion Dollar Reinvestment Model (TDRM)," primarily because of two assumptions it makes. First, I assume that the CMS will manage a Fund of no less than one trillion dollars every year. Incidentally, as the model shows, we must borrow 100% of the costs during the first two years. That means two trillion dollars plus some extra for interest, operating costs, and the initial costs to set everything up. Starting with year three, we begin to receive early revenues from services provided in year one. That is therefore the first year we do not need to borrow 100% of our costs. Year four brings in more of that revenue and so on.

The model shows us that even in the worst case **the total amount of money needed to implement the TDRM is under four trillion dollars**. That amount covers the first six years of CMS operations (reduce this to five years and a bit less money in the best case scenario), after which the CMS annual revenue exceeds one trillion dollars per year so borrowing can stop altogether. Starting in year seven the CMS makes enough money to continue offering one trillion dollars per year in services without borrowing any additional funds. It also starts repaying its debt in that year. **The worst case TDRM result shows all debt repaid in the 18th year of CMS operations.** The best case scenario does this in the 12th year. That means the program has paid off all its debt and continues to provide one trillion dollars of services per year, or more, without any further outside contribution.

This point brings me to the second major assumption of the TDRM. The year after the debt is paid off under either the best or worst case scenario, the CMS will have more than one trillion dollars in cash reserves available annually. I have called it the Trillion Dollar Reinvestment Model (TDRM) because we reinvest some portion of the cash reserves above one trillion dollars back into CMS services. In other words, after repaying its debt, the CMS Fund starts to grow on its own. This means the CMS's impact on the economy starts to increase as well. This reinvestment is the second assumption I referred to.

By the way, the TDRM does not assume we will reinvest the entire surplus. The part of the surplus that we do not reinvest becomes new revenue (payback) for the government to use. How do we decide how much to pay back and how much to reinvest? Like a professional money manager, the model sets up rules for payback versus reinvestment. My worst case rule says that **once the annual CMS fund exceeds $1.5 trillion, 50% of the money in the Fund over this $1.5 trillion mark is to be paid back into the U.S. government as new revenue each year!** The best case rule I used is more conservative. It calls for us to pay 25% of the Fund in excess of $2 trillion to the government as revenue. The results in the long run between these two sets of numbers are dramatically different, although it is a choice between great and super awesome. **In the worst case scenario, the government starts receiving CMS revenues in the 24th year of its operations. Five years later in the 29th year, this revenue grows to nearly $350 billion per year. By the 34th year, CMS revenue exceeds $550 billion annually.** In the best case scenario, CMS begins producing government revenue in its 17th year of operations. Five years later in the 22nd year of CMS operations, this annual revenue grows to $486 billion. By the 27th year, CMS revenue in the best case just clears $1 trillion per year.

What about the very long run? The worst case scenario appears to approach an upper limit of an annual Fund just under $2.5 trillion, which includes an annual government revenue contribution of just under $1 trillion. To do this, the CMS must take in annual revenues of just under $3.5 trillion. The program approaches this mark around year 50, but never quite reaches it as government payments and annual cost increases decrease growth to nearly zero. In order to continue CMS Fund growth further, we would need to tighten the payback rules. That means we would allow the CMS to keep a bit more of it profits each year for reinvestment.

We can see the effect of tighter payback rules in the best case scenario because that case pays a smaller percentage back to the government and sets a higher Fund threshold. The TDRM shows us that letting the CMS keep more of its money for reinvestment allows the Fund to become really big. The punch line here is that best case rules never produce an upper limit in the first 41 years of CMS operations. I stopped at 41 years because that is the year that CMS government payments equal today's entire government budget of about $3.5 trillion.

With the luck of the best case scenario, income tax goes away 41 years from the start of our original $1 trillion CMS program. I know reality will be different, but this illustration is still valid to show that we can achieve this goal just by managing a few factors. The reality is that reinvestment rules will change regularly. We could be even more aggressive than my best case assumes, for instance. That would allow us to achieve income tax independence without all of the other good fortune the best case scenario assumes.

I have talked about costs and revenues, the traditional focal points of interest in commercial business plans. However, our original motivation for the entire strategy did not center on either of these. My mandate was to create jobs and lower the unemployment rate. Of course, we cannot accomplish this even in Magnified Capitalism without improving the whole economy. So we are also interested in how our plan affects the GDP. Here are those results.

In the worst case scenario, the TDRM takes unemployment from the current rate of 8.2% to 6.5% in the first year. In the second and third years it drops further to 5.8% and 5.6% respectively. Unemployment falls just a bit more and stays roughly the same for the next 15 years or so. During this entire time I project that the CMS will directly produce just short of three million new jobs (gross) each year. GDP pops in the first years from today's meager 2.2% to 3.7% in year 1, 4.6% in year 2, and 5.1% in the 3rd year. GDP gets only a little better from there, never quite reaching 6% until after we pay off the CMS debt.

Now, recall that in the 18th year of CMS operations we completely pay off the CMS debt (in the worst case). At this point the Fund will start to enlarge beyond the $1 trillion mark annually. This produces a larger and ever-growing impact on the economy in subsequent years. My model conservatively projects a further lowering of the unemployment rate to around 4.5% over the next 20 years (years 19 through 38). GDP rates grow in parallel to as high as 9%. The model improves neither unemployment nor GDP much beyond these levels because of the topping-out effect I mentioned earlier. We would have to change the reinvestment rules to let the CMS Fund grow more in order to see further improvements.

The best case scenario shows us what happens when the CMS Fund grows even fatter. But first let me describe what the earlier years look like in this scenario. Best case TDRM shows the unemployment rate dropping to nearly 4.6% within the first 3 years, when GDP growth hits a 6.6% quarterly rate in that same year. Unemployment levels off just below this point for many years until we pay off the CMS debt, which occurs in year 12 in this scenario. After that the economy goes on another improvement run. The CMS Fund never stops growing under the best case rules, so there is no plateau in this scenario. For instance, by the 25th year of CMS operations the annual Fund size grows to over $4 trillion, the government is earning over $800 billion in CMS revenue, the GDP quarterly growth rate has cleared 10%, and unemployment is below 4%. Essentially, it is hard to imagine an economy sustaining a level much better than that. I want to emphasize an important point here. The economy is on fire in this scenario because it is getting a $4 trillion boost every year right into the heart of our capitalist machine.

Had enough talk about numbers? Me, too. Some people prefer their numbers in tables, so I'll close out this dialog with a summary in the form of a table below. In addition to restating some of the projections we just discussed, I have included some alternative ways of interpreting the same data. I have also included average values which represent an "expected projection", as well as a brief interpretation of each financial measure.

Magnified Capitalism Trillion Dollar Reinvestment Model (TDRM) Summary Table:
All dollar figures shown in billions of dollars (U.S.)

Financial Measure	Best Case	Expecte d	Worst Case	Interpretation
Total Funding Required - amount borrowed	**$3,622**	**$3,738**	**$3,854**	Total cost of CMS including setup costs and debt interest
# Years Negative Cash Flow - until payback begins	**5**	**6**	**6**	Last year CMS needs money; after this it pays its own way
Year # that Debt is Repaid - with debt repaid, Fund grows after this year	**12**	**15**	**18**	Repaid with interest; next year CMS Fund grows > $1T
Year # that Government Revenue Begins - using reinvestment rules stated in text	**17**	**21**	**24**	CMS Fund > threshold beyond which a portion is paid to gov't as revenue
Gov't Revenue in year 25	**$804**	**$483**	**$162**	Gov't revenue grows each year
Gov't Revenue in year 40	**$3,343**	**$2,032**	**$722**	Worst case approaches plateau
Total CMS Funds Value in year 40	**$39,550**	**$23,623**	**$7,697**	If CMS stopped providing services and just collected what was due for 6 years

Economic Measure	Best Case	Expected	Worst Case	Interpretation
Unemployment Rate Yr 1	**6.2%**	**6.4%**	**6.5%**	Year 0 is 8.2%, fast progress
Unemployment Rate Yr 3	**4.7%**	**5.2%**	**5.7%**	Stays near this until Fund ...
Unemployment Rate Yr 10	**4.7%**	**5.1%**	**5.4%**	... grows when debt repaid
Unemployment Rate Yr 25	**3.7%**	**4.2%**	**4.7%**	Fund has grown > $1T here
Qtly GDP Change – Year 1	**4.2%**	**3.9%**	**3.7%**	Year 0 is 2.2%, fast progress
Qtly GDP Change – Year 3	**6.6%**	**5.8%**	**5.1%**	GDP growth slows a bit ...
Qtly GDP Change – Year 10	**8.7%**	**7.3%**	**5.9%**	... ~ year 10, then picks ...
Qtly GDP Change – Year 25	**10.8%**	**9.2%**	**7.7%**	... up again when Fund > $1T

Financial Conclusions

The numbers are positive. Even the worst case scenario is still a great success. Unemployment rates fall fastest in the early years, just what we want from a strategy whose main purpose is to fix this problem. The unemployment rate keeps falling fast under any scenario for several years. The only difference between worst case and best case scenarios is the level at which this rate finally settles, either a fairly good level or a really good level. Either way, we win. The GDP figures support the same sort of conclusion.

Interestingly, even the cost of the whole program shows a strong result. How is that? In both the best and worst case scenarios, the total cost stays in a pretty tight, predictable range. Both cases give us a number close to but under $4 trillion, the total amount we need to borrow to conduct this $1 trillion annual strategy. The program will take a bit more than $2 trillion for the first two years, then a bit less than that for the next three or four years, depending on how lucky (or efficient) we are. After that, the bleeding stops and the CMS starts repaying the $4 trillion setup cost. Somewhere between the 12th and 18th years, we will repay all of that money. From then on, the CMS will provide its services at a profit, completely out of debt. At this point we allow the Fund to grow larger than $1 trillion annually. Between year 17 and 24, the CMS Fund will grow so much that it will be able to start paying revenue back to the United States government, yet it will still grow each year. Comparing the best case reinvestment rules to the worst case ones shows us how we can manage the Fund to replace income taxes completely, if we want to. Or we can take a bigger share of the CMS Fund and limit its growth to an amount that is still amazingly large.

For those who are interested in comparing this model to the commercial world, here are a few interesting reference points. By borrowing around $3.8 trillion to implement Magnified Capitalism, I am roughly saying that I expect the CMS to manage a $3.8 trillion fund. Does anything like exist that today? As of 2011, the Vanguard Fund stood as the largest fund management company in the world. Its fund value is estimated to be worth $1.7 trillion. This is not too far from what we expect to accomplish.

How do the CMS's earnings compare to the commercial world? In the worst case scenario the TDRM assumes that the CMS captures a gross annual return on investment (ROI) of 9%. Essentially, that means the Fund returns 9% interest, compounded annually. In the best case scenario, I used the more optimistic ROI figure of 15%. How does that compare with traditional commercial venture capital (VC) companies? Depending on how well it is run, a VC can expect to make between 11% and 17% ROI. I have discounted this range because I expect the CMS to offer non-profit-driven incentives and otherwise take a slightly smaller share of the profits than the VC partners it serves. If we think the actual ROI ought to be in the middle of this range, then we should be very happy with the worst case projections that assume so much less.

Eliminating Income Taxes

Finally, what can we do about eliminating income taxes? The financial analysis has taught us a few things. It shows us we need to let the annual Fund grow to somewhere between $10 and $15 trillion in order to generate government revenue equal to today's federal budget. The best case scenario accomplishes this in 41 years; the worst case scenario never grows the Fund much beyond $2.5 trillion annually in the same time frame. That means if we want to replace income taxes we need to either reduce how much the CMS pays back to the government, or borrow more up front and make a bigger initial investment. The advantage here is that many CMS costs are fixed. If we make a bigger up-front investment, these costs shrink as a percentage of the whole package. We could also take other more creative actions like reducing the speed at which we repay the CMS debt. The TDRM assumes all profit over the $1 trillion needed per year goes to debt repayment. In other words, it repays debt about as fast as it can. Slowing down repayment would allow the Fund to grow beyond $1 trillion much sooner. In any case, the exact strategy is up to us.

Through one approach or another, we can reasonably craft a strategy to replace income taxes in about fifty years, or a bit longer if we cannot help but use a bit more of the CMS money in the meantime. The TDRM financial model shows us that we have choices. The good news is that there is plenty of room for variation. This is a sign that the overall strategy is extremely effective. The only bad news is that this variation is bound to become political fodder. Hopefully the need to pick a reasonable solution will win out over the political desire to beat the other side down. Here I am an optimist. I think compromise over how much to turn the knob is relatively easy once we all agree that the knob needs turning.

"If someone tells you 'there is no way you can lose', they are either naïve or lying. It is striking how often people in the most advantageous situations regularly manage to find a path to failure. One of the best ways to invite failure is to gain an advantage and then blindly count on victory going forward. One of the best ways to invite success is to be persistent in chasing the goal no matter your current situation. Accumulate as many advantages as possible. Prepare for as many pitfalls as you can think of. Keep going when you are knocked back, as long as you are still in the game. Always assume the other side is brilliant and surprising. Avoid or minimize your losses by trying to anticipate what may go wrong and be ready with a mitigation plan once you notice the prerequisite conditions are met."

- Future V.P. of CMS Risk Management Division -

VIII. Risk Management

I am not a politician. A politician may be well advised to mention only their plan's upside and its high odds of success. When asked about the risks, a politician might prefer to dismiss the long odds for failure. This may make for good rhetoric and posturing, but for a planner it is dangerously bad form.

The truth is that nothing is free. The price of real opportunity is a measure of risk. The smartest investors and entrepreneurs take risks with big potential benefits, yet they also prepare for the worst case scenario. How do they do that? They either plan for it or they are just lucky. Luck does happen, but we cannot count on it, so I will focus on how to construct a plan that manages risk.

There is an accepted method for planning for the possibility that things may not go well. It begins with listing every risk we can think of. Then, for each risk, we consider what would happen if our plan encountered that problem. Usually, new information will become available to help us see a problem coming before the situation blows up. This information is important. We want to know what the markers are for each risk so that we can keep an eye on their status. If these markers tell us there is a problem brewing then we can prepare to kick off a risk mitigation plan (or a risk reduction plan). Other markers might warn us that failure is imminent, so we better exit now while our program is still largely intact. The difference between these two situations is like the difference between trying to restart the jet engine when it first fails, and parachuting out of the plane as it falls below 2,000 feet. If we prepare for bad fortune, we will succeed or at least be sure to survive. This kind of preparation helps make the entire endeavor a very good bet.

Before I list the major risks I want to point out that the ones I will discuss come in two primary categories: the known risks and the unknown risks. I will deal with each type separately. Also, we may recall that the SWOT analysis listed many risks, along with mitigation strategies for each. These were all strategic risks - risks that had to do with whether or not the whole plan would work. We are not concerned about those risks anymore because they were addressed with plan modifications. At this point we can assume that our plan will work if we complete its steps successfully. The risks we are worried about in this chapter are situational risks. What surprises or bad luck might pop up to trip the plan unexpectedly? Also, we are not just worried about issues that will make us fail in a black and white sense. We are also concerned about situations that might cause delays, increase costs, or otherwise reduce the plan's effectiveness.

Known Risks

Known risks are just what they sound like - the risks we ought to be able to think of in advance. Unknown risks are trickier, but we will deal with those a bit later. For now, here is my list of known risks along with the primary markers we can look for to warn us they are looming. I have listed them in no particular order.

Known Risk	**Warning Signs/Markers to Watch**
Budget Overruns, Under-Budgeting	Budget milestones, contractor targets, project timeline milestones
Legal Problems	Legal process milestones, legal team analysis, external legal filings, protests on legal grounds
Political Roadblocks or Delays	Project timeline milestones, congressional actions or stalling tactics or unwillingness to compromise, protests or other organized opposition acts
CMS Effectiveness too Low (impact, cost, or ROI)	Operating budget milestones, employee (org size) targets, operational timeline milestones, internal reports of conflict, critical external analysis or reports, reports of micromanagement, reports of: lack of oversight, lack of performance incentives, lack of transparency, lack of legal enforcement, lack of testing/QA, other abuses or misappropriation
Scope Creep (plan requirements grow beyond what is planned for)	Change Management Procedures/Plan issues, Congress adds unnecessary details or additional plan requirements, reports that change management process is not working, project timeline milestones
Abuse (scams by customers or CMS people), under-enforcement of Ts & Cs	Quarterly CMS reports for fraud rates – settlements – 2nd opinions (escalations) – complaints, external reports, especially from law enforcement (FBI), media reports or protests of abuse, legal actions
Customer Dissatisfaction, Declining Service Uptake	Quarterly reports for customer satisfaction – complaints, external analysis and media reports on fairness – rating system – redressing procedures, external reports of customer successes vs. failures, legal actions, protests

Unknown Risks

One practical definition for an unknown risk is any risk that is not on the list of known risks. The way to reduce unknown risks then becomes apparent: Just make the known risk list bigger! If we cannot think of any new ones, there is an answer for that, too. We do not need to think of everything ourselves. Just invite everyone who cares to contribute to do so.

The main solution has two simple parts: First, go through a process of collecting more risk ideas. They can come from teams, meetings, expert outsiders, congressional input, and even online contributions. The second part involves formally owning the list. Make sure someone compiles and tracks the details. Furthermore, do not stop maintaining a risk list once the program gets going. New risks will pop up. We will put away, or mitigate, some risks. If we are diligent in managing risks this way, we will almost never be caught completely unprepared. Sure, some surprises will pop up that leave less time to prepare than others. But it is extremely unusual for any risk to come completely out of the blue with zero warning signs and therefore no time to prepare. As long as reasonable people focus on this problem all the time they can usually insure enough warning time to respond.

Many project planners like to assess risks with by assigning an estimated-probability-percentage, or alternately, a level-of-risk-score (probability combined with impact). The bigger the list, the more important this kind of assessment is. As these lists grow it quickly becomes difficult to tell what order of attention everything deserves without some way to compare. A rating system allows us to prioritize risks no matter how many we collect. In total, the solution is to conduct a formal, ongoing risk management process. We can call the people responsible the Risk Management Team. This team can then provide regular updates on risks that have changed recently. They would provide these reports to the stakeholders, such as CMS management and the Board, as well as posting them to the public.

Risk Mitigation

Now that we have decided to form a Risk Management Team, a convenient solution for risk mitigation planning arises. I do not need to spell out what to do in every possible situation. That is not even appropriate for an executive briefing like this. What I can say, however, is that the Risk Management Team should prepare a complete response to each risk on their list. This same team should also be responsible for monitoring the markers associated with each risk. The status of these markers will raise or lower the probability of any related risks. The execution of any risk mitigation actions, as well as the results of such actions, will also affect risk probabilities. The result is simple from this standpoint: The solution to risk mitigation is to put a team in place whose whole job is to track and address risks.

Addressing risks includes two types of action. Preventive actions are those we can take before a risk becomes a full-blown problem. We trigger these actions when our risk markers change to increase the odds of the risk happening above some threshold. The second type of action is to make or improve our planned response. In other words, we make sure the organization is ready so it can act quickly and effectively when a problem pops up.

The Risk Management Team must also have enough authority and access to top management to insure the organization follows all its plans. This is sufficient. Effective risk management must be proactive. It is not difficult to understand, but it is easy to ignore or minimize. As long as we pay attention and incentivize the Risk Management Team to be comprehensive, we should catch most problems early. The team will make sure we take preventive actions and are ready to handle problems that do pop up before they get too bad.

Plan Constraints

A constraint is a limit we cannot change that might affect our plan. I have listed them here primarily for completeness. Also, for those who want to further analyze this proposal, I have provided these items in the form of a table to help them understand what I considered to be the most important constraints.

Constraint	Comments
Initial CMS Funding has limits; replacing income taxes immediately is not practical	I propose a $1 trillion annual fund. About ten times that amount is enough to pay for the federal budget without taxes in about six years, but that is far too high an amount to borrow (a total of around $35 trillion over 6 years) and expect political passage. Rather, I propose to borrow a practical amount ($3.8 trillion over 6 years), pay that debt off quickly, then save enough over several decades to eventually replace income taxes (if that becomes a goal).
Unemployment Rate cannot be zero, i.e., there is an "employment saturation" effect	What would the unemployment rate be if anyone who wanted a job received ten job offers a day? I do not really know. No one does. It still would not be zero, though. There will always be people "in between" jobs who do not need to work, at least for a while: those who are incapacitated, those who want to hold out for the perfect offer, or those just procrastinating. In my model I had to estimate what I labeled the "employment saturation" effect. The answer my calculations gave was that 3% unemployment was amazing, but with enough capital we might be able to push it to as low as 2.5%. Before correcting for employment saturation, my earlier models projected a negative unemployment rate in some cases! Joking to myself, I decided that meant we would have to hire people from other countries and ship them in during work hours. Regardless, unemployment is an open issue at some very high levels of capital magnification. It starts to matter as the Fund grows beyond about $5 trillion annually.

Major Plan Modification (protection)	This proposal is complete and should work if we implement it as described. What are the odds that the plan will change between now and implementation? Probably near 100%. The real question is whether such changes will be properly considered, weighed, simulated, tested, and validated. Eliminate simulation testing to save money (as one obvious example) and I can just about guarantee the whole thing will fail. The constraint here is an extension of the strategic and situational risks we have already discussed. It is a question of, "How much discipline will Congress apply?" in passing the needed legislation. If our leaders insist on twisting a good idea into a bad one by cutting corners, we will have a problem.
High GDP Resistance	Just as my early financial models showed a negative unemployment rate (see Employment Saturation above) when the CMS Fund grew really huge, so did these models also project GDP growth rates that exceeded the historic record (over 18%) in some cases. I modified the model to estimate a "natural" added resistance for GDP growth when it goes above 9% quarterly. Since the problem of having so much money available for business growth has never actually occurred in history over sustained periods, nobody knows exactly how this will affect GDP. The good news is that it does not really matter. If GDP turns out to be 14% when I projected 10% I will gladly admit I was way off. To be honest, I cut the numbers way back on purpose. I estimated the fabulous cases with lower numbers lest no one believe the answers at all.
Early National Disaster	This plan does not account for a major national disaster, especially one that occurs during the formation and setup of the CMS. It might turn out that continuing with the plan would actually help tremendously, or it could be better to wait until we have dealt with the immediate problems, especially if the disaster were severe enough to prevent a large portion of people from working whether they wanted to or not. In any case, these are just thoughts. I have neither modeled nor fully considered this case. No risk mitigation would be likely to address a disaster that was both sufficiently severe, early in the plan timeline (before services begin generating income), and surprising (not enough warning time to prepare). I would add, as I mentioned previously, that an established and profitable CMS would have the opposite impact in a major disaster. We could use its considerable resources (the Fund) to pay for major recovery efforts. This is the national insurance policy benefit that I discussed. However, this insurance only avails itself after the CMS is operating for at least a few years, preferably a few decades.

Closing Thoughts on Risk

It is natural after considering all the risks in a plan to become anxious or frightened. In truth, such a reaction should be inverted. Look at what we will do.

VIII. Risk Management

We will not just consider all the risks listed here. We will assign a professional team to monitor them, track their triggers and markers, and keep considering an ever-larger list perpetually. This team will always be working on new plans to address emerging risks. These plans will be transparent to the public. The CMS management should be under constant pressure to address any emerging threats before the risks trip the system up too badly. CMS management will want this kind of preparation. We should all want it. It represents a professional way to take a bold action.

If we hear a bear in a dark cave we are exploring, we deploy our soldiers to the front. Good thing our Risk Management Team brought the audio amplifier (to monitor distant cave sounds). Do not be scared that there might be a bear there. Instead, be glad we considered the possibility ahead of time. The Risk Management Team insured we hired soldiers with huge guns, personal armor, gas grenades, and special ops training, to fend off or even capture the bears. As soon as we heard the bear sound, we deployed our special ops people to deal with the situation appropriately. It is normal to be scared of dark caves, but that is also where the good stuff lies. Good thing we went into the cave prepared.

There is a grand lesson in capitalism, and it is the opposite of what some people think. The winners are the companies that refuse to declare victory. Their management knows a market never stands still. Many stock investors are still fooled into buying a company's stock due to a management focus on improving profit margins. After all, this can improve a company's short-term value. What these investors miss is that the price of doing so is essentially a mortgage on that company's future. Most investments based on a company's profitability improvements should be reserved for day traders who plan to sell their stock as soon as they make their profit. The long-term investor knows to look for companies with a strategy to build market leadership, or extend it. They look for companies that keep innovating and delivering what customers want. These are the companies worth investing in.

IX. Next Steps and Beyond U.S. 2.0

It is a misunderstanding that capitalism is synonymous with greed. Investors who buy stock in companies focused on near-term profits can make money that way, but these investors do not drive our capitalist economy. The businesses themselves drive the economy. Sometimes businesses become focused on maximizing profit above all else. This is the kind of disposition that greed suggests. That focus on profit can occur because shareholders demand it, or because new management anticipates they will, or for a variety of other reasons. Stockholders occasionally even vote to install new management that takes this tack, although this is not as common as some would think.

But guess what? These companies and their stockholders are taking themselves out of the real game. Profit-driven executives and their stockholders often milk their company for a few years, sell their stock at a somewhat higher price (if they catch it in time), then watch the underlying company degrade itself into irrelevance. Most often the executives responsible for the damage collect their bonuses and leave, to go on to rape some other business. Why should they care if the company they once managed takes another five or ten years to finish its downfall? On their resume they will claim the success of improved profit margins in the short time they were there. It usually takes many years for a profit-focus to ruin an established business, especially when the company is very large or once was a much-respected market leader. Sometimes board of directors recognizes the downtrend in time and brings in new visionary management to correct the problem. I am not saying management with a profit priority is rare. This situation happens all the time. But the companies that drive our economy are not these types, at least not by the time they adopt such a profit-driven strategy. On the contrary, this is common management error. The more successful long-term investors already know this.

In time I expect more and more people will understand this concept. As a result, even shorter-term investors will be increasingly reluctant to support such profit-only strategies. Why is greed a bad management strategy? A new company cannot expect to break into an existing market with such a foundation. That is why we primarily see this focus in older, more established companies. The more pretentious a business is about its market position, the more tempted its management will be to focus on profits above all else.

These companies are misguided to undertake such an approach. Their products and services are sure to decline in competitiveness because a profit-driven strategy means management will conduct a variety of "efficiency improvement measures". This will include hiring reductions, freezes and/or layoffs. It also means reduced investment in the company's future, such as deferring or reducing spending on newer technology, updated systems, research and development, and effective testing and inspections. This strategy gives sales and marketing the goals of discounting less, raising prices, and finding new ways to charge customers for "extra services". A priority on profit can produce dictums from management that pressure their employees in many other negative ways. Employees are likely to conclude it is better to take shortcuts and save money, too. This can result in "unintended" problems in safety, quality control, and many other aspects of a business. Eventually, the attraction of such companies' products and services necessarily declines in their markets. They create ever larger openings for competitors to offer better solutions. The attitudes of their overworked and threatened employees can easily attest to this.

Consider investors who buy up a company's stock after that company announces layoffs, for example. Such a buy-up is a common, although not an automatic, reaction to layoff announcements. The usual explanation for this response is that the company in question is trying to get its costs under control so it is better positioned to survive. Regardless, traders trying to buy up such companies cannot be interested in the long run. Layoffs are bad news. Everyone inside such a company knows it. If the company is in real trouble, and must lay off employees just to survive a bit longer, it is fundamentally unstable. Such a company is on the verge of bankruptcy. Investors should run away. That is not the usual reason for layoffs, however. Many companies enact layoffs just to improve their margins. In other words, they are trying to tweak their financial analysis. These companies usually deserve to be punished for such actions both in the value of their stock and in the markets that they compete in. They are trading in their future prospects for some degree of financial positioning today. Management has lost experienced employees, distressed the remaining people with higher workloads and a narrower outlook, and probably canceled, delayed or jeopardized projects that would have improved various aspects of their future. Customers should run away. Investors should sell their stock. Those stockholders who want to hold the company stock should learn to replace such management, not reward them.

The real business drivers of our economy are the companies who are in it to compete. These businesses come in three flavors. First there are the newer companies that have innovated their way to success. These are the superstars and headliners. Lately, they tend to be tech companies, although we can find them in every branch of the business world. Then there are the old stalwarts that have found some reasonable, long-term balance between profit and innovation. Often these older companies adopt a strategy of buying the up-and-comers, since it is easier to justify their innovations and growth this way. It is not as sad a strategy as it may seem. These buy-ups inject new ideas into the older companies, producing a market that helps entrepreneurs. In other words, one way to generate wealth is to start a company that is designed to be bought out once it proves itself sufficiently.

The third kind of capitalist engine comprises most of the remaining ordinary businesses. This group includes the little guys, the medium-sized ones and even some of the larger companies that we have never heard of. They are not leaders and their stock may not even be public, or if it is, it is not widely traded. These businesses are all over the place. They account for a large portion of our economy. Sure, all companies need a decent profit margin to survive and thrive, but these have not established themselves by cutting costs, reducing services and raising prices. Most companies make it because they find a niche they can serve well. They did something right or they got lucky enough. Either way, to make their impact they need to keep improving or they will go away, too.

Business markets are a jungle. Greed can push people to risk their business for a few more dollars. This happens most often when a company hits a pause in its growth and runs out of ideas for jump-starting expansion again. However, these plateauing or declining companies are not the drivers of our economic future. Rather, the ones who are best at understanding and meeting the customers' needs drive our economy onward. The lesson here is about change. Business leadership means mastering the ability to regularly adapt and improve. The greedy are just the vultures at the margins, eating up the profits of those companies that have lost their way.

Why all this discussion about what kind of company really drives a capitalist economy? Because you, Mr. President, have asked for a business plan in the spirit of a commercial company. A professional commercial business plan does not just offer a single solution or strategy; it offers a path to the future. It lays down a trail that leads towards possibilities for constant innovation. In this proposal we have a way to make a healthy profit to pay for our efforts and to keep our CMS business financially strong. But to stay ahead of all the other countries in the world, we must do much more than that. We have to keep improving faster than they do. Now, we could argue this is unnecessary. Once we are doing well, why not take a break in our plan until we run into another problem later? But this is the same kind of argument made by those businesses that fade away in the long run. If you want the opinion of this capitalist, Mr. President, we will have more self-respect and success if we stop thinking that way. Frankly, it is that kind of thinking that got us to this point in the first place.

Thinking that we have arrived is a losing attitude. We reached the top and stopped changing because it is easy to think that way at the top. This was an error that most people have failed to recognize. It is not a concession to admit we have to keep changing. It is a concession to our competitors if we stand still. This plan represents our collective reawakening. Americans know how to manage a business. We should use those same principles to manage our country. Tomorrow we can innovate ourselves towards success with Magnified Capitalism. After that we should innovate another aspect of ourselves. Then we should do so again and again for as long as we possibly can. That is how we lead and stay in the lead. Truthfully, this is the real American formula for success.

Next Steps

Mr. President, I trust I have convinced you to go forward. The matter before us now is, "What do we do about it?" You may recall that I addressed this question in large part in previous discussions. In *Chapter V: CMS Operational Plan Overview*, I provided several relevant details, including a timeline with key milestones, as well as a discussion of how to set up the CMS through a two-step congressional program. Of course, the very next step centers around gaining political consensus, or establishing a populist momentum for Magnified Capitalism. In that case we might refer to the discussion in *Chapter III: SWOT Analysis* under the weakness titled "Congressional Seizure." There we assumed that Congress might become a roadblock inhibiting this proposal. It would be wise to start out with this assumption anyway. Therefore, we could immediately implement the steps I outlined as a way to get the process going as fast as possible. With a few additional comments, here are the three measures I mentioned there that we can begin executing immediately:

1. **Sign Up Political Champion(s)** – Who will be motivated to make a political bet on Magnified Capitalism first? Will it be an established President seeking re-election in a weak economy, who is still without a believable plan for fixing our problems? Will it be the challenger who claims to know how to create jobs better, but is similarly vague about how he will do that? Or should we instead still assume the challenger's promised tax cutting and fiscal conservativeness is supposed to create all the needed jobs? Perhaps some other high-level force will grab the reins of leadership. Unless the two leading presidential candidates jump on board quickly, there will be room for an existing or up-and-coming congressional leader to wave the Magnified Capitalism flag first and then claim most of the accolades to aid in their ambitions. The advantage goes to the first, the loudest, and the most aggressive, in that order. My hope is that the actual situation will include all of the above. The best case would involve a competition for who is first to

rally the masses and how quickly we can implement this plan. Of course, I would not be surprised if we end up with some delay in implementation. The top choices for champion are just as likely to study the matter as they are to embrace it in short order, if only to avoid some perceived error. This is why am triggering the next two steps, hopefully with your tacit support, Mr. President. These may help convince you that becoming a champion would be politically advantageous as well as truly cogent.

2. **Acquire Political Action Funding** - There are many beneficiaries in Magnified Capitalism who currently have strong resources (money). I admit some pride that this strategy is good for the country yet it does not demonize anyone (analytical criticisms not withstanding). This plan is based on the principle that making money with new business concepts is such a good idea, we need to pump it up. We should encourage those who currently enable business growth to do so even more. These are the same people who should be demanding that their political representatives enact the legislation needed for this program. I want to help them. My first step is to set up a website where they can share their input: www.magnifiedcapitalism.com. It should be operational by the time you read this, Mr. President. Additionally, I will publish this written proposal openly so anyone can access it. Hopefully it will receive enough attention to attract the resources we need to start a formal Magnified Capitalism Political Action Committee (PAC). We will see. Our efforts to form a Magnified Capitalism PAC may be greatly aided by success in the next step.

3. **Start a Grass Roots Campaign** - Ultimately, the best way to be sure of implementing our strategy is to have everyone demand it. Everyone should. There are no losers, although I expect many doubters, especially at first. Mostly, however, I anticipate the main hurdle to be one of gaining widespread awareness. That is the reason for publishing this writing. I need every reader's help, especially early on. If I have done anything to awaken hope in my readers, I ask them to please take at least one or two steps to help spread the word. We can all post our opinions online or ask our friends to read this proposal. Some other ways to help include asking a journalist or news organization to follow up; calling into a radio show; writing to a favorite talk show or state or federal representative. If each reader can help a few others to learn about this strategy, we can make it happen. Politicians will not ignore a reasonable plan that the majority of voters want us to pursue. This is how it can work in the United States first. Here, more than anywhere, the people can make a specific goal happen if enough of us demand it. This sort of outcome does not happen very often because politicians increasingly position issues as divisive. Everything seems to be about us versus them, left versus right, incumbent versus challenger.

> Not this time. Magnified Capitalism should fit everyone's agenda: the Tea Party, the Occupiers (a. k. a., the Occupy Wall Street movement or the 99%), independents who just want the economy fixed, the unemployed who want real action, the employed or retired who are worried that the economy is headed into trouble. Everyone is demanding a solution, but until now no one has put forward a plan that really solves our problems. The only people we should hear speaking out against Magnified Capitalism are those who doubt it will work to such a degree that they expect it to cause even more problems. To those people I say, "I understand your concern, but respectfully you should reconsider." If rereading this proposal does not convince you, then refer this concept to some economists for analysis. Let them run their numbers and examine the plan closely. Some may say they do not expect it to work. Most should say the opposite. None should tell you there is a serious downside to trying, as long as we do not take shortcuts. That is why I have been so careful in drafting a professional plan. I have considered and accounted for downsides. Now I just need everyone's help to spread the word.

Assuming the above steps generate the political will, I suggest we take some additional steps. Most important is to quickly and correctly enact Magnified Capitalism legislation as I have outlined. A brief political skirmish about the details will not do much harm, but we should not wallow in this kind of activity. Once it is clear that we can gain legislative passage, we should pause the arguing for everyone's good. Well-intended representatives of all sides should enter a brief negotiation on this strategy's details with the intent of producing prompt compromise. This plan allows us to defer most ideological arguments or assign them to the separate issue of managing CMS incentives. That is OK. We can decide CMS incentives close to the last minute. The plan even expects them to change annually and in response to emergencies. Ideally, we should treat the matter of Magnified Capitalism itself as an issue of national security. We need to implement this plan now. It is a good excuse to work together and transform our country into a new kind of world competitor.

Although it is not absolutely required, I also strongly suggest enacting additional measures to improve banking regulation. Some will assume this position is left-leaning, but I do not look at it that way. My idea of regulation is probably different than most Democrats imagine. Here is what I mean.

To me it is a matter of implementing our plan correctly. Magnified Capitalism needs the banking system to work both efficiently and ethically. United States 2.0 does not benefit from banks that make extra money through shady practices that risk our future. The kind of bank regulation I want to see encompasses two simple issues: banking transparency and penalties for fraud. I am not necessarily calling for outlawing or restricting any particular bank's investment strategy. In my version of banking regulation, banks will have little to complain about. All I want to see is that our banks' actions (and financial investment statements) are both illuminated and summarized. It should be easy for an ordinary American to understand their bank's investment portfolio and strategy at all times. It should also be easy for an independent analyst to verify such claims through details the bank makes public.

Second, the bank's employees and management should personally certify this information, subject to severe penalties for falsifying or failing to disclose information. Neither rule prevents any kind of investment strategy banks may want to take. It just means they will have trouble misleading anyone about what they are doing, even as they are doing it. We should all want this kind of common sense regulation, rather than rules that try to cage bank investment strategies. I think transparency will fix most problems far better because it will let the people decide what kind of bank they want. Arm the market with information and let the market decide. Regardless of how we organize the new regulations, leaving banking rules as they are is dangerous. It is one of the few issues that could trip up an otherwise properly implemented Magnified Capitalism strategy.

United States 3.0

Implementing Magnified Capitalism is how we form United States 2.0. Our next major improvement strategy will elevate the country to version 3.0. In the beginning of this chapter I made the case that a good commercial strategy involves not just a single step, but a roadmap toward the future. Magnified Capitalism provides a roadmap of sorts in that it inherently handles ongoing changes, especially with regard to policy-based incentives. I compared these incentives to a new steering wheel for our rocket-modified racecar.

This is not what I meant about a roadmap, though. I meant that we, as a country, should pursue regular change in the way we manage ourselves, even after we launch this program. We should demand fundamental upgrades that improve our global competitiveness regularly, even when things are going well - especially when things are going well. Why? Because when we are on top it is far less risky to make change than if we wait until we are struggling. Leaders can afford to make a misstep from time to time, especially if they are careful in their planning. Also, we tend to be more careful in such planning when there is less pressure to hurry up. The payoff for taking some risk by changing is to stay in the lead, to be prosperous, to enable real happiness, and to keep growing as the clear example for others to follow.

We have shown the world two kinds of leadership in the last hundred years or so. The first kind is the one that sets the example of managing a country built on top of innovative business leadership. Freedom enables capitalism which in turn enhances freedom and prosperity (when at its best). It is a circular cycle of some beauty. The United States will conduct this kind of business with any country that is reasonably behaving itself, and those countries and their citizens will benefit from it. That benefit is not just monetary, either. These countries we trade with also benefit from the interaction, the model, the example we set. It makes me very proud that this kind of exchange with other countries has made us the envy of most of the world's people. It is not the envy of our government, but the envy of our people. Being an American means having freedom of opportunity. This comes from our recognition of the importance of capitalism.

Second, we have also repeatedly shown military leadership over the last hundred years. Certainly, we have learned much from this sort of leadership, too. While we are the supreme superpower today, our use of military might has received mixed reviews over the years. I will not otherwise offer an analysis except to point out that this kind of leadership is trickier than people sometimes imagine it to be. We can be both right and wrong at the same time. Pursuing military leadership itself is extremely advantageous, but we can probably all agree that its application rarely works as expected, except when the situation is absolutely dire anyway. But those dire cases are also the times there is no doubt the other side asked for it. We earn a moral bonus in such very rare cases.

I think we owe it to those who do the sacrificing to remember that. I believe that part of the responsibility of being a military leader is to set the highest moral standard for the use of military might. That does not mean we do not fight. It does mean we should be proud to explain to God, or our children, why we supported the need to, and in the manner we did it.

Otherwise, I mention military leadership for two reasons. First, we still hold this important kind of leadership. Second, we must realize that business leadership does more to sway the hearts and minds of the world's citizenry than military leadership does. Similarly, if we want to follow through in winning freedom for the whole world, we cannot do so primarily through the military. The military aspect is necessary primarily to keep other countries from being tempted by stupid acts of conquest. A strong military therefore enables a focus on business, for the most part. But the lesson is this: We win by showing others how to be prosperous with capitalism. Want to try to really beat the U.S.? The only way to do that is to compete with us in business. Oh, if you want to do that you will need to enable more freedom for your own people.

Magnified Capitalism gains us a renewed and increased advantage in being the world leader in business. Our strategy establishes a new starting point for the roadmap to ongoing change. We want a more effective government that enables and empowers its citizens and businesses without any handouts. In other words, this approach pursues an increase in personal freedom. By making our sources of money both more powerful and more accessible, this plan focuses on changing our capitalist infrastructure. Then it sets the stage for what can come next.

It sets an example for how we can provide government functions through a different kind of organization that is responsive to its people. Other U.S. government organizations might later benefit from combining commercial goals with social ones by being citizen-owned, transparently managed, and metric driven. The Capital Magnification Service will become a proof of concept model. It will demonstrate that we can upgrade the nature of our government operations to take advantage of modern commercial processes without compromising any democratic principles. On the contrary, it will show us we can embrace the features of capitalism that drive our private sector's commercial success.

Previously, those who considered privatizing government functions in the United States focused on an outsourcing model. They considered whether it makes sense to hire a private company to fulfill this or that function. The problem with such an approach has become apparent: It has little built-in incentive for quality of service or effective results. This outsourcing approach has succeeded in only a few very narrow service categories, such as prison management. However, Magnified Capitalism shows us there is a hybrid organization possible that acts like the best of both worlds - part commercial and part government. The citizen company may be applicable to a wide range of government services, if not most of them.

There is one big problem hindering any measure that is so bold: the nature of politics. I have argued that we have a strong need for urgency today. Once the economy is running well, this urgency will disappear. Given our country's current state, it would not be difficult to project a return to the kind of partisanship that keeps us from passing any other transformative legislation.

Change to Help Change: Term Limits with a Grandfather Clause

There is a partial solution to this problem, but politicians have fought it and won at the national level. The solution is found in term limits. We can blame much congressional gridlock on the fact that once someone is elected, their ability to be reelected approaches certainty. Historically, House members in a given election year have had a minimum of an 85% chance for reelection, with many election years reaching 96% to 98% odds (since the 1960's). Senators who stay in office three times longer than House members per election cycle have had to fight a bit harder. Their odds of reelection since 1982 have been no less than 75% in a given year, although in half of those election years their odds have been above 90%.

Many people do not realize that there is a reason reelection odds are so high. The average congressional member spends most of his or her workday building their next reelection fund, either directly or indirectly. Doing that from office is a big advantage over the next challenger. This is especially true since fundraising causes them to meet a lot of supporters. The politicians know that making lots of promises that these supporters want to hear tends to improve campaign donations.

Why blame congressional gridlock on the lack of term limits? The people who stay in office perpetually are the ones who have the most trouble working with the other side to reach compromise. They will deny it, though. This problem is simply and absolutely due to human nature. If the politicians could only stay in office for just a short time, they would fight to be effective in the time they had. That requires compromise and everyone knows it. But if they are spending over 50% of their time making deals for reelection funding, then they have to lock themselves down to harder positions. They tend to make populist promises that cater to their targeted supporters, especially those with the money.

This dynamic encourages politicians to demonize their opponents with greater vigor. This way, they receive more money and support from those on the other side of an issue. Long-term politicians can lose perspective on why they were elected in the first place, although people in these positions will often rationalize their actions. They will say things like, "The problem with term limits is that my state would not be better served by the next person. I know what I am doing. My state would lose its seniority and experience (in this matter or that)." So they have killed past attempts at congressional term limits with justifications that paint them as being selfless.

My solution is simple: We should pass legislation that imposes term limits on only the new people who have yet to be elected. In other words, let those currently in office keep those offices as long as they are able. Lawyers call this kind of arrangement a grandfather clause. Let us not ask our politicians to shoot themselves in the foot, as it were. A term limit law with a grandfather clause just might pass, and that would be far better than nothing. Then maybe our Congress will eventually become more amenable to enacting real change in a way that benefits us all instead of being so worried about reelection that they put up a good fight to gain their constituents' next round of money. I know this sort of legislation will not eliminate all gridlock, but it will bring the problem down a few notches. That should be enough to deliver us a more functional and productive Congress over time.

Also, because United States 2.0 requires a new habit of political change in America, we really need term limits or else our progress will once again plateau until the next crisis. After we enact Magnified Capitalism, term limits should be the next thing that we Americans demand of our representatives. A brief aside might help us appreciate the point here.

I often say that George Washington is one of the people I respect most from history. "One of the most respected?" people typically reply, wondering why I would feel that way about a man associated with a cherry tree fable, a notorious general who lost almost every battle he led. What many Americans do not realize is that democracy was not unique to the United States. Furthermore, there are many countries since then and even today that call themselves democracies but whom most of us would scoff at. Russia, the new Egypt, Iran, all of these and more have parliaments and Presidents (and/or Prime Ministers) with "democratic elections". Our country could have followed a much less remarkable path if not for George Washington. In one of his earliest acts as President of the United States he supported the set of amendments to the Constitution known as the Bill of Rights. These laws form a critical legal basis for our personal freedoms. Later, and perhaps most importantly, he voluntarily left the office of U.S. President after two terms, setting the precedent for how a citizen-led country should operate. He did not have to do this, as the people would have kept reelecting him. But George thought it was the right thing to do so he gave up his office to illustrate his philosophy, that no one should hold a powerful political office for life. Thank God.

Most historians agree that the expectation that our President will only serve two terms has contributed greatly to our country's success. It is one of the biggest differences between our democracy and others' less impressive implementations. George Washington believed that holding an office for life was a core cause of the problems he saw in other countries' governments. That he walked away from his office to prove this point makes me especially proud that he was our first President. To me, that one act made him a great man. He chose the right thing over personal gain.

He was right, so much so that when Franklin D. Roosevelt broke the convention by holding office for four terms, it took only a few years after F.D.R.'s death to fix the system properly with the 22nd Amendment to the Constitution. Presidential term limits became law. People loved F.D.R. but the fact that he decided to become President for life scared them anyway. We should pay attention to history. The benefit of term limits can be hard to explain. The implications are not always the same from person to person. The impact can also be so subtle that it is hard to prove. The effect on the presidency is most important and therefore easiest to understand. But even the people who lived through the F.D.R. years only got the message after he died. Let me be clear on this. We have the same problem with every political office; it is just most obvious when we consider the most powerful positions.

Menu of U.S. 3.0 Considerations

Once we have congressional term limits in place, we will be ready to adopt a habit of strategic governmental change. If we can accomplish this we will be nearly impossible to catch. What changes am I talking about? Truthfully, we should form a new group equivalent to what a commercial company might call "Strategic Planning", "Business Development", or some similar name. By any name their purpose is this. They come up with proposals not unlike this one. They compare a company's (or country's) vision with the direction in which it is heading. Then they propose specific plans for how to deliver this vision more directly. We should form a Strategic Planning group regardless of the ideas that follow. But I cannot help myself. I do have a shortlist of ideas, so I will present them for early consideration.

U.S. 3.0 Consideration #1: Citizen Company (CC) Model

I mentioned this possibility several times so it deserves to be listed first as a natural follow-up. I expect the Capital Magnification Service will prove that we can model government functions in a new way. It should serve as a paradigm for how a citizen company can replace a standard government bureaucracy. Of course there is a natural political problem with attempting this. Government is amazingly effective at protecting the status quo. If we decided that the IRS, for example, would be a good candidate for such a conversion, there would be trouble. Every current IRS employee would have some good cause to protest such a conversion, as would any politician with something to gain by siding with them.

I am not picking on the IRS. We could just as well target the Treasury Department, Education, Commerce, or God forbid one of the military services. Any of these would offer similar, if not stronger political resistance.

My suggestion therefore is to avoid tipping the table over with such a scary proposition. There are probably far smoother ways to plan for conversion to services provided by a citizen company. As a first step, we can form new CCs designed to provide support services to existing agencies. The existing bureaucracy can purchase services similar to the way they might use outsourcing. The main difference is that the outsourcing company itself is a citizen company, and therefore has the kind of management structure needed to resist a profit-only priority. Over time we can transition more and more services from the existing bureaucratic agency to the citizen company.

This approach to change would provide two benefits. First, it would allow the citizen company to prove its efficiency and capabilities within a selected scope. Second, it would allow existing government employees to find appropriate positions in the new company as its scope gradually grew larger. The result should be a measured transition that leaves most people comfortable, including many of those directly affected.

The casual observer might ask, "Why do we want to convert the government functions to the CC model?" The primary answer to that is twofold.

The first reason is that government services from a citizen company should be far more effective than a traditional bureaucracy. Recall that *effective* in a business context means a combination of attractive and cost-efficient. Thus we should be able to provide the same services for less money and/or fewer people. Also, these same services should end up having a deeper or more positive impact.

The second reason for using a CC is that such a company is encouraged to make a profit, or at least some revenue, if that is at all justified. We want it to make some money to offset its costs, as long as this income does not impede the purpose of its existence. Give capitalists the license and incentive to make money and watch them find a way to do it. Notice that the CC is not driven to make money as a top goal. We must define one or more performance metrics to displace profits as a primary goal. The FDA, for example, does food packing inspections anyway. Why not allow them to offer optional inspection preparation services for a fee? Food manufacturers will probably appreciate and make good use of these optional services to better prepare them for the official inspections. Such an organization could also offer training classes, as well as automated monitoring services, cooperative programs, and even resource or system certifications. All such measures could both improve food quality and reduce related costs for the commercial vendors. I would expect a food packer's insurance costs to drop with the use of such services, too.

As another example, the Federal Emergency Management Agency (FEMA) provides emergency response services during major regional disasters. But they could also provide emergency planning integration services that insure coordination between commercial companies and the government under various scenarios. Would any business really pay for that? Absolutely. There are disaster management companies in various market segments today. The computer industry uses them extensively. A disaster management firm that was tightly integrated with FEMA might offer advantages to its customers. The same sort of cooperation would end up making the government more effective in meeting its goals, thus we hit two birds with one stone.

There are many other possibilities for agencies to provide optional services for a fee. Our military could offer a large menu of new services, from coordination with private companies to services for other countries. The U.S. Department of the Treasury could provide secure money printing services for other countries. NORAD or NASA could extend spacecraft tracking and communications services to both private companies and other nations. The Coast Guard and various police forces (or the FBI) could offer training, coordination, optional inspection or certification, and security system integration. The list of commercial services that our government could and should be able to provide is staggering. We would select these services carefully so as to help, not hinder, the non-revenue part of the organizations' current operations. It is not hard to explain how we can do this, but it is too involved for this brief summary.

By the way, I am aware that the government charges for some services today. However, the way this is done is completely out of step with how a CC would operate. For example, the National Park Service charges entrance fees for using a number of the more elaborate or well-maintained parks. I am sure a citizen company would change that completely. It would probably make more sense to make entry to all parks free. Visitors should even be offered some free services or gifts for visiting, but each site's sponsors would provide these. Each park might have a unique combination of several commercial companies that have made a deal to provide some free services to visitors as well as paying for limited commercial rights at the park's entrance. Here the business can sell some gear, food, or other products that meet with park regulations. They can also offer visitors a free piece of gear or service, claim sponsorship on the park's marketing material, and otherwise be responsible for certain negotiated aspects of the park's services (like marketing and waste disposal at the entrance).

So I bite my tongue and will not elaborate further here. This is a topic of serious depth and potential. Sure, some people will be scared to take such a direction. To them I extend my sympathy. There is no doubt that a plan to convert government services to those sourced from CCs would be fraught with complexity and risk. But that is no reason to reject the idea. It is only a motivation to create a well-considered plan. Risk avoidance is not the American way. Risk management is. Regardless, this is a topic worth further study and serious consideration. If we do it correctly we could end up reducing the cost of running the government to surprisingly low levels. The services we receive for this reduced cost should also end up being far superior in ways that are hard to predict. Many of the paid services would invite commercial businesses to become more closely integrated with government services. Even though part of the purpose of the shift to CCs is to generate income and offset costs, the result could also produce an even more effective government capability than we were shooting for.

U.S. 3.0 Consideration #2: Capital Remagnification, or Magnified Capitalism Part II
Can we make more fundamental improvements to Magnified Capitalism? Sure we can. These improvements can come from a number of directions including changes in existing CMS services, new CMS services, changes to CMS structure, significant improvements to service modeling, and changes to rules that limit CMS growth. It is unnecessary to address most of these issues right now. However, once United States 2.0 has been purring along for a while, there will be room to do much more. Our original strategy calls for a complete breakout, a new kind of citizen company that offers a novel set of services. The transition to Part II can be far more gradual. I will just touch on what I mean by each type change I listed above.

The existing CMS services have plenty of room to evolve. We can add options. We can spawn derivatives to better serve various segments of business and society. We can add new functions to the point that we hardly recognize the original service menu. How about some specific examples. An easy case is to offer all the services I mentioned in new flavors geared to strategic business types. Business planners call this a vertical market strategy. Consider an illustrative example. Imagine we want to beef up the use of CMS services by biotech companies. Biotech is the name of our vertical market. The CMS now creates a modified version of its Venture Capital Participation service that caters just to biotechs.

Why bother? Because every industry has special considerations. Gearing a financial service to specific industries (or vertical markets) will align that service better with those customers' needs. In this case, the Ts & Cs will more precisely align with the requirements of the people who are seeking funding in bio-technology businesses. This alignment will likely result in better risk estimates, more accurate company valuations, better deal terms when the deal deserves it, better service by deal managers who understand the industry, and no doubt much more. The point is not that I know the details of what each industry will need so much as that it is not hard to predict that eventually various industries will push for changes that help them.

Totally new CMS services are also easy to predict, but can be similarly hard to describe today. When a company serves its customers well, it learns what they want. Eventually, people will ask for financial services that are not on the CMS menu. Or perhaps some people will imagine new services that are compatible with both the CMS mission and structure. Regardless, if I knew of them I would list them here and then they would not be new. The prediction is only that we will invent these services and find them both useful and profitable.

Changes to CMS structure offer a similar problem again. I know they will arise. I do not yet know what the best candidates are. These will come largely from people's experience working at and with the CMS. They will see what works well and what should work better. Then they will offer solutions for optimization. It should not take long to start hearing the good ideas.

Improvements in service modeling are a bit easier to imagine. By service modeling I mean computer market simulations and related testing systems. I predict that the simulation testing systems will become so effective at helping us tune CMS services that they will produce unanticipated positive results. These are the kinds of results that would make an analyst say, "Wow! If we change this or that then something great happens." I do not know what the "this or that" is or even what the "something great" will be. I can only be sure that those who continue to improve the automated testing and market modeling systems will make such discoveries regularly.

Finally we must consider the rules for CMS growth. There will be lots of rules. I have talked about some, and we will negotiate others when we set the CMS up. One rule I talked about is the regulation that limits CMS services to U.S. citizens. It is a good policy for now. Later it might not be. How is that? By thirty years from now Magnified Capitalism will have fixed our economy decades earlier. The CMS Fund may become so large that we will be challenged to find enough good investments under the existing rules. We will have to make a choice. Either we will have to force the CMS's profitability down to some degree, or allow the CMS to offer services to new people who were not previously eligible. The obvious new people will be those who are not citizens. At this point in the future, loosening such a limit might be fine as long as we handle the details carefully. This is just one example.

How much money the government receives from the CMS is another rule that will change. I have not dictated this policy, but I modeled two different versions in my financial analysis. The point is not which rule we decide on. The point is that whatever we agree on today, in the future a different regulation will make more sense. That change may have a profound impact on the CMS, though.

There will certainly be many other rules that will make sense early on, but that later on we will want to change. Taken together, the body of changes will transform this plan into something new. It will likely be profound from today's vantage point. I hope to live to see some of them.

U.S. 3.0 Consideration #3: Multi-dimensional Government Agencies

My original concept for a multi-dimensional government agency focused on the evolution of the military. The idea of multi-dimensions is that a single agency can handle multiple functions that overlap in the skills and resources needed to deliver that function. In other words, we can do many different jobs using the same people, tools, and equipment.

Having a multi-dimensional government means that we purposefully design the same resources to tackle more than one kind of problem. A three-dimensional strategy is one designed to handle three kinds of problems with one set of resources. We could even go higher to four dimensions or more, although much beyond five or six would probably be a stretch.

Applying this concept to the military seems easiest to imagine, although we could consider the same principle for any agency function. My example here will focus on the Army.

Imagine in the future that we rarely use the Army for the kinds of wars we have engaged in until now. It is not hard to see this coming, as it has already begun. The war in Afghanistan is a perfect example of a transition for the military in general and the Army in particular. The daily activity there is nothing like it was in World War II. The Army's focus is no longer battle-oriented. It includes a great deal of cross-training and coordination with the local and national government. There is an aspect of policing, infrastructure improvement and building, political coordination, and much more. These are hard skills to expect the Army to provide. As an organization it is certainly not optimized for all of this, at least not yet. To their credit, they are working on it, though. One way they might be able to more effectively achieve their goals is if someday we reorganized the Army into a multi-dimensional agency.

The kind of changes we would see might well be illustrated by the example of equipment procurement. Instead of ordering up a new single-purpose rifle, we would have greater need for a multi-purpose one. The new rifles would still do what the old ones could do, perhaps even better. However, they would include new functions for the support of the new multi-role challenges. They might support a wider range of non-lethal ammunition. These new rifles could include more communications functions, like automated voice translators or some type of optional warning system. They might be designed to do a better job of doubling as a hand-to-hand weapon or providing a means to detain and secure. The point is not to pick on the rifle so much as to focus on the basic concept of multi-purpose uses. The multi-dimensional strategy drives us to produce fewer steak knives and instead make more Swiss army knives (which are multi-function tools).

The multi-dimensional agency strategy takes this same approach up to the organizational level. A military troop will purposely cross-train in multiple, closely-related functions. A military division will include many different types of multi-purpose troops so that as a division they can implement a staggering variety of security strategies. This would include standard warfare, naturally. But it would also provide for policing, special coordination with local forces, and the many other new challenges the military faces today.

Let us move away from the pure military example now. It is possible to implement the same sort of strategy with other agencies, resulting in some merging in many cases. For example, some of the interoperation between the Army and the Afghans is arguably overlapping with the State Department's foreign relations duties. Why not merge the functions formally with a multi-dimensional strategy? We could probably achieve our goals more efficiently with less total resources.

I do not mean to focus on the military. They merely represent a convenient example. Analysis may reveal the specific suggestions I put forward here are problematic. That is OK. The point is not that we should enact the exact military examples I mentioned, but that there are bound to be many good cases for applying multiple-use strategies in government. The examples I gave here simply illustrate the point clearly.

U.S. 3.0 Consideration #4: Severe Emergency Deterrence & Planning
We already have the Federal Emergency Management Agency (FEMA), which is responsible for handling national emergencies. What I am proposing here is probably different enough to justify a new agency, or perhaps more realistically, a new dimension for FEMA to take on. It would turn FEMA into a new animal, however. Regardless, the purpose is a bit different from the reactionary mission of today's FEMA. It is also not limited to the United States for good reason. I will elaborate a bit.

Severe Emergency Deterrence & Planning (SEDP) does not focus on helping out in a local disaster. Its purpose is to stop a global catastrophe from either killing everyone, or destroying enough of us to destabilize the world for generations. We could argue that this is more of a State Department function than it is a FEMA extension, but that is a detail. The point is that SEDP tries to anticipate and rate all possible threats to the world, or to entire countries. Its priority is the United States, but it is too simplistic to only focus on us alone. Any pandemic threat that could upset the stability of the United States is just as likely to ruin much of the world. A moderately-sized asteroid threat might take out one country, or even just a part of it. But the aftereffects might still throw the world off balance enough to destabilize food production, energy and other vital activities. And what about a rogue nuclear strike? Is it impossible to imagine some North Korean act of desperation, an odd terrorist effort, or an errant Iranian launch?

Who is planning for dealing with these risk scenarios? Some people are probably working on it. I expect they are buried too deep in a larger organization to make a dent in these big issues. We might mention some obscure military analysts working on one specific example of such an event. It would be counterproductive to have someone in charge of an effort when few people recognize their authority, though. If we elevated the matter to a higher level, deterrence efforts would become transformed both politically and effectively. A well-known group led by the United States could become a very useful vehicle for us to coalesce with other countries. These are matters for all people of the world to come together around. We should take advantage of that global spirit so that we actually achieve this goal.

The impact would be more profound than simply being ready for a rogue comet strike, for example. The launching and maintaining of a ring of distant space monitoring systems to prepare for such a remote possibility would require a sort of international cooperation that will remind us of a more important concept: We are all ultimately on the same team. Thus the argument for undertaking this project is stronger than the risk assessment alone would suggest. It has been pointed out that if the world were threatened by an external problem, we would all stop fighting each other to fight the threat as one. This effort leverages this dynamic in two ways.

First, we should prepare for a menu of global risks just in case, using the same risk management technique I talked about for this plan. We should list the known risks so we can make an assessment of each. Second, let us start creating the risk mitigation plans for those risks. Some of these plans could be dual or triple use, like those space monitors. Putting monitoring systems out beyond Mars to detect comets may seem expensive given that the risk is probably very low. But if we needed similar technology for tracking asteroids, making scientific discoveries, undertaking commercial space projects, and perhaps other reasons, then the payback is more diverse. Roll it all up into one project and we get interesting value.

The subtle effect is not that we will have a bit more warning of errant bodies flying through space, but that we will have a reason to convince the whole world to cooperate on something external, even if many find it trivial. I picked an outlandish case on purpose. If we can see the logic in this example, it is much easier to see why this kind of effort is justified for the more likely but still hopefully rarc global disaster threats.

U.S. 3.0 Consideration #5: War Obsolescence Planning

Some might call me naïve for putting the word war next to obsolete. I am not suggesting we get rid of the military. Such a move would probably invite war. However, there is a tactic no one has ever tried or even been in a position to try: to attempt to make it more advantageous for a growing body of countries to avoid ever starting a war. Not by dictating terms with a hammer threat, though. Rather, this approach would weave interdependencies of services and trade in such a way that *starting* a war would threaten a country's infrastructure. However, we would gain great advantage in both times of peace and in the call to defend a partner or a people. This would be a system where partnerships with the United States are formed under such terms that eventually it a stupendously horrible idea for those partners to start a war. The idea is similar in some ways to a pact, like NATO, only it has a different emphasis. The focus is not so much on a military agreement as it is based on the trade of services, especially ones between governments.

We could design these coalitions to respond to military outbreaks the way a defense agreement normally does. However, we would couple them with trade agreements, cooperative government services and business relationships. In other words, if a country is going to do business with us, they should join us in real defense. Then we sweeten the coalition packages over time to make it an ever-improving advantage. Consider, for example, the case where the CMS is not supposed to offer business services to people from other countries. Maybe the way to begin relaxing that limitation is to first allow CMS services with those who have comprehensive war obsolescence agreements with us. Truthfully, the terms of such agreements would be far more complicated than I can even summarize here. The intention is to work on an effective strategy that uses business principles and trade, not to presume to tell anyone exactly what that strategy will be without first going through the complete strategic analysis.

U.S. 3.0 Consideration #6: Oceanic, Underground and Space Commercialization
Recall that I used COMSAT as an example of the U.S. government starting a private company. Their mission was to jumpstart the commercial satellite industry in the 1960's, a mission they succeeded at. We should consider similar efforts, perhaps using lessons learned from Magnified Capitalism, to jumpstart the commercialization of deep ocean, underground, and outer space environments.

The oceanic aspect would include activities such as collecting methane from deep ocean floor deposits. It is well known that a huge energy store is available in the form of methane hydrate at the bottom of moderately deep cold ocean waters. While there are many technical and scientific issues to consider, weigh and overcome in order to utilize this energy, one thing is certain. There is more energy available in this form than double the oil reserves on earth. If any scientific research is worth serious support from the government, this is.

There are two main issues with such a project. How do we bring the hydrates up from the ocean floor cost effectively? And is there a way to utilize this energy in a way that would not have serious environmental consequences? The latter is an issue because methane hydrate represents a large store of carbon dioxide. Burning it for fuel is easy. But doing that is nearly as bad for our atmosphere as what we do with our oil. Because there is so much of it, if we burned all this methane for energy we would certainly increase our risk of climate change more than we already have. It would be wise to find a way to use this energy source in a green manner before we develop an industry around using it. There are many possible solutions to investigate. Money and resources would make a big difference. Given how energy-driven our country is and the whole world is becoming, this seems like an obvious direction to pursue soon.

Of course there are also other reasons to explore the oceans, especially the deeper parts. One of the great values of scientific research is the discovery of information we could not have predicted. I believe science has generally served us well. We can always pick on science for either its more trivial benefits, or the ones that have brought danger to society. Let us not be thrown by such narrow political attacks. It makes sense to do research in an ongoing manner even when the return from that research superficially appears to be a poor investment. History has shown us that those who justify doing less research in favor of using their money "more productively" have consistently been the losers for it. The issue to me, therefore, is not whether we spend research money, but where and how smartly.

Many people intuitively appreciate the pure science of space exploration in particular. I do, too. But if we think we need to learn how to explore and commercialize outer space, there is an important corollary that we should accept. All the reasons for exploring space apply to a higher degree to the oceans, and deep underground exploration on earth as well. This is because we know so little about the parts of the earth that are hard for us to reach. Yet, that is exactly why we need to study those spaces. We are sure to discover many useful things we could not have guessed unless we go there. These include solving practical engineering problems, like how to travel to deep ocean (or underground) locations, how people can stay there for extended periods, what resources are hidden there, and what special capabilities we gain if we do all this. Note that high pressures and odd environments can enable useful properties in biology, chemistry, and the physics of material production. Doing the science will inevitably create commercial opportunities.

This brings the matter back full circle. The science of exploring and commercializing deep oceans and underground is related to the exploration of space. Much of the science and engineering required for all three overlap in fascinating ways. Breakthroughs in any one discipline can often be usefully extended to applications in the other two. As my point about multi-dimensional government suggested, if we have overlapping targets, functions and benefits, we have a special opportunity. Rather than separately pursuing related efforts, let us take advantage of the fact that these sciences have so much in common. Let us use the same organization to instigate and promote the development of all three. Spawning one or more new commercial companies, or perhaps a citizen company, is one possible approach.

U.S. 3.0 Consideration #7: Unlocking Gridlock

Democracy has essentially won. It is now only a matter of time before real democracy becomes ubiquitous. There is one caveat, however. Democracy won because we showed it can work. Winning itself represents a mere point in time, though. We can win today and still lose tomorrow. One way we could lose is if we show the world how a successful democracy can produce such a complete congressional seizure that the legislature becomes unable to serve its people effectively. That risk has warning markers that we are seeing today.

Primarily, this danger is visible in the growing polarization of the political parties. There is an increasing inclination for politicians to demonize those with the opposing view and then make inflexible promises to underscore their positions. If we keep going down this path our frustrations of today will be tiny compared to those of tomorrow. I can make a case that this is such a damaging trend that it threatens the stability of the United States as a functional government model. Regardless of whether gridlock results in some future downfall, or whether it merely produces the perpetual inability to act towards the greater good, we should address it.

This is an important enough topic that I suggested we address the matter immediately after Magnified Capitalism using a new bill limiting congressional term limits. That should help. There is probably much more that we could do. My suggestion here is to form a team to investigate the options towards this end and present them to the people for consideration. I do not know the menu of options. But I would love to have some bright people work on producing such a menu.

Final Thoughts on Next Steps

After going through the considerations I just listed, I found myself wanting to make the same kind of point with each one. That would be some version of, "This is just an idea I think is worth working on. I have developed a complete plan for Magnified Capitalism. It has stood up to critical thinking. This particular new idea I am talking about now (U.S. 3.0) will need a similar treatment. Do not judge it until it receives equivalent handling from some well-qualified business planner."

When coming up with ideas it is very useful to separate the brainstorming from the plan development and plan judgment (or the decision to enact the plan). Considering something creative is almost free until we spend real money on it. Many if not all of the ideas I listed for United States 3.0 could end up failing to produce as strong a plan as Magnified Capitalism has. That is OK. Let us brainstorm some other worthy goals, then. But let's revisit these too, from time to time when someone suggests a new strategy to address the same goal. We must keep trying to develop, keep aiming for improvement and change. It is not that United States 3.0 must have this element or that, but that we must keep looking for the answer until we find it, no matter the answer or the method used. The danger lies in standing still. The danger lies in thinking it is safer not to change and improve.

The people of the world will always change. We can be the example of how to successfully change. Or we can declare that we have arrived and therefore, since we are the best, we no longer need to change. This is the perfect recipe for planned obsolescence on our part. Our fall will then be only a matter of time. What a waste that would be. We are experts at managing change in our businesses. We are well positioned to lead change management in national governance, too. Let us be bold about it because that is the best way forward.

"The American people are amazing for a particular reason. Often underestimated, we regularly produce a surprise breakout whenever we are challenged. The reason we break out keeps varying, but that we do so does not. We broke out in our independence from the British and then again later in the forming of our Constitution. We sealed the deal in the War of 1812 when the British thought to take one last try. Then came our long-brewing internal strife that could only be settled through the Civil War. Certainly, like most challenges, that war led to our ultimate strengthening. Resolving this conflict led directly to unprecedented business growth and world economic leadership that has lasted over 100 years to this day. Then the two World Wars essentially compelled us into building up our military leadership to superpower status. During these wars the opposition was surprised again and again that our freedom did not produce the softness they expected, but rather the opposite. Not only did we have something to fight for, but we consistently produced an extra energy and creativeness. Unavoidably, all this history in combination proved something important to most of the world by the end of the 20th Century. This is the idea that freedom through a secular democracy in promotion of capitalism is the best solution to national governance. Most of the world sees it, although holdouts see room for great variance. Today, our strength wanes as China is preparing to retake its old position as the top economy. Good for them. They have earned their gains through peaceful internal improvements. We, however, do not need to stand still. I know of no American, no matter their party, who wants to stand still. The time is ripe for our next breakout. We have shown again and again that America does not cower unresponsive to its challenges, ever. I declare to the people of the world, "Do not be fooled by our politics. We know how to put these issues aside when the matter is clear." That matter is clear today, right now. The next surprise American breakout is here. That breakout has a name. It is called Magnified Capitalism."

- Suggested text you are welcome to use in your next speech, Mr. President -

X. Conclusion

I have presented so much information, Mr. President, that you would be forgiven for feeling a bit overwhelmed. I will try to simplify the matter here.

The United States certainly has serious problems today. For some it is not that terrible, yet for others it is. Even for those citizens not under direct financial pressure, many worry about the future and our direction. If this country were a business evaluating itself, we would talk about our status in a totally different way. We would say we are the market leader, but our leadership is threatened and under attack by competitors. The management of our country is not yet mobilizing us for change while the competition is changing as fast as they can to beat us. That is a big problem. The good news is that there is still time to make a move, but we have to actually get our butts in gear and do something big. Sooner would be better.

X. Conclusion

I have more good news. You hold in your hands a specific plan for how make a breakout. With it we take advantage of our strengths. We compromise nothing of our standards, our beliefs, or our principles. On the contrary, we turn them up. This strategy leverages the American people, our greatest asset. We must stop the self-loathing and infighting for a moment and do something to elevate ourselves. Magnified Capitalism is the answer. There is no reason to delay.

Credit will go to the one who recognizes the urgency first. The public should rightfully punish the laggards. There are many reasons to implement this plan. It comes from neither the right nor the left. It leverages the principles that made us strong - freedom and the right to pursue happiness. That is equivalent to saying we have a right to work hard for our success, to take risks towards innovation, to start a new business, sell a new idea, or expand an existing enterprise. We do these things to make money, but they work primarily because of the reward markets give us for delivering something good. Once that is done, the next reward goes to the newer and better thing. Our capitalist system is fair because it is free and essentially impartial. It rewards risk and innovation and penalizes those who seek to stifle or stand still. The strategy you are reviewing, Mr. President, is a new way to turn up the volume on these principles.

The United States has been finished with its first phase for a little while now. We can declare a victory of sorts for the people of the world. They are all following one or more aspects of our example. Now it is time to recognize our own foundation. Taking a cue from the capitalism that has elevated our country, we should embrace our next phase. That means changing how we govern ourselves in innovative ways. It does not mean abandoning the principles that we know and love. It means improving our processes in useful and fundamental ways so as to serve our collective prosperity. It is time to erect a pillar of survivable success.

Our people are shrewder than some mistakenly assume. We know that both sides of the political body are rhetorically walking away from each other right now. We know one side promises the same failed methods they had already tried when they won the last few times. Yet the other side is no better. They seem to only demonize the others for their positions. Until now it appeared we only had two choices: those most assume are either wrong or misguided, and those who have no cogent economic strategy at all. Is there any wonder that frustration rules the political air?

Magnified Capitalism is a breakout strategy. It provides cover for both sides to come together, as we all know we should. It is bold. It is aggressive. Is it too expensive?

Can we afford a plan that costs just under $4 trillion in total? I remind you that we spent about one-fifth of that four years ago on the Emergency Economic

Stabilization Act of 2008. This so-called Obama bailout was widely criticized as a terribly managed act of desperation, yet it saved us from the brink nonetheless. What of a plan that costs five times as much over six years, but pays it all back quickly? Yet this plan is no stop-gap measure. Expertly managed, it will be well worth the $4 trillion deposit. The main benefit is that this strategy will keep us from ever ending up in such a desperate position again. That is what a pillar of survivable success does for us. It leaves a legacy for our children that is stronger than the one we were given, yet it also serves us well today. How well?

This plan can be launched and active about one year from the date Congress passes the first bill. Admittedly, that is an optimistic timeline, but there is little excuse for the process to take much more time than that. Just the fact that this real solution is coming will have an immediate impact. A positive effect on most markets should appear as soon as the bill passes. This near-immediate improvement in the economy will take place solely due to positive psychology, just as the soldiers on the front line becoming energized when they receive word that the Air Force and artillery are about to shell the other side. The tide starts to turn just from the change in expectations.

The first day that the new Capital Magnification Service opens its doors for business formally marks the launch of our strategy. On that day the website goes live. The network of Certified Business Valuators has been trained and is ready for their customers. The menu of services rolls out. There is something for everyone. Venture capitalists are at the spearpoint of new job creation. They receive a CMS offering to let them make more money and make more deals.

Bankers are next. Their CMS service encourages them to make more loans, especially for businesses, education, and a variety of investments. Banking activity finally breaks out of its current defensive position.

Existing businesses receive a CMS service which offers them a carrot for expanding. The carrot is bigger if they utilize incentives like keeping much of their expansion within the United States, as well as using U.S. suppliers and services.

Then there are the rest of us. We all have access to CMS services if we need them. In fact, we have our own menu. A mini version of the venture capital offering, private venture funding, is available to the wealthy or those who might form investor groups for collaboration. Not only will these services encourage such activity, but other services will be available to make it easy for people to join up with each other to back new business.

Existing small businesses that are under pressure will find it easy to obtain funding for investments they need to grow themselves.

X. Conclusion

Those brilliant people with patentable ideas will now receive a two-sided benefit. They will no longer have to be rich to pursue a patent. They will also have an easier time selling those patents as new markets form from investors looking to buy them up. Bang. An entirely new process develops to help the inspired grow their ideas into wealth. Along the way the rest of us are assured immediate benefit from such inspiration. That is side one.

Side two is that the companies who today pay very little to employees for their patentable ideas will be forced to change their policies. If they do not, they will lose those great ideas to the new process. This is just fine. Now inventors will have a choice. The companies they work for will finally make it worth their trouble to provide extraordinary inventions. They can choose to take these new better deals, or go with side one if the offer is not good enough. America wins either way.

And finally there is the coup de grâce. The Prototype Development Network will be the online meeting place for the unemployed, underemployed, and underappreciated to establish new opportunities for themselves. By using the PDN prototypers will help launch thousands of new businesses that would otherwise never see the light of day. Entrepreneurs will gain access to a new work force. Workers will have a chance to prove themselves in new ways. All will share in the possibility of making it big.

In the process, without even realizing it, the American workforce will be stepping it up. Productivity will jump. The average skill set will improve. Even the average level of education will rise. Look for the biggest educational surge to occur in the middle where there is need but not necessarily hard requirements for higher degrees. The United States will blossom into its 2.0 era.

Why should we care? The reason is almost intuitive when we follow the logic of the strategy. We identified the targets of job creation. Then we created a new organization whose purpose was to offer those job sources new services that amplify their capability. I will spell out the results so as to be crystal clear.

Unemployment will drop like a rock, fast and hard. The cold edge of our difficult times will vaporize about as fast as we can reasonably imagine. The unemployment rate itself will shed nearly two percentage points each of the first two years that the CMS is running. Then, as it approaches the comfortable level associated with far better times, the rate of improvement will understandably slow down and stabilize. Other measures of the economy, like the GDP, will show similar improvements. Although this plan focuses on the sources of job creation, there is just no avoiding it. The whole of the economy will necessarily recover and then flourish in the process.

Then there are the many secondary benefits. We will have a new economic policy steering wheel. CMS incentives will prove a new and important power that our government will learn to use to address the disadvantaged as well as our strategic interests. This means bringing production and jobs back to the United States, making new advances in key technologies, and developing new solutions to problems that aid our geopolitical standing.

We will strengthen our overall economy. More than that, we will surge back. In the process we will address social inequities. We can head off the impending bankruptcy of entitlement programs. We will gain an inherent improvement of healthcare and retirement benefits just from competition. Our level of innovation will take off due to the ease of patenting and the great increase in new business development. With economic growth even comes an increase in our ability to influence other countries.

A bit later we get a special benefit. Shortly after its debts are repaid the CMS will start feeding our government with a new growing source of income. With just a little discipline this income will eventually displace much if not all income tax revenue.

The most important secondary benefit is the amalgamation of all these positives. When we surge as an economic leader we put off China's ability to overtake us as the world's top economy. We will regain our position as the most competitive nation by a wide margin. All the other nations will collectively gasp at our profound resurgence, and then most will cheer. At first they will cheer because when we do well, so does everyone else. We are not alone in our economic woes. Most nations are either struggling or concerned that their neighbors are struggling. Our recovery will spread just from improved international money flow. Certainly our closest friends and business partners will be the biggest immediate benefactors. But economic recovery in the United States will provide a boost to every nation to some degree.

Shortly after the world cheers us for basic economic recovery, they will cheer for another reason. We will have shown them that democracy has another gear to shift into. The foundation of capitalism is not limited to what we have already witnessed.

What about the details? Is there a plan? Do the numbers make sense? Can we pass a bill to make this work? Mr. President, I hope I have plainly answered such concerns. There is enough detail here to take the next step. I have addressed every major risk factor with steps for mitigation. We only need a champion, a strong political movement, or the voice of enough people demanding it. Any of these will provide the required energy.

X. Conclusion

As for the numbers, yes, they are big enough to be scary. Frankly, if anyone claimed a solution without big numbers they would necessarily be either lying or misguided. But I have addressed these concerns, as the strategy repays all borrowed funds in the manner of a real business plan.

We can extract a storyline from our plan. It will play out in a natural progression whose details we should now understand. However, there is a lesson I have not mentioned before. The moral of this story is that freedom is not just a philosophy for the individual. The holdout communist and pseudo-fascist countries of the world sometimes demonize capitalism and its democratic infrastructure. Their logic often focuses on the apparent self-serving individualism that democracy suggests. They offer the counter-logic that their own systems are superior because they work for the greater good. Their logic calls on some sort of self-sacrifice on the part of their population in return for a claim of superior infrastructure for the entire country.

While this logic has been shown to be doomed to failure in many examples throughout the twentieth century, we have left an opening. China in particular has managed to compromise its own old communist philosophy with an update that adds aspects of both democracy and the freedoms democracy requires. By making such compromises the Chinese have benefited greatly from improvements in their resulting capitalist efforts. Their modern hybrid-communism allows enough freedom to let businesses grow, albeit in some constricted ways. Yet China's government makes even these upgrades grudgingly, still claiming that they retain the primary features and benefits of a communist philosophy. Magnified Capitalism will destroy that logic as well as that of similar holdouts.

Capitalism and freedom are intertwined. This bold new strategy makes that apparent. In order to turn up our economic success we must take freedom to a new level. Magnifying capitalism is equivalent to magnifying freedom. Anyone can become wealthy in United States 2.0. All they need to do is work for it and be willing to take some risks. It is the entrepreneur's bet, only now that bet will be available to people who never imagined they could take it before. Furthermore, we do not need the majority of people to have such a nature. The rest of us will benefit just from the freedom offered to those who take the risks. Business creation and expansion will boom. Innovation will take a new surge. Investment will at first reinvigorate, then take off, and then surge into an acceleration. Even education will be elevated by the desire to take full advantage of the choices available.

Freedom will win. It will become completely obvious that freedom is not just a benefit for the individual, but it also has a strong social benefit in the form of a capitalist infrastructure. While some will argue this has already been shown, it has not been demonstrated so clearly that it was beyond debate. Once we establish United States 2.0, the remaining murkiness of freedom's value as a governing philosophy will crystalize. Freedom is not just what the world's people deserve as individuals. Freedom in a secular democracy with a Magnified Capitalism program will become the new gold standard set proudly by the United States of America. Freedom magnified will be shown to produce runaway prosperity and success. This success must be shared by the governing country with its people. That is an American future to smile about.

I turn to you now, Mr. President. I suggest we start with small steps and go from there. Will you help create this future?

Appendix A: TDRM Financial Model (detail)

This appendix contains a printout of the Magnified Capitalism Trillion Dollar Reinvestment Model (TDRM). This is the financial analysis I created and refer to extensively in *Chapter VII: Financials*. For better viewing please download the electronic version of this file at www.magnifiedcapitalism.com. If a password is requested for access to the document, it will be in order to provide some evidence that you have read this proposal first. In that case the password will be "mcread". Some minor notes I made to myself are not shown here but are visible in the full electronic version.

The model has four tabs: Summary & Analysis, Assumptions, Detail of Best-Case, and Detail of Worst-Case. Each tab is shown in order as follows.

Magnified Capitalism - Financials Support

Version 1.1 · © 2012 by Peter Naleszkiewicz, All rights reserved

Rendering: Trillion Dollar Reinvestment Model (TDRM) · Re-Invests any Fund surplus

Page: **Summary & Analysis**

Comparing the Financial Assumptions and Results of Magnified Capitalism in two cases:

Best Case Scenario vs. Worst Case Scenario

All figures shown in Billions of U.S. Dollars

Assumptions Comparison: *	Best Case	Worst Case	* simplified in this summary to show the primary variables
CMS Annual Operating Costs **	$ 0.25	$ 1.00	** with subsequent annual increases
CMS Setup Costs including simulation testing ***	$ 0.50	$ 1.00	*** with subsequent annual maintenance costs
Average Fund Annualized Return On Investment (ROI)	15.00%	9.00%	This is the main measure of Fund Performance
CMS Fund Size, kept constant year over year	$ 1,000.00	$ 1,000.00	Borrowed until income > Fund size, later years the Fund grows larger
Fund threshold before CMS generates Gov't Revenue	$ 2,000.00	$ 1,500.00	If CMS Fund ends the year with more than this, part of it is paid to Gov't
Percentage over Fund threshold paid to gov't	25.00%	50.00%	Best Case grows the CMS Fund larger

Both cases use Q2 2012 U.S. Economic status as a starting point for considering economic impact.
The Worst Case assumes less optimistic values for year over year job retention and GDP retention as well as a higher basis for how many new jobs it takes to move the unemployment figures.

Financial Analysis Summary:	Best Case	Worst Case	
Total Amount of Money Borrowed to Fund CMS	$ 3,621.58	$ 3,853.79	needed until CMS reaches positive cash flow
CMS Operating year that begins positive cash flow	5	6	in this year CMS makes more money than Fund size & stops borrowing
Year of operation that all debt incurred is paid off	12	18	in this year the CMS is debt free
CMS Operating year that begins Gov't Revenue	17	24	in this year CMS Fund savings have grown > threshold in assumptions
CMS Annual Gov't Revenue 5 years later	$ 486.18	$ 349.74	5 years after revenue begins, this is the annual contribution
... Gov't Revenue 10 years later	$ 1,020.06	$ 555.95	The annual contribution continues to grow
Ultimate limit of Gov't revenue for Best Case -->	Provides total current gov't budget ($3.5T) by the 41st year, with potential growth beyond		
Ultimate limit of Gov't revenue for Worst Case -->	Provides nearly $1 Trillion annual revenue before topping out due to aggressive payback rules and growing costs		
CMS Fund savings ... after 25 years of CMS	$ 4,129.97	$ 1,553.73	CMS Fund money reserve which is fully reinvested each year
... after 40 years	$ 11,299.79	$ 2,199.03	
CMS Fund Value ... after 40 years (est. savings x 3.5)	$ 39,549.27	$ 7,696.59	CMS stops services and just collects what is due

U.S. Economic Impact Analysis Summary:	Best Case	Worst Case	Average	Here, *Average* is similar to *Expected*
Unemployment Rate				
Year 0 (before CMS Starts)	8.20%	8.20%	8.20%	
Year 1	6.15%	6.50%	6.33%	
Year 2	5.13%	5.83%	5.48%	
Year 3	4.61%	5.56%	5.09%	
... Year 10	4.63%	5.38%	5.01%	
... Year 25 (converged target)	3.66%	4.69%	4.17%	
Gross Domestic Product (GDP quarterly growth rate)				
Year 0 (before CMS Starts)	2.20%	2.20%	2.20%	
Year 1	4.20%	3.70%	3.95%	
Year 2	5.60%	4.60%	5.10%	
Year 3	6.58%	5.14%	5.86%	
... Year 10	8.68%	5.93%	7.30%	
... Year 25 (converged target)	10.84%	7.66%	9.25%	

Magnified Capitalism - Financials Support

Rendering: Trillion Dollar Reinvestment Model (TDRM) - Re-Invests any Fund surplus

Page: **Assumptions** Note: User Changeable Values shown in GREEN

Calculated Values shown in **DARK BLUE**

Preset Annual CMS Fund Levels ... in Billions of Dollars - Always invests at least this much unless surplus allows more

Year 1	Year 2	Year 3	Year 4	Year 5	Year 6	Year 7	Year 8	Year 9	Year 10
$ 1,000.0	$ 1,000.0	$ 1,000.0	$ 1,000.0	$ 1,000.0	$ 1,000.0	$ 1,000.0	$ 1,000.0	$ 1,000.0	$ 1,000.0

Cost of Money (U.S. Federal borrowing rate = 10 year T-Notes rate. Year 1 is rate is as in 2012)

Year 1	Year 2	Year 3	Year 4	Year 5	Year 6	Year 7	Year 8	Year 9	Year 10
1.50%	1.75%	2.00%	2.25%	2.50%	2.75%	3.00%	3.25%	3.50%	3.75%

Costs...

Recurring costs, dollars in $1,000's (except in conversion collum)

	Best Case	...in billions	Worst Case	...in billions
Number of CMS Employees	1,000		2,000	
Average annual pay including benefits and bonuses	$ 200		$ 400	
Total Annual Employee Costs	$ 200,000		$ 800,000	
Facility and infrastructure (offices)	$ 20,000		$ 80,000	
... ave cost per employee	$ 20		$ 40	
Computer and communications (lease/service/budget)	$ 30,000		$ 120,000	
... ave cost per employee	$ 30		$ 60	
Total Year 1 Annual Operating Costs ($1,000's)	$ 250,000	$ 0.25	$ 1,000,000	$ 1.00
Annual increase in CMS Ops Budget	5.00%		7.00%	

Startup Costs - to be amortized (repaid with interest), dollars in $1,000's

	Best Case	...in billions	Worst Case	...in billions
Computer Systems and Network	$ 100,000		$ 200,000	
Software Development	$ 250,000		$ 500,000	
Acceptance Testing	$ 100,000		$ 200,000	
Organization incl Legal and Misc.	$ 50,000		$ 100,000	
Total Startup Costs ($1,000's)	$ 500,000	$ 0.50	$ 1,000,000	$ 1.00
Portion of fixed costs that recur for maintenance	20.00%		40.00%	

Revenues...

	Best Case	Worst Case
Annualized Return on Investment (ROI) over all services	15.00%	9.00%

Schedule of ave recievables from year 1 through year 6 for a given year's services

	Year 1	Year 2	Year 3	Year 4	Year 5	Year 6	checksum
	0.00%	10.00%	20.00%	40.00%	20.00%	10.00%	100.00%
Accrued ROI of original fund							
Best Case	15.00%	32.25%	52.09%	74.90%	101.14%	131.31%	
Worst Case	9.00%	18.81%	29.50%	41.16%	53.86%	67.71%	
Schedule of recievables with ROI Applied for a given year's services							Gross ROI
Best Case	0.00%	3.23%	10.42%	29.96%	20.23%	13.13%	76.96%
Worst Case	0.00%	1.88%	5.90%	16.46%	10.77%	6.77%	41.79%

Rules for returning revenue back to fed government - Using $millions

	Best Case	Worst Case	
- Before revenue is returned, Fund surplus must exceed:	$ 2,000	$ 1,500	<-- Fund Threshold
- Percent of Fund Threshold overage returned	25.00%	50.00%	

U.S. Economic Impact...

	Q1 2012	Best Case	Worst Case
Year 0 (starting):			
GDP (quarterly growth)	2.20%	2.20%	2.20%
Unemployment Rate	8.20%	8.20%	8.20%
MC Impact:			
GDP rate increase per Trillion in Fund		2.00%	1.50%
Delta GDP Retention year over year		70.0%	60.0%
Added Resistance to GDP over 9%		75.0%	80.0%
Jobs Created per Trillion Funding		3,200,000	2,880,000
CMS Jobs Retention year over year		50.0%	40.0%
Saturation Correction Threshold Rate		5.00%	6.00%
Saturation Correction - Optimal limit		2.50%	3.00%
Annual Jobs to unemployment rate conversion			
New Jobs needed to hold steady		2,280,000	2,500,000
Delta Jobs needed to decrease 1%		1,560,000	1,700,000
Saturation Correct. Thres Mill Jobs		4.0	3.5
Saturation Correct. % over Jobs		15.0%	10.0%

Appendix A: TDRM Financial Model (detail)

Note that the following pages show 40 years of projections for each case (2 pages per case, 1 extra year for best case). The website version covers more years (60 total) in the Worst-Case.

Magnified Capitalism - Financials Support

Version 1.1 - © 2012 by Peter Naleszkiewicz, All rights reserved

Rendering: Trillion Dollar Reinvestment Model (TDRM) - Re-Invests any Fund surplus

Page: **Detail of Best Case**

*GREEN = From Assumptions, **Dark Blue** = Calculated*

All figures in Billions of Dollars unless noted otherwise

--> With Year 11 onward this model simply uses the year 10 rates and assumptions

	Year 1	Year 2	Year 3	Year 4	Year 5	Year 6	Year 7	Year 8	Year 9	Year 10	Year 11	Year 12	Year 13	Year 14	Year 15	Year 16	Year 17	Year 18
CMS Fund Level at Start of Each Year	$ 1,000.0	$ 1,000.0	$ 1,000.0	$ 1,000.0	$ 1,000.0	$ 1,000.0	$ 1,000.0	$ 1,000.0	$ 1,000.0	$ 1,000.0	$ 1,000.0	$ 1,000.0	$ 1,331.7	$ 1,769.1	$ 1,769.0	$ 1,812.9	$ 1,971.6	$ 2,252.5
Costs ... (Negative = debt)					--> CMS becomes profitable, debt begins pay down							--> CMS Debt completely repaid						
Fund Balance (Debt) from previous year	$ -	$ (1,015.8)	$ (2,051.4)	$ (2,977.9)	$ (3,621.6)	$ (3,573.1)	$ (3,118.7)	$ (2,420.0)	$ (1,704.5)	$ (968.1)	$ (206.5)	$ 562.6	$ 1,331.7	$ 1,769.1	$ 1,769.0	$ 1,812.9	$ 1,971.6	$ 2,252.5
Fund level applied this year (for svcs)	$ (1,000.0)	$ (1,000.0)	$ (1,000.0)	$ (1,000.0)	$ (1,000.0)	$ (1,000.0)	$ (1,000.0)	$ (1,000.0)	$ (1,000.0)	$ (1,000.0)	$ (1,000.0)	$ (1,000.0)	$ (1,331.7)	$ (1,769.1)	$ (1,769.0)	$ (1,812.9)	$ (1,971.6)	$ (2,252.5)
Fixed Costs (CMS Setup)	$ (0.50)	$ (0.10)	$ (0.10)	$ (0.10)	$ (0.10)	$ (0.10)	$ (0.10)	$ (0.10)	$ (0.10)	$ (0.10)	$ (0.10)	$ (0.10)	$ (0.10)	$ (0.10)	$ (0.10)	$ (0.10)	$ (0.10)	$ (0.10)
Operating Costs (Budget)	$ (0.25)	$ (0.26)	$ (0.28)	$ (0.29)	$ (0.30)	$ (0.32)	$ (0.34)	$ (0.35)	$ (0.37)	$ (0.39)	$ (0.41)	$ (0.43)	$ (0.45)	$ (0.47)	$ (0.49)	$ (0.52)	$ (0.55)	$ (0.57)
Receivables by end of year	$ -	$ -	$ 132.3	$ 436.4	$ 1,136.0	$ 1,538.3	$ 1,769.6	$ 1,769.6	$ 1,769.6	$ 1,769.6	$ 1,769.6	$ 1,769.6	$ 1,769.6	$ 1,769.6	$ 1,813.5	$ 1,972.2	$ 2,337.3	$ 2,782.5
Fund Balance w/o interest	$ (1,000.8)	$ (2,016.1)	$ (2,919.5)	$ (3,541.9)	$ (3,486.0)	$ (3,035.2)	$ (2,349.5)	$ (1,650.9)	$ (935.4)	$ (199.0)	$ 562.6	$ 1,331.7	$ 1,769.1	$ 1,769.0	$ 1,812.9	$ 1,971.6	$ 2,336.7	$ 2,781.8
Interest applied (%) to outstanding debt	1.5%	1.8%	2.0%	2.3%	2.5%	2.8%	3.0%	3.3%	3.5%	3.8%	3.8%	3.8%	3.8%	3.8%	3.8%	3.8%	3.8%	3.8%
Debt Interest	$ (15.01)	$ (35.28)	$ (58.39)	$ (79.69)	$ (87.15)	$ (83.47)	$ (70.49)	$ (53.65)	$ (32.74)	$ (7.46)	$ -	$ -	$ -	$ -	$ -	$ -	$ -	$ -
Total Fund Balance w/ interest applied	$ (1,015.8)	$ (2,051.4)	$ (2,977.9)	$ (3,621.6)	$ (3,573.1)	$ (3,118.7)	$ (2,420.0)	$ (1,704.5)	$ (968.1)	$ (206.5)	$ 562.6	$ 1,331.7	$ 1,769.1	$ 1,769.0	$ 1,812.9	$ 1,971.6	$ 2,336.7	$ 2,781.8
Gain (or loss) from last year	$ (1,015.8)	$ (1,035.6)	$ (926.5)	$ (643.7)	$ 48.5	$ 454.4	$ 698.7	$ 715.5	$ 736.4	$ 761.7	$ 769.1	$ 769.1	$ 437.3	$ (0.0)	$ 43.8	$ 158.7	$ 365.1	$ 445.2
U.S. Government Revenue ...																	--> CMS Fund Exceeds	
Portion of Fund Exceeding threshold	$ -	$ -	$ -	$ -	$ -	$ -	$ -	$ -	$ -	$ -	$ -	$ -	$ -	$ -	$ -	$ -	$ 336.7	$ 781.8
Revenue paid to government	$ -	$ -	$ -	$ -	$ -	$ -	$ -	$ -	$ -	$ -	$ -	$ -	$ -	$ -	$ -	$ -	$ 84.2	$ 195.5
Revenue / Gross Profit ...																		
Receivables from services	$ -	$ -	$ 132.3	$ 436.4	$ 1,136.0	$ 1,538.3	$ 1,769.6	$ 1,769.6	$ 1,769.6	$ 1,769.6	$ 1,769.6	$ 1,769.6	$ 1,769.6	$ 1,769.6	$ 1,813.5	$ 1,972.2	$ 2,337.3	$ 2,782.5
- From 6 years ago	$ -	$ -	$ -	$ -	$ -	$ -	$ 231.3	$ 231.3	$ 231.3	$ 231.3	$ 231.3	$ 231.3	$ 231.3	$ 231.3	$ 231.3	$ 231.3	$ 231.3	$ 231.3
- From 5 years ago	$ -	$ -	$ -	$ -	$ -	$ 402.3	$ 402.3	$ 402.3	$ 402.3	$ 402.3	$ 402.3	$ 402.3	$ 402.3	$ 402.3	$ 402.3	$ 402.3	$ 402.3	$ 535.7
- From 4 years ago	$ -	$ -	$ -	$ -	$ 699.6	$ 699.6	$ 699.6	$ 699.6	$ 699.6	$ 699.6	$ 699.6	$ 699.6	$ 699.6	$ 699.6	$ 699.6	$ 699.6	$ 931.7	$ 1,237.6
- From 3 years ago	$ -	$ -	$ -	$ 304.2	$ 304.2	$ 304.2	$ 304.2	$ 304.2	$ 304.2	$ 304.2	$ 304.2	$ 304.2	$ 304.2	$ 304.2	$ 304.2	$ 405.1	$ 538.1	$ 538.1
- From 2 years ago	$ -	$ -	$ 132.3	$ 132.3	$ 132.3	$ 132.3	$ 132.3	$ 132.3	$ 132.3	$ 132.3	$ 132.3	$ 132.3	$ 132.3	$ 132.3	$ 176.1	$ 234.0	$ 234.0	$ 239.8
- From last year	$ -	$ -	$ -	$ -	$ -	$ -	$ -	$ -	$ -	$ -	$ -	$ -	$ -	$ -	$ -	$ -	$ -	$ -
Portion of Revenue as Gross Profit	$ -	$ -	$ 32.3	$ 136.4	$ 436.0	$ 638.3	$ 769.6	$ 769.6	$ 769.6	$ 769.6	$ 769.6	$ 769.6	$ 769.6	$ 769.6	$ 780.3	$ 829.0	$ 973.9	$ 1,173.4
U.S. Economic Impact ...																		
GDP	4.20%	5.60%	6.58%	7.27%	7.75%	8.08%	8.32%	8.48%	8.60%	8.68%	8.73%	8.77%	9.12%	9.39%	9.44%	9.47%	9.56%	9.71%
- Starting point (year 0)	2.20%	2.20%	2.20%	2.20%	2.20%	2.20%	2.20%	2.20%	2.20%	2.20%	2.20%	2.20%	2.20%	2.20%	2.20%	2.20%	2.20%	2.20%
- Last year's CMS delta	0.00%	2.00%	3.40%	4.38%	5.07%	5.55%	5.88%	6.12%	6.28%	6.40%	6.48%	6.53%	6.57%	6.92%	7.19%	7.24%	7.27%	7.36%
- Retention of last year's delta	0.00%	1.40%	2.38%	3.07%	3.55%	3.88%	4.12%	4.28%	4.40%	4.48%	4.53%	4.57%	4.60%	4.84%	5.04%	5.07%	5.09%	5.15%
- This year's CMS impact	2.00%	2.00%	2.00%	2.00%	2.00%	2.00%	2.00%	2.00%	2.00%	2.00%	2.00%	2.00%	2.66%	3.54%	3.54%	3.63%	3.94%	4.50%
- Total delta over starting point	2.00%	3.40%	4.38%	5.07%	5.55%	5.88%	6.12%	6.28%	6.40%	6.48%	6.53%	6.57%	7.27%	8.38%	8.57%	8.70%	9.04%	9.66%
- Add'l resistance >9%	0.00%	0.00%	0.00%	0.00%	0.00%	0.00%	0.00%	0.00%	0.00%	0.00%	0.00%	0.00%	0.35%	1.18%	1.33%	1.42%	1.68%	2.14%
Unemployment Rate	6.15%	5.13%	4.61%	4.63%	4.63%	4.63%	4.63%	4.63%	4.63%	4.63%	4.63%	4.63%	4.09%	4.17%	4.13%	4.13%	4.08%	4.03%
- Starting point (year 0)	8.20%	8.20%	8.20%	8.20%	8.20%	8.20%	8.20%	8.20%	8.20%	8.20%	8.20%	8.20%	8.20%	8.20%	8.20%	8.20%	8.20%	8.20%
- Last year's CMS delta	0.00%	2.05%	3.08%	3.59%	3.57%	3.57%	3.57%	3.57%	3.57%	3.57%	3.57%	3.57%	3.57%	4.11%	4.03%	4.07%	4.07%	4.12%
- Retention of last year's delta ****	0.00%	1.03%	1.54%	1.52%	1.52%	1.52%	1.52%	1.52%	1.52%	1.52%	1.52%	1.52%	1.52%	1.31%	1.35%	1.33%	1.33%	1.30%
- This year's CMS impact	2.05%	2.05%	2.05%	2.05%	2.05%	2.05%	2.05%	2.05%	2.05%	2.05%	2.05%	2.05%	2.59%	2.72%	2.72%	2.74%	2.79%	2.87%
* Gross new jobs - Millions	3.20	3.20	3.20	3.20	3.20	3.20	3.20	3.20	3.20	3.20	3.20	3.20	4.26	5.66	5.66	5.80	6.31	7.21
* Net new jobs - Millions ****	3.20	3.20	3.20	3.20	3.20	3.20	3.20	3.20	3.20	3.20	3.20	3.20	4.04	4.25	4.25	4.27	4.35	4.48
- Total delta over starting point	2.05%	3.08%	3.59%	3.57%	3.57%	3.57%	3.57%	3.57%	3.57%	3.57%	3.57%	3.57%	4.11%	4.03%	4.07%	4.07%	4.12%	4.17%

The sheet below depicts years 19 through 41 of the Best-Case.

Year 19	Year 20	Year 21	Year 22	Year 23	Year 24	Year 25	Year 26	Year 27	Year 28	Year 29	Year 30
$2,586.4	$2,801.6	$2,964.5	$3,158.2	$3,458.5	$3,811.2	$4,130.0	$4,412.2	$4,703.8	$5,060.2	$5,470.1	$5,889.2
$2,586.4	$2,801.6	$2,964.5	$3,158.2	$3,458.5	$3,811.2	$4,130.0	$4,412.2	$4,703.8	$5,060.2	$5,470.1	$5,889.2
$ (2,586.4)	$ (2,801.6)	$ (2,964.5)	$ (3,158.2)	$ (3,458.5)	$ (3,811.2)	$ (4,130.0)	$ (4,412.2)	$ (4,703.8)	$ (5,060.2)	$ (5,470.1)	$ (5,889.2)
$ (0.10)	$ (0.10)	$ (0.10)	$ (0.10)	$ (0.10)	$ (0.10)	$ (0.10)	$ (0.10)	$ (0.10)	$ (0.10)	$ (0.10)	$ (0.10)
$ (0.60)	$ (0.63)	$ (0.66)	$ (0.70)	$ (0.73)	$ (0.77)	$ (0.81)	$ (0.85)	$ (0.89)	$ (0.93)	$ (0.98)	$ (1.03)
$3,069.5	$3,286.7	$3,545.0	$3,945.5	$4,415.8	$4,840.8	$5,217.2	$5,606.1	$6,081.2	$6,627.9	$7,186.6	$7,729.7
$3,068.8	$3,286.0	$3,544.2	$3,944.7	$4,415.0	$4,840.0	$5,216.3	$5,605.1	$6,080.2	$6,626.8	$7,185.6	$7,728.6
3.8%	3.8%	3.8%	3.8%	3.8%	3.8%	3.8%	3.8%	3.8%	3.8%	3.8%	3.8%
$ -	$ -	$ -	$ -	$ -	$ -	$ -	$ -	$ -	$ -	$ -	$ -
$3,068.8	$3,286.0	$3,544.2	$3,944.7	$4,415.0	$4,840.0	$5,216.3	$5,605.1	$6,080.2	$6,626.8	$7,185.6	$7,728.6
$ 286.9	$ 217.2	$ 258.2	$ 400.5	$ 470.3	$ 425.0	$ 376.4	$ 388.8	$ 475.1	$ 546.6	$ 558.7	$ 543.1
threshold to begin paying revenue back into U.S. Government											
$1,068.8	$1,286.0	$1,544.2	$1,944.7	$2,415.0	$2,840.0	$3,216.3	$3,605.1	$4,080.2	$4,626.8	$5,185.6	$5,728.6
$ 267.2	$ 321.5	$ 386.1	$ 486.2	$ 603.7	$ 710.0	$ 804.1	$ 901.3	$1,020.1	$1,156.7	$1,296.4	$1,432.2
$3,069.5	$3,286.7	$3,545.0	$3,945.5	$4,415.8	$4,840.8	$5,217.2	$5,606.1	$6,081.2	$6,627.9	$7,186.6	$7,729.7
$ 308.0	$ 409.2	$ 409.2	$ 419.3	$ 456.0	$ 521.0	$ 598.2	$ 648.0	$ 685.7	$ 730.5	$ 800.0	$ 881.6
$ 711.6	$ 711.6	$ 729.3	$ 793.1	$ 906.1	$1,040.4	$1,127.0	$1,192.5	$1,270.4	$1,391.3	$1,533.2	$1,661.4
$1,237.6	$1,268.3	$1,379.3	$1,575.9	$1,809.4	$1,960.0	$2,074.0	$2,209.5	$2,419.6	$2,666.4	$2,889.3	$3,086.8
$ 551.4	$ 599.7	$ 685.2	$ 786.7	$ 852.2	$ 901.7	$ 960.6	$1,052.0	$1,159.3	$1,256.2	$1,342.1	$1,430.8
$ 260.7	$ 297.9	$ 342.0	$ 370.5	$ 392.1	$ 417.7	$ 457.4	$ 504.0	$ 546.2	$ 583.5	$ 622.1	$ 669.2
$ -	$ -	$ -	$ -	$ -	$ -	$ -	$ -	$ -	$ -	$ -	$ -
$1,315.1	$1,411.3	$1,507.7	$1,671.5	$1,876.8	$2,069.0	$2,235.0	$2,396.9	$2,594.5	$2,828.6	$3,073.7	$3,310.9
9.91%	10.05%	10.16%	10.27%	10.44%	10.65%	10.84%	11.02%	11.20%	11.40%	11.65%	11.90%
2.20%	2.20%	2.20%	2.20%	2.20%	2.20%	2.20%	2.20%	2.20%	2.20%	2.20%	2.20%
7.51%	7.71%	7.85%	7.96%	8.07%	8.24%	8.45%	8.64%	8.82%	9.00%	9.20%	9.45%
5.26%	5.40%	5.49%	5.57%	5.65%	5.77%	5.91%	6.05%	6.17%	6.30%	6.44%	6.61%
5.17%	5.60%	5.93%	6.32%	6.92%	7.62%	8.26%	8.82%	9.41%	10.12%	10.94%	11.78%
10.43%	11.00%	11.42%	11.89%	12.57%	13.39%	14.17%	14.87%	15.58%	16.42%	17.38%	18.39%
2.72%	3.15%	3.47%	3.81%	4.33%	4.94%	5.53%	6.06%	6.59%	7.21%	7.94%	8.69%
3.95%	3.93%	3.89%	3.85%	3.78%	3.72%	3.66%	3.61%	3.55%	3.48%	3.41%	3.34%
8.20%	8.20%	8.20%	8.20%	8.20%	8.20%	8.20%	8.20%	8.20%	8.20%	8.20%	8.20%
4.17%	4.25%	4.27%	4.31%	4.35%	4.42%	4.48%	4.54%	4.59%	4.65%	4.72%	4.79%
1.27%	1.23%	1.22%	1.20%	1.18%	1.13%	1.09%	1.05%	1.02%	0.98%	0.93%	0.87%
2.98%	3.04%	3.09%	3.15%	3.24%	3.35%	3.45%	3.54%	3.63%	3.74%	3.86%	3.99%
8.28	8.97	9.49	10.11	11.07	12.20	13.22	14.12	15.05	16.19	17.50	18.85
4.64	4.74	4.82	4.92	5.06	5.23	5.38	5.52	5.66	5.83	6.03	6.23
4.25%	4.27%	4.31%	4.35%	4.42%	4.48%	4.54%	4.59%	4.65%	4.72%	4.79%	4.86%

Year 31	Year 32	Year 33	Year 34	Year 35	Year 36	Year 37	Year 38	Year 39	Year 40	Year 41
$6,296.5	$6,711.8	$7,170.8	$7,679.9	$8,219.4	$ 8,770.9	$ 9,339.6	$ 9,946.0	$ 10,601.4	$ 11,299.8	$12,030.1
$6,296.5	$6,711.8	$7,170.8	$7,679.9	$8,219.4	$ 8,770.9	$ 9,339.6	$ 9,946.0	$ 10,601.4	$ 11,299.8	$12,030.1
$ (6,296.5)	$ (6,711.8)	$ (7,170.8)	$ (7,679.9)	$ (8,219.4)	$ (8,770.9)	$ (9,339.6)	$ (9,946.0)	$(10,601.4)	$(11,299.8)	########
$ (0.10)	$ (0.10)	$ (0.10)	$ (0.10)	$ (0.10)	$ (0.10)	$ (0.10)	$ (0.10)	$ (0.10)	$ (0.10)	$ (0.10)
$ (1.08)	$ (1.13)	$ (1.19)	$ (1.25)	$ (1.31)	$ (1.38)	$ (1.45)	$ (1.52)	$ (1.60)	$ (1.68)	$ (1.76)
$8,283.6	$8,895.6	$ 9,574.6	$10,293.9	$11,029.3	$ 11,787.6	$ 12,596.2	$ 13,470.1	$ 14,401.4	$ 15,375.2	$16,390.8
$8,282.4	$8,894.4	$ 9,573.3	$10,292.5	$11,027.8	$ 11,786.1	$ 12,594.6	$ 13,468.5	$ 14,399.7	$ 15,373.4	$16,388.9
3.8%	3.8%	3.8%	3.8%	3.8%	3.8%	3.8%	3.8%	3.8%	3.8%	3.8%
$ -	$ -	$ -	$ -	$ -	$ -	$ -	$ -	$ -	$ -	$ -
$8,282.4	$ 8,894.4	$ 9,573.3	$10,292.5	$11,027.8	$ 11,786.1	$ 12,594.6	$ 13,468.5	$ 14,399.7	$ 15,373.4	$16,388.9
$ 553.8	$ 612.0	$ 678.9	$ 719.3	$ 735.3	$ 758.2	$ 808.5	$ 873.9	$ 931.3	$ 973.7	$1,015.5
					...(in yr 41)--> CMS Revenue = US Budget					
$6,282.4	$6,894.4	$7,573.3	$8,292.5	$ 9,027.8	$ 9,786.1	$ 10,594.6	$ 11,468.5	$ 12,399.7	$ 13,373.4	$14,388.9
$1,570.6	$1,723.6	$1,893.3	$2,073.1	$2,257.0	$ 2,446.5	$ 2,648.7	$ 2,867.1	$ 3,099.9	$ 3,343.4	$3,597.2
$8,283.6	$8,895.6	$ 9,574.6	$10,293.9	$11,029.3	$ 11,787.6	$ 12,596.2	$ 13,470.1	$ 14,401.4	$ 15,375.2	$16,390.8
$ 955.3	$1,020.6	$1,088.0	$1,170.4	$1,265.3	$ 1,362.2	$ 1,456.4	$ 1,552.5	$ 1,658.6	$ 1,776.4	$1,901.2
$1,774.9	$1,892.2	$2,035.6	$2,200.5	$2,369.0	$ 2,532.9	$ 2,700.0	$ 2,884.6	$ 3,089.4	$ 3,306.4	$3,528.3
$3,290.8	$3,540.1	$3,826.9	$4,120.1	$4,405.0	$ 4,695.6	$ 5,016.7	$ 5,372.9	$ 5,750.3	$ 6,136.1	$6,534.0
$1,539.2	$1,663.9	$1,791.3	$1,915.2	$2,041.6	$ 2,181.2	$ 2,336.0	$ 2,500.1	$ 2,667.9	$ 2,840.9	$3,025.3
$ 723.4	$ 778.8	$ 832.7	$ 887.6	$ 948.3	$ 1,015.7	$ 1,087.0	$ 1,159.9	$ 1,235.2	$ 1,315.4	$1,402.0
$ -	$ -	$ -	$ -	$ -	$ -	$ -	$ -	$ -	$ -	$ -
$3,547.6	$3,806.6	$4,096.6	$4,407.7	$4,726.4	$ 5,052.5	$ 5,397.9	$ 5,771.8	$ 6,172.5	$ 6,592.5	$7,029.5
12.15%	12.40%	12.67%	12.97%	13.29%	13.63%	13.97%	14.33%	14.72%	15.14%	15.58%
2.20%	2.20%	2.20%	2.20%	2.20%	2.20%	2.20%	2.20%	2.20%	2.20%	2.20%
9.70%	9.95%	10.20%	10.47%	10.77%	11.09%	11.43%	11.77%	12.13%	12.52%	12.94%
6.79%	6.96%	7.14%	7.33%	7.54%	7.77%	8.00%	8.24%	8.49%	8.77%	9.06%
12.59%	13.42%	14.34%	15.36%	16.44%	17.54%	18.68%	19.89%	21.20%	22.60%	24.06%
19.38%	20.39%	21.48%	22.69%	23.98%	25.31%	26.68%	28.13%	29.70%	31.37%	33.12%
9.44%	10.19%	11.01%	11.92%	12.88%	13.88%	14.91%	16.00%	17.17%	18.42%	19.74%
3.27%	3.20%	3.11%	3.04%	2.93%	2.87%	2.76%	2.68%	2.56%	2.47%	2.36%
8.20%	8.20%	8.20%	8.20%	8.20%	8.20%	8.20%	8.20%	8.20%	8.20%	8.20%
4.86%	4.93%	5.00%	5.09%	5.16%	5.27%	5.33%	5.44%	5.52%	5.64%	5.73%
0.81%	0.76%	0.70%	0.62%	0.56%	0.45%	0.39%	0.28%	0.20%	0.07%	-0.04%
4.12%	4.24%	4.39%	4.54%	4.71%	4.88%	5.05%	5.24%	5.44%	5.66%	5.88%
20.15	21.48	22.95	24.58	26.30	28.07	29.89	31.83	33.92	36.16	38.50
6.42	6.62	6.84	7.09	7.35	7.61	7.88	8.17	8.49	8.82	9.17
4.93%	5.00%	5.09%	5.16%	5.27%	5.33%	5.44%	5.52%	5.64%	5.73%	5.84%

Appendix A: TDRM Financial Model (detail)

Magnified Capitalism - Financials Support

Version 1.1 - © 2012 by Peter Naleszkiewicz, All rights reserved

Rendering: Trillion Dollar Reinvestment Model (TDRM) - Re-Invests any Fund surplus

Page: **Detail of Worst Case**

*GREEN = From Assumptions, **Dark Blue** = Calculated*

All figures in Billions of Dollars unless noted otherwise

--> With Year 11 onward this model simply uses the year 10 rates and assumptions

	Year 1	Year 2	Year 3	Year 4	Year 5	Year 6	Year 7	Year 8	Year 9	Year 10	Year 11	Year 12	Year 13	Year 14	Year 15	Year 16	Year 17	Year 18
CMS Fund Level at Start of Each Year	$ 1,000.0	$ 1,000.0	$ 1,000.0	$ 1,000.0	$ 1,000.0	$ 1,000.0	$ 1,000.0	$ 1,000.0	$ 1,000.0	$ 1,000.0	$ 1,000.0	$ 1,000.0	$ 1,000.0	$ 1,000.0	$ 1,000.0	$ 1,000.0	$ 1,000.0	$ 1,000.0
Costs ... (Negative = debt)						--> CMS becomes profitable, debt begins pay down												--> CMS De
Fund Balance (Debt) from previous year	$ -	$ (1,017.0)	$ (2,053.8)	$ (2,995.3)	$ (3,700.5)	$ (3,853.8)	$ (3,704.6)	$ (3,387.2)	$ (3,067.9)	$ (2,745.0)	$ (2,416.7)	$ (2,076.2)	$ (1,723.1)	$ (1,356.9)	$ (977.2)	$ (583.4)	$ (175.0)	$ 239.6
Fund level applied this year (for svcs)	$ (1,000.0)	$ (1,000.0)	$ (1,000.0)	$ (1,000.0)	$ (1,000.0)	$ (1,000.0)	$ (1,000.0)	$ (1,000.0)	$ (1,000.0)	$ (1,000.0)	$ (1,000.0)	$ (1,000.0)	$ (1,000.0)	$ (1,000.0)	$ (1,000.0)	$ (1,000.0)	$ (1,000.0)	$ (1,000.0)
Fixed Costs (CMS Setup)	$ (1.00)	$ (0.40)	$ (0.40)	$ (0.40)	$ (0.40)	$ (0.40)	$ (0.40)	$ (0.40)	$ (0.40)	$ (0.40)	$ (0.40)	$ (0.40)	$ (0.40)	$ (0.40)	$ (0.40)	$ (0.40)	$ (0.40)	$ (0.40)
Operating Costs (Budget)	$ (1.00)	$ (1.07)	$ (1.14)	$ (1.23)	$ (1.31)	$ (1.40)	$ (1.50)	$ (1.61)	$ (1.72)	$ (1.84)	$ (1.97)	$ (2.10)	$ (2.25)	$ (2.41)	$ (2.58)	$ (2.76)	$ (2.95)	$ (3.16)
Receivables by end of year	$ -	$ -	$ 118.8	$ 377.8	$ 942.4	$ 1,250.2	$ 1,417.9	$ 1,417.9	$ 1,417.9	$ 1,417.9	$ 1,417.9	$ 1,417.9	$ 1,417.9	$ 1,417.9	$ 1,417.9	$ 1,417.9	$ 1,417.9	$ 1,417.9
Fund Balance w/o interest	$ (1,002.0)	$ (2,018.5)	$ (2,936.6)	$ (3,619.1)	$ (3,759.8)	$ (3,605.4)	$ (3,288.6)	$ (2,971.4)	$ (2,652.2)	$ (2,329.3)	$ (2,001.2)	$ (1,660.8)	$ (1,307.9)	$ (941.9)	$ (562.3)	$ (168.6)	$ 239.6	$ 653.9
Interest applied (%) to outstanding debt	1.5%	1.8%	2.0%	2.3%	2.5%	2.8%	3.0%	3.3%	3.5%	3.8%	3.8%	3.8%	3.8%	3.8%	3.8%	3.8%	3.8%	3.8%
Debt interest	$ (15.03)	$ (35.32)	$ (58.73)	$ (81.43)	$ (93.99)	$ (99.15)	$ (98.66)	$ (96.57)	$ (92.83)	$ (87.35)	$ (75.0)	$ (62.3)	$ (49.0)	$ (35.3)	$ (21.1)	$ (6.3)	$ -	$ -
Total Fund Balance w/ interest applied	$ (1,017.0)	$ (2,053.8)	$ (2,995.3)	$ (3,700.5)	$ (3,853.8)	$ (3,704.6)	$ (3,387.2)	$ (3,067.9)	$ (2,745.0)	$ (2,416.7)	$ (2,076.2)	$ (1,723.1)	$ (1,356.9)	$ (977.2)	$ (583.4)	$ (175.0)	$ 239.6	$ 653.9
Gain (or loss) from last year	$ (1,017.0)	$ (1,036.8)	$ (941.5)	$ (705.2)	$ (153.3)	$ 149.2	$ 317.3	$ 319.3	$ 322.9	$ 328.3	$ 340.5	$ 353.1	$ 366.2	$ 379.8	$ 393.8	$ 408.4	$ 414.5	$ 414.3
U.S. Government Revenue ...																		
Portion of Fund Exceeding threshold	$ -	$ -	$ -	$ -	$ -	$ -	$ -	$ -	$ -	$ -	$ -	$ -	$ -	$ -	$ -	$ -	$ -	$ -
Revenue paid to government	$ -	$ -	$ -	$ -	$ -	$ -	$ -	$ -	$ -	$ -	$ -	$ -	$ -	$ -	$ -	$ -	$ -	$ -
Revenue / Gross Profit ...																		
Receivables from services	$ -	$ -	$ 118.8	$ 377.8	$ 942.4	$ 1,250.2	$ 1,417.9	$ 1,417.9	$ 1,417.9	$ 1,417.9	$ 1,417.9	$ 1,417.9	$ 1,417.9	$ 1,417.9	$ 1,417.9	$ 1,417.9	$ 1,417.9	$ 1,417.9
- From 6 years ago	$ -	$ -	$ -	$ -	$ -	$ -	$ 167.7	$ 167.7	$ 167.7	$ 167.7	$ 167.7	$ 167.7	$ 167.7	$ 167.7	$ 167.7	$ 167.7	$ 167.7	$ 167.7
- From 5 years ago	$ -	$ -	$ -	$ -	$ -	$ 307.7	$ 307.7	$ 307.7	$ 307.7	$ 307.7	$ 307.7	$ 307.7	$ 307.7	$ 307.7	$ 307.7	$ 307.7	$ 307.7	$ 307.7
- From 4 years ago	$ -	$ -	$ -	$ -	$ 564.6	$ 564.6	$ 564.6	$ 564.6	$ 564.6	$ 564.6	$ 564.6	$ 564.6	$ 564.6	$ 564.6	$ 564.6	$ 564.6	$ 564.6	$ 564.6
- From 3 years ago	$ -	$ -	$ -	$ 259.0	$ 259.0	$ 259.0	$ 259.0	$ 259.0	$ 259.0	$ 259.0	$ 259.0	$ 259.0	$ 259.0	$ 259.0	$ 259.0	$ 259.0	$ 259.0	$ 259.0
- From 2 years ago	$ -	$ -	$ 118.8	$ 118.8	$ 118.8	$ 118.8	$ 118.8	$ 118.8	$ 118.8	$ 118.8	$ 118.8	$ 118.8	$ 118.8	$ 118.8	$ 118.8	$ 118.8	$ 118.8	$ 118.8
- From last year	$ -	$ -	$ -	$ -	$ -	$ -	$ -	$ -	$ -	$ -	$ -	$ -	$ -	$ -	$ -	$ -	$ -	$ -
Portion of Revenue as Gross Profit	$ -	$ -	$ 18.8	$ 77.8	$ 242.4	$ 350.2	$ 417.9	$ 417.9	$ 417.9	$ 417.9	$ 417.9	$ 417.9	$ 417.9	$ 417.9	$ 417.9	$ 417.9	$ 417.9	$ 417.9
U.S. Economic Impact ...																		
GDP	3.70%	4.60%	5.14%	5.46%	5.66%	5.78%	5.85%	5.89%	5.91%	5.93%	5.94%	5.94%	5.95%	5.95%	5.95%	5.95%	5.95%	5.95%
- Starting point (year 0)	2.20%	2.20%	2.20%	2.20%	2.20%	2.20%	2.20%	2.20%	2.20%	2.20%	2.20%	2.20%	2.20%	2.20%	2.20%	2.20%	2.20%	2.20%
- Last year's CMS delta	0.00%	1.50%	2.40%	2.94%	3.26%	3.46%	3.58%	3.65%	3.69%	3.71%	3.73%	3.74%	3.74%	3.75%	3.75%	3.75%	3.75%	3.75%
- Retention of last year's delta	0.00%	0.90%	1.44%	1.76%	1.96%	2.08%	2.15%	2.19%	2.21%	2.23%	2.24%	2.24%	2.25%	2.25%	2.25%	2.25%	2.25%	2.25%
- This year's CMS impact	1.50%	1.50%	1.50%	1.50%	1.50%	1.50%	1.50%	1.50%	1.50%	1.50%	1.50%	1.50%	1.50%	1.50%	1.50%	1.50%	1.50%	1.50%
- Total delta over starting point	1.50%	2.40%	2.94%	3.26%	3.46%	3.58%	3.65%	3.69%	3.71%	3.73%	3.74%	3.74%	3.75%	3.75%	3.75%	3.75%	3.75%	3.75%
- Add'l resistance >9%	0.00%	0.00%	0.00%	0.00%	0.00%	0.00%	0.00%	0.00%	0.00%	0.00%	0.00%	0.00%	0.00%	0.00%	0.00%	0.00%	0.00%	0.00%
Unemployment Rate	6.50%	5.83%	5.56%	5.45%	5.41%	5.39%	5.39%	5.39%	5.38%	5.38%	5.38%	5.38%	5.38%	5.38%	5.38%	5.38%	5.38%	5.38%
- Starting point (year 0)	8.20%	8.20%	8.20%	8.20%	8.20%	8.20%	8.20%	8.20%	8.20%	8.20%	8.20%	8.20%	8.20%	8.20%	8.20%	8.20%	8.20%	8.20%
- Last year's CMS delta	0.00%	1.70%	2.37%	2.64%	2.75%	2.79%	2.81%	2.81%	2.81%	2.82%	2.82%	2.82%	2.82%	2.82%	2.82%	2.82%	2.82%	2.82%
- Retention of last year's delta ****	0.00%	0.68%	0.95%	1.06%	1.10%	1.12%	1.12%	1.12%	1.13%	1.13%	1.13%	1.13%	1.13%	1.13%	1.13%	1.13%	1.13%	1.13%
- This year's CMS impact	1.70%	1.69%	1.69%	1.69%	1.69%	1.69%	1.69%	1.69%	1.69%	1.69%	1.69%	1.69%	1.69%	1.69%	1.69%	1.69%	1.69%	1.69%
* Gross new jobs - Millions	2.88	2.88	2.88	2.88	2.88	2.88	2.88	2.88	2.88	2.88	2.88	2.88	2.88	2.88	2.88	2.88	2.88	2.88
* Net new jobs - Millions	2.88	2.88	2.88	2.88	2.88	2.88	2.88	2.88	2.88	2.88	2.88	2.88	2.88	2.88	2.88	2.88	2.88	2.88
- Total delta over starting point	1.70%	2.37%	2.64%	2.75%	2.79%	2.81%	2.81%	2.81%	2.82%	2.82%	2.82%	2.82%	2.82%	2.82%	2.82%	2.82%	2.82%	2.82%

The sheet below depicts years 19 through 40 of the Worst-Case.

Year 19	Year 20	Year 21	Year 22	Year 23	Year 24	Year 25	Year 26	Year 27	Year 28	Year 29
$ 1,000.0	$ 1,068.0	$ 1,413.9	$ 1,413.6	$ 1,421.4	$ 1,479.8	$ 1,553.7	$ 1,662.1	$ 1,725.3	$ 1,768.2	$ 1,801.7
ebt completely repaid										
$ 653.9	$ 1,068.0	$ 1,413.9	$ 1,413.6	$ 1,421.4	$ 1,479.8	$ 1,553.7	$ 1,662.1	$ 1,725.3	$ 1,768.2	$ 1,801.7
$ (1,000.0)	$ (1,068.0)	$ (1,413.9)	$ (1,413.6)	$ (1,421.4)	$ (1,479.8)	$ (1,553.7)	$ (1,662.1)	$ (1,725.3)	$ (1,768.2)	$ (1,801.7)
$ (0.40)	$ (0.40)	$ (0.40)	$ (0.40)	$ (0.40)	$ (0.40)	$ (0.40)	$ (0.40)	$ (0.40)	$ (0.40)	$ (0.40)
$ (3.38)	$ (3.62)	$ (3.87)	$ (4.14)	$ (4.43)	$ (4.74)	$ (5.07)	$ (5.43)	$ (5.81)	$ (6.21)	$ (6.65)
$ 1,417.9	$ 1,417.9	$ 1,417.9	$ 1,426.0	$ 1,484.7	$ 1,612.6	$ 1,829.7	$ 1,956.3	$ 2,042.6	$ 2,109.9	$ 2,206.5
$ 1,068.0	$ 1,413.9	$ 1,413.6	$ 1,421.4	$ 1,479.8	$ 1,607.5	$ 1,824.2	$ 1,950.5	$ 2,036.4	$ 2,103.3	$ 2,199.5
3.8%	3.8%	3.8%	3.8%	3.8%	3.8%	3.8%	3.8%	3.8%	3.8%	3.8%
$ -	$ -	$ -	$ -	$ -	$ -	$ -	$ -	$ -	$ -	$ -
$ 1,068.0	$ 1,413.9	$ 1,413.6	$ 1,421.4	$ 1,479.8	$ 1,607.5	$ 1,824.2	$ 1,950.5	$ 2,036.4	$ 2,103.3	$ 2,199.5
$ 414.1	$ 345.9	$ (0.3)	$ 7.8	$ 58.4	$ 127.6	$ 216.7	$ 126.3	$ 85.9	$ 67.0	$ 96.1
					--> CMS Fund Exceeds threshold to begin paying revenue back into U.S. Government					
$ -	$ -	$ -	$ -	$ -	$ 107.5	$ 324.2	$ 450.5	$ 536.4	$ 603.3	$ 699.5
$ -	$ -	$ -	$ -	$ -	$ 53.7	$ 162.1	$ 225.3	$ 268.2	$ 301.7	$ 349.7
$ 1,417.9	$ 1,417.9	$ 1,417.9	$ 1,426.0	$ 1,484.7	$ 1,612.6	$ 1,829.7	$ 1,956.3	$ 2,042.6	$ 2,109.9	$ 2,206.5
$ 167.7	$ 167.7	$ 167.7	$ 167.7	$ 167.7	$ 167.7	$ 167.7	$ 179.1	$ 237.1	$ 237.1	$ 238.4
$ 307.7	$ 307.7	$ 307.7	$ 307.7	$ 307.7	$ 307.7	$ 328.6	$ 435.1	$ 435.0	$ 437.4	$ 455.4
$ 564.6	$ 564.6	$ 564.6	$ 564.6	$ 564.6	$ 603.0	$ 798.3	$ 798.2	$ 802.6	$ 835.6	$ 877.3
$ 259.0	$ 259.0	$ 259.0	$ 259.0	$ 276.6	$ 366.2	$ 366.1	$ 368.2	$ 383.3	$ 402.4	$ 430.5
$ 118.8	$ 118.8	$ 118.8	$ 126.9	$ 168.0	$ 168.0	$ 168.9	$ 175.8	$ 184.6	$ 197.5	$ 205.0
$ -	$ -	$ -	$ -	$ -	$ -	$ -	$ -	$ -	$ -	$ -
$ 417.9	$ 417.9	$ 417.9	$ 419.2	$ 429.7	$ 461.3	$ 525.7	$ 569.1	$ 598.6	$ 615.4	$ 642.0
5.95%	6.05%	6.63%	6.98%	7.20%	7.42%	7.66%	7.97%	8.25%	8.48%	8.67%
2.20%	2.20%	2.20%	2.20%	2.20%	2.20%	2.20%	2.20%	2.20%	2.20%	2.20%
3.75%	3.75%	3.85%	4.43%	4.78%	5.00%	5.22%	5.46%	5.77%	6.05%	6.28%
2.25%	2.25%	2.31%	2.66%	2.87%	3.00%	3.13%	3.28%	3.46%	3.63%	3.77%
1.50%	1.60%	2.12%	2.12%	2.13%	2.22%	2.33%	2.49%	2.59%	2.65%	2.70%
3.75%	3.85%	4.43%	4.78%	5.00%	5.22%	5.46%	5.77%	6.05%	6.28%	6.47%
0.00%	0.00%	0.00%	0.00%	0.00%	0.00%	0.00%	0.00%	0.00%	0.00%	0.00%
5.38%	5.26%	4.94%	4.80%	4.75%	4.72%	4.69%	4.67%	4.64%	4.62%	4.61%
8.20%	8.20%	8.20%	8.20%	8.20%	8.20%	8.20%	8.20%	8.20%	8.20%	8.20%
2.82%	2.82%	2.94%	3.26%	3.40%	3.45%	3.48%	3.51%	3.53%	3.56%	3.58%
1.13%	1.13%	1.17%	1.31%	1.36%	1.38%	1.39%	1.40%	1.41%	1.43%	1.43%
1.69%	1.81%	2.09%	2.09%	2.09%	2.10%	2.12%	2.13%	2.15%	2.15%	2.16%
2.88	3.08	4.07	4.07	4.09	4.26	4.47	4.79	4.97	5.09	5.19
2.88	3.08	3.56	3.56	3.56	3.58	3.60	3.63	3.65	3.66	3.67
2.82%	2.94%	3.26%	3.40%	3.45%	3.48%	3.51%	3.53%	3.56%	3.58%	3.59%

Year 30	Year 31	Year 32	Year 33	Year 34	Year 35	Year 36	Year 37	Year 38	Year 39	Year 40
$ 1,849.7	$ 1,907.1	$ 1,955.1	$ 1,992.9	$ 2,023.6	$ 2,055.9	$ 2,090.5	$ 2,123.3	$ 2,151.7	$ 2,176.0	$ 2,199.0
$ 1,849.7	$ 1,907.1	$ 1,955.1	$ 1,992.9	$ 2,023.6	$ 2,055.9	$ 2,090.5	$ 2,123.3	$ 2,151.7	$ 2,176.0	$ 2,199.0
$ (1,849.7)	$ (1,907.1)	$ (1,955.1)	$ (1,992.9)	$ (2,023.6)	$ (2,055.9)	$ (2,090.5)	$ (2,123.3)	$ (2,151.7)	$ (2,176.0)	$ (2,199.0)
$ (0.40)	$ (0.40)	$ (0.40)	$ (0.40)	$ (0.40)	$ (0.40)	$ (0.40)	$ (0.40)	$ (0.40)	$ (0.40)	$ (0.40)
$ (7.11)	$ (7.61)	$ (8.15)	$ (8.72)	$ (9.33)	$ (9.98)	$ (10.68)	$ (11.42)	$ (12.22)	$ (13.08)	$ (13.99)
$ 2,321.7	$ 2,418.2	$ 2,494.4	$ 2,556.4	$ 2,621.6	$ 2,691.3	$ 2,757.6	$ 2,815.2	$ 2,864.7	$ 2,911.5	$ 2,958.0
$ 2,314.2	$ 2,410.2	$ 2,485.9	$ 2,547.3	$ 2,611.9	$ 2,681.0	$ 2,746.5	$ 2,803.3	$ 2,852.0	$ 2,898.1	$ 2,943.6
3.8%	3.8%	3.8%	3.8%	3.8%	3.8%	3.8%	3.8%	3.8%	3.8%	3.8%
$ -	$ -	$ -	$ -	$ -	$ -	$ -	$ -	$ -	$ -	$ -
$ 2,314.2	$ 2,410.2	$ 2,485.9	$ 2,547.3	$ 2,611.9	$ 2,681.0	$ 2,746.5	$ 2,803.3	$ 2,852.0	$ 2,898.1	$ 2,943.6
$ 114.7	$ 96.0	$ 75.7	$ 61.4	$ 64.6	$ 69.1	$ 65.6	$ 56.8	$ 48.7	$ 46.0	$ 45.5
$ 814.2	$ 910.2	$ 985.9	$ 1,047.3	$ 1,111.9	$ 1,181.0	$ 1,246.5	$ 1,303.3	$ 1,352.0	$ 1,398.1	$ 1,443.6
$ 407.1	$ 455.1	$ 492.9	$ 523.6	$ 555.9	$ 590.5	$ 623.3	$ 651.7	$ 676.0	$ 699.0	$ 721.8
$ 2,321.7	$ 2,418.2	$ 2,494.4	$ 2,556.4	$ 2,621.6	$ 2,691.3	$ 2,757.6	$ 2,815.2	$ 2,864.7	$ 2,911.5	$ 2,958.0
$ 248.2	$ 260.6	$ 278.8	$ 289.3	$ 296.5	$ 302.2	$ 310.2	$ 319.8	$ 327.9	$ 334.2	$ 339.4
$ 478.1	$ 511.5	$ 530.9	$ 544.1	$ 554.4	$ 569.2	$ 586.9	$ 601.6	$ 613.3	$ 622.7	$ 632.7
$ 938.5	$ 974.1	$ 998.4	$ 1,017.3	$ 1,044.4	$ 1,076.8	$ 1,103.9	$ 1,125.3	$ 1,142.6	$ 1,160.9	$ 1,180.4
$ 446.9	$ 458.0	$ 466.6	$ 479.1	$ 494.0	$ 506.4	$ 516.2	$ 524.1	$ 532.5	$ 541.4	$ 549.9
$ 210.1	$ 214.1	$ 219.8	$ 226.6	$ 232.3	$ 236.8	$ 240.4	$ 244.3	$ 248.4	$ 252.3	$ 255.6
$ -	$ -	$ -	$ -	$ -	$ -	$ -	$ -	$ -	$ -	$ -
$ 676.3	$ 706.5	$ 730.6	$ 748.9	$ 767.6	$ 788.1	$ 808.2	$ 825.9	$ 840.9	$ 854.7	$ 868.4
8.86%	9.01%	9.05%	9.08%	9.11%	9.14%	9.17%	9.19%	9.22%	9.24%	9.26%
2.20%	2.20%	2.20%	2.20%	2.20%	2.20%	2.20%	2.20%	2.20%	2.20%	2.20%
6.47%	6.66%	6.86%	7.05%	7.22%	7.37%	7.50%	7.64%	7.77%	7.89%	8.00%
3.88%	3.99%	4.11%	4.23%	4.33%	4.42%	4.50%	4.58%	4.66%	4.73%	4.80%
2.77%	2.86%	2.93%	2.99%	3.04%	3.08%	3.14%	3.18%	3.23%	3.26%	3.30%
6.66%	6.86%	7.05%	7.22%	7.37%	7.50%	7.64%	7.77%	7.89%	8.00%	8.10%
0.00%	0.04%	0.20%	0.33%	0.45%	0.56%	0.67%	0.77%	0.87%	0.96%	1.04%
4.59%	4.58%	4.57%	4.56%	4.54%	4.54%	4.52%	4.52%	4.51%	4.50%	4.49%
8.20%	8.20%	8.20%	8.20%	8.20%	8.20%	8.20%	8.20%	8.20%	8.20%	8.20%
3.59%	3.61%	3.62%	3.63%	3.64%	3.66%	3.66%	3.68%	3.68%	3.69%	3.70%
1.44%	1.44%	1.45%	1.45%	1.46%	1.46%	1.47%	1.47%	1.47%	1.48%	1.48%
2.17%	2.18%	2.18%	2.19%	2.20%	2.20%	2.21%	2.21%	2.22%	2.22%	2.23%
5.33	5.49	5.63	5.74	5.83	5.92	6.02	6.12	6.20	6.27	6.33
3.68	3.70	3.71	3.72	3.73	3.74	3.75	3.76	3.77	3.78	3.78
3.61%	3.62%	3.63%	3.64%	3.66%	3.66%	3.68%	3.68%	3.69%	3.70%	3.71%

Index

Acknowledgements

Foremost I want to thank my wonderful wife Sherry, and our son Blaise, to whom I dedicate this writing.

Our amazing son has given me the motivation to try to leave this world a better place regardless of the odds. Blaise, you are a gem beyond anything I could have imagined.

Aside from bearing the gift of our son, my dear Sherry has provided love and support during this entire effort. Such help is so critical that without it I would have had neither the strength nor the opportunity to complete the journey. Thank you sweetheart, you continue to make me feel so very lucky.

Laura Perry deserves particular mention. She is a good friend and the primary editor for this work whose efforts greatly elevated its quality.

Friends and family, most of whom do not even realize their contributions, that have helped me either recently or through efforts long past include:

Phillip Seaver and Suzanne Rezelman and family, Eddie and Jennifer Maise and family, Betty Hampton, Helmut and Silvia Feischl, Bernie & Birgit Kraemer, Gabe and Korina Adams, Edward "Van" and Katie VanBuren and family, Connie Hampton, Dylan Hampton, Casey and Misty Hampton and family, Mike and Nika Hinton and family, John Naleszkiewicz, Kristopher Naleszkiewicz, Alexandra Naleszkiewicz, Nicole Naleszkiewicz, Mark and Teresa Rivard and family, Carrie Hampton and Mike Mongeon and family, Aaron and Tara Hampton and family, Bogdan "Bogie" and Elizabeth Naleszkiewicz, and to the truly many others who I have failed to mention yet deserve my appreciation.

Belated thanks to my mom and dad, Krystyne and Wladimir, as well as one of my most influential mentors, Bob Baron. I know I underappreciated you all when I had the chance. Even though you are no longer with us, it is with profound gratitude that I thank you for your efforts to try to make me a better person despite your challenges to the contrary. I hope God finds your souls well.

And to you who are reading this, I thank you too. We can change the world. All that is needed is for us to dare step in that direction.

www.ingramcontent.com/pod-product-compliance
Lightning Source LLC
Chambersburg PA
CBHW031822170526
45157CB00001B/157

* 9 7 8 1 4 7 9 1 2 8 5 4 9 *